FreeCAD 0.19

Basics Tutorial

Tutorial Books

Contents

INTRODUCTION

FreeCAD, as a topic of learning, is very vast and has a broad scope. It is a package of many workbenches delivering exceptional value to enterprises. It offers a set of tools, which are easy-to-use to design, document, and simulate 3D models. Using this software, you can design your products free of cost.

This book provides a step-by-step approach for users to learn FreeCAD. It is aimed at those with no previous experience with FreeCAD. The user is guided by starting a FreeCAD session to creating parts, assemblies, and drawings. Each chapter has components explained with the help of real-world models.

Scope of this book

This book is written for students and engineers who are interested to learn FreeCAD for designing mechanical components and assemblies, and then create drawings.

This book provides a step-by-step approach to learning FreeCAD. The topics include Getting Started with FreeCAD, Basic Part Modeling, Creating Assemblies, Additional Modeling Tools, and Creating Drawings.

Chapter 1 introduces FreeCAD. The user interface and terminology are discussed in this chapter.

Chapter 2 takes you through the creation of your first FreeCAD model. You create simple parts.

Chapter 3 teaches you to create assemblies. It explains the Top-down and Bottom-up approaches for designing an assembly. You create an assembly using the Bottom-up approach.

Chapter 4: In this chapter, you learn the sketching tools.

Chapter 5: In this chapter, you learn additional modeling tools to create complex models.

Chapter 6 teaches you to create drawings of the models created in the earlier chapters.

Chapter 7 teaches you to create a sheet metal model.

Chapter 1: Getting Started with FreeCAD

This tutorial book brings in the most commonly used features of FreeCAD.

In this chapter, you will:

- Understand the FreeCAD terminology
- Start a new file
- Understand the User Interface
- Understand different workbenches in FreeCAD

In FreeCAD, you create 3D parts and use them to create 2D drawings and 3D assemblies.

FreeCAD is Feature Based. Features are shapes that are combined to build a part. You can modify these shapes individually.

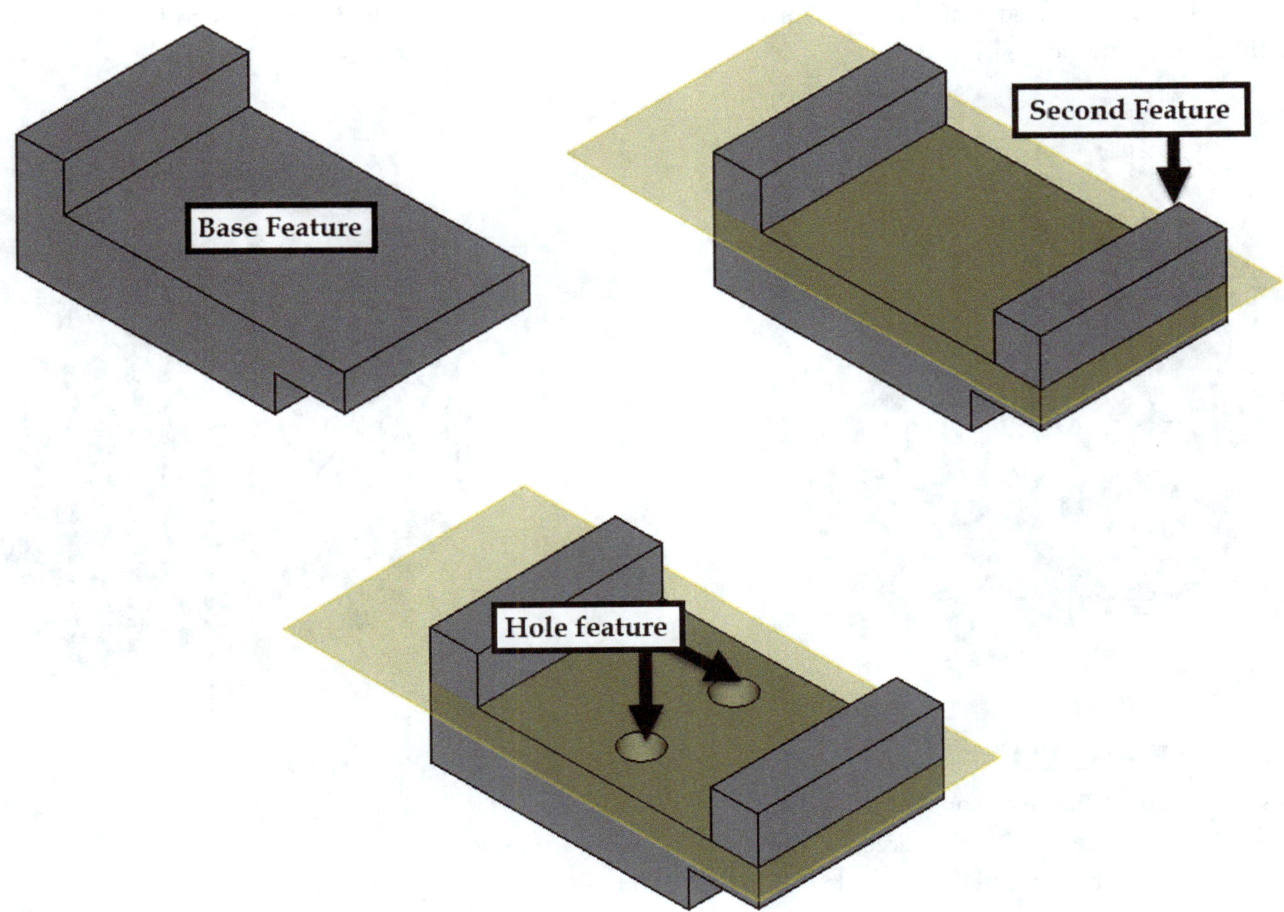

Most of the features are sketch-based. A sketch is a 2D profile and can be extruded, revolved, or swept along a path to create features.

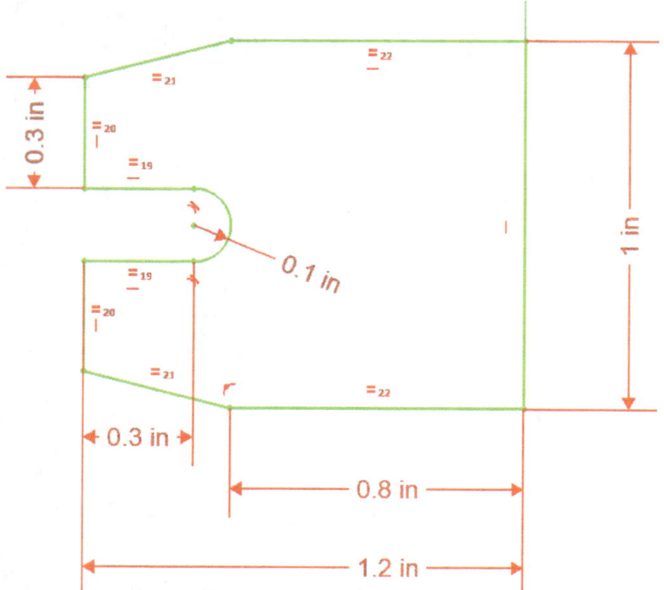

FreeCAD is parametric. You can specify standard parameters between the elements. Changing these parameters changes the size and shape of the part. For example, see the design of the body of a flange before and after modifying the parameters of its features.

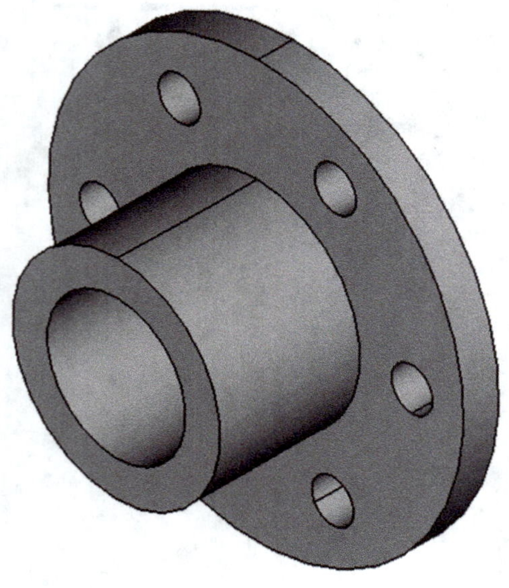
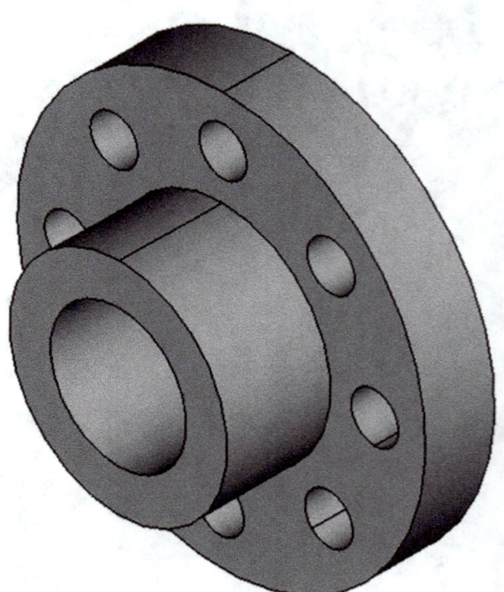

Starting FreeCAD

- Click the Windows icon on the taskbar.
- Click **F** > **FreeCAD 0.19** > **FreeCAD**.
- On the ribbon, click **File > New** to start a new part file.

Notice these essential features of the FreeCAD window.

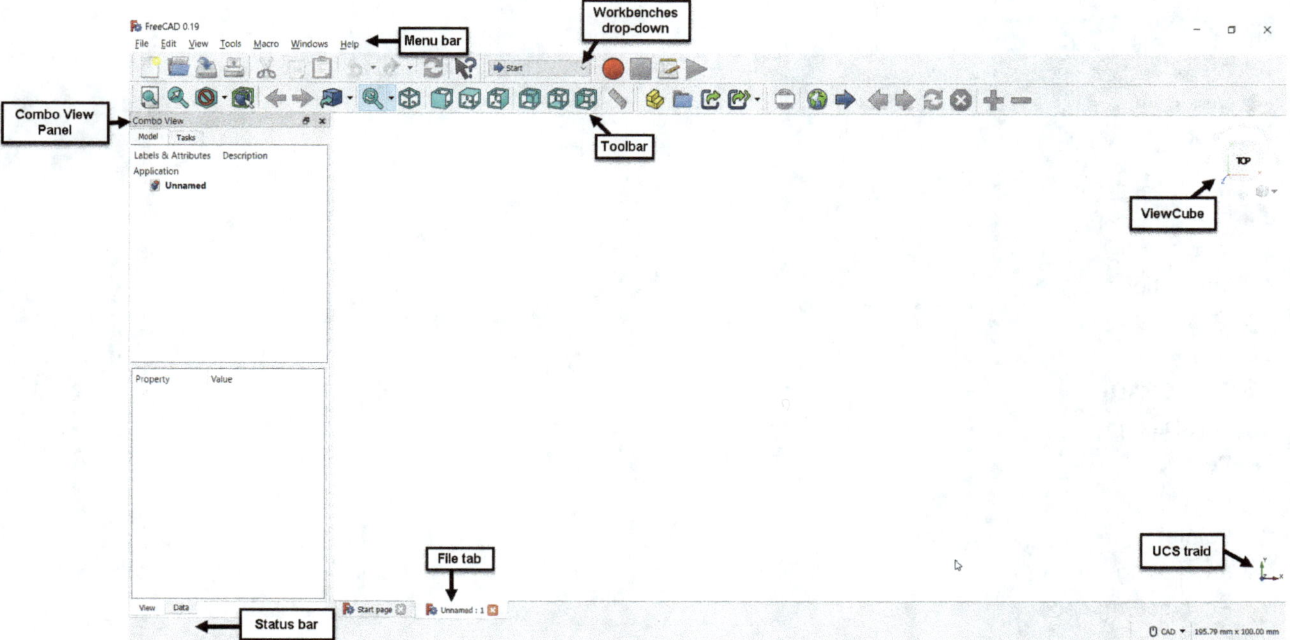

Workbenches in FreeCAD

A workbench is a set of tools and environments that can be used to create parts, assemblies, drawings, and so on. There are many workbenches available in FreeCAD. You can activate different workbenches by using the **Workbenches** drop-down located on the top-left corner.

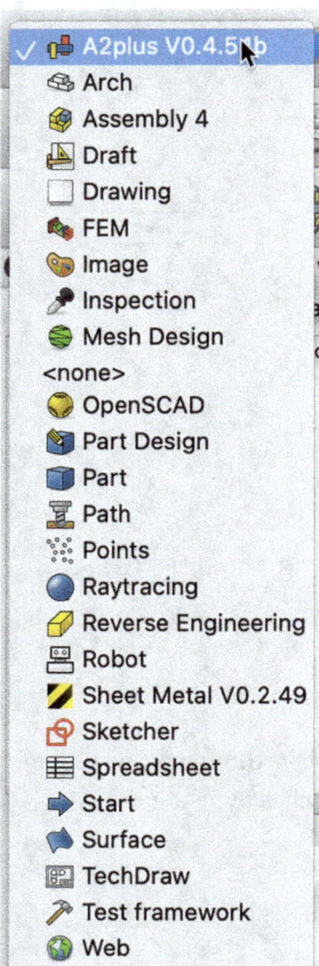

User Interface

Various components of the user interface are discussed next.

Menu bar

The menu bar is located at the top of the window. It has various options (menu titles). When you click on a menu title, a drop-down appears. Select an option from this drop-down.

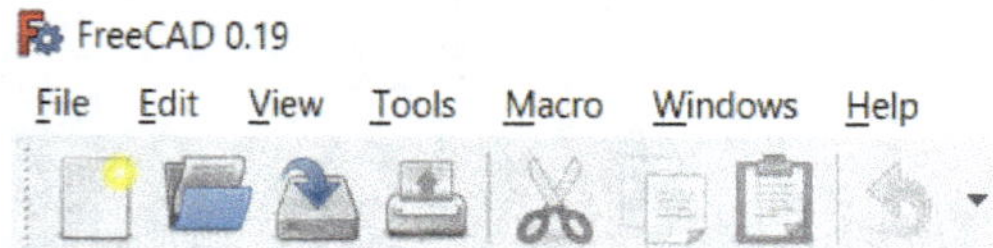

File Menu

The **File Menu** appears when you click on the **File** option located at the top left corner of the window. This menu contains the options to open, print, export, save, and close a file.

Toolbar

A toolbar is a set of tools, which help you to perform various operations. Various toolbars available in different workbenches are given next.

Start Toolbars	
Workbench	This toolbar has a drop-down to change the workbench.
Macro	This toolbar has tools to create and execute macros.
File	This toolbar has tools to create, open, and save files. You can also print, cut, copy, paste, undo, redo, recompute, and seek help.
View	This toolbar has tools to manipulate the view of the model.
Structure	It has tools to create or open part files.
Navigation	It has tools to open a website in FreeCAD.
Sketcher Toolbars	
Sketcher	This toolbar has tools to start or exit a sketch.

Sketcher geometries	This toolbar has tools to create sketch elements.
Sketcher constraints	This toolbar has tools to apply constraints between sketch elements.
Sketcher B-spline tools	This toolbar has tools to create and edit B-splines.
Sketcher Virtual Space	This toolbar helps you to hide or show constraints.
Sketch Tools	This toolbar has various selection tools and options that aid you in creating sketch elements very fast.
Part Design Toolbars	
Part Design Helper	This toolbar has tools to create new bodies, datum points, axis, datum planes, and clones. You can also create or leave a sketch.
Part Design Modeling	This toolbar has commands to create solid features based on the sketch geometry.

Assembly 2 Toolbars	
Assembly 2	This toolbar has tools to create components or insert existing components into an assembly. This toolbar also has tools to apply constraints between components.
Assembly 2 Shortcuts	This toolbar has tools to change the direction of the constraints, lock rotation, and insert multiple bolts into holes.
TechDraw Toolbars	
TechDraw Views	This toolbar has tools to generate standard views of a 3D geometry.
TechDraw Clips	It has tools to add or remove clips to the drawing sheet.
TechDraw Pages	The tools on this toolbar help you to add a new page.
TechDraw Dimensions	The tools on this toolbar help you to add dimensions to the drawing views.
TechDraw File Access	This toolbar helps you to export the drawing page

		to the SVG format.
TechDraw Decoration		The tools on this toolbar help you to change the hatch patterns and insert images.
Sheet Metal Toolbars		
My Commands		The tools on this toolbar help you to create a sheetmetal model.
FEM Toolbars		
Model		It has tools to define materials and element geometry of the model.

Mechanical Constraints	It has tools to define mechanical constriants.
Thermal Constraints	It has tools to add thermal constraints.
Mesh	It has tools to mesh the model.
Fluid Constraints	It has tools to add fluid constraints.
Electronstatic Constraints	It has tools to add electrostatic constraints.
Solve	It has tools to perform the finite element analysis.
Results	It has tools display the results of finite element analysis.
Utilities	It has tools to clip and unclip faces.
Path Toolbars	

Project Setup 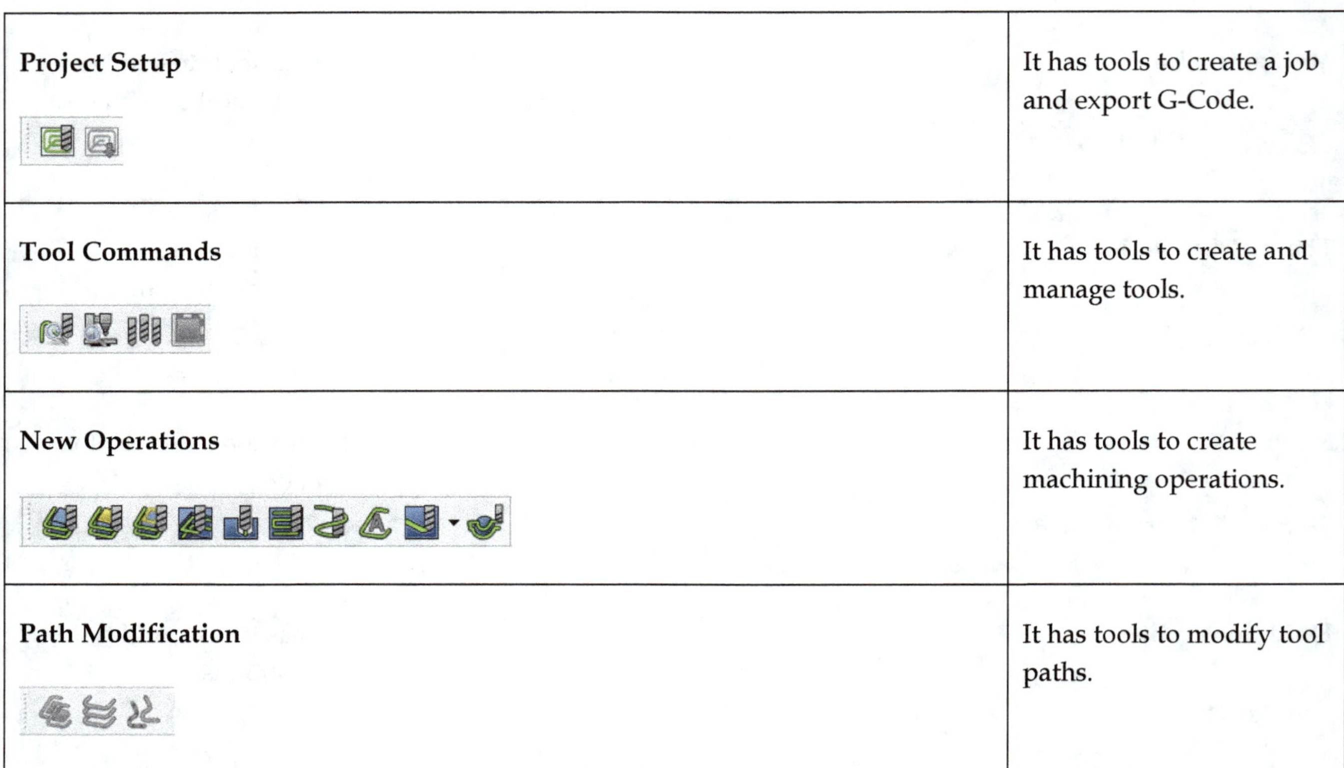	It has tools to create a job and export G-Code.
Tool Commands	It has tools to create and manage tools.
New Operations	It has tools to create machining operations.
Path Modification	It has tools to modify tool paths.

You can hide or show toolbars in the application window. To do this, click **View > Toolbars**, and then select the toolbar name from the list displayed.

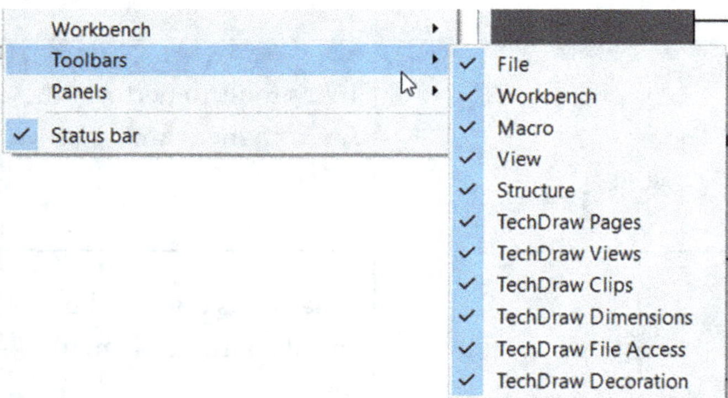

Status bar

The Status bar is available below the graphics window. It shows the action taken while using the commands.

Model tab

It contains the list of operations carried while constructing a part.

Dialog

When you click any tool in FreeCAD, the dialog related to it appears in the **Tasks** tab of the **Combo View** panel. A dialog has various options. The following figure shows various components of a dialog.

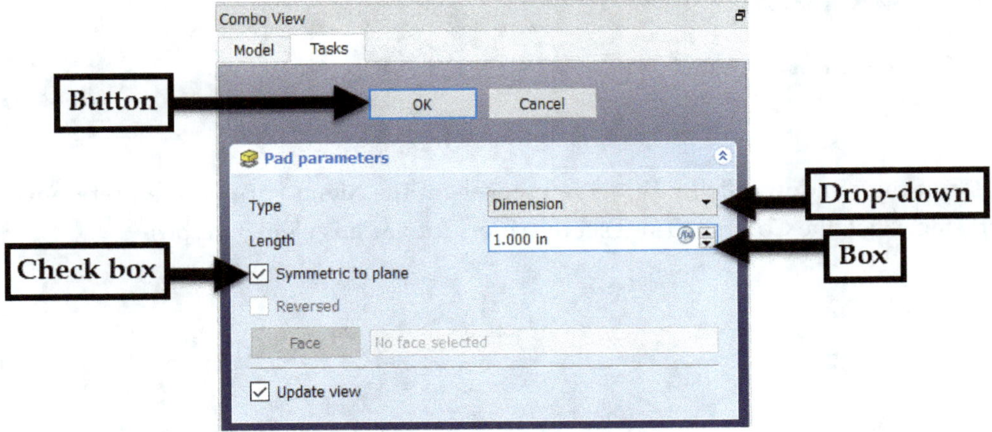

This book uses the default options on the dialog.

Navigation Styles

FreeCAD provides you with different types of mouse navigation styles: **OpenInventor, CAD, Revit, Blender, MayaGesture, Touchpad, Gesture,** and **Open Cascade**. You can select the desired navigation style from the drop-down located at the bottom right corner.

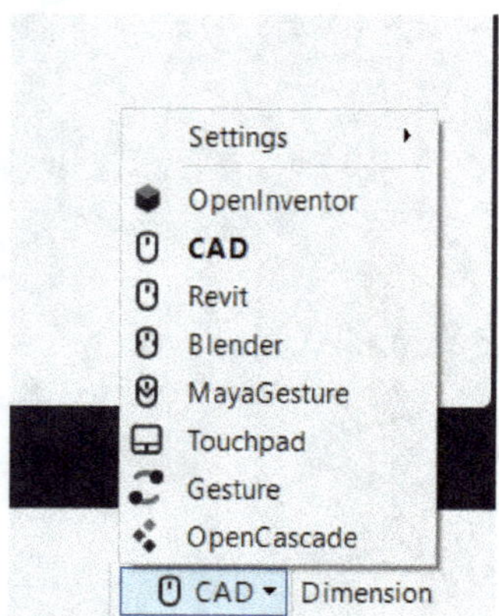

This book uses the CAD Navigation Style for your mouse. Select the **CAD** option from the **Navigation Styles** drop-down. Next, place the mouse cursor on the drop-down; the various mouse functions are displayed.

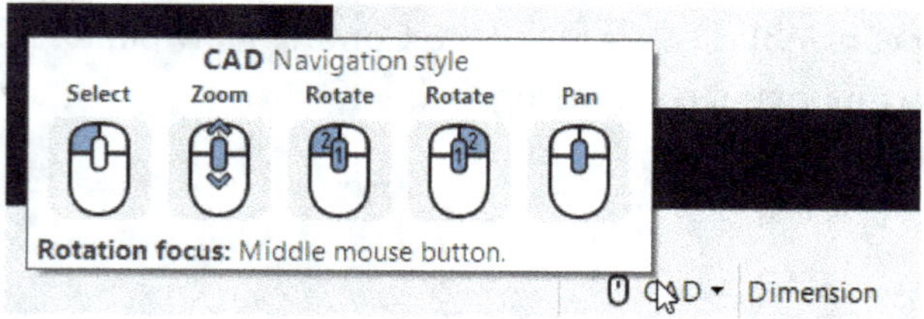

Background

To change the background color of the window, click **Edit > Preferences** on the Menu bar. On the **Preferences** dialog, click **Display** on the left side. Click the **Colors** tab and set the colors for various element types.

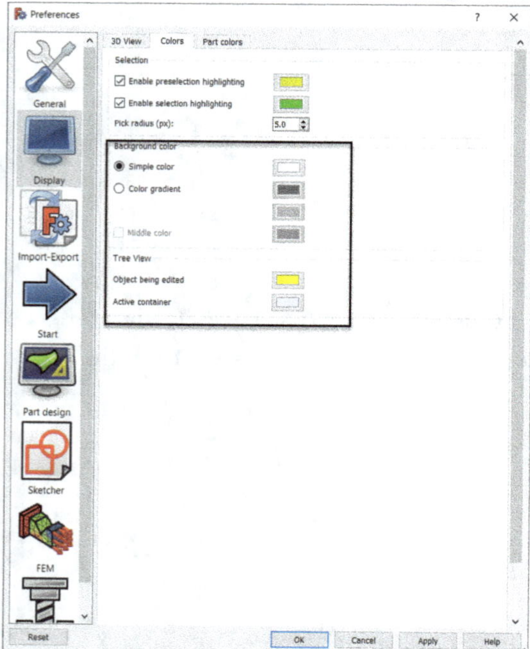

To change the color of sketch elements, click **Sketcher** on the left side, and then click the **Colors** tab. Next, change the **Sketch colors**. Click **OK** to apply the changes.

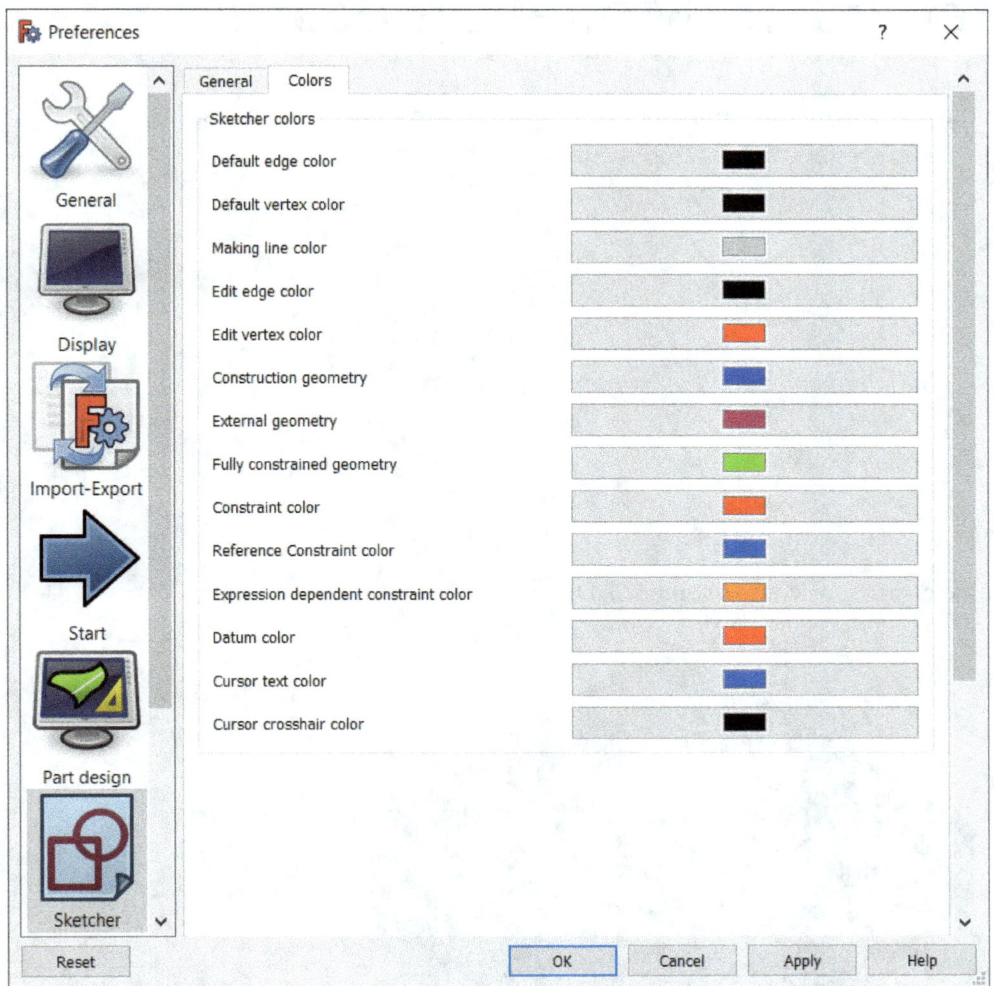

Chapter 2: Part Modeling Basics

This chapter takes you through the creation of your first FreeCAD model. You create simple parts:

In this chapter, you will:

- Create Sketches
- Create a base feature
- Add another feature to it
- Add fillets
- Shell the model
- Create Pocket features

TUTORIAL 1

This tutorial takes you through the creation of your first FreeCAD model.

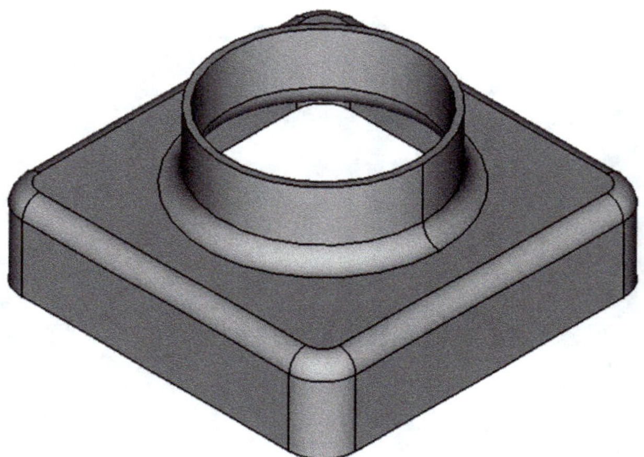

Starting a New Part File

1. To start a new part file, click **File > New** on the Menu Bar (or) click the **New** icon on the **File** toolbar.

A new model window appears.

2. On the **Workbench** toolbar, select **Workbench** drop-down > **Part Design** (or) select **View > Workbench > Part Design** on the Menu bar.

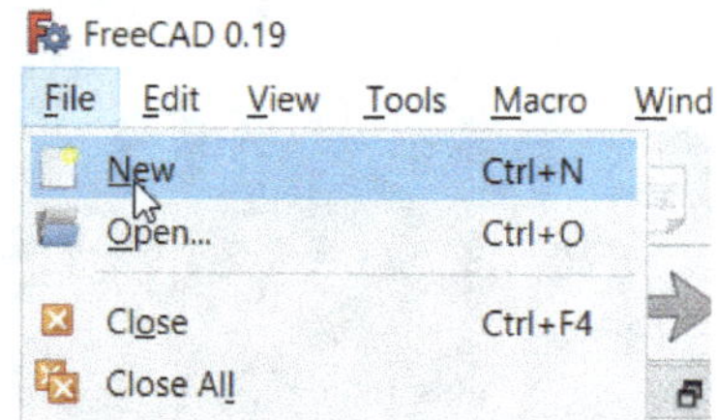

(or)

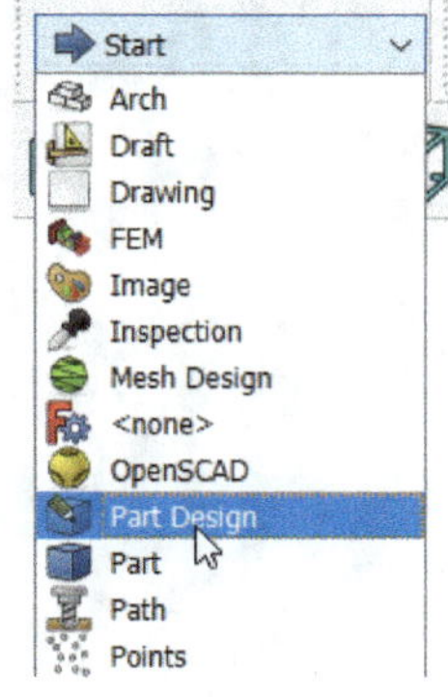

(or)

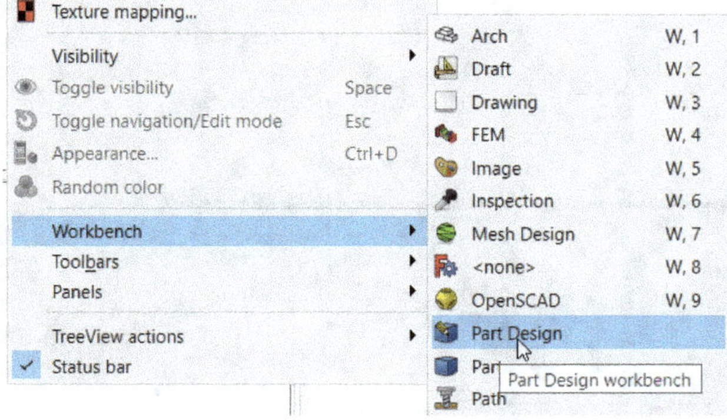

Starting a Sketch

1. To start a new sketch, click **Part Design Helper toolbar > Create New Sketch** (or) click **Sketch > Create Sketch** on the Menu bar.

2. Select the **XY_Plane**, and then click **OK**. The sketch starts.

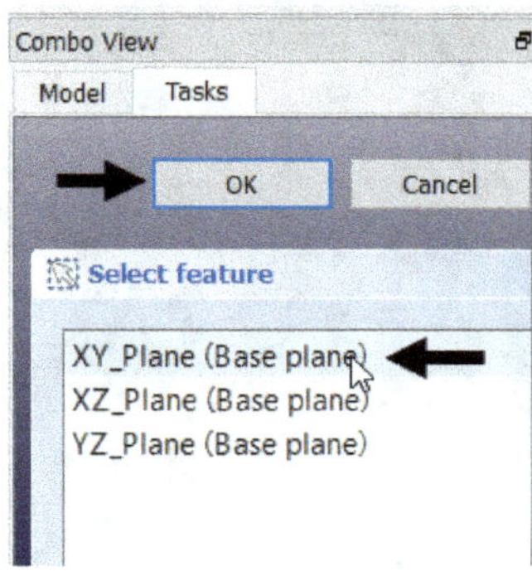

Notice that:
- The grid and sketch origin appear.
- The **Sketcher, Sketcher geometries, Sketcher constraints, Sketcher tools, Sketcher B-spline tools**, and **Sketcher virtual space** toolbars are displayed.
- "**Empty Sketch**" appears in the **Solver Messages** section in the **Combo View** panel.

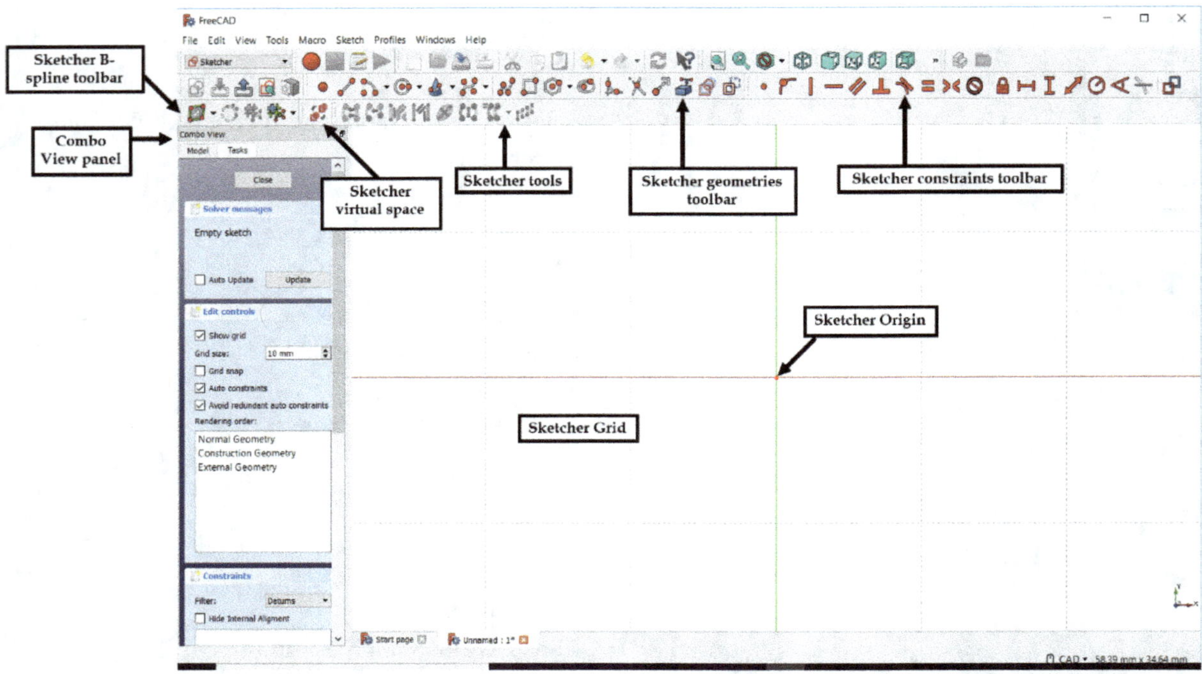

Before you begin sketching, make sure that your FreeCAD settings match the settings used in this tutorial.

3. Click **Edit > Preferences** on the Menu bar. The **Preferences** dialog box appears.
4. On the **Preferences** dialog box, click the **General** option at the left side and then click the **Units** tab.
5. Select **User System > Standard (mm/kg/s/degree)**.
6. Type **2** in the **Number of decimal** box.
7. Click **OK**.
8. In the **Edit Controls** section of the **Tasks** tab of the **Combo View** panel, make sure that the **Show grid** checkbox is selected.

The first feature is an extruded feature from a sketched rectangular profile. You begin by sketching the rectangle.

9. On the **Sketcher geometries** toolbar, click the **Rectangle** icon (or) click **Sketch > Sketcher geometries > Create Rectangle**.

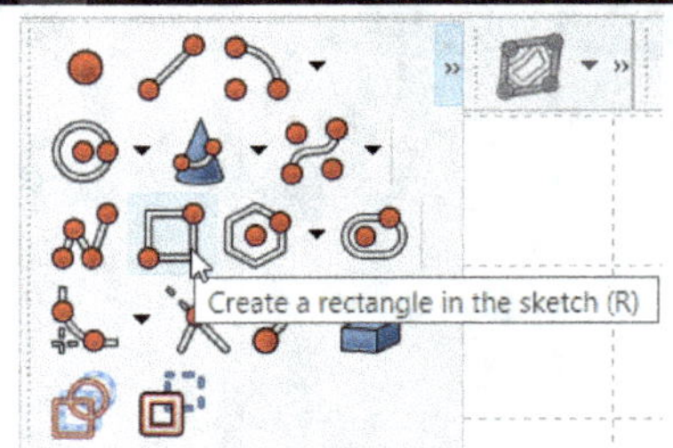

10. Move the cursor to the sketch origin located at the center of the graphics window, and then click on it.
11. Drag the cursor towards the top right corner, and then click to create a rectangle.

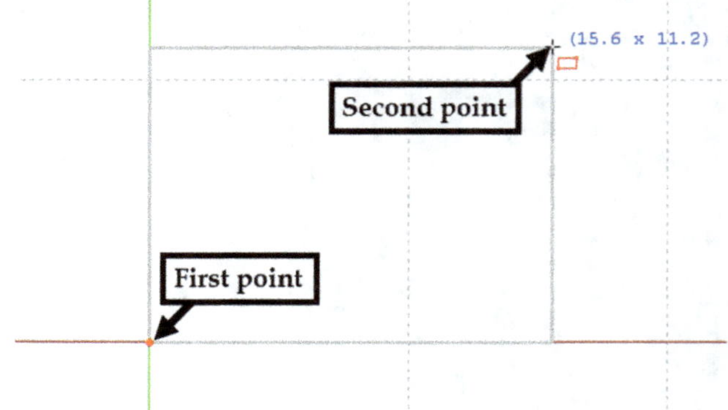

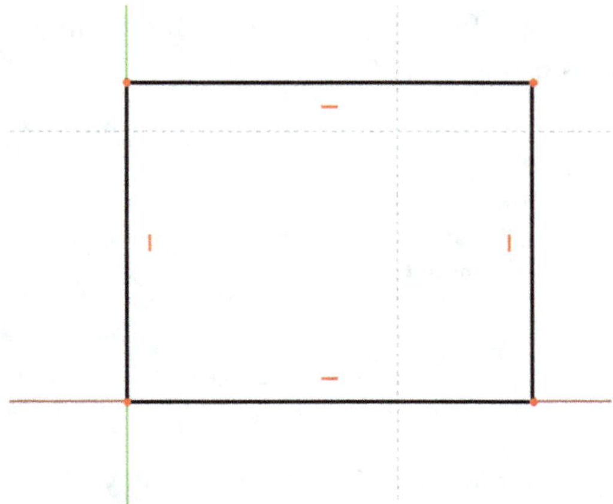

12. Press **ESC** to deactivate the tool.

Adding Constraints

In this section, you specify the size of the sketched rectangle by adding constraints. As you add constraints, the sketch can attain any one of the following states:

Fully Constrained sketch: In a fully constrained sketch, the positions of all the entities are fully described by constraints. In a fully constrained sketch, all the entities are a green color.

Under Constrained sketch: Additional constraints are needed to specify the geometry completely. In this state, you can drag under constrained sketch entities to modify the sketch. An under constrained sketch entity is in black.

If you add any more constraints to a fully constrained sketch, a message appears in the Solver messages section of the **Combo View** panel. It shows that constraint over constraints the sketch. Also, it prompts you to delete anyone of the constraints. Select any one of the constraints and press **Delete** on your keyboard. You can also convert any one of the constraints into a reference constraint. To do this, select the constraint and click the **Toggle reference/driving constraint** icon on the **Sketcher constraints** toolbar.

1. Click **Sketcher constraints** toolbar > **Constrain vertical distance** ⏸ (or) click **Sketch** > **Sketcher constraints** > **Constrain vertical distance** on the menu bar.
2. Select the right vertical line of the rectangle.
3. Enter **100** in the **Length** box of the **Insert Length** dialog and click **OK**.
4. Click **Sketcher constraints** toolbar > **Constrain horizontal distance** ⊢⊣ (or) click **Sketch** > **Sketcher constraints** > **Constrain horizontal distance** on the menu bar.
5. Select the bottom horizontal line of the rectangle.
6. Enter **100** in the **Length** box of the **Insert Length** dialog and click the **OK** button.

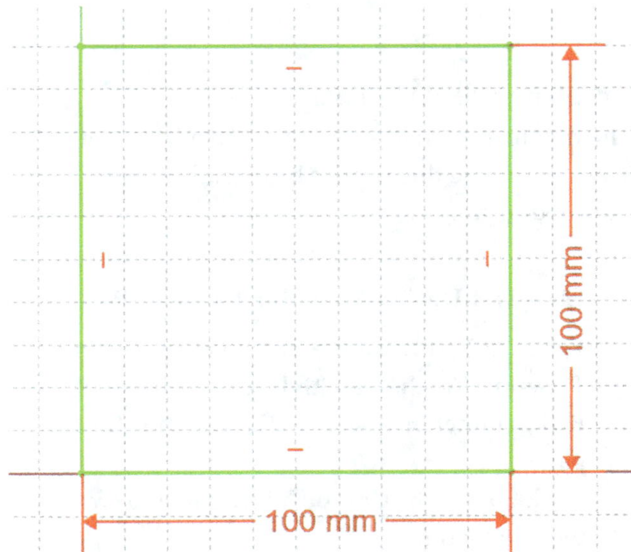

7. Press **Esc** to deactivate the **Constrain horizontal distance** tool.
8. To display the entire rectangle at full size and to center it in the graphics area, use one of the following methods:

   • Click **Fit All** 🔍 on the **View** toolbar.
   • Click **View** > **Standard Views** > **Fit All** on the Menu bar.

9. Click **Close** on the **Combo View** panel.

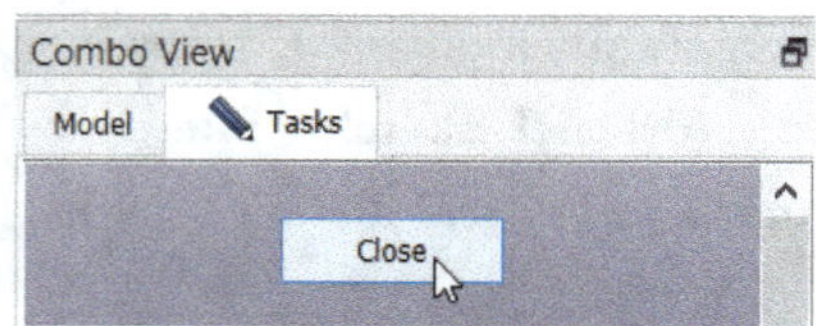

10. Again, click **Fit All** 🔍 on the **View** toolbar.

Creating the Base Feature

The first feature in any part is called a base feature. You now create this feature by extruding the sketched rectangle.

1. Click **Part Design Modeling** toolbar **> Pad**
   (or) click **Part Design > Pad** on the Menu bar.
2. Type-in 25 in the **Length** box available on the **Pad parameters** dialog on the **Combo View** panel.
3. Click **OK** on the **Combo View** panel to create the pad feature.
4. On the **View** toolbar, click the **Isometric** icon.

Notice the new feature, **Pad**, in the **Model** tab of the **Combo View** panel.

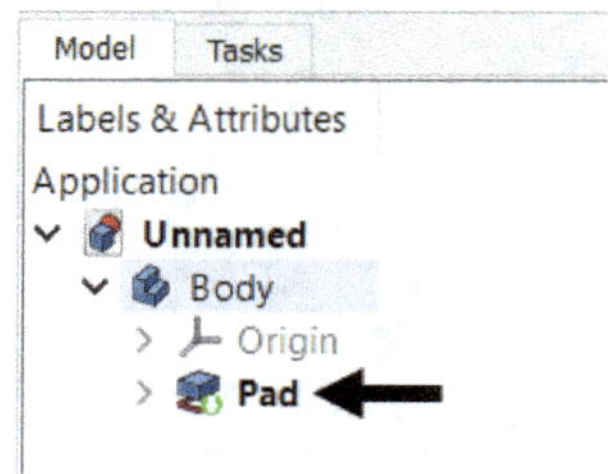

To magnify a model in the graphics area, you can use the zoom tools available on the **Zoom** submenu in the **View** menu of the Menu bar.

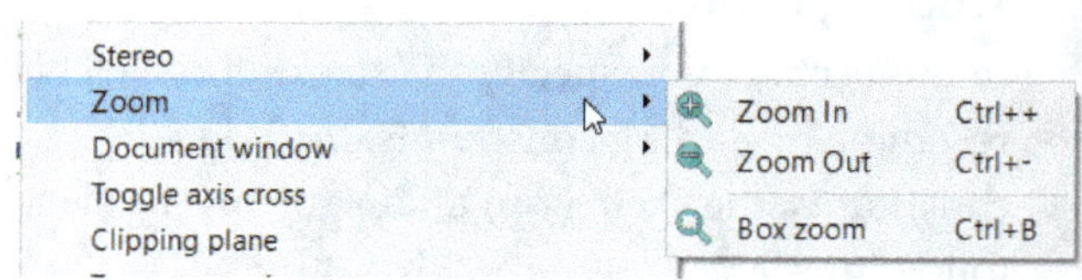

Click **Zoom In** to zoom into the model.

Click **Zoom Out** to zoom out of the model.

Click **Box Zoom**, and then drag the pointer to create a rectangle; the area in the rectangle zooms to fill the window.

The **View** toolbar has two more zoom tools: **Fit All** and **Fit Selection**.

Click **Fit All** 🔍 to display the full part size in the current window.

Click on a vertex, an edge, or a feature, and then click **Fit Selection** 🔍 ; the selected item zooms to fill the window.

To display the part in different draw styles, select the options in the **Draw Style** drop-down on the **View** toolbar.

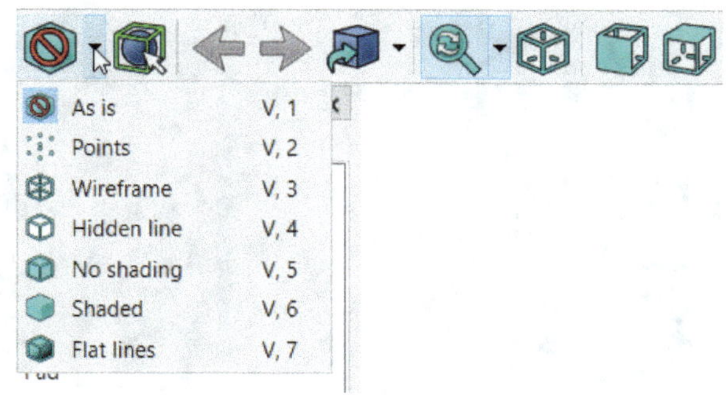

Normal Mode

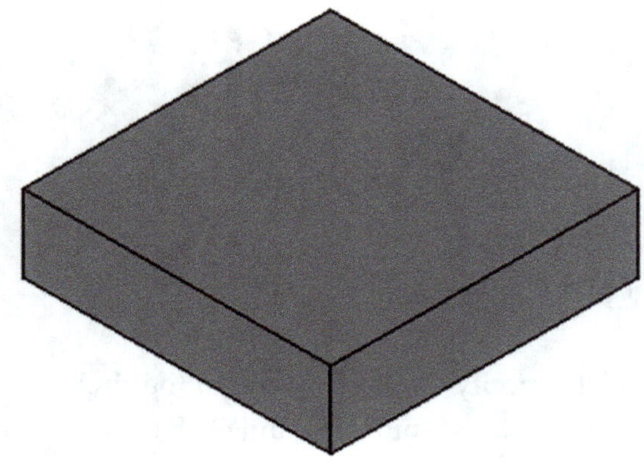

Flat lines

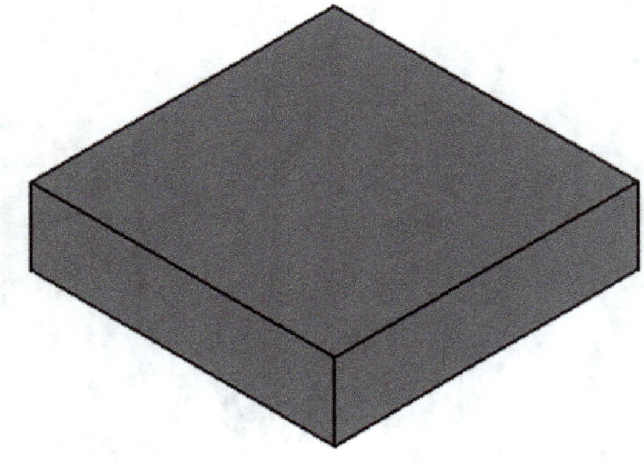

Shaded

Wireframe

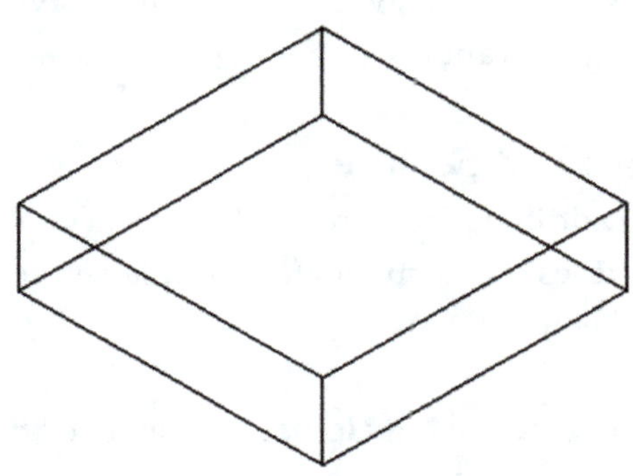

Points

Hidden Line

No Shading

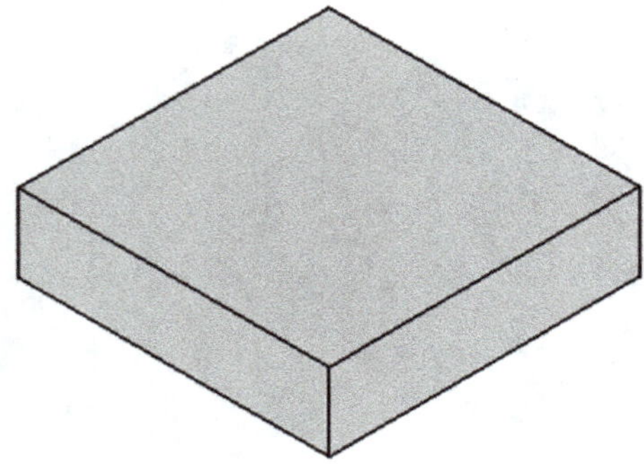

The default draw style for parts and assemblies is **Normal Mode**. You may change the draw style whenever you want.

Adding a Pad Feature

To create additional features on the part, you need to draw sketches on the model faces or planes, and then extrude them.

1. On the **Part Design Helper** toolbar, click the **Create a new datum plane** ◇ icon.
2. Click on the top face of the first feature.

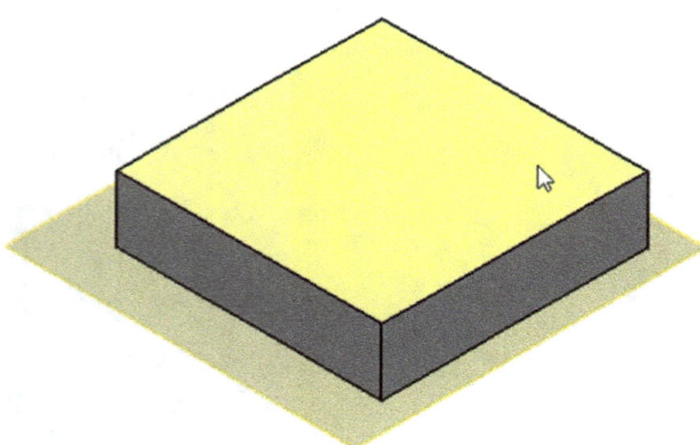

3. Click **OK** on the **Tasks** tab of the **Combo View** panel.
4. Click **Create Sketch** on the **Face tools** section of the **Tasks** tab. A new sketch is started.

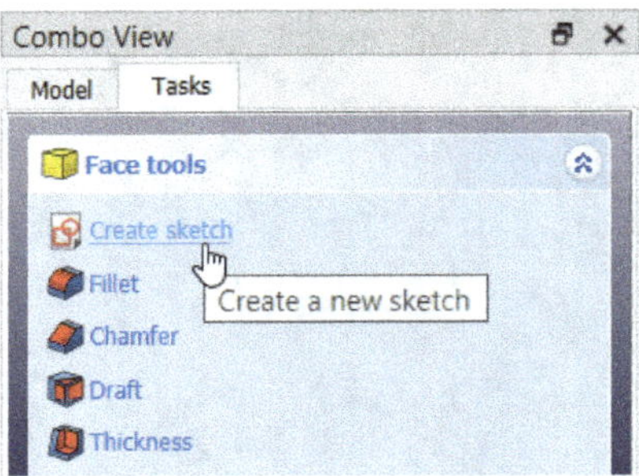

5. On the **Sketcher geometries** toolbar, click **Circle** drop-down > **Center and rim point.**

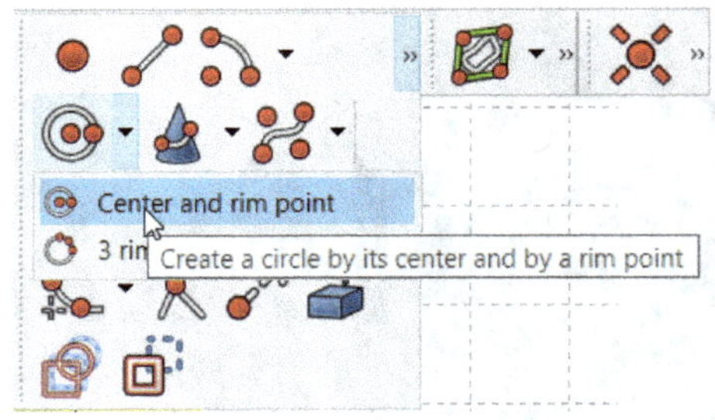

6. Click to specify the center point of the circle.
7. Move the pointer outward and click to create the circle.

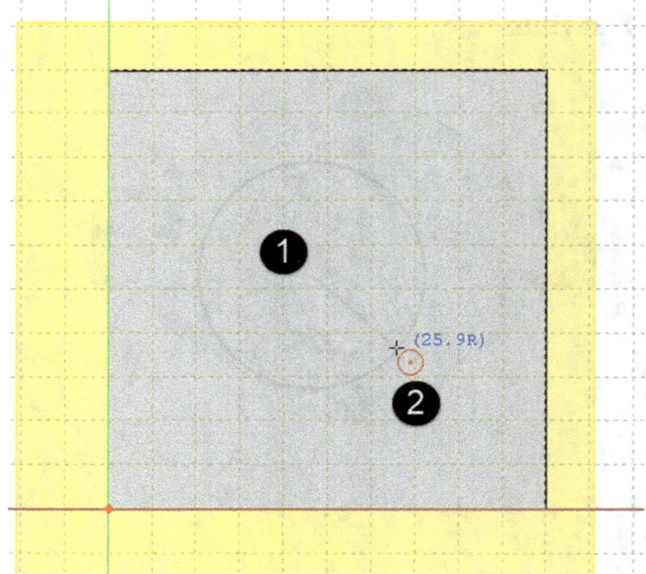

8. On the **Sketcher constraints** toolbar, click the **Constrain distance** ✐ icon.
9. Select the center point of the circle.
10. Select the horizontal axis of the sketch.
11. Type **50** in the **Length** box of the **Insert Length** dialog.
12. Click **OK**.

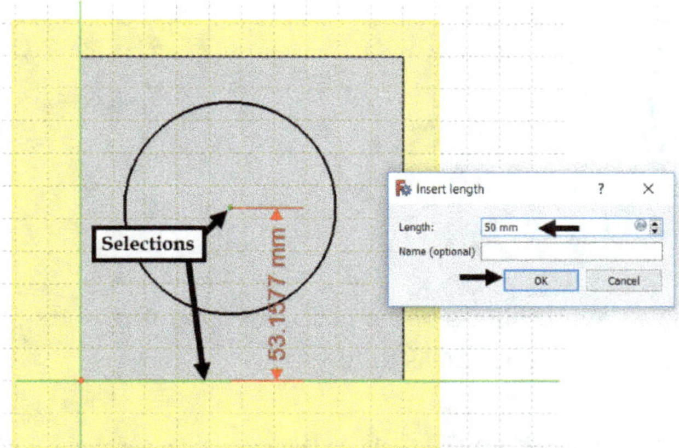

13. Select the center point of the circle and the vertical axis of the sketch.
14. Type **50** in the **Length** box and click **OK**.

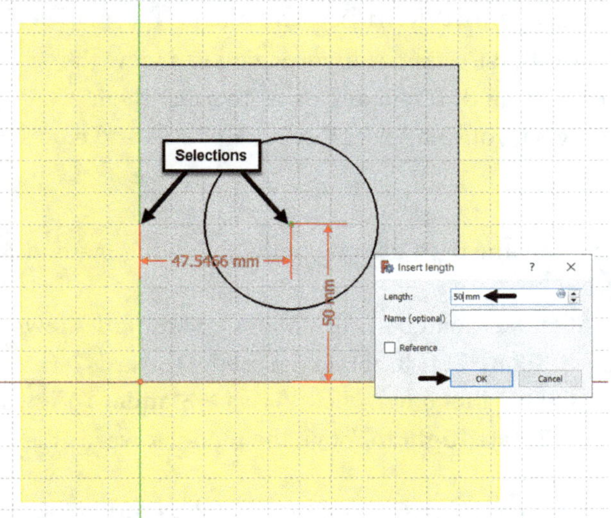

15. On the **Sketcher constraints** toolbar, click the **Constrain radius** ⊘ icon.
16. Select the circle and type **30** in the **Radius** box of the **Change Radius** dialog.

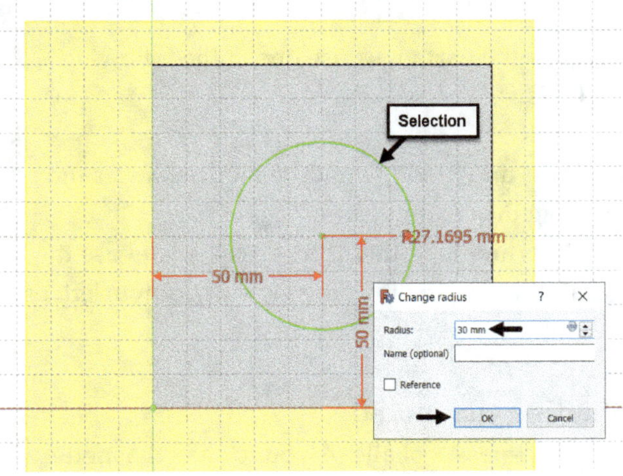

17. Click **OK**.
18. On the **Sketcher** toolbar, click the **Leave Sketch** icon.
19. On the **Part Design Modeling** toolbar, click the **Pad** icon.
20. Type **20** in the **Length** box of the **Pad Parameters** dialog.
21. Click **OK**.

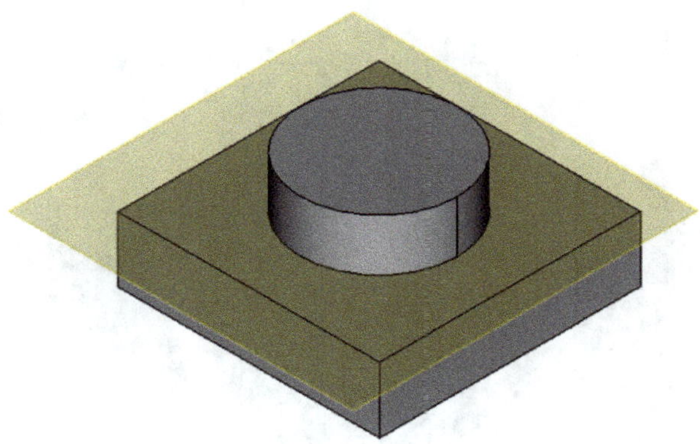

Filleting the Corners

The **Fillet** tool allows you to fillet the corners of the model.

1. Click on the datum plane displayed on the model.
2. On the Menu bar, click **View > Visibility > Hide Selection**.
3. On the **View** toolbar, select **Draw style > Wireframe**.
4. Press and hold the Ctrl key and select the vertical edges of the model, as shown.

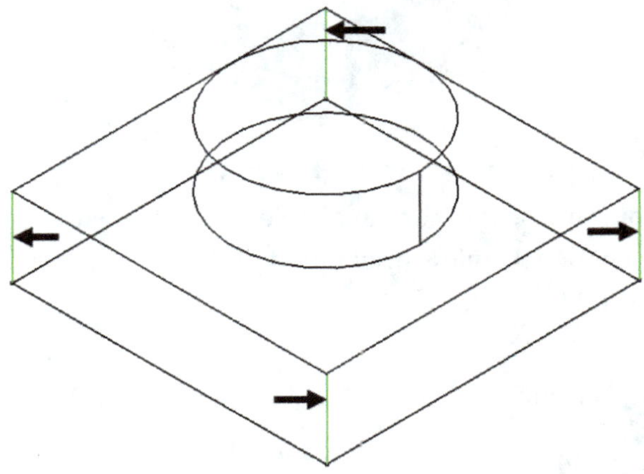

5. On the **Part Design Modeling** toolbar, click the **Fillet** icon.
6. Type **10** in the **Radius** box.
7. Click **OK**.
8. On the **View** toolbar, select **Draw style > Flat lines** .
9. Click on the horizontal face of the model, as shown.

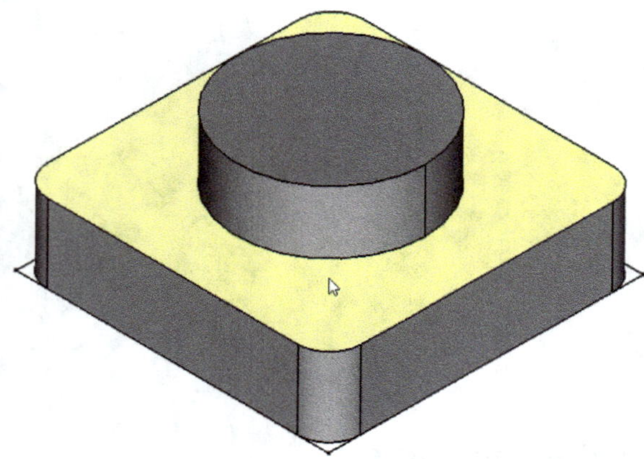

10. Click the **Fillet** icon on the **Part Design Modeling** toolbar.
11. Type **5** in the **Radius** box and click **OK**.

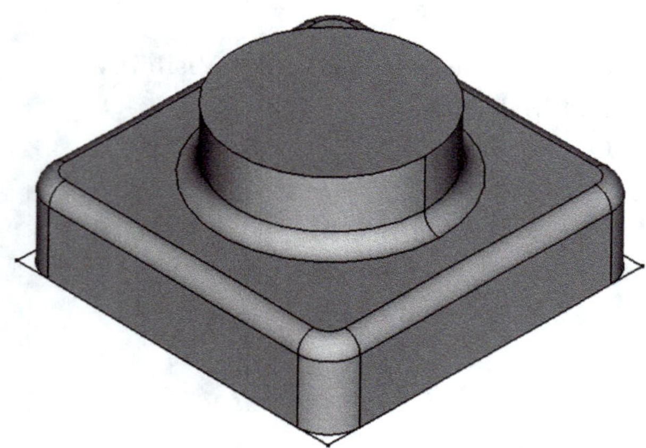

Changing the View Orientation

You can use the icons available on the **View** toolbar to change the view orientation of the sketch, part, or assembly.

Front

Top

Right

Rear

Bottom

Left

Isometric

The default planes of the part corresponding to the standard views are as follows:

- **XZ Plane - Front** or **Back**
- **YZ Plane - Top** or **Bottom**
- **XY Plane - Right** or **Left**

Rotating and Moving the Part

In addition to standard views, you can view the model from different angles by rotating them. By doing so, you can select the hidden faces and edges easily.

To rotate the part, use one of the following methods:

- On the Menu bar, click **View > Standard Views > Rotate Left** to rotate the model towards left.
- On the Menu bar, click **Views > Standard Views > Rotate Right** to rotate the model towards the right.
- Press and hold the middle and the right mouse buttons. Next, drag the cursor to rotate the model.
- To rotate the part in 90° increments, press and hold the **Shift** key and use the arrow keys.

To move the part view, use one of the following methods:

- Press and hold the middle mouse button and drag the cursor.
- Press and hold the **Alt** or **Ctrl** key and use the arrow keys to move the view up, down, left, or right.

Shelling the model

The **Thickness** tool allows you to shell the model.

Part Modeling Basics

1. Press and hold the middle and right mouse buttons.
2. Drag the cursor upward to display the bottom face.
3. Click on the bottom face.

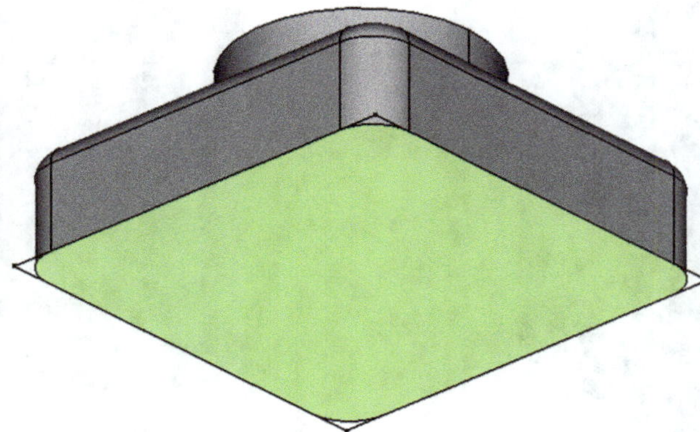

4. On the **Part Design Modeling** toolbar, click the **Thickness** icon.
5. In the **Thickness Parameters** dialog, select **Mode > Skin**.
6. Select **Join Type > Intersection**.
7. Type **2** in the **Thickness** box.
8. Check the **Make thickness inwards** option.
9. On the **View** toolbar, click the **Isometric** icon.
10. On the **Thickness parameters** dialog, click the **Add face** button.
11. Select the top face of the second feature.

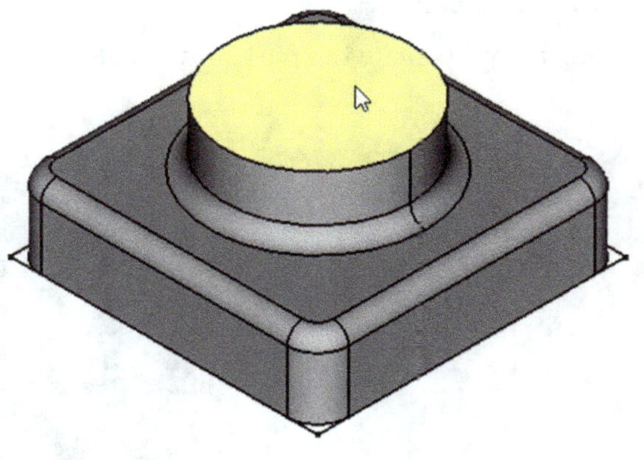

12. Click **OK**.

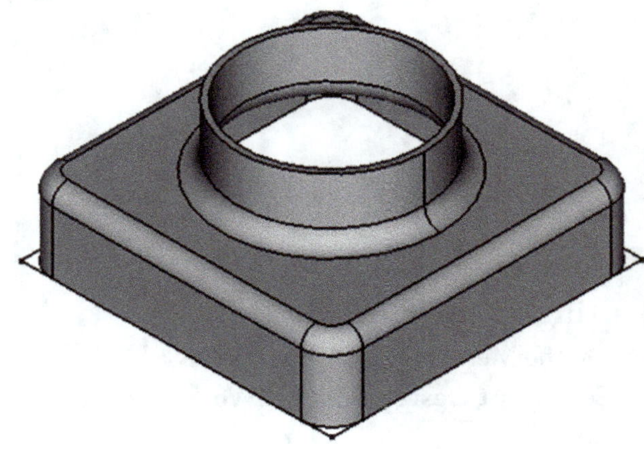

Saving the Part

1. Click **File > Save** on the Menu bar.
2. On the **Save As** dialog, type-in **Tutorial1** in the **File name** box.
3. Click **Save** to save the file.
4. Click **File Menu > Close**.

Note:

*.FCStd is the file extension for all the files that you create in FreeCAD.

TUTORIAL 2

In this tutorial, you create the part shown below.

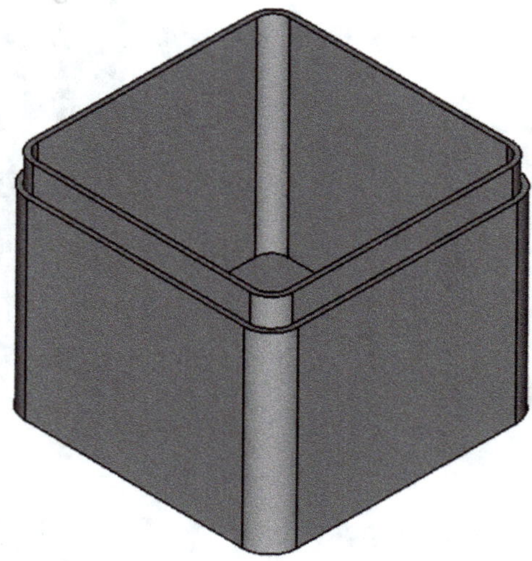

Starting a New File

1. On the Menu bar, click **File > New**.
2. Select **Part Design** from the **Workbench** drop-down.

Sketching for the Pad Feature

1. Click **Create Sketch** icon on the **Part Design Helper** toolbar.
2. Select the XY plane.
3. Click **OK**.
4. Click **Rectangle** on the **Sketcher geometries** toolbar.
5. Create a rectangle, shown in the figure.

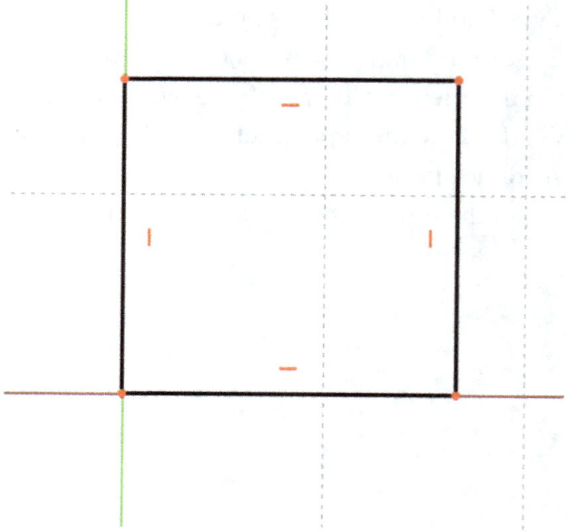

6. Add vertical and horizontal distance constraints to the rectangle, as shown.

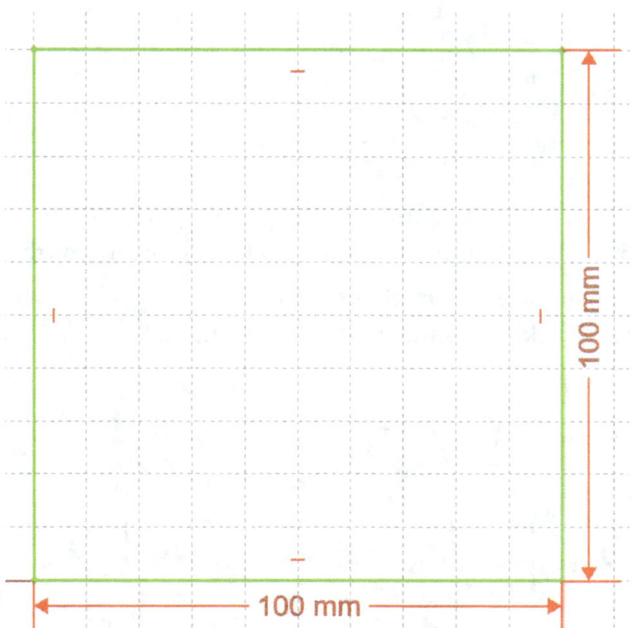

7. Click the **Leave Sketch** icon on the **Sketcher** toolbar.

8. Click **Pad** on the **Create** panel.

9. Type **80** in the **Length** box and click **OK**.

10. Click the **Isometric** icon on the **View** toolbar.

11. Select **Draw Style > Wireframe** on the **View** toolbar.

12. Press and hold the Ctrl key and select the vertical edges.

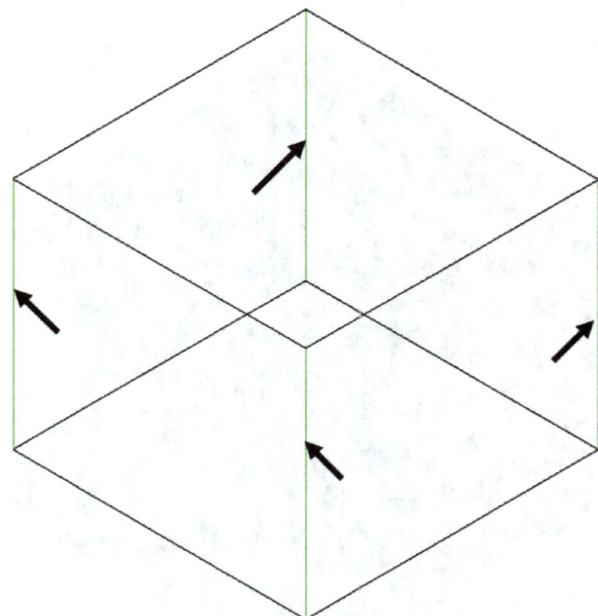

13. On the **Part Design Modeling** toolbar, click the **Fillet** icon.

14. Type 10 in the **Radius** box.

15. Click **OK**.

16. On the **View** toolbar, select **Draw Style > Flat lines**.

17. Click on the top face of the model.

18. Click the **Thickness** icon on the **Part Design Modeling** toolbar.

19. Type 4 in the **Thickness** box.

20. Select **Join Type > Intersection**.

21. Check the **Make thickness inwards** option.

22. Click **OK**.

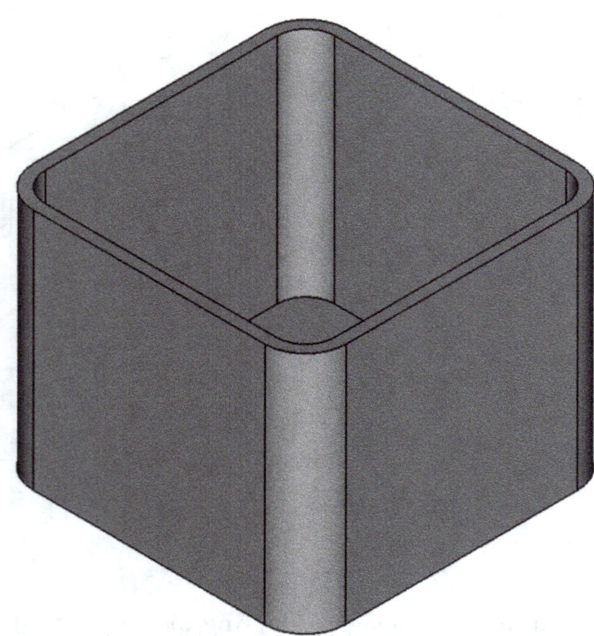

Creating the Cut Feature

1. On the **Part Design Helper** toolbar, click the **Create a new datum plane** ⬦ icon.
2. Click on the top face of the first feature.

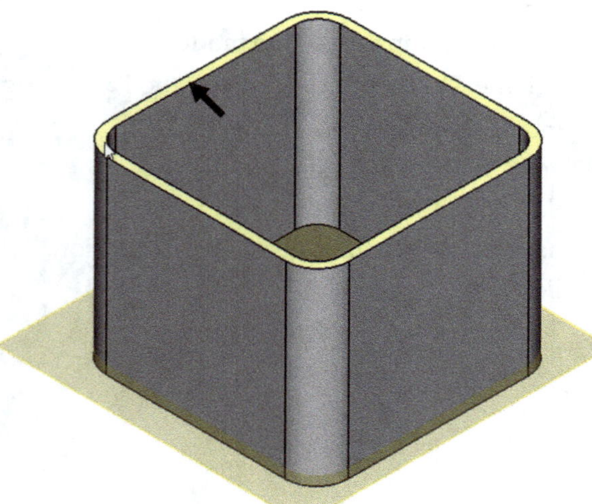

3. Click **OK** on the **Tasks** tab of the **Combo View** panel.
4. Click **Create Sketch** on the **Face tools** section of the **Tasks** tab. A new sketch is started.

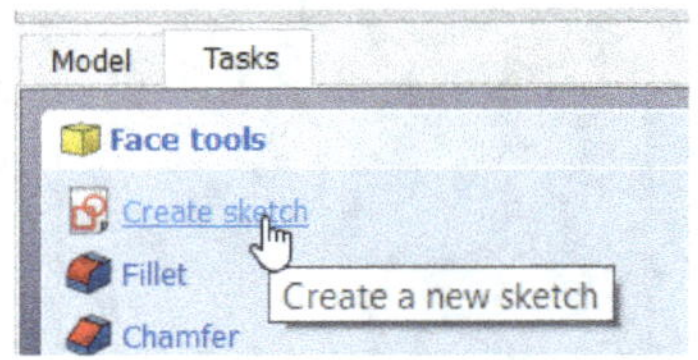

5. Click the **External geometry** icon on the **Sketcher geometries** toolbar.
6. Click on the inner edges of the model.

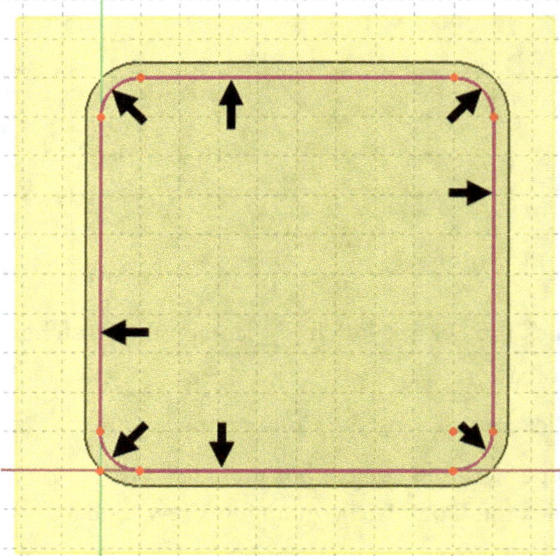

7. Click the **Rectangle** icon on the **Sketcher geometries** toolbar.
8. Create a rectangle, as shown.

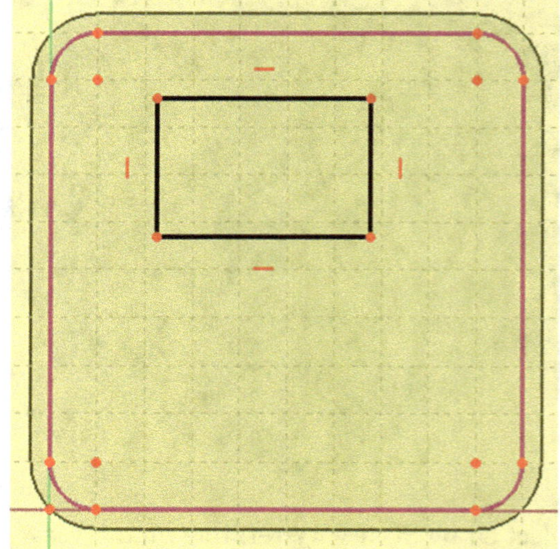

9. Click the **Create fillet** icon on the **Sketcher geometries** toolbar.
10. Click on the left vertical and the top horizontal line.

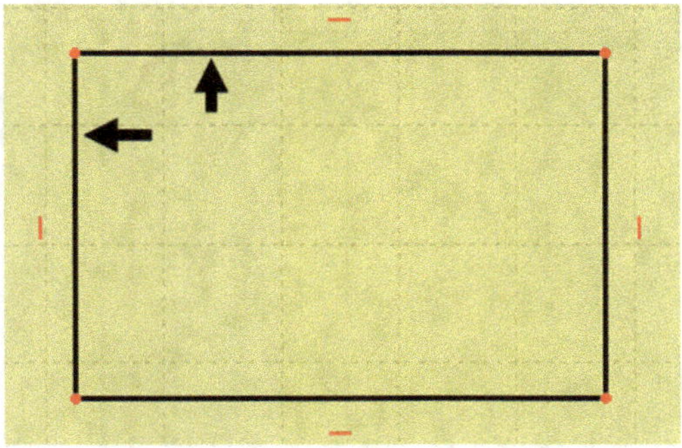

A fillet is created at the corner.

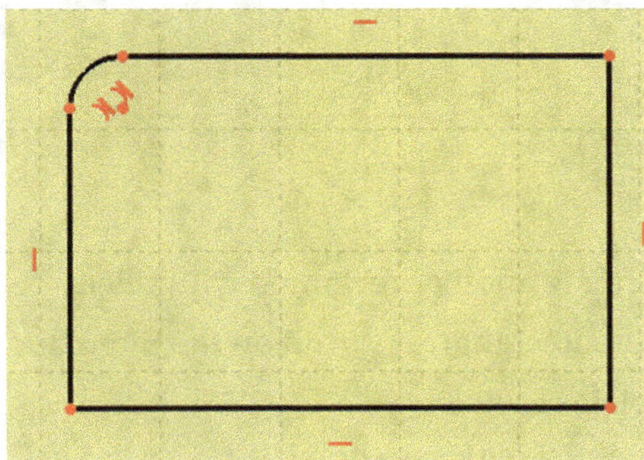

11. Likewise, create fillets at the remaining corners, as shown.

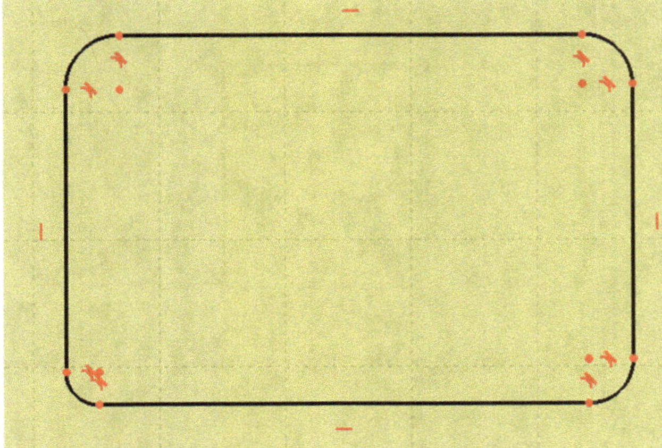

12. Click the **Constrain equal** icon on the **Sketcher constraints** toolbar.
13. Select the top -right and top-left fillets of the rectangle; the fillets are made equal.
14. Select the top-left and bottom-left fillets of the rectangle.
15. Select the bottom-left and the bottom-right fillets of the rectangle.

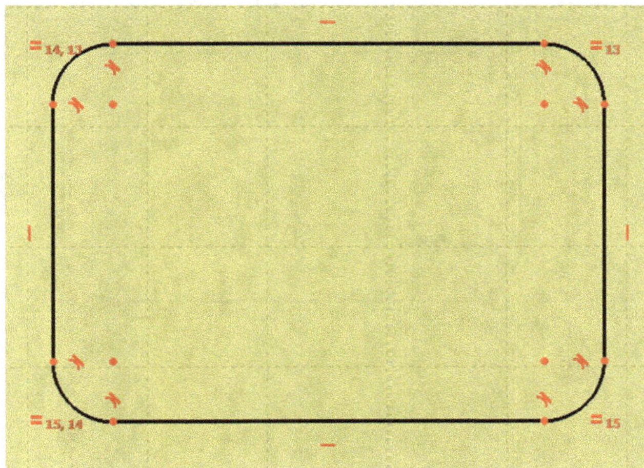

16. Click the **Constrain Coincident** icon on the **Sketcher constraints** toolbar.
17. Select the center point of the top right fillet of the rectangle.
18. Select the center point of the top right fillet of the external geometry.

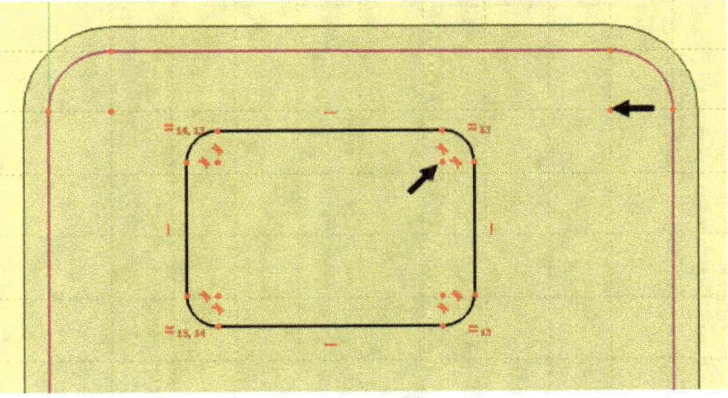

19. Select the center point of the bottom-left fillet of the rectangle.
20. Select the center point of the bottom-left fillet of the external geometry.

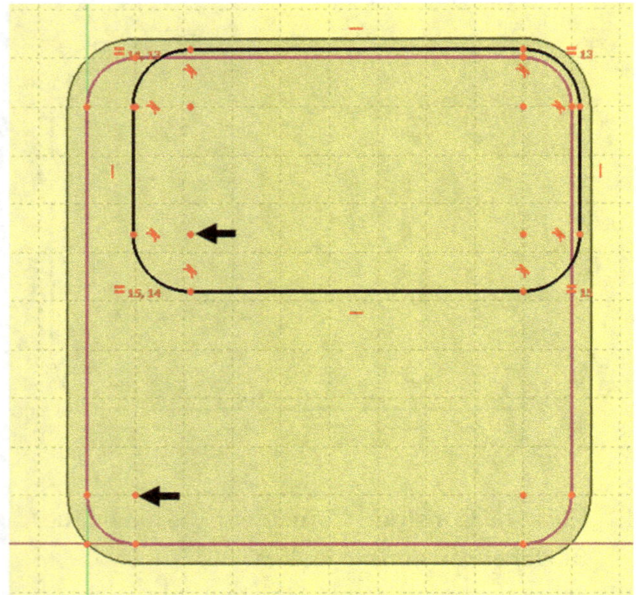

The centerpoints of the fillets are coincident with each other.

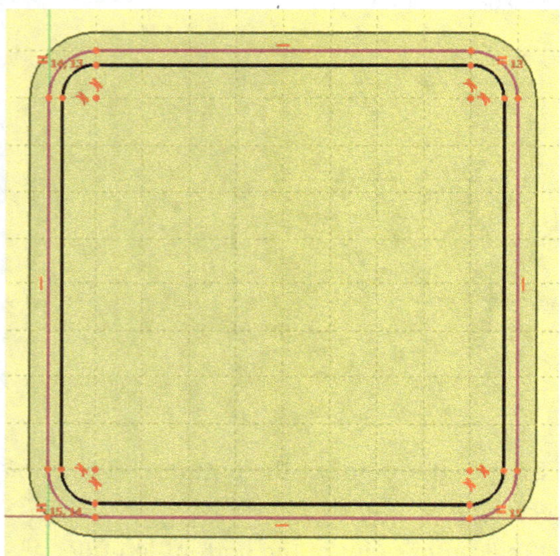

21. Click **Constrain radius** ⊘ on the **Sketcher constraints** toolbar.
22. Select any one of the fillets of the rectangle.
23. Type 8 in the **Radius** box.
24. Click **OK**.

25. Likewise, create another rectangle with fillets.
    - Click the **Rectangle** ▢ icon on the **Sketcher geometries** toolbar.
    - Create a rectangle, as shown.

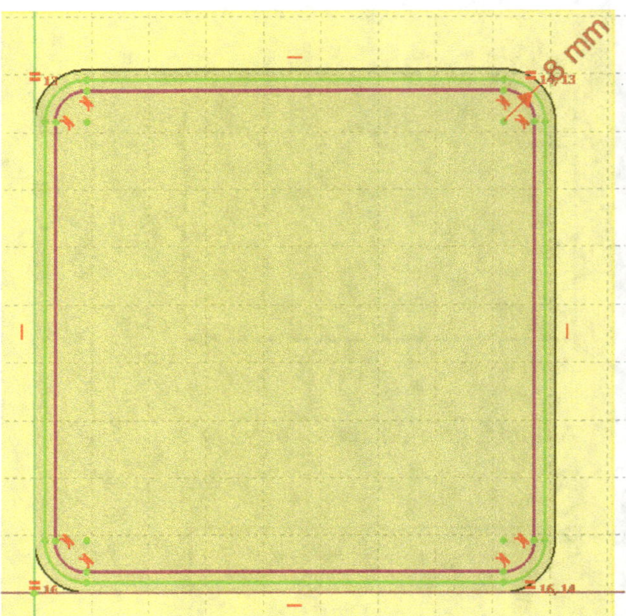

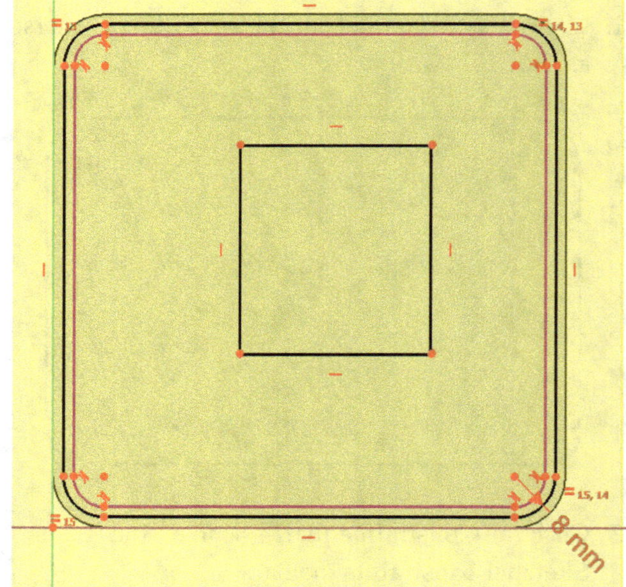

    - Click the **Create fillet** icon on the **Sketcher geometries** toolbar.
    - Create fillets at the corners of the rectangle, as shown.

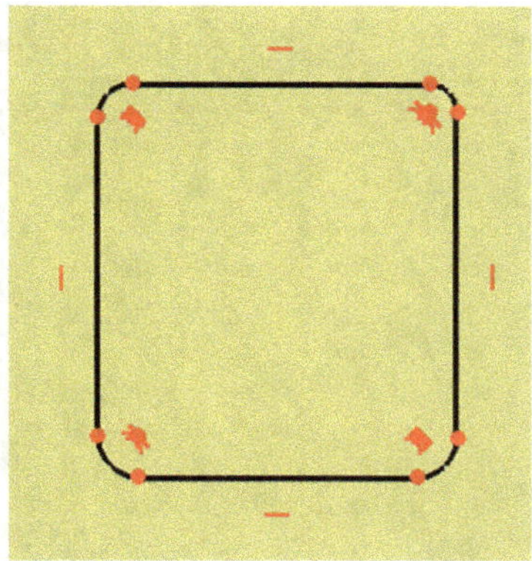

- Click the **Constrain equal** ≡ icon on the **Sketcher constraints** toolbar.
- Select the top -right and top-left fillets of the rectangle; the fillets are made equal.
- Select the top-left and bottom-left fillets of the rectangle.
- Select the bottom-left and the bottom-right fillets of the rectangle.

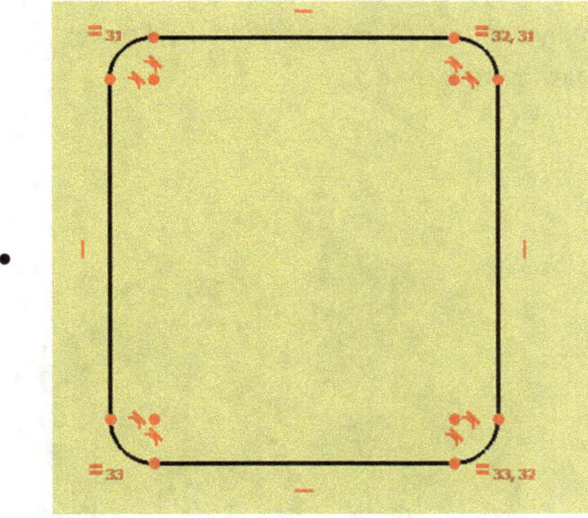

-
- Click the **Constrain Coincident** ◦ icon on the **Sketcher constraints** toolbar.
- Select the center point of the top right fillet of the rectangle.
- Select the center point of the top right fillet of the external geometry.

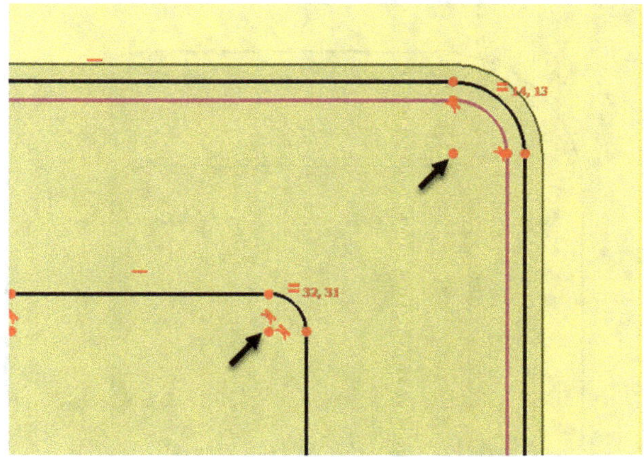

- Select the center point of the bottom-left fillet of the rectangle.
- Select the center point of the bottom-left fillet of the external geometry.

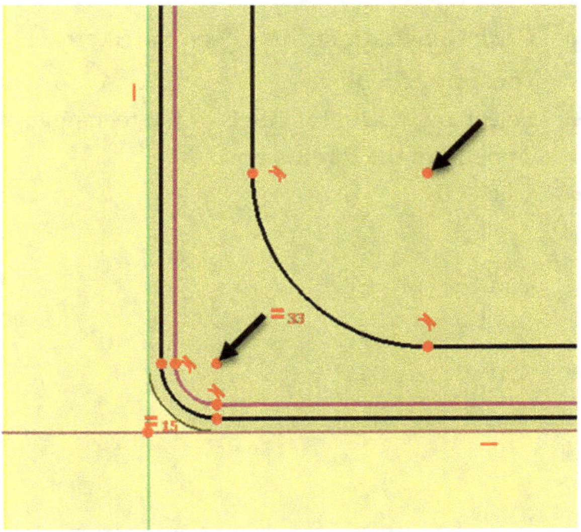

- The centerpoints of the fillets are coincident with each other.

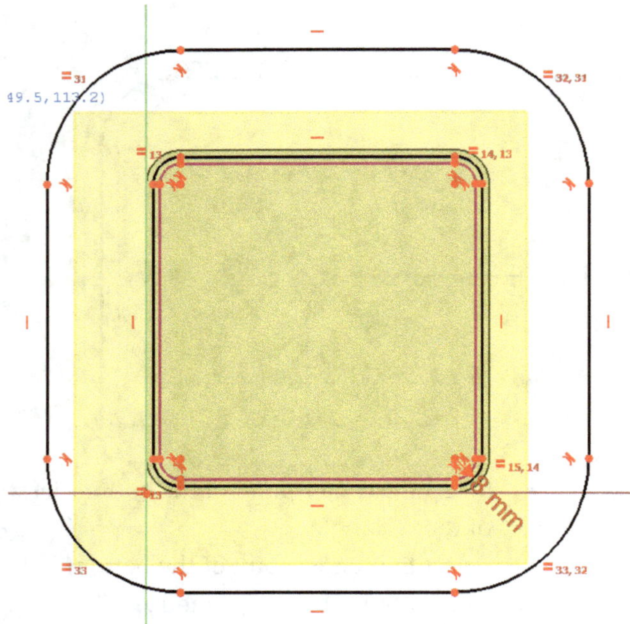

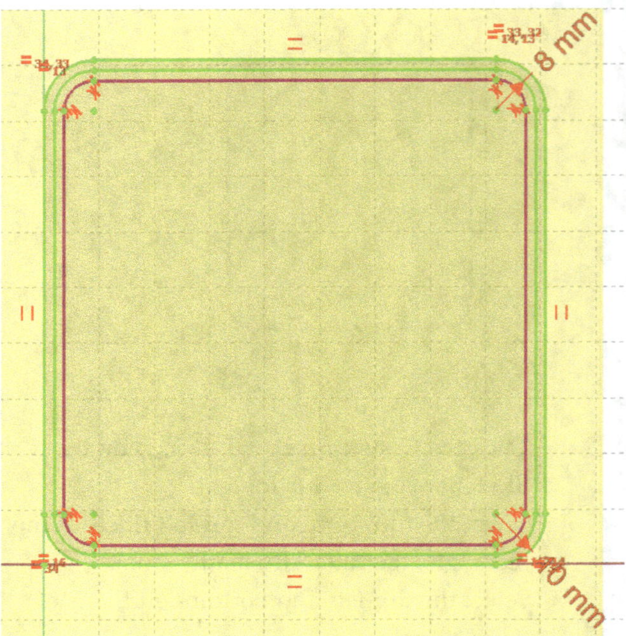

- Click **Constrain radius** ⊘ on the **Sketcher constraints** toolbar.
- Select any one of the fillets of the rectangle.
- Type 10 in the **Radius** box.
- Click **OK**.

26. Click **Leave Sketch** on the **Sketcher** toolbar.
27. Click the **Pocket** icon on the **Part Design Modeling** toolbar.
28. Type **10** in the **Length** box in the **Pocket parameters** dialog.
29. Click **OK**.

30. Save and close the file.

Chapter 3: Assembly Basics

In this chapter, you will:

- Add Components to assembly
- Apply constraints between components

TUTORIAL 1

This tutorial takes you through the creation of your first assembly.

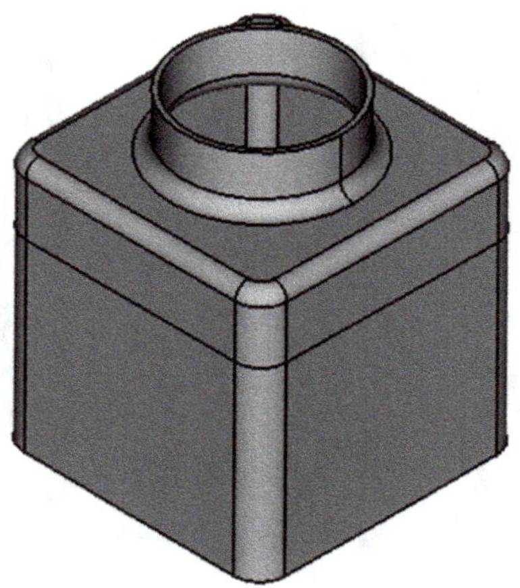

Starting a New Assembly File

1. Open the **FreeCAD** application.
2. Click **Tools > Addon Manager** on the Menu bar.
3. On the **Addon Manager** dialog, click the **Workbenches** tab.
4. Select **A2plus** from the list.
5. Click **Install/Update**.
6. Click **Close**.
7. Close the FreeCAD application, and then restart it.
8. Click **File > New** on the Menu bar.
9. Select **Workbenches** drop-down > **Assembly 2**.

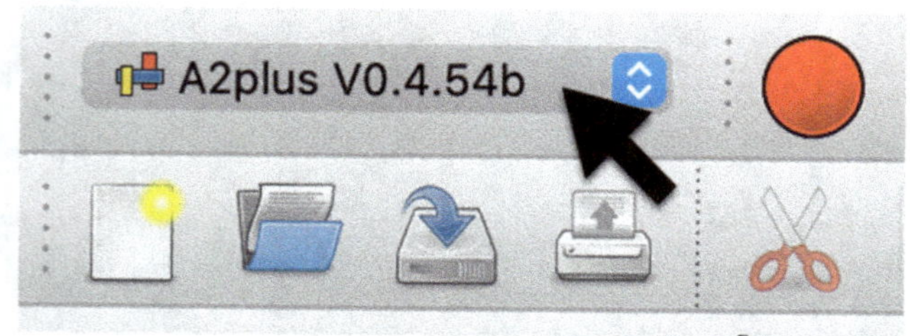

Inserting the Base Component

1. Click **File > Save** on the menu bar.
2. Type **Assembly_tutorial** in the **File name**.
3. Click **Save**.
4. To insert the base component, click the **Add a part from an external file** icon on the **A2p_Part** toolbar.

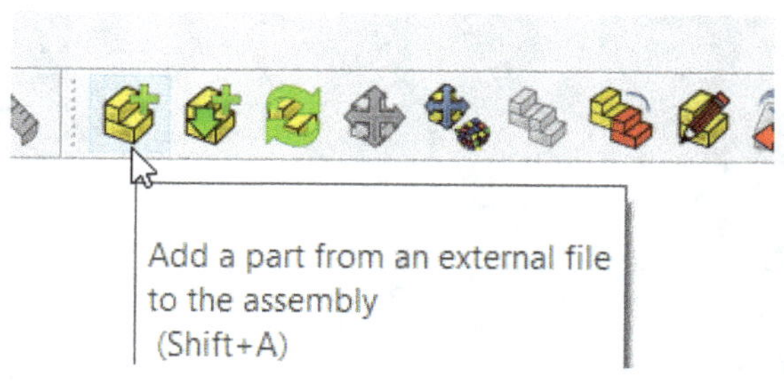

5. Browse to the location of the **Tutorial 2** file of Chapter 1, and then double-click on it.

6. Click the **Isometric** icon on the **View** toolbar.

Adding the second component

1. To insert the second component, click **A2plus > Add a part from an external file** on the Menu bar.
2. Browse to the location of the **Tutorial** 1 file of Chapter 1, and then double click on it.
3. Click in the window to place the component.

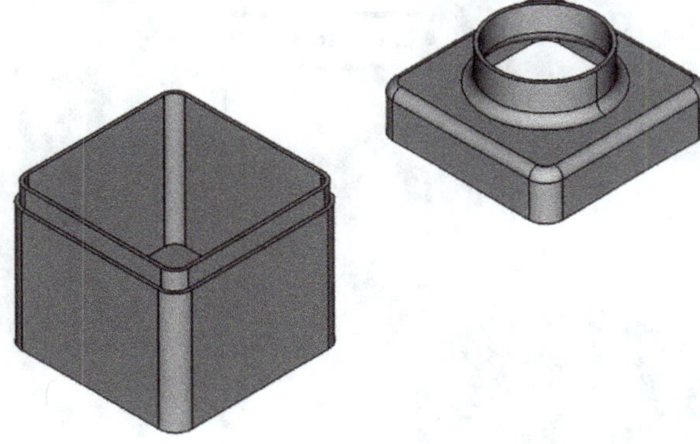

Applying Constraints

After adding the components to the assembly environment, you need to apply constraints between them. By applying constraints, you establish relationships between components.

The **A2p_Constraint** toolbar has various tools to apply constraints between the components.

Different assembly constraints that can be applied are given next.

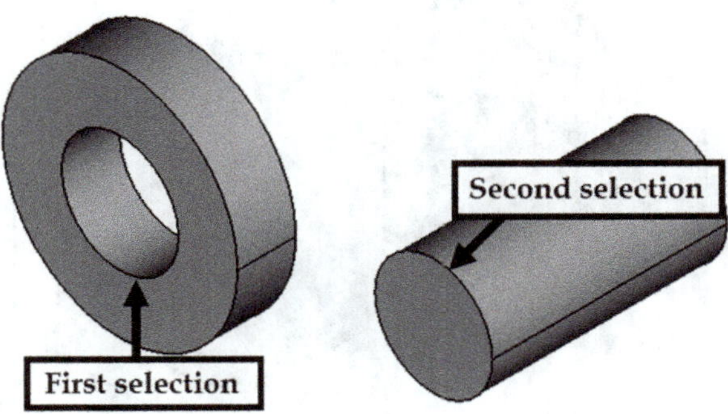

Add circularEdge constraint: This constraint is used to make two circular edges concentric.

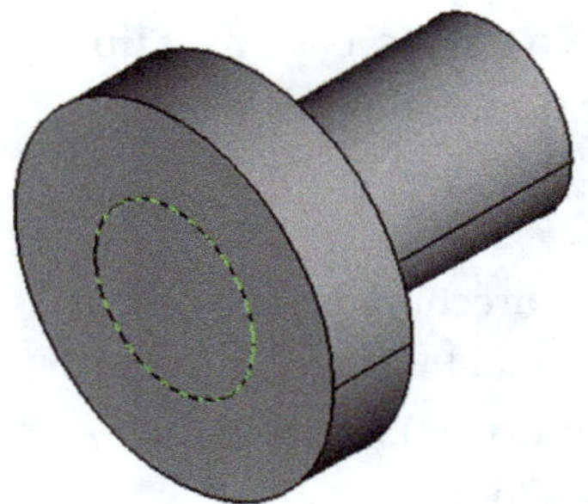

Click the **Flip direction** button on the **Constraint Properties** dialog to reverse the direction.

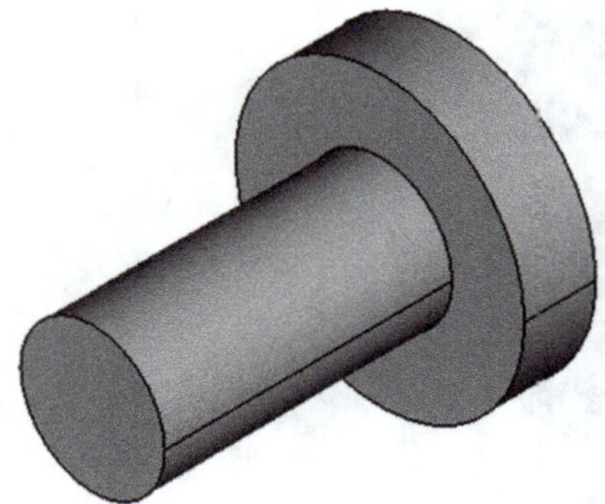

Click the **Toggle** button on the **Constraint Properties** dialog to lock/unlock the rotation of the component.

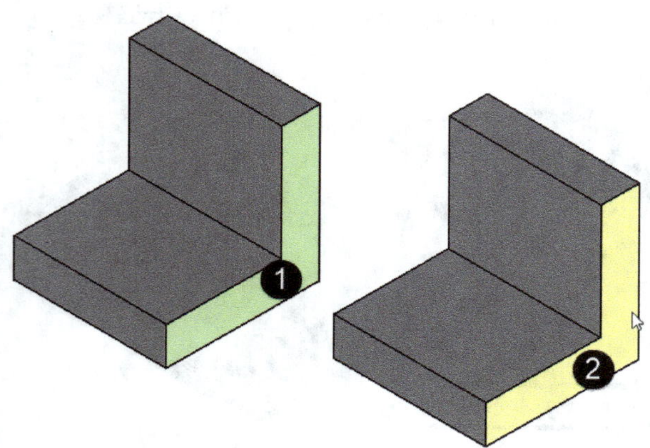

Add planeCoincident Constraint: Using this constraint, you can make two planar faces coplanar to each other.

You can change the direction in which the planar faces touch each other. To do this, click the **Flip direction** button on the **Constraint Properties** dialog.

You can also change the direction by using the **Direction** drop-down. To do this, select an option from the **Direction** drop-down located in the **Constraint Properties** dialog.

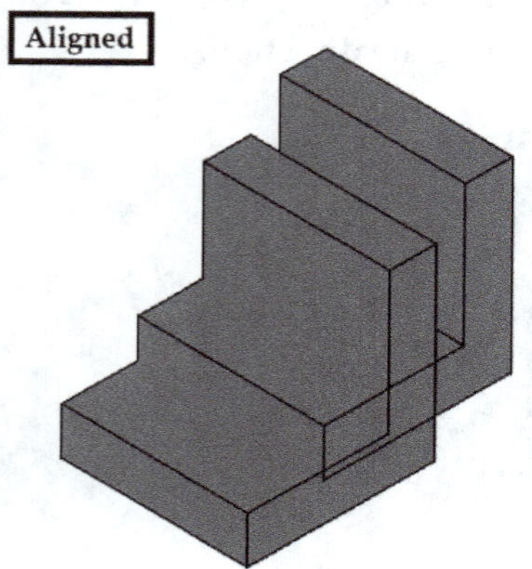

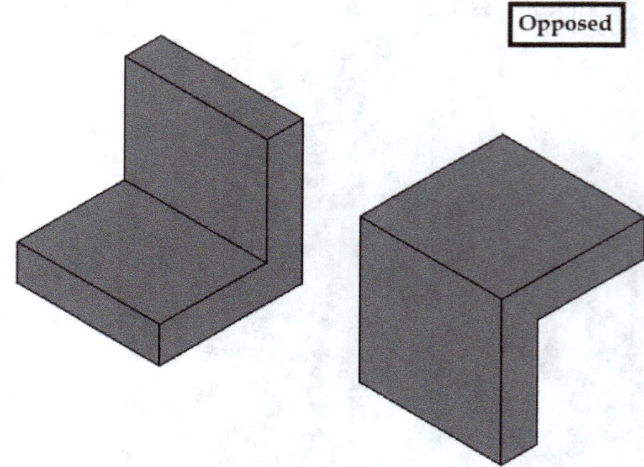

Add axial Coincident Constraint: This constraint allows you to align the centerlines of the round faces. Select the two cylindrical faces to be aligned.

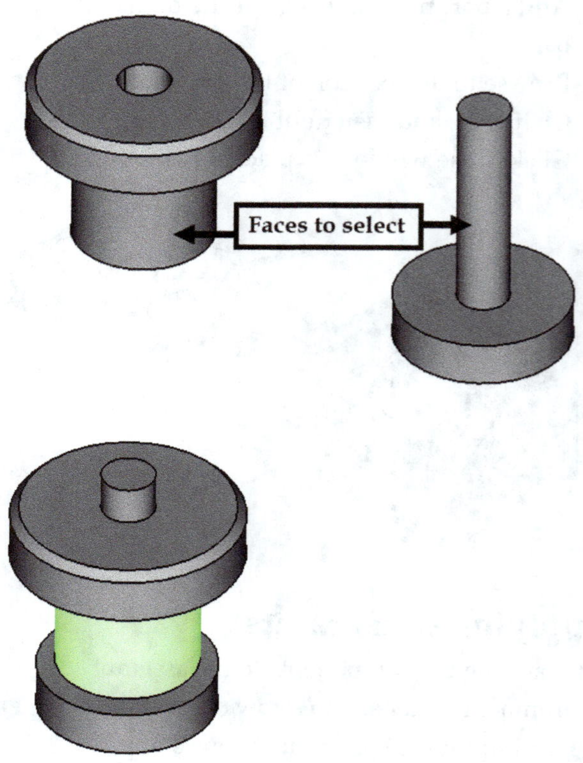

Click the **Flip direction** button on the **Constraint Properties** dialog; the axes of the selected round faces are positioned in the direction opposite to each other.

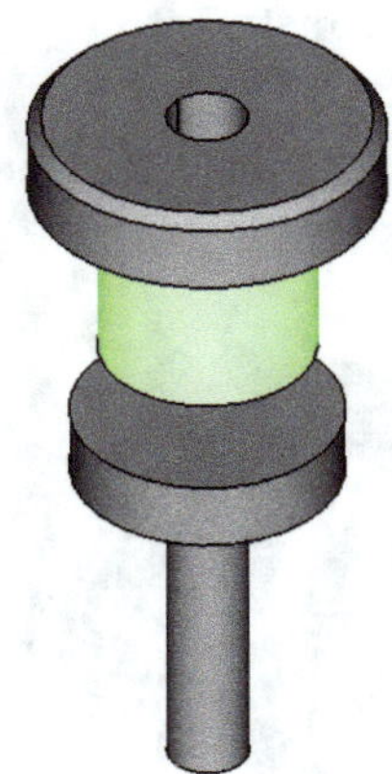

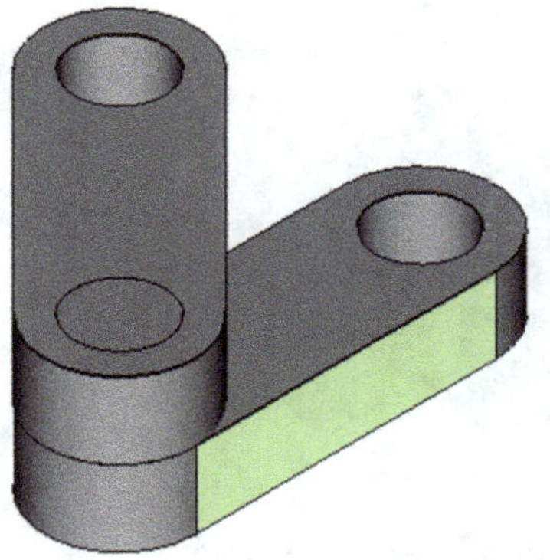

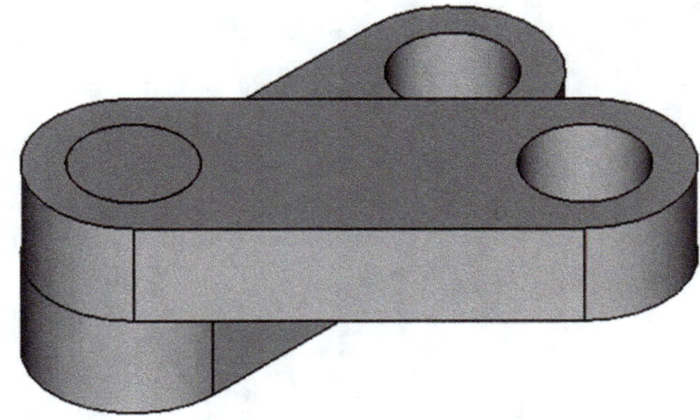

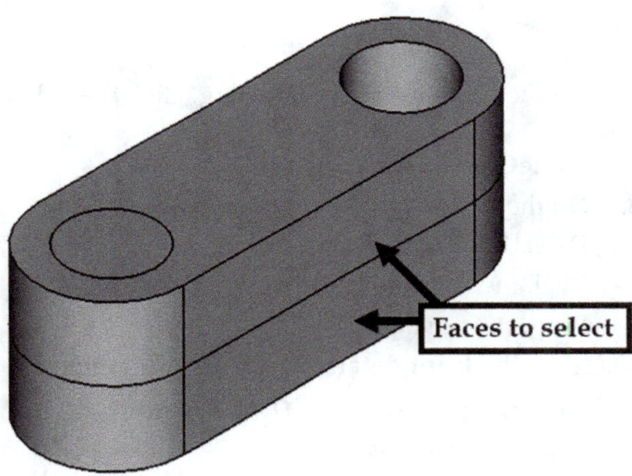

Add angledPlanes constraint: Applies the angle constraint between two components. Activate the Define Constraints command select the faces to be constrained.

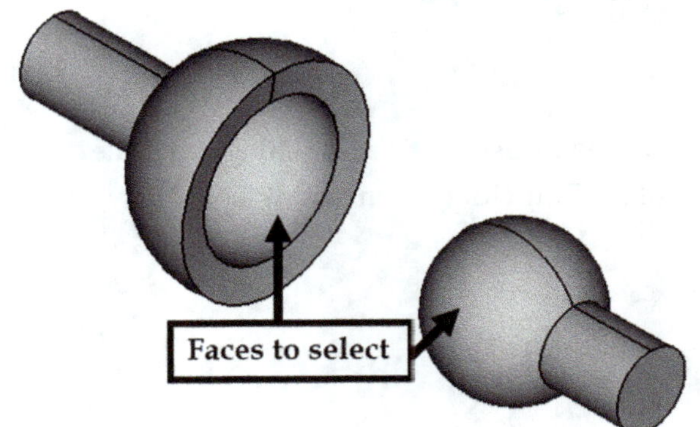

Add sphereCenterIdent constraint: This constraint is used to align two spherical surfaces.

On the **Constraint Tools** dialog, click the **Add angledPlanes constraint** icon. On the **Constraints Properties** dialog, type 45 in the **Angle** box. Click the **Accept** button.

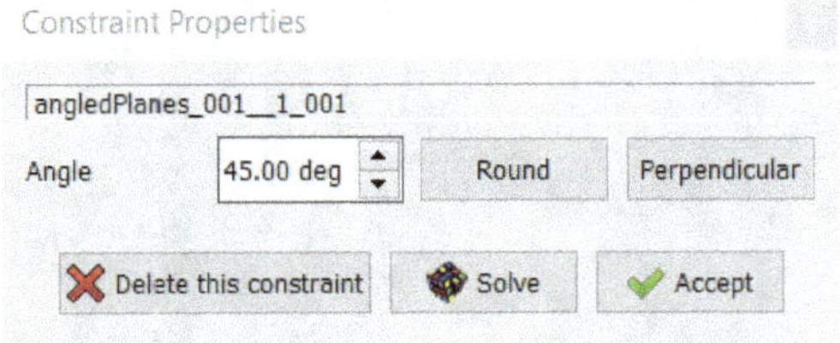

Constraint Properties

angledPlanes_001__1_001

Angle | 45.00 deg | Round | Perpendicular

Delete this constraint | Solve | Accept

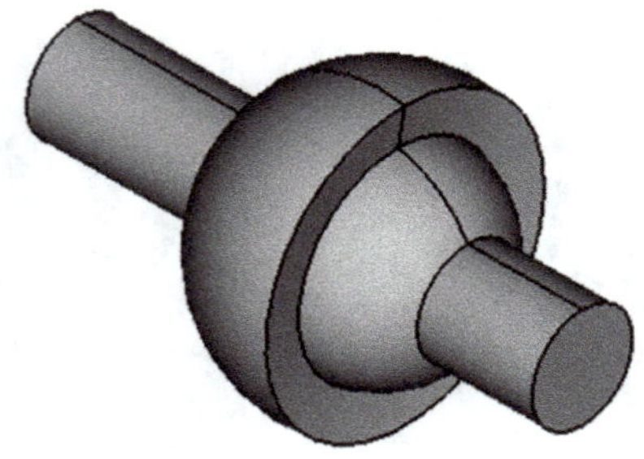

1. Click the **Define Constraints** icon on the **A2p_Constraint** toolbar.

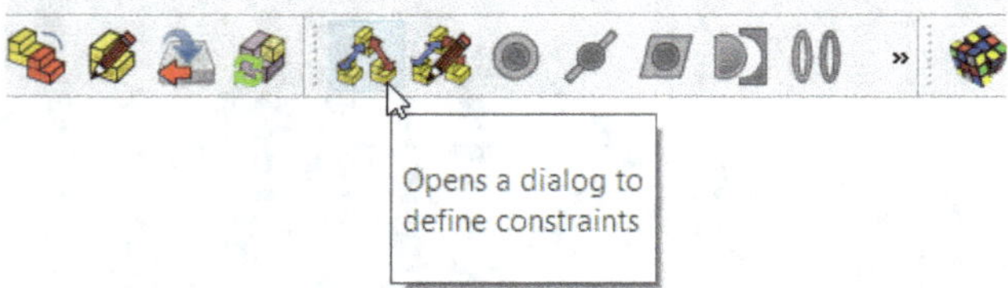

2. Press and hold the CTRL key, and then click on the planar faces of the two parts, as shown.

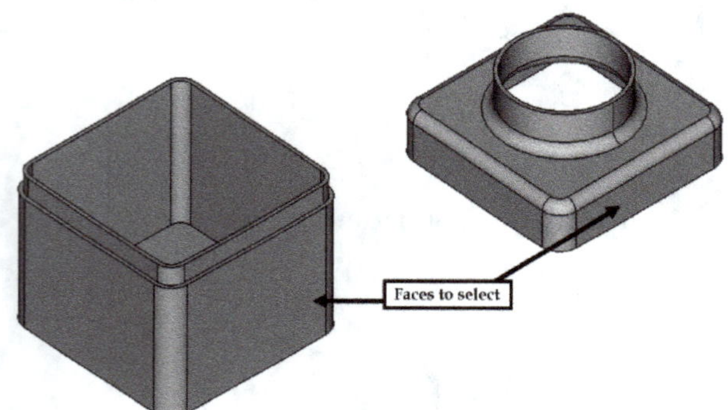

3. On the **Constraint Tools** dialog, click the **Add planeCoincident Constraint** icon.

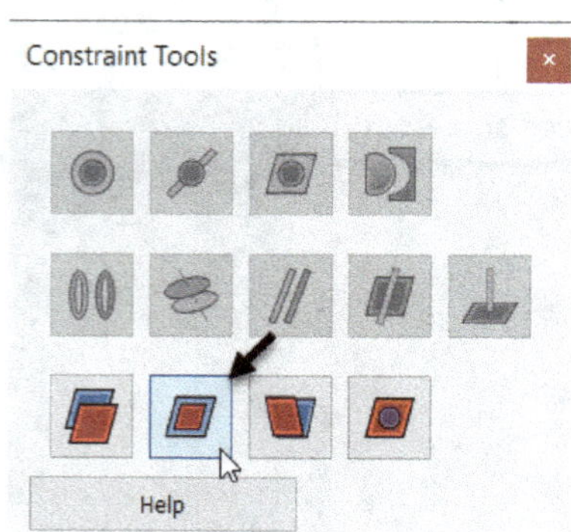

4. On the **Constraint Properties** dialog, select **Direction > aligned**.

5. Click the **Accept** button on the **Constraint Properties** dialog.
6. Press and hold the CTRL key, and then select the planar faces of the two parts, as shown.

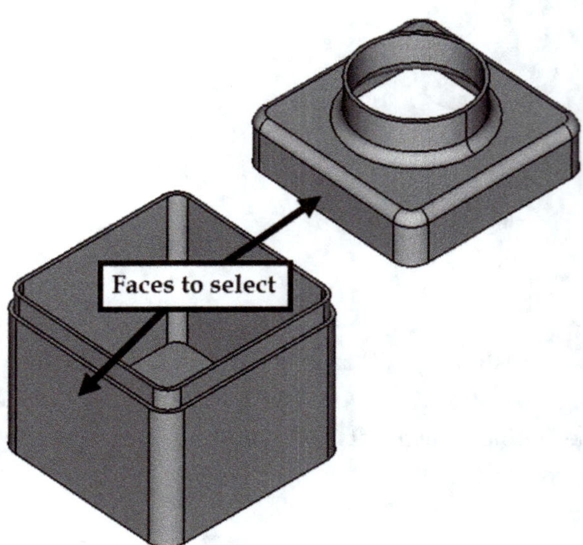

7. On the **Constraint Tools** dialog, click the **Add planeCoincident Constraint** icon.
8. On the **Constraint Properties** dialog, select **Direction > aligned**.
9. Click the **Accept** button on the **Constraint Properties** dialog.
10. Click the **Print detailed DOF information** icon on the **A2p_Solver** toolbar. The degrees of freedom are displayed.

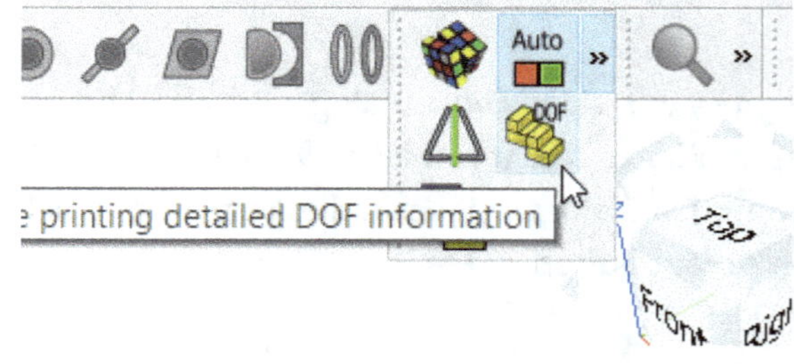

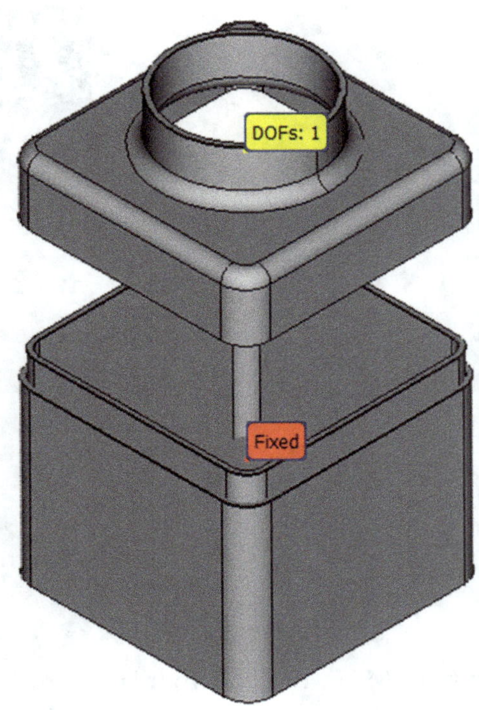

You need to remove this degree of freedom.

11. Press and hold the CTRL key and select the first face.

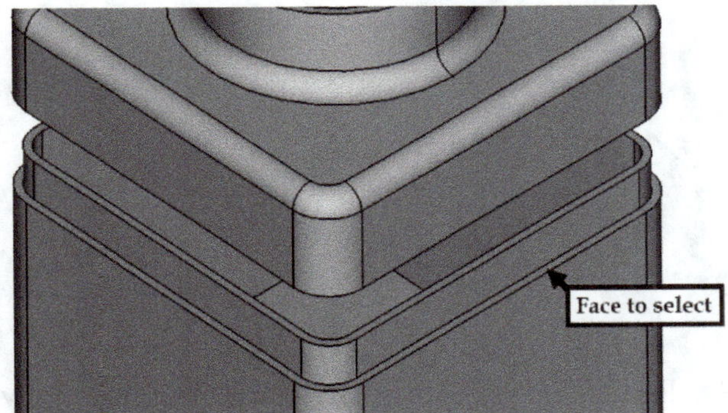

12. Press and hold the CTRL key and select the second face, as shown.

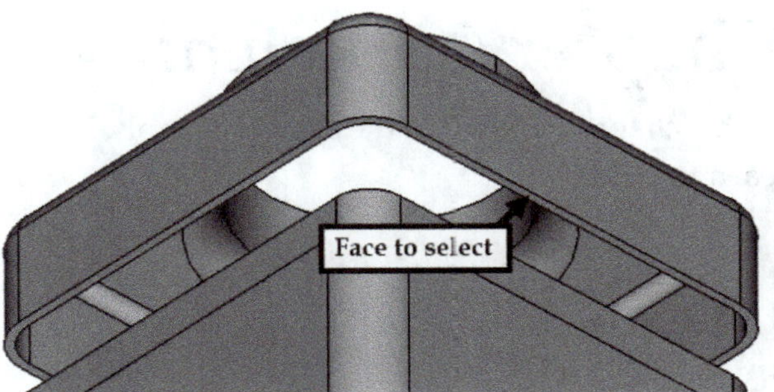

13. On the **Constraint Tools** dialog, click the **Add planeCoincident Constraint** icon.
14. On the **Constraint Properties** dialog, select **Direction > opposed**.
15. Click the **Accept** button on the **Constraint Properties** dialog.
16. Close the **Constraint Tools** dialog.
17. Click the **Print detailed DOF information** icon on the **A2p_Solver** toolbar.

The assembly is constrained fully.

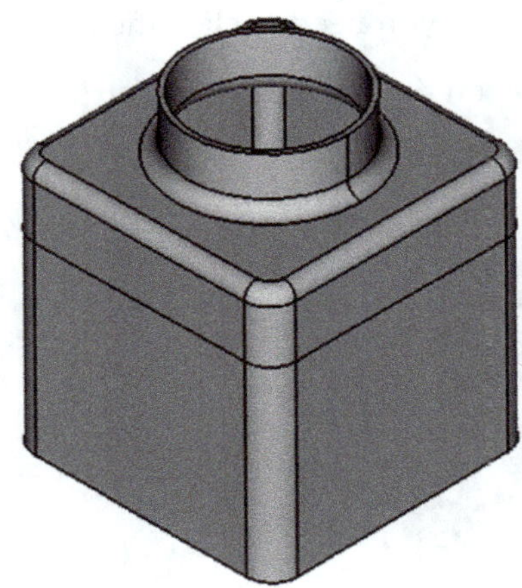

18. Click **File > Save** on the Menu bar.
19. Click **File > Close** on the Menu bar.

Chapter 4: Sketching

In this chapter, you learn the sketching tools. You learn to create:

- Polylines
- Polygons
- Slots
- Constraints
- B-Splines
- Ellipses
- Circles
- Trim
- Extend
- Toggle Construction geometry

Creating Polylines

The **Create Polyline** tool is the most commonly used while creating a sketch.

1. To activate this tool, you need to click the **Create Polyline** icon on the **Sketcher geometries** toolbar.
2. Click in the graphics window and move the pointer.
3. Click to create a line. Notice that another line is attached to the cursor.

4. Move the pointer and click to create another line.

5. Press the **M** key on your keyboard.
6. Move the pointer and click to create a line perpendicular to the previous line.

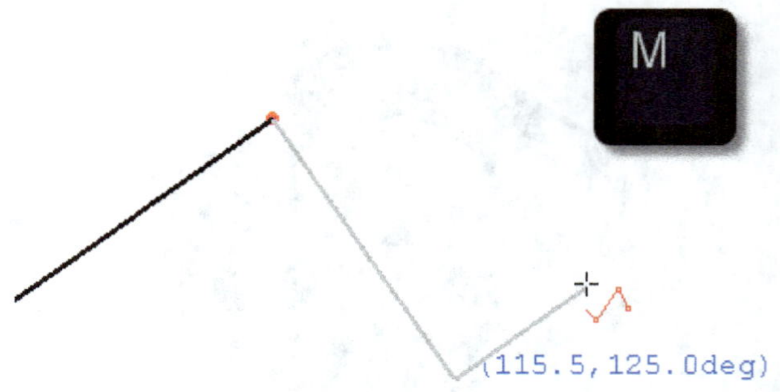

7. Press the **M** key twice on your keyboard.
8. Move the pointer and click to create a line colinear to the previous line.

9. Press the **M** key thrice on your keyboard; a grey arc tangent to the previous line appears.

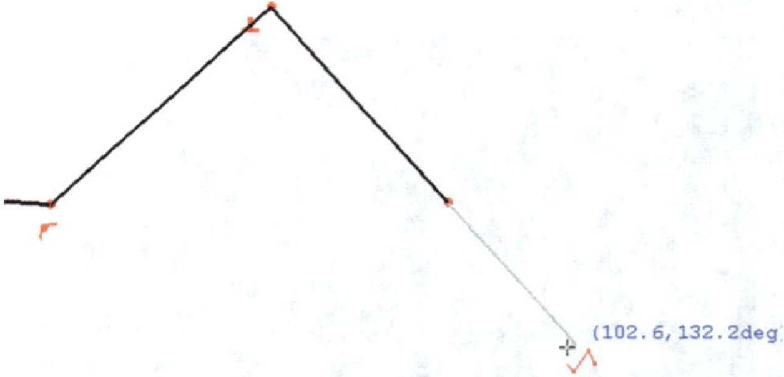

10. Move the pointer and click to create an arc tangent to the previous line.

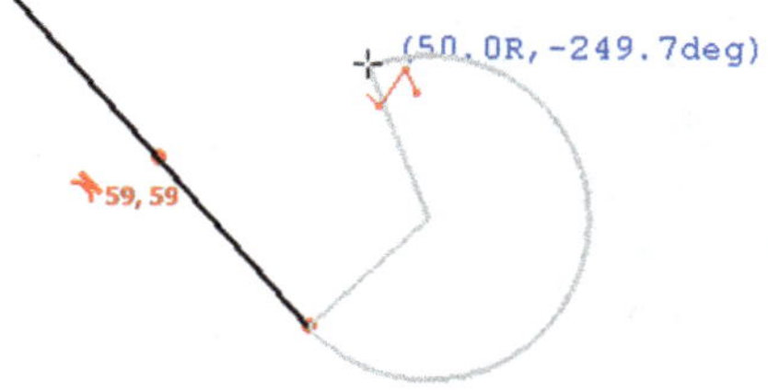

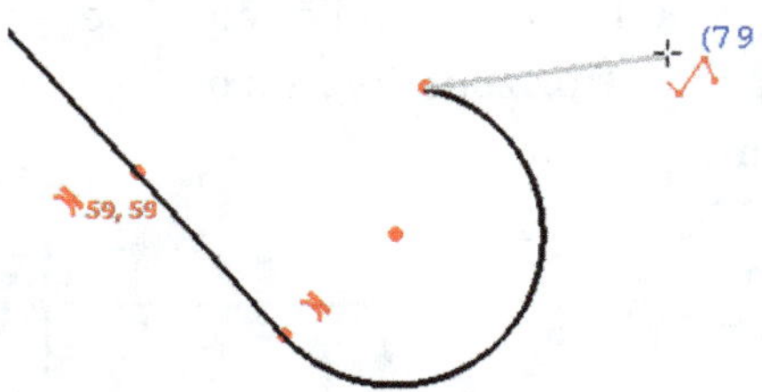

11. Press the **M** key four times to display an arc normal to the previous line.
12. Again, press the **M** key to change the direction of the normal arc.

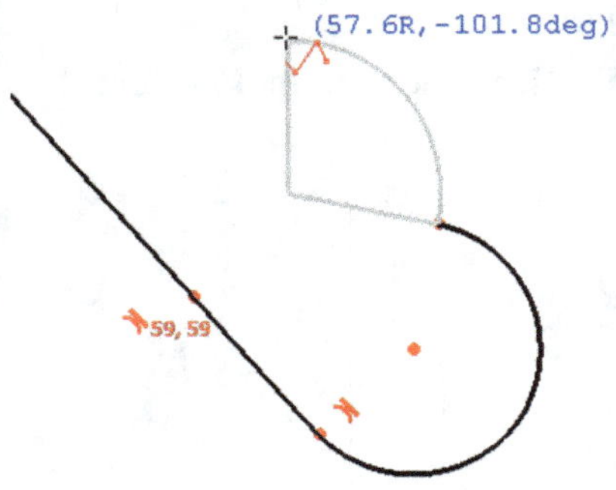

13. Click to create the normal arc.
14. Right click to end the line chain.
15. Again, right click to deactivate the **Create Polyline** tool.

Creating Polygons

A Polygon is a shape having many sides ranging from 3 to 1024. In FreeCAD, you can create regular polygons having sides with equal length. Follow the steps given next to create a polygon.

1. Click the **Create Sketch** icon on the **Sketcher** toolbar.
2. On the **Sketcher geometries** toolbar, select

   Polygon > Regular Polygon .
3. On the **Create array** dialog, type **8** in the **Number of Sides** box.
4. Click **OK**.
5. Click to define the center of the polygon.
6. Move the pointer and click to define the size and angle of the polygon.

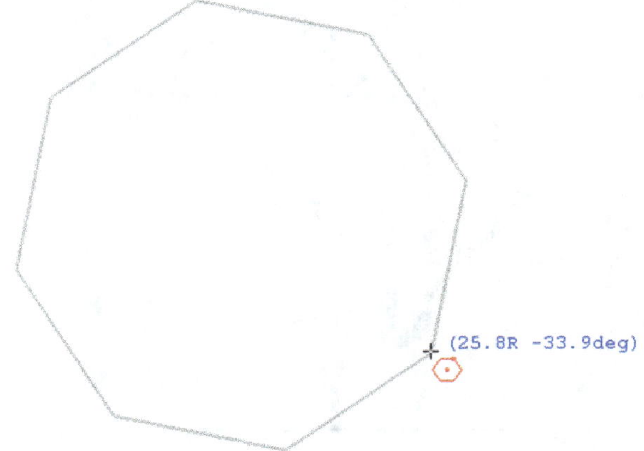

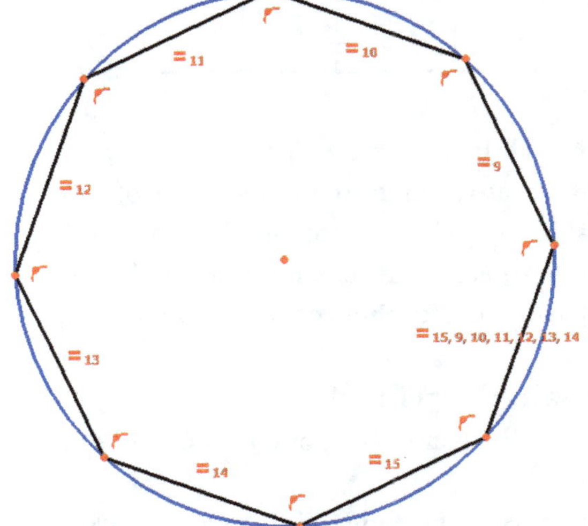

Creating a Slot

The **Create Slot** tool is used to create slots.

1. Click the **Create Slot** icon on the **Sketcher geometries** toolbar.
2. Click to specify the centerpoint of the first semicircle.
3. Move the pointer and click to specify the endpoint of the second semicircle.

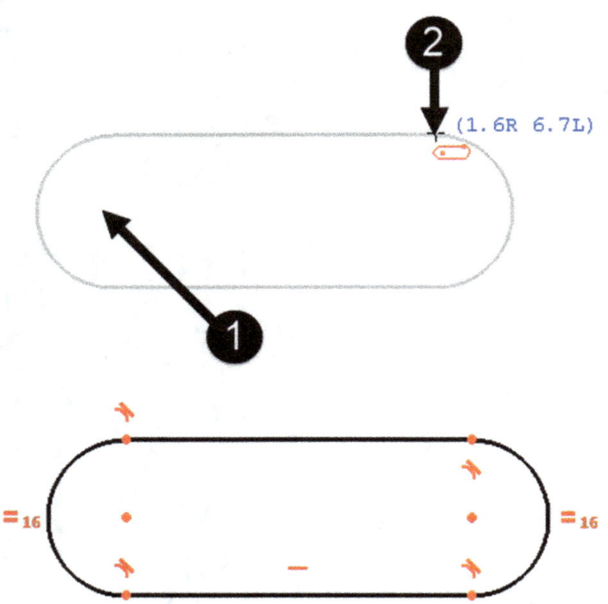

Constraints

Constraints are used to control the shape of a sketch by establishing relationships between the sketch elements. You can add constraints using the tools available on the **Sketcher constraints** toolbar.

Constrain Coincident

This constraint connects a point to another point.

1. On the **Sketcher constraints** toolbar, click

    Constrain Coincident 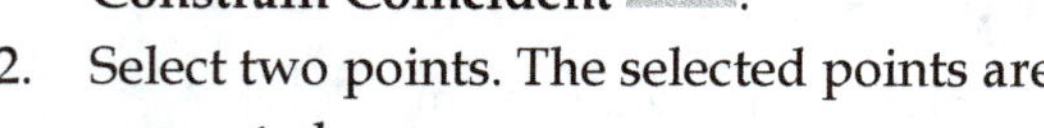.
2. Select two points. The selected points are connected.

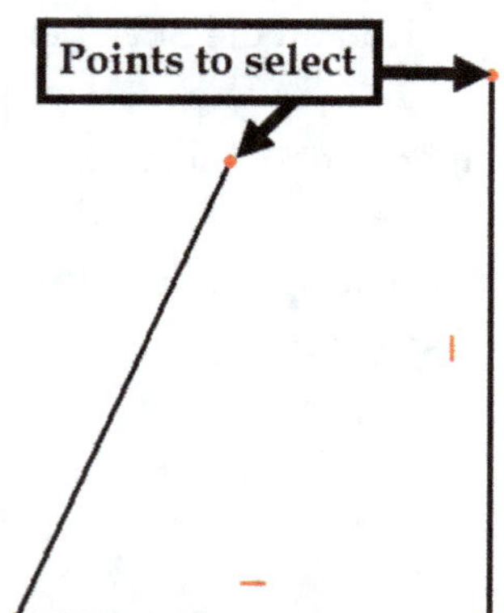

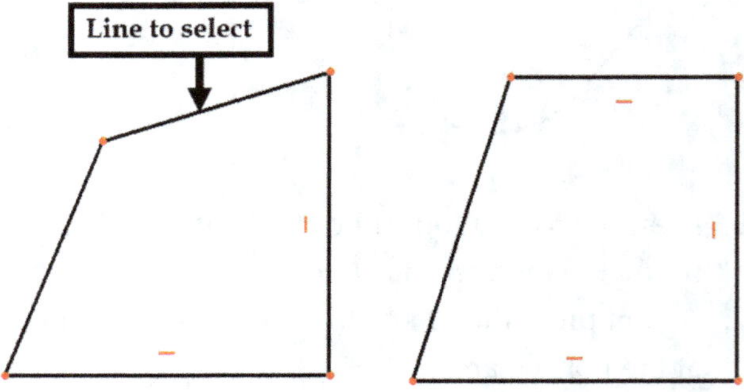 Constrain horizontally

To apply the **Horizontal** constraint, click on a line and click the **Constrain Horizontally** icon on the **Sketcher constraints** toolbar.

Constrain Vertically

Use the **Constrain Vertically** icon to make a line vertical.

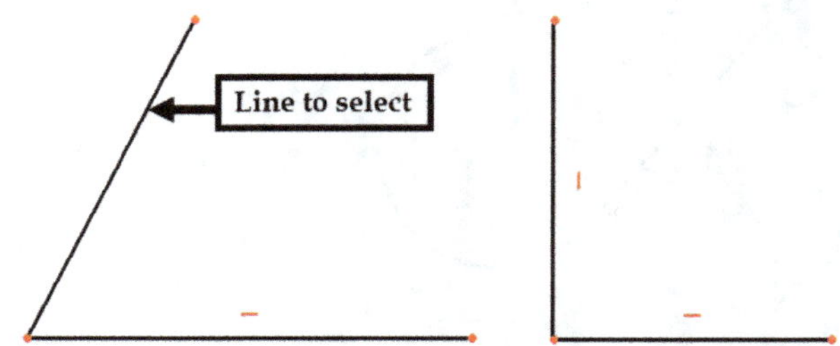

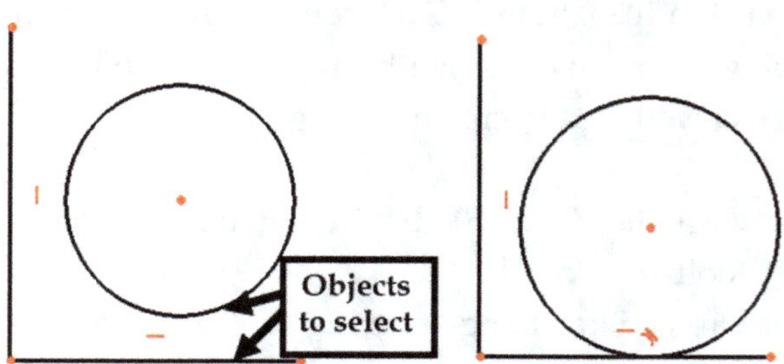 Constrain tangent

This constraint makes an arc, circle, or line tangent to another arc or circle. Click the **Constrain Tangent** icon on the **Sketcher constraints** toolbar. Select a circle, arc, or line. Next, select another circle or arc; the two elements are tangent to each other.

Constrain Parallel

Use the **Constrain Parallel** icon to make two lines parallel to each other. To do this, click the **Constrain Parallel** icon on the **Sketcher constraints**. Next, select the two lines to be parallel.

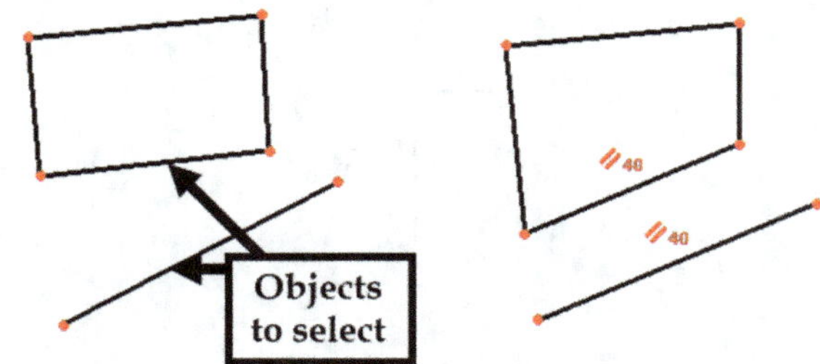

Constrain Perpendicular

Use the **Constrain Perpendicular** icon to make two entities perpendicular to each other.

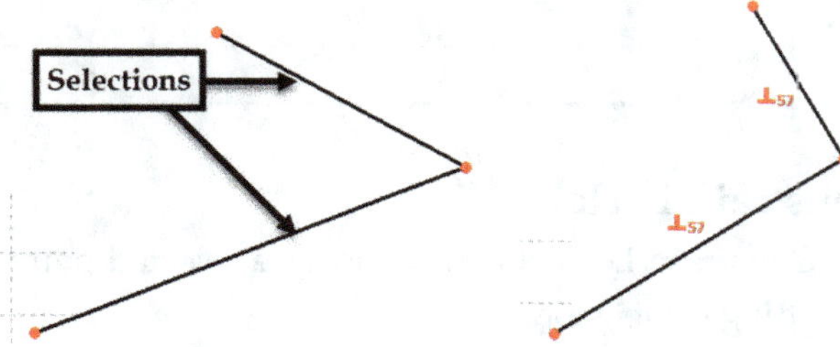

Auto Constraints

FreeCAD automatically adds constraints when you create sketch elements.

1. Start a new sketch and activate the **Create Polyline** tool from the **Sketcher geometries** toolbar.
2. Click to specify the start point of the line.
3. Move the pointer in the horizontal direction and notice the **Horizontal** constraint flag.
4. Click to create a line with the **Horizontal** constraint.

5. Move the pointer vertically in the upward direction and notice the **Vertical** constraint flag.
6. Click to create a line with the **Vertical** constraint.

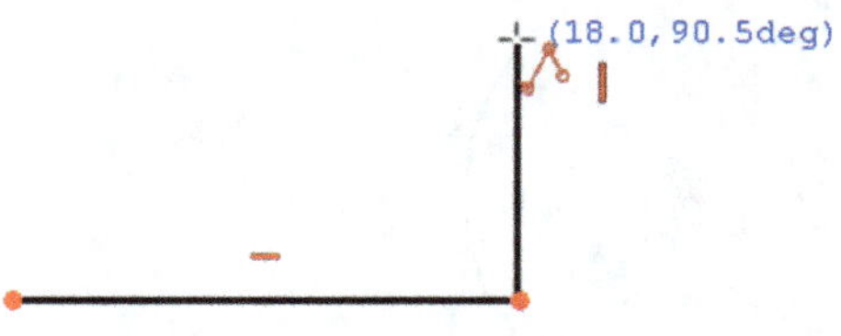

7. Create an inclined line, as shown.

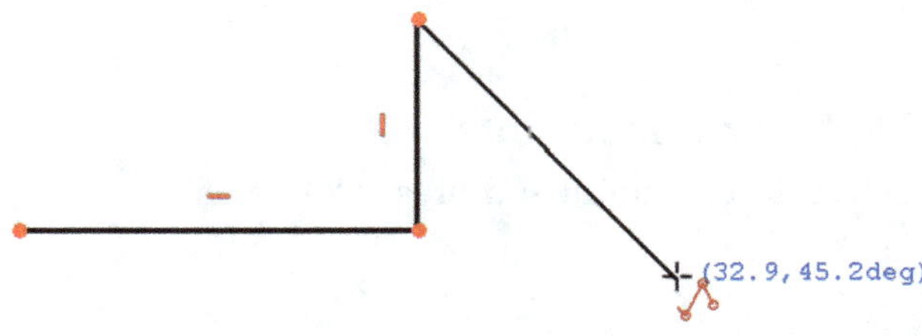

8. Press **Esc** twice to deactivate the tool.
9. On the **Sketcher geometries** toolbar, click the **Create Circle** icon, and then create a circle.
10. Activate the **Create Line** tool and click on the circle.
11. Move the pointer around the circle and notice that the line maintains the **Tangent** constraint with the circle.

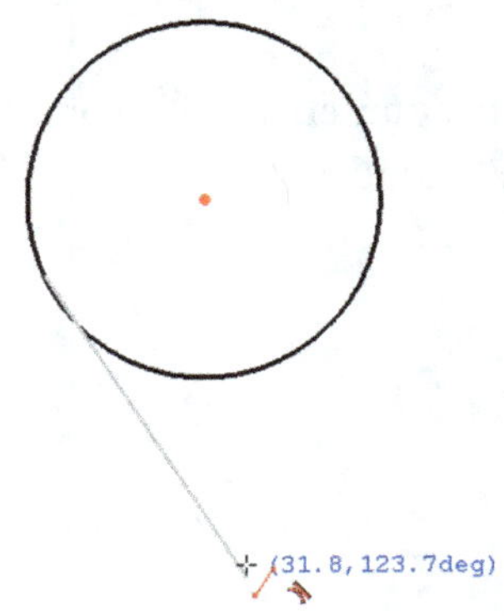

12. Click to create a line that is tangent and coincident to the circle. Right click to deactivate the **Create Line** tool.

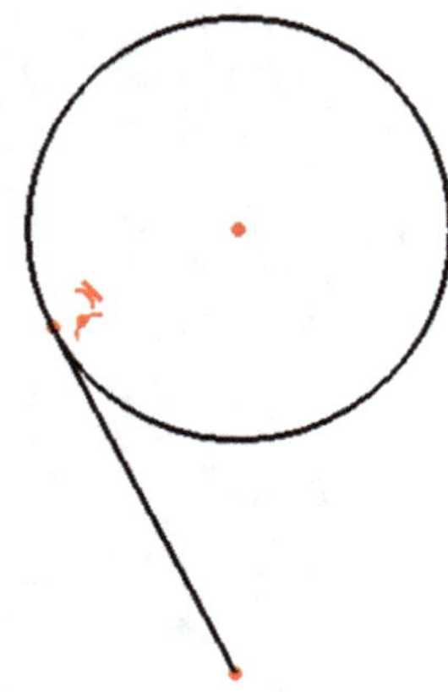

Deleting Constraints

Select the constraint and press **Delete** on your keyboard.

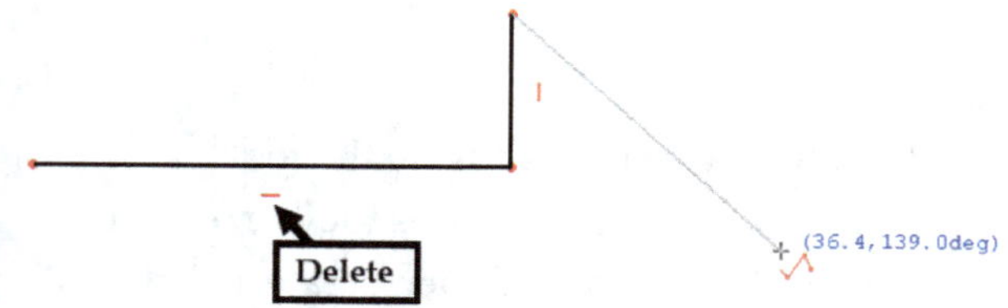

Constrain symmetrical

Use the **Constrain symmetrical** tool to make two sketch elements symmetric about a centerline.

1. Click on the elements to make symmetric.
2. Click on the d
3. Click the **Constrain symmetrical** icon on the **Sketcher constraints** toolbar.

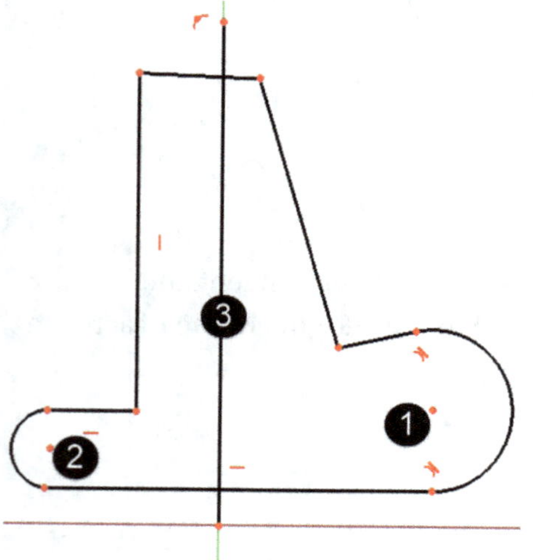

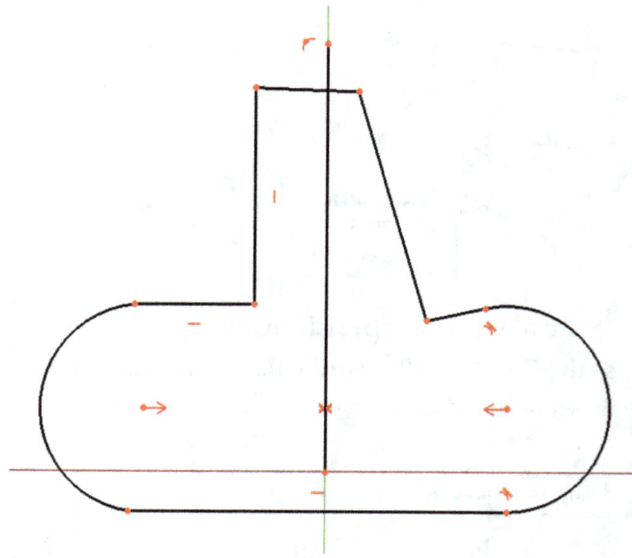

Constrain Lock

The **Constrain Lock** constraint locks a selected point by adding dimensions to it.

1. On the **Sketcher constraint** toolbar, click the **Constrain Lock** icon.
2. Select a point from the sketch.

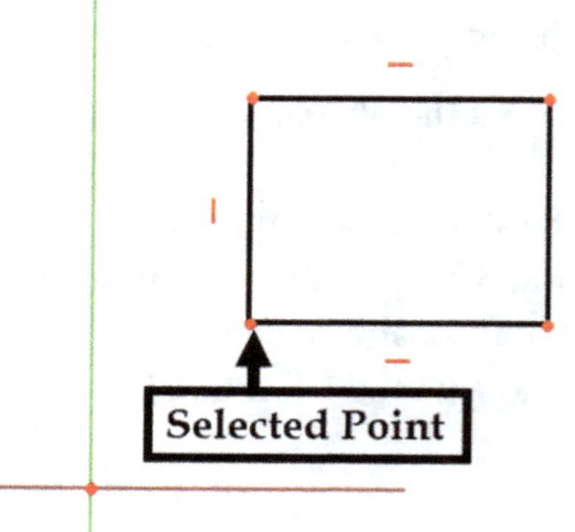

Dimensions are created between the selected point and the origin.

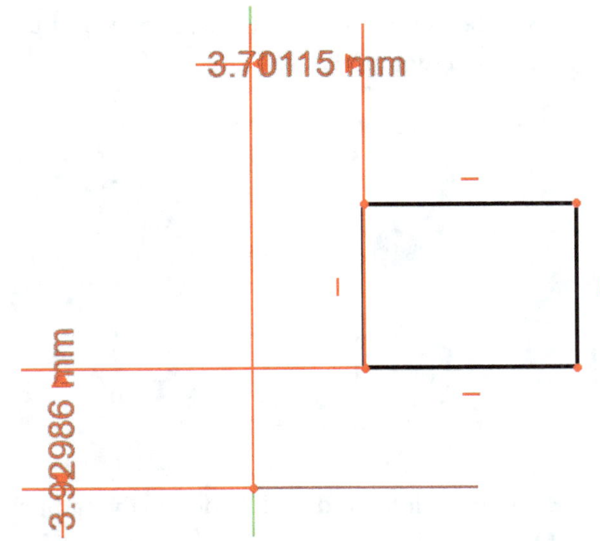

Constrain Block

This constraint fixes the sketch object at its location.

1. Click the **Constrain Block** 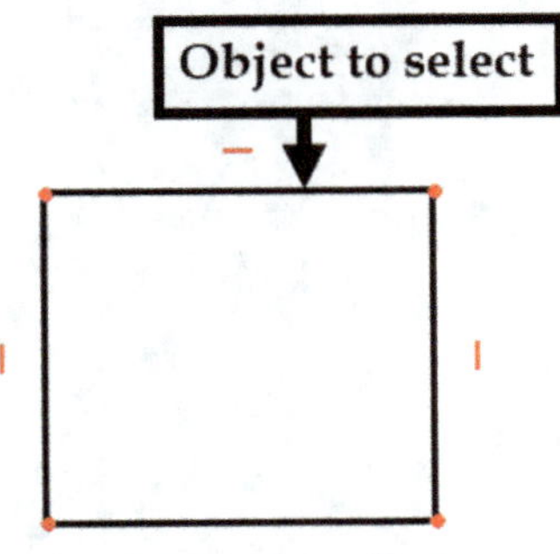 icon on the **Sketcher constraints** toolbar.
2. Select an object from the sketch.

3. Click the object and drag; notice that it is fixed at its location.

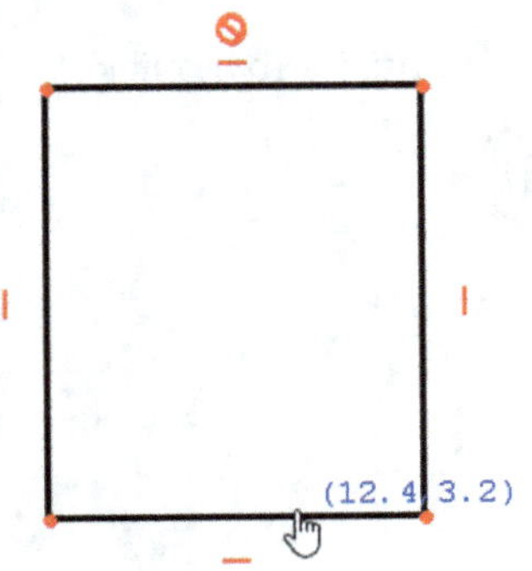

Hiding Constraints

To hide sketch constraints, uncheck the checkbox next to it in the **Constraints** section located in the **Combo View** panel.

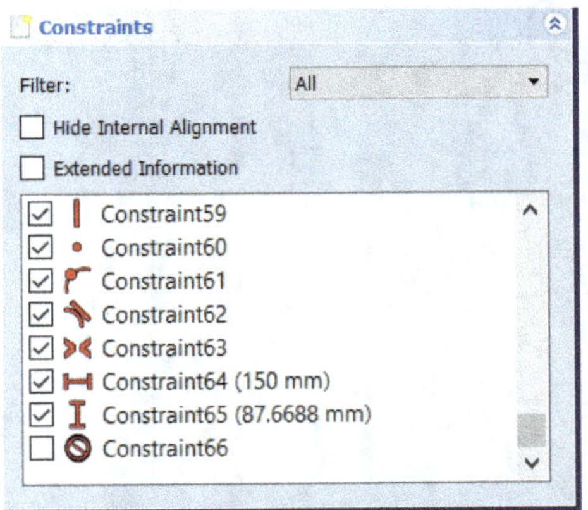

 ## Create B-Spline

This command creates a smooth B-spline curve using the control points you select.

1. On the **Sketcher geometries** toolbar, click **B-Spline** drop-down > **Create B-Spline**.
2. Click to define points in the graphics window.

3. Right click to create a spline controlled by the selected points.
4. Press Esc to deactivate this command.

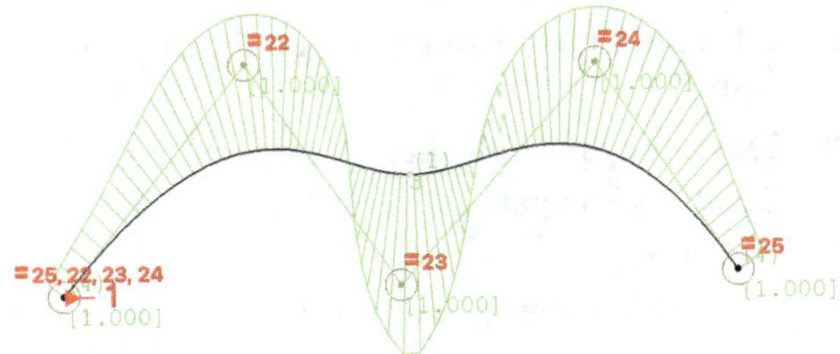

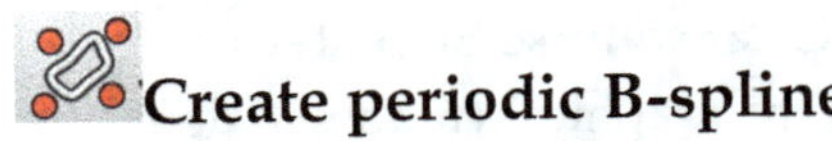 ## Create periodic B-spline

If you want to create a closed B-spline, then click the **B-spline** drop-down > **Create periodic B-spline** on the **Sketcher geometries** toolbar. Next, specify the control points. Right click to create a closed B-spline.

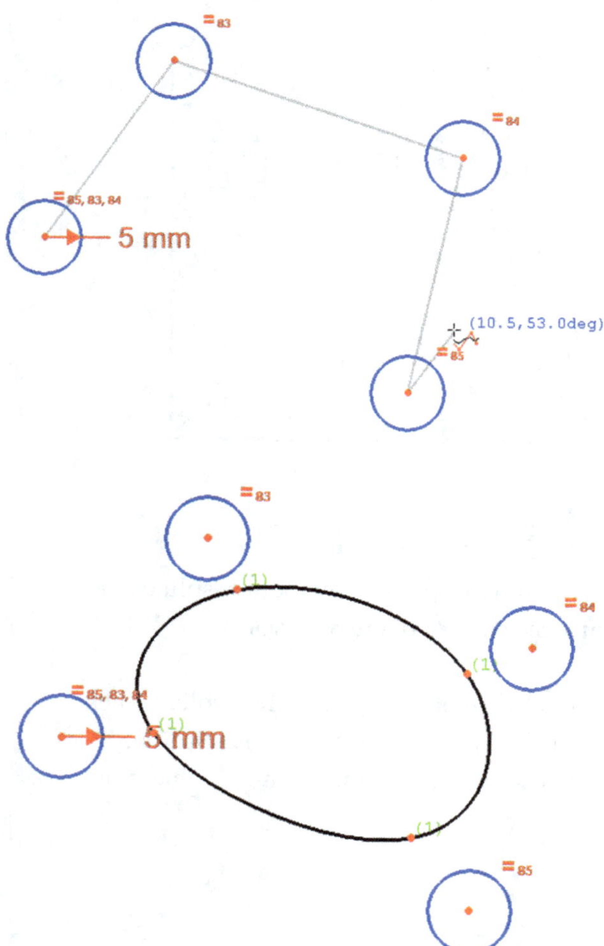

Ellipses

Ellipses are also non-uniform curves, but they have a regular shape. They are splines created in regular closed shapes.

1. Click the **Create Sketch** icon on the **Sketcher** toolbar.
2. Select any one of the datum planes from the **Combo View** panel.
3. Click **OK**.
4. On the **Sketcher geometries** toolbar, click **Conic** drop-down > **Create ellipse by center** .
5. Pick a point in the graphics window to define the center of the ellipse.

6. Move the pointer and click to define the radius and orientation of the first axis.

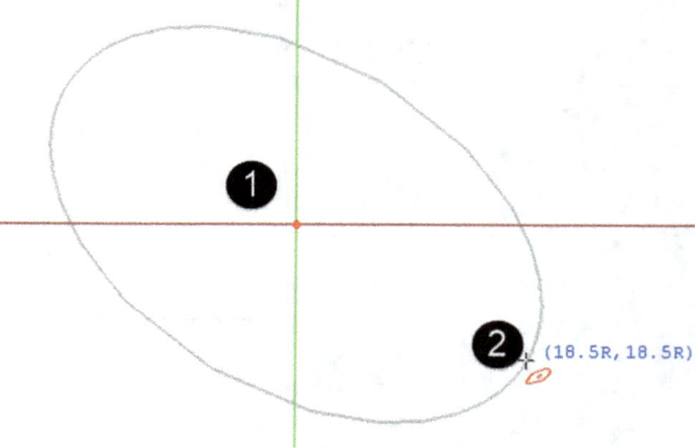

7. Move the pointer and click to define the radius of the second axis.

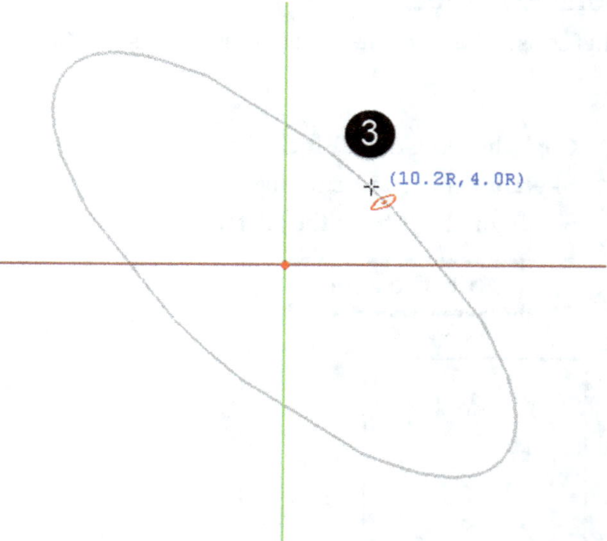

Click and drag the ellipse to notice that it is under-defined. You need to add dimensions and constraints to fully define the ellipse.

8. On the **Sketcher constraints** toolbar, click

Constrain angle 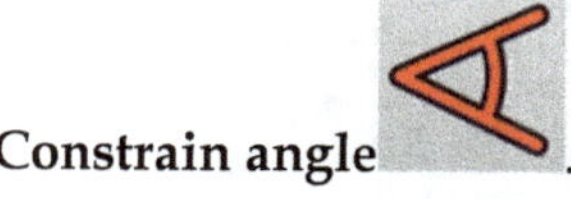.

9. Select the lines, as shown.

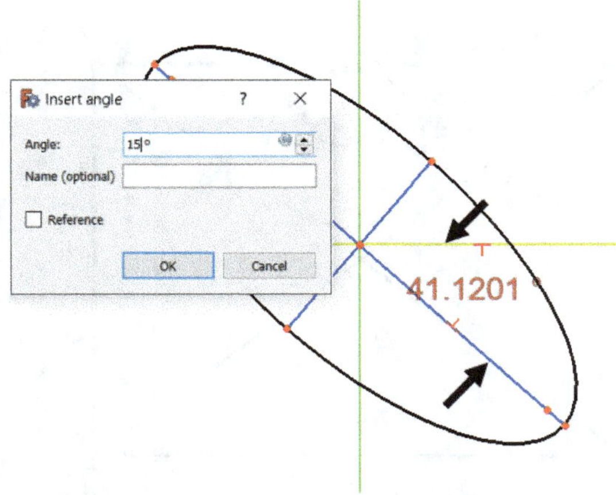

10. Type 15 in the **Angle** box and click **OK**.

11. Click the **Constrain distance** icon on the **Sketcher constraints** toolbar.

12. Select the major axis line.

13. Type 25 in the **Length** box and click the **OK** button.

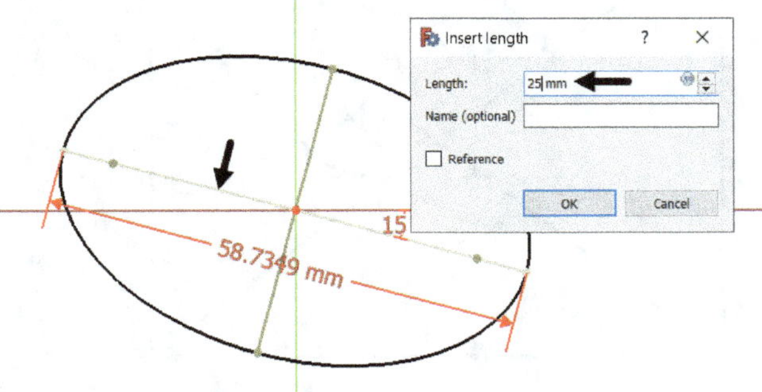

14. Likewise, add the distance constrain to the minor axis. The sketch is fully defined.

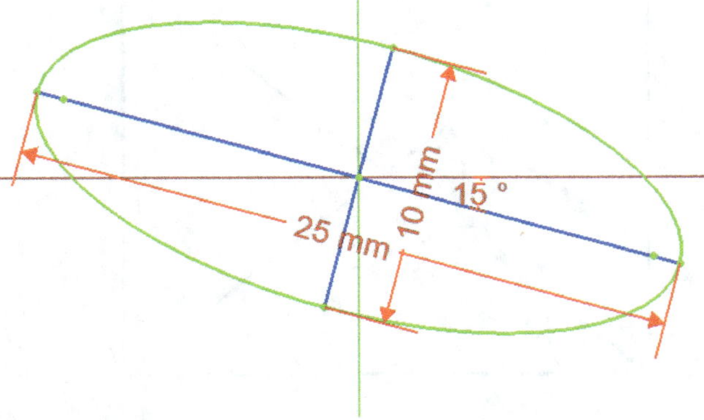

Extend Edge

The **Extend Edge** tool is used to extend lines, arcs, and other open entities to connect to other objects.

1. Create a sketch, as shown below.

2. Click the **Extend edge** icon on the **Sketcher geometries** toolbar.

3. Select the horizontal open line.

4. Select the arc; the line is extended up to the arc.

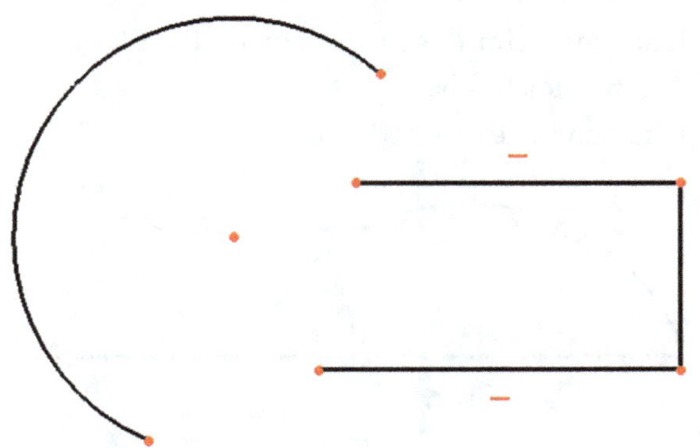

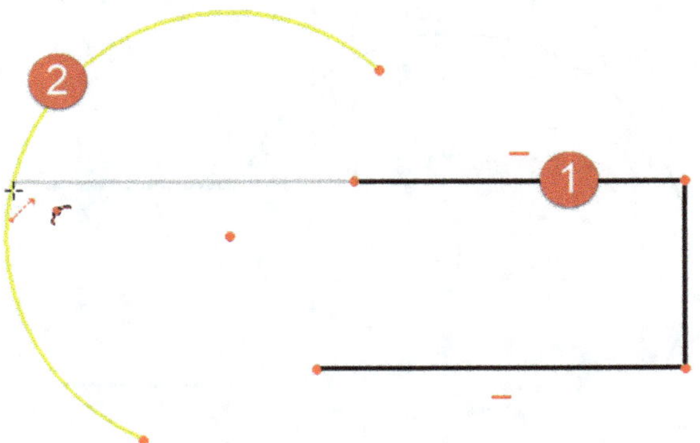

Likewise, extend the other elements, as shown.

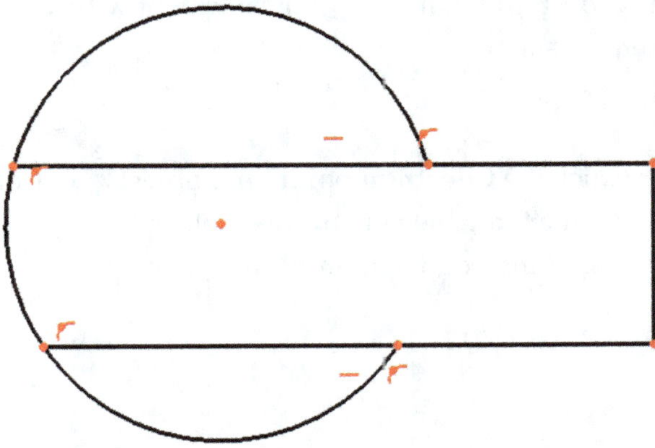

Trim Edge

The **Trim Edge** tool is used to trim the unwanted portions of the sketch using an intersecting edge.

1. Click the **Trim Edge** 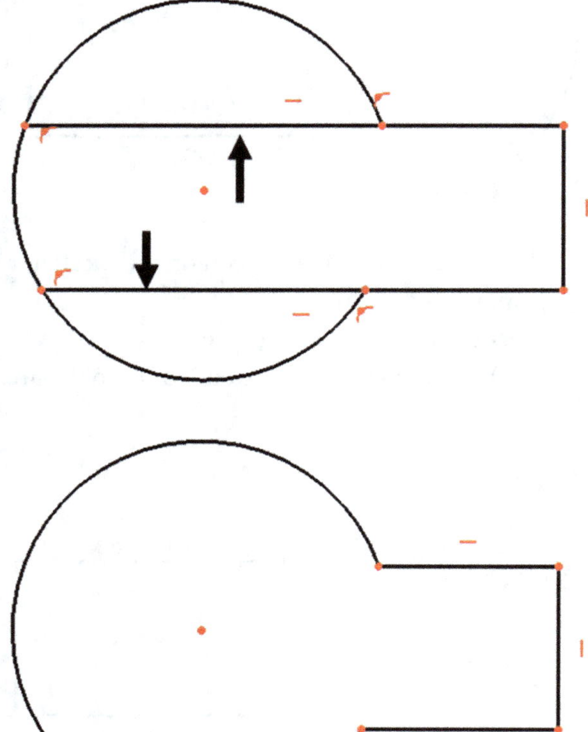 icon on the **Sketcher geometries** toolbar.
2. Click on the edges to trim.

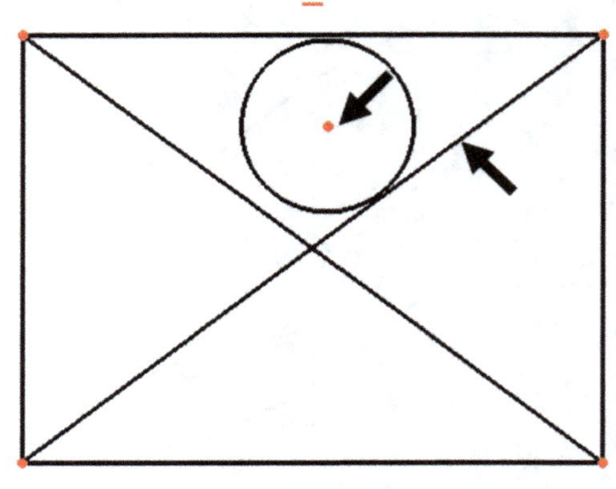

The point is made coincident with the object. Likewise, make the point coincident with another object, as shown.

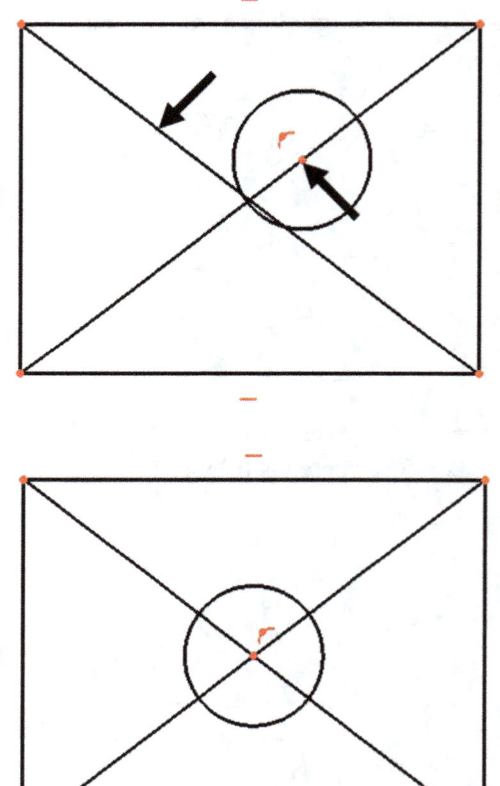

Constrain point onto object

This constraint makes a point coincident with a sketch element.

1. Click the **Constrain point onto object** icon on the **Sketcher constraints** toolbar.
2. Select the point and object, as shown.

Toggle Construction geometry

This command converts a standard sketch element into a construction element. Construction elements support you to create a sketch of a desired shape and size. To convert a standard sketch element to construction element, click on it and select **Toggle Construction geometry** 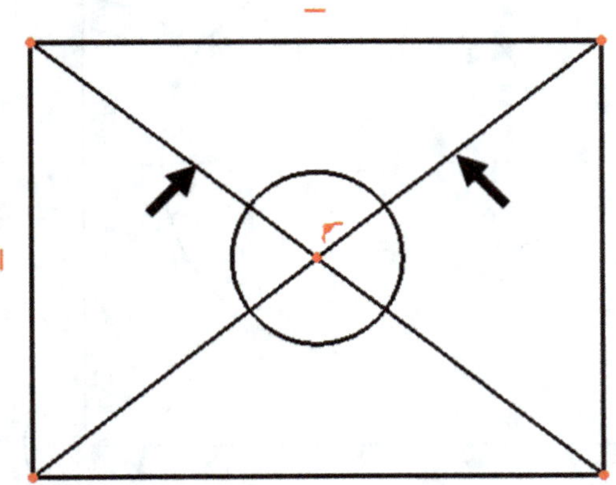 on the **Sketcher geometries** toolbar.

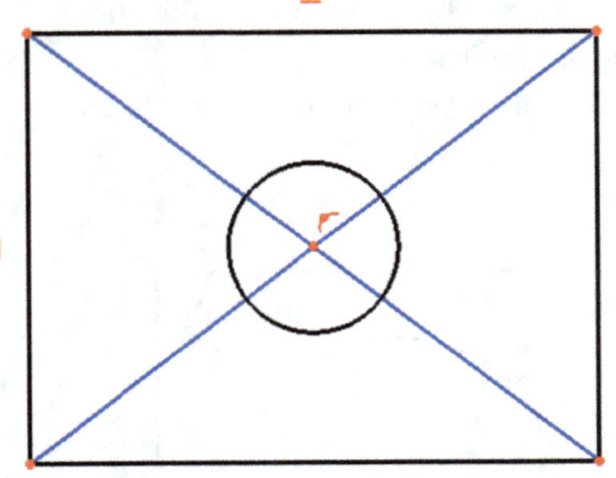

You can also convert it back to a standard sketch element by clicking on it and selecting the **Toggle Construction geometry** icon on the **Sketcher geometries** toolbar.

TUTORIAL 1

In this tutorial, you create the sketch shown in the figure.

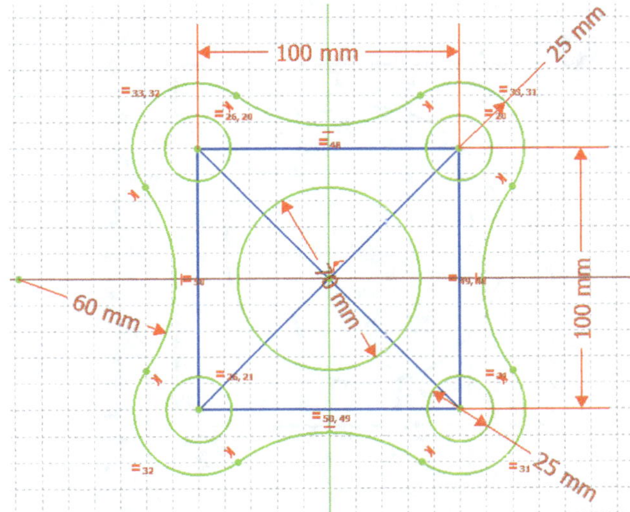

1. Open the FreeCAD application.
2. Click **File > New** on the Menu bar.
3. Select the **Part Design** option from the **Workbenches** drop-down.
4. Click the **Create sketch** icon on the **Part Design Helper** toolbar, and then select the XY Plane.
5. Click **OK** to start the sketch.
6. Click the **Create Circle** icon on the **Sketcher geometries** toolbar.
7. Select the origin point of the sketch.
8. Move the pointer outward and click to create a circle.
9. On the **Sketcher geometries** toolbar, click the **Rectangle** icon (or) click **Sketch > Sketcher geometries > Create Rectangle**.

10. Click in the second quadrant of the sketch.
11. Drag the cursor towards the bottom right corner, and then click to create a rectangle.

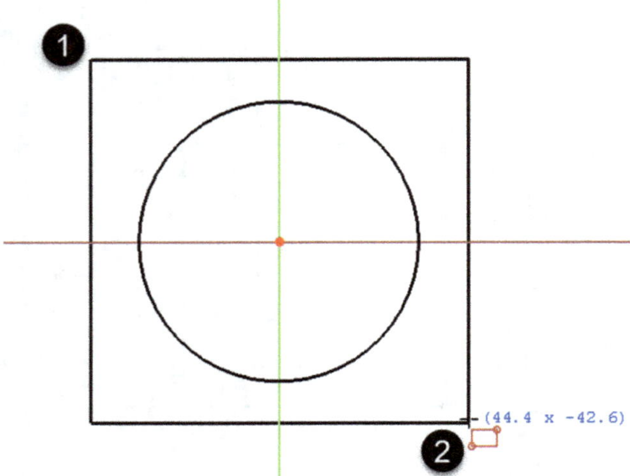

12. Click the **Create Circle** icon on the **Sketcher geometries** toolbar.
13. Select the top-left corner point of the rectangle.
14. Move the pointer outward and click to create a circle.

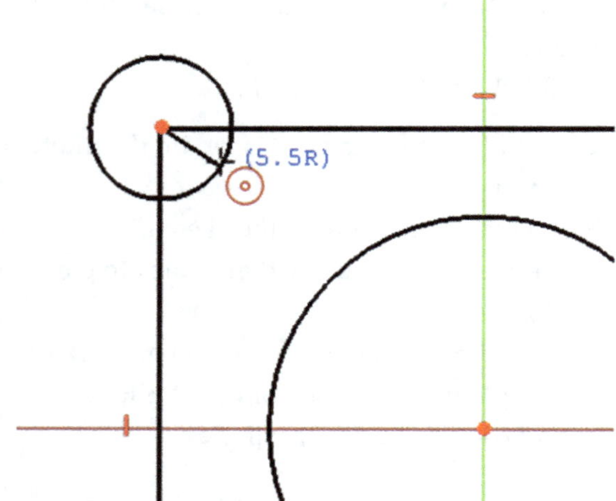

15. Likewise, create three more circles on the remaining corners.

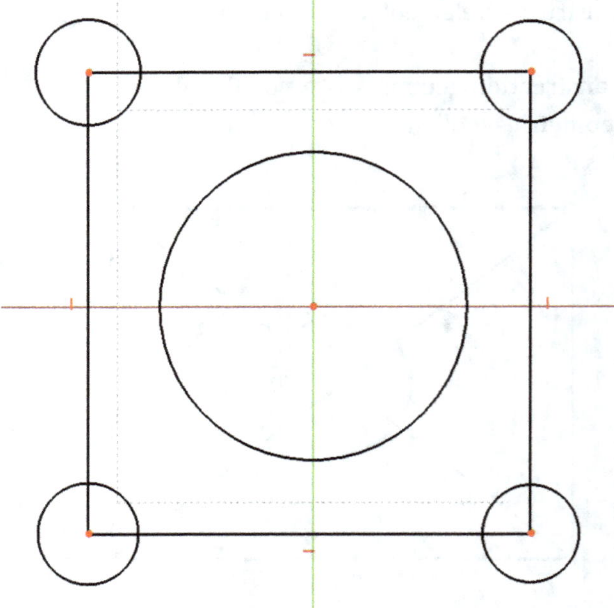

16. Click the **Create Line** icon on the **Sketcher geometries** toolbar.
17. Select the corner points of the rectangle, as shown.

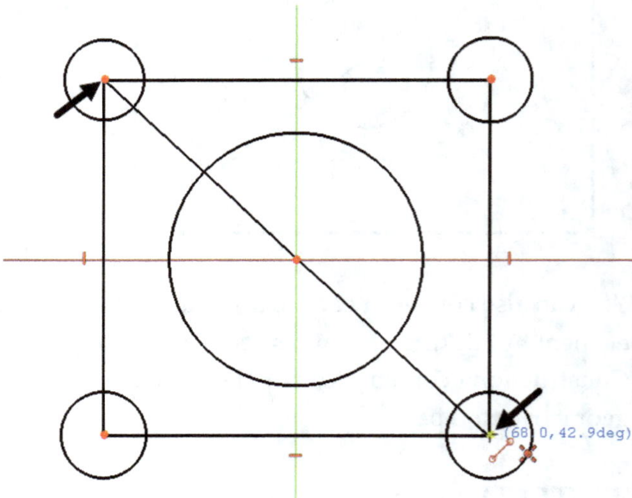

18. Select the two corner points of the rectangle, as shown.

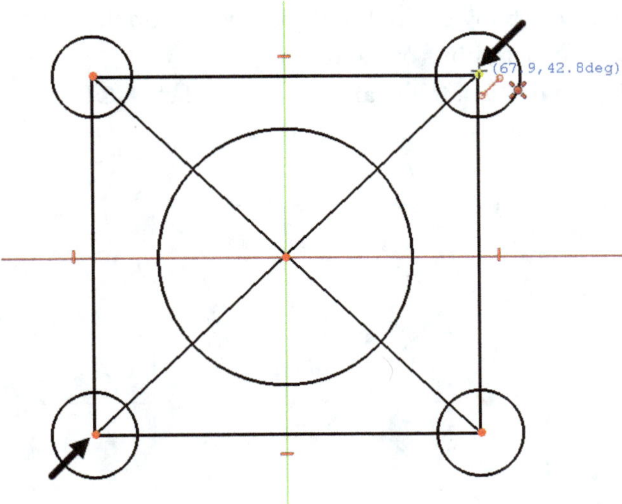

19. Click the **Constrain point onto object** icon on the **Sketcher constraints** toolbar.
20. Select the origin point and the diagonal line, as shown.

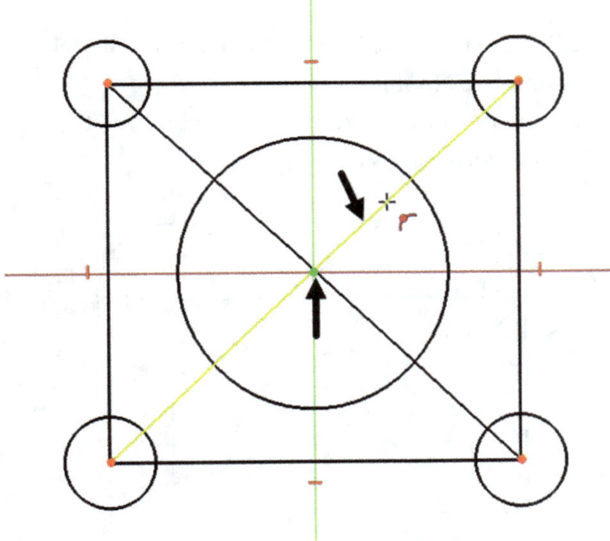

21. Select the origin point and another diagonal line.
22. Press ESC.
23. Select the lines of the rectangle and the two diagonal lines.
24. Click **Toggle Construction geometry** on the **Sketcher geometries** toolbar.

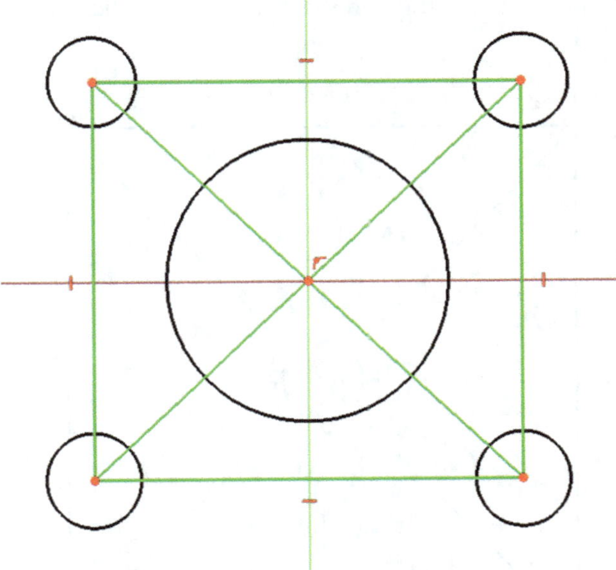

25. Click the **Constrain equal** icon on the **Sketcher constraints** toolbar.
26. Select the circles located on the corner points of the rectangle (start from the top-left corner circle).
27. Select the bottom-left and top-left circles; the diameters of the circles are made equal.

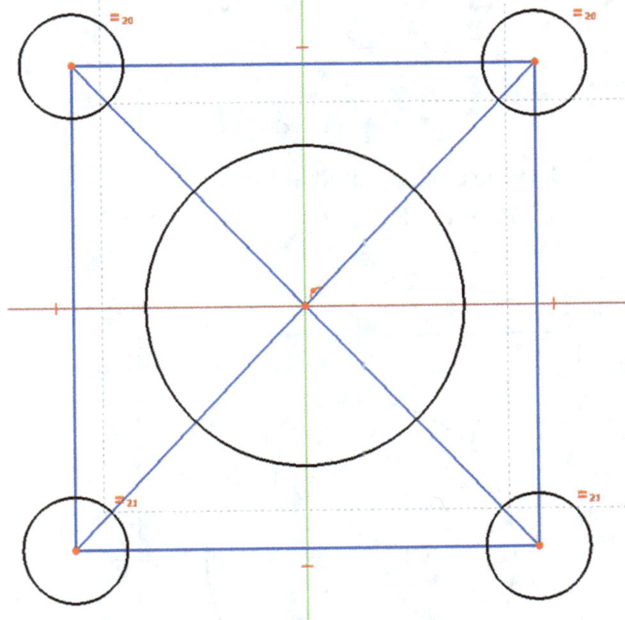

28. Click **Constrain distance** on the **Sketcher constraints** toolbar.
29. Select the vertical line of the rectangle.
30. Type 100 in the **Length** box, and then click **OK**.
31. Select the horizontal line of the rectangle.

32. Type 100 in the **Length** box, and then click **OK**.

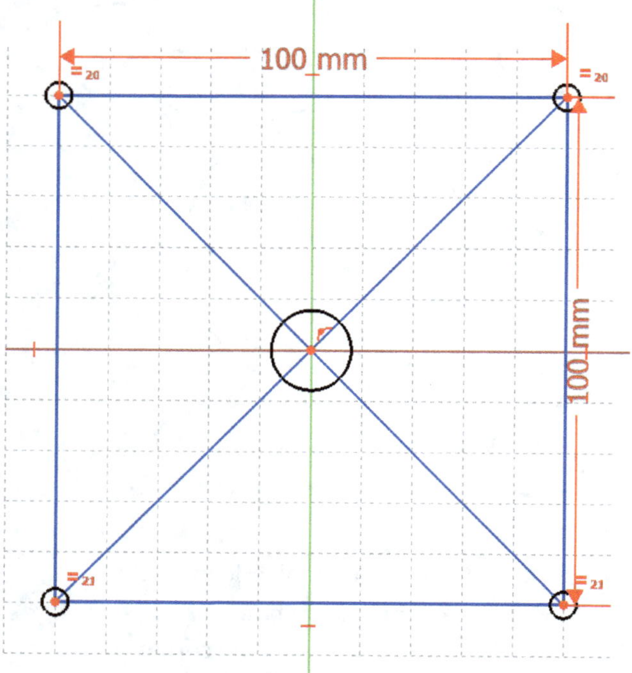

33. Click the **Constrain radius drop-down >
Constrain diameter** on the **Sketcher constraints**
toolbar.

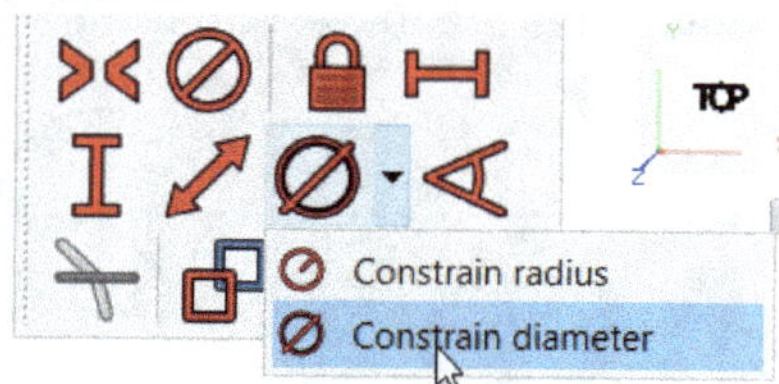

34. Select the circle located at the center.
35. Type **70** in the **Diameter** box and click **OK**.

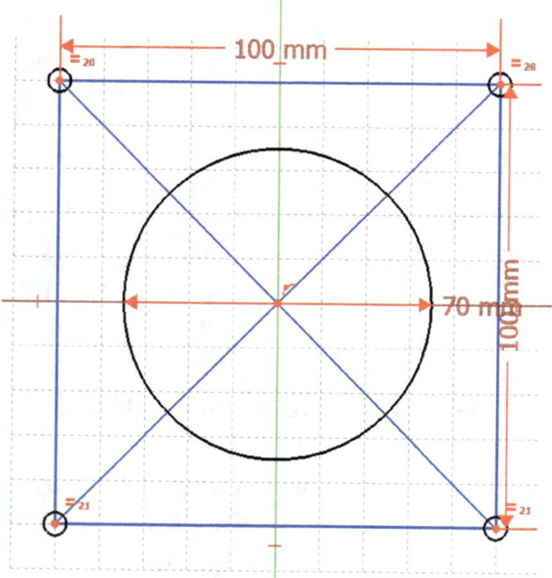

36. Select any one of the circles located on the
corner points of the rectangle.
37. Type **25** in the **Diameter** box, and click **OK**.

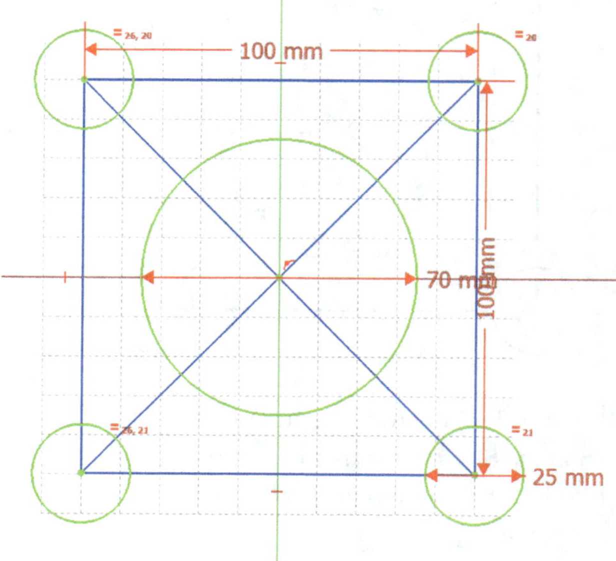

38. Click the **Create Circle** icon on the **Sketcher
geometries** toolbar.
39. Create two circles on the corner points of the
rectangle, as shown.

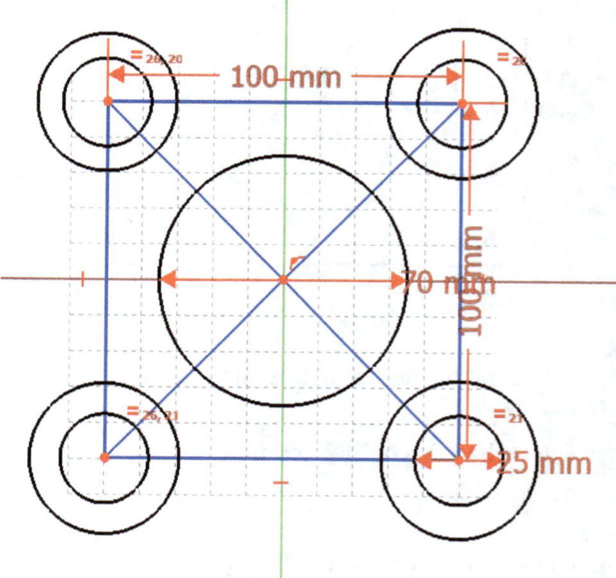

40. Click the **Constrain equal** icon on the
Sketcher constraints toolbar.
41. Select the newly created circles.
42. Select the bottom-left and top-left circles; the
diameters of the circles are made equal.

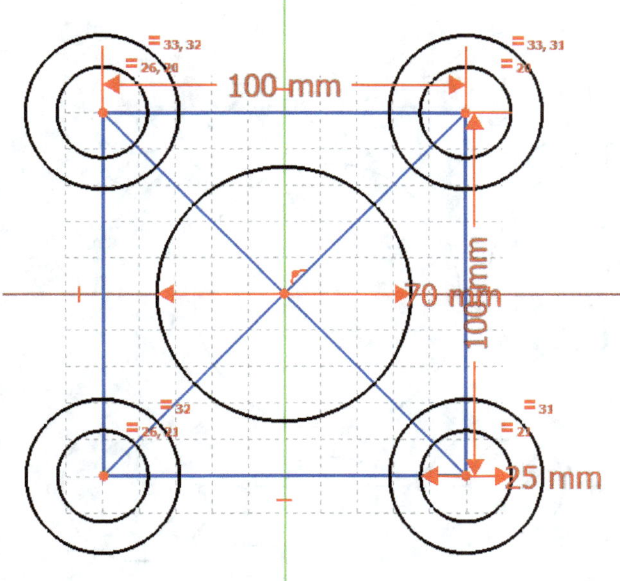

43. Click **Arc** drop-down > **End points and rim point** on the **Sketcher geometries** toolbar.

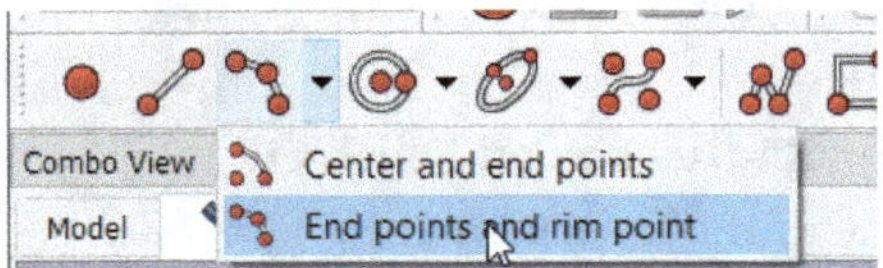

44. Select the outer circle located on the top-left corner.
45. Select the outer circle located on the bottom-left corner.

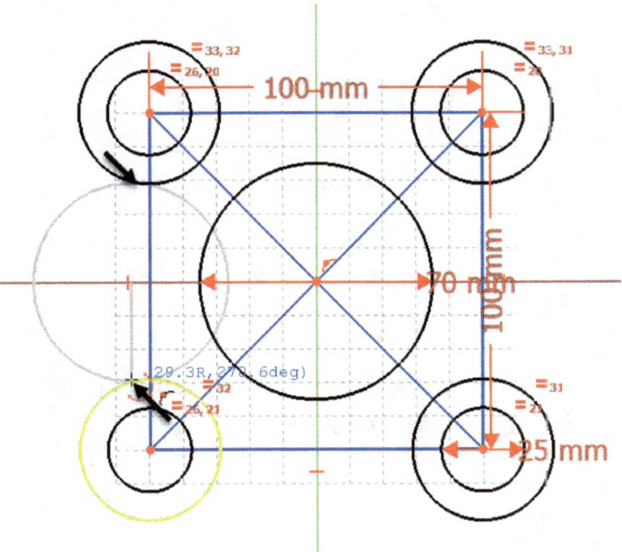

46. Move the pointer toward the right and click to create an arc.

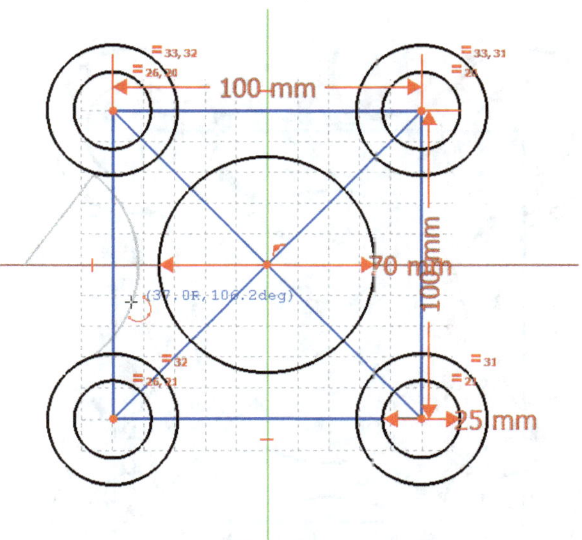

47. Likewise, create three more arcs, as shown.

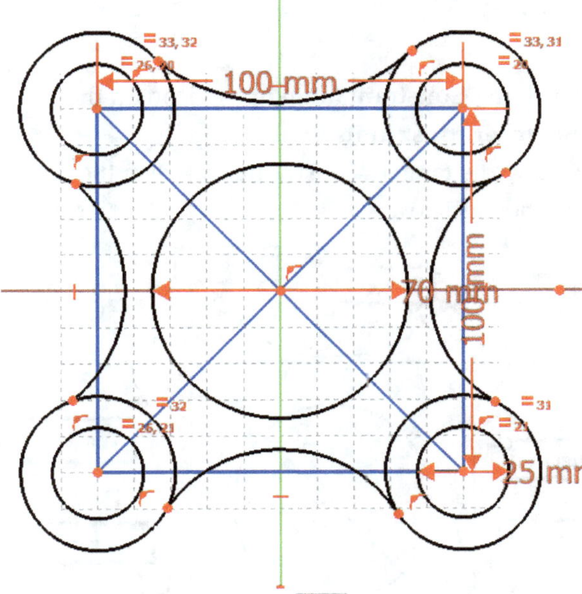

48. Click the **Trim Edge** icon on the **Sketcher geometries** toolbar.
49. Click on the edges to trim, as shown.

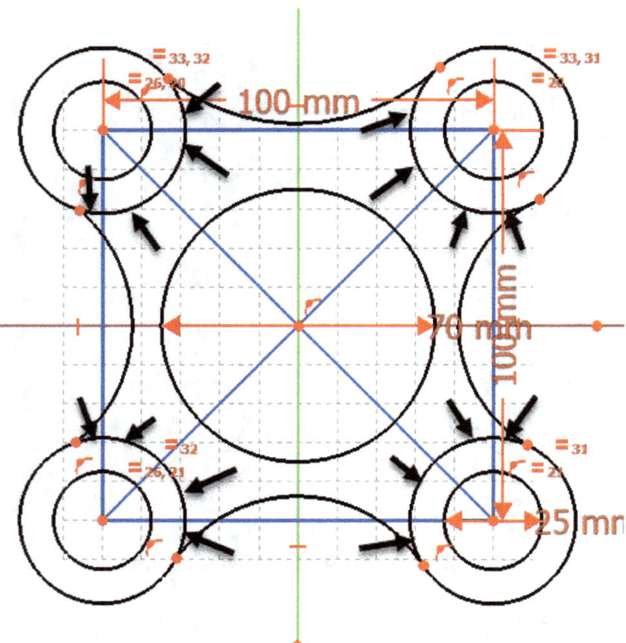

50. Click the **Constrain tangent** icon on the **Sketcher constraints** toolbar.
51. Create the tangent constraints between the entities, as shown.

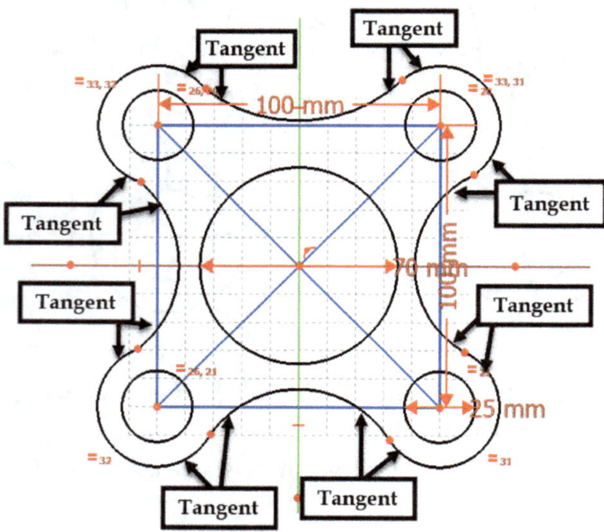

52. Click the **Constrain equal** icon on the **Sketcher constraints** toolbar.
53. Make the arcs equal, as shown.

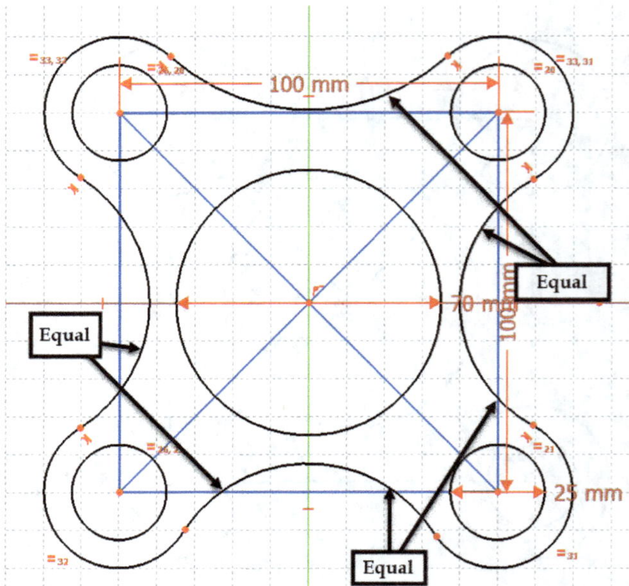

54. Click the **Constrain radius** icon on the **Sketcher constraints** toolbar.
55. Select any one of the arcs concentric to the circles.
56. Type **25** in the **Radius** box and click **OK**.
57. Select any one of the tangent arcs.
58. Type 60 in the **Radius** box and click **OK**.

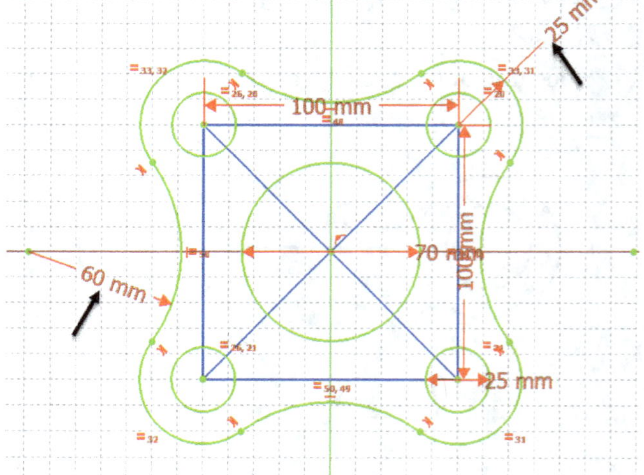

59. Click **Leave Sketch** on the **Sketcher** toolbar.
60. Save and close the file.

Chapter 5: Additional Modeling Tools

In this chapter, you create models using additional modeling tools. You learn to:

- Create slots
- Create circular patterns
- Create holes
- Create chamfers
- Create shells
- Create coils
- Create a loft feature
- Create a sweep feature

TUTORIAL 1

In this tutorial, you create the model shown in the figure:

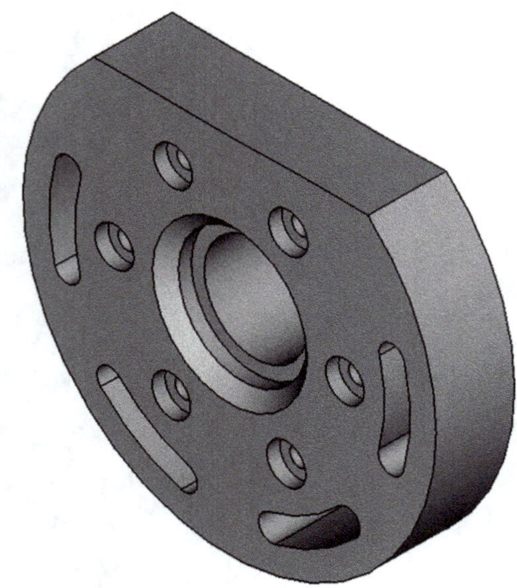

Creating the First Feature

1. Open the FreeCAD application.
2. Click **File > New** on the Menu bar.
3. Select the **Part Design** option from the **Workbenches** drop-down.
4. On the Menu bar, click **Edit > Preferences**.
5. Click the **Units** tab on the **Preferences** dialog.
6. Select **User system > Imperial decimal**.

7. Type **3** in the **Number of decimals** box.
8. Click **OK**.
9. Click the **Create sketch** icon on the **Part Design Helper** toolbar, and then select the XZ Plane.
10. Click **OK** to start the sketch.
11. Deactivate the **Toggle Construction geometry** icon on the **Sketcher geometries** toolbar.
12. Click the **Create Circle** icon on the **Sketcher geometries** toolbar.
13. Select the origin point of the sketch.
14. Move the pointer outward and click to create a circle.

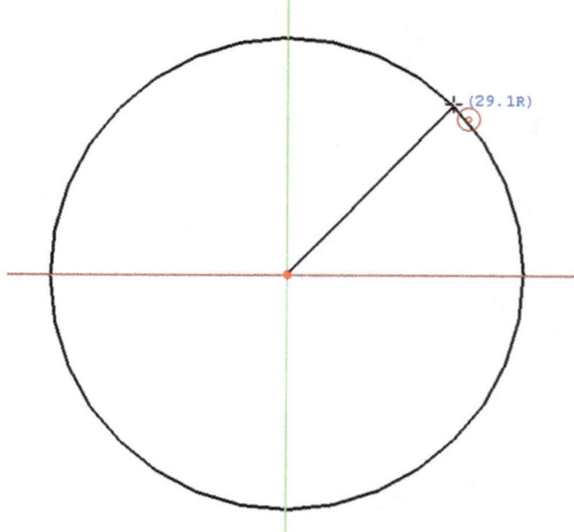

15. Click the **Create Line** icon on the **Sketcher geometries** toolbar.
16. Specify a point at the location outside the circle, as shown.

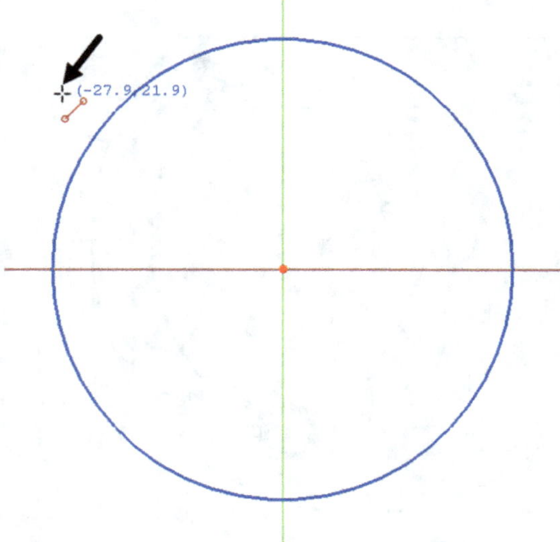

17. Move the pointer horizontally and notice the Horizontal constraint symbol.
18. Click outside the circle — Press Esc to deactivate the **Create Line** tool.

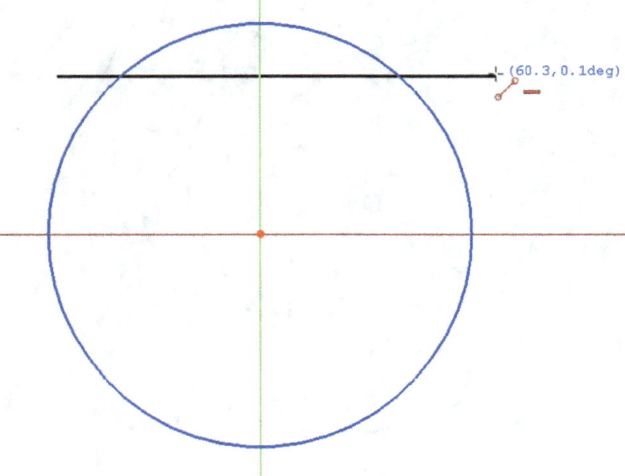

19. Click the **Trim Edge** icon on the **Sketcher geometries** toolbar.
20. Click on the portions of the sketch to be trimmed, as shown below.

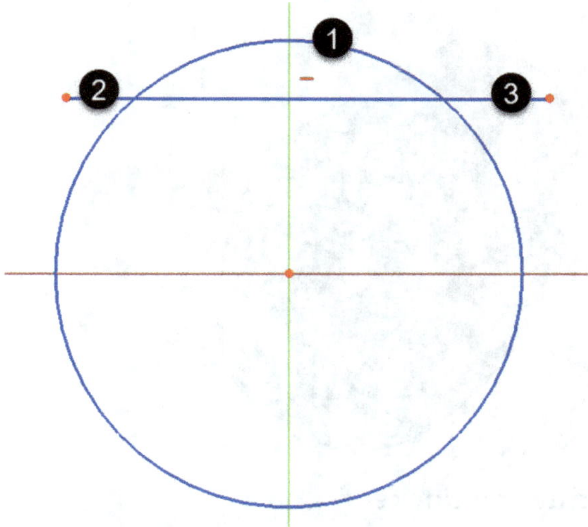

21. Add the **Radius** and **Horizontal Distance** constraints to the sketch.

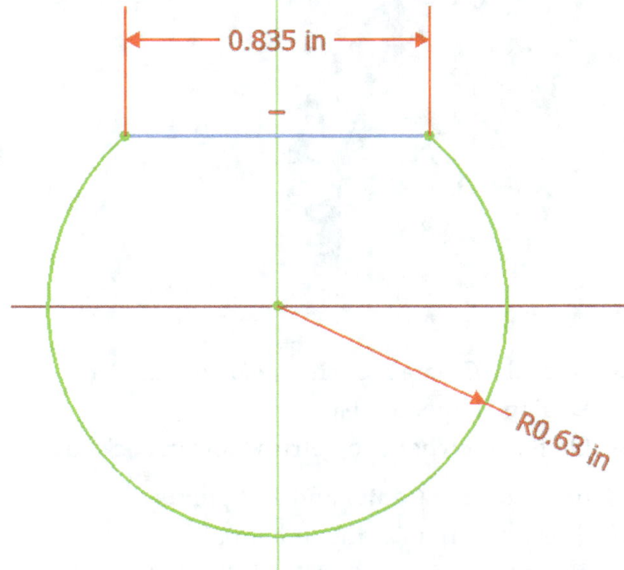

22. Click the **Close** button on the **Combo View** panel.
23. Click the **Pad** icon on the **Part Design Modeling** toolbar.
24. Type **0.236** in the **Length** box and click **OK**.

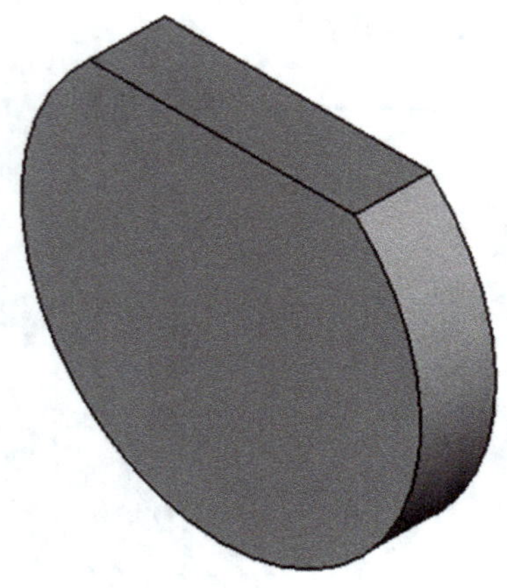

Creating the Pocket feature

1. Click on the front face of the model.

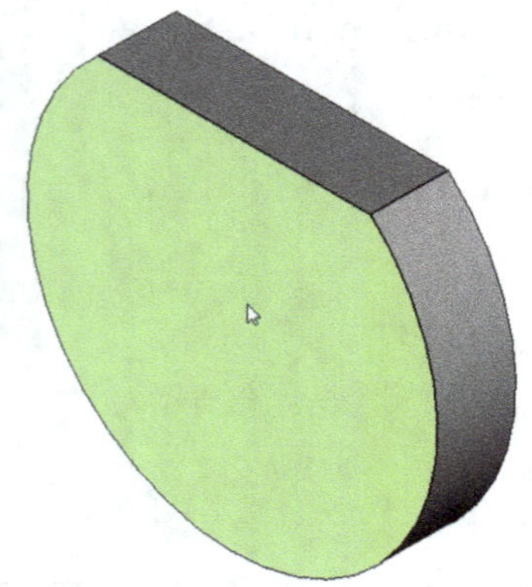

2. Click the **Create Sketch** icon on the **Part Design Helper** toolbar.
3. On the **Sketcher geometries** toolbar, click **Arc drop-down > Center and end points**.
4. Select the origin as the center point.
5. Move the cursor outside and click in the first quadrant of the circle to specify the start point of the arc.
6. Move the cursor and click in the fourth quadrant of the circle to specify the endpoint of the arc.

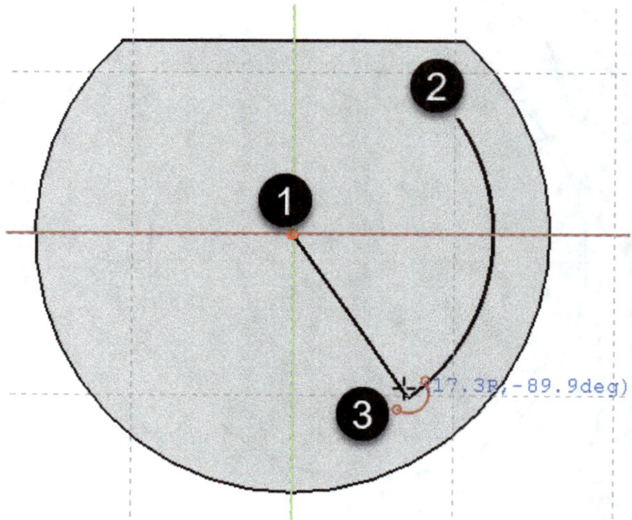

7. Likewise, create another centerpoint arc, as shown.

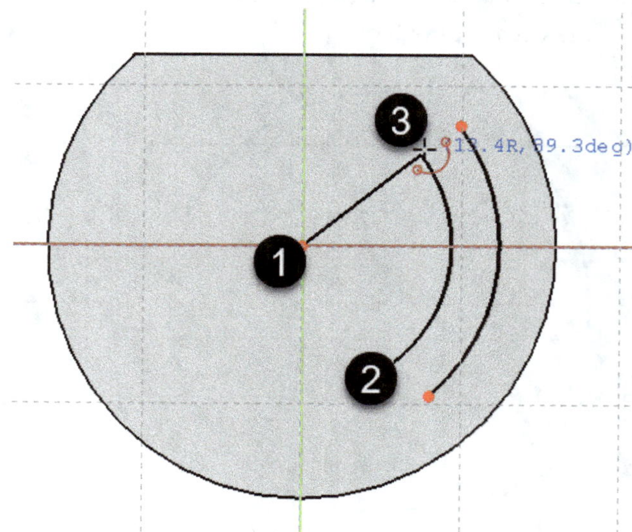

8. On the **Sketcher geometries** toolbar, click **Arc drop-down > End points and rim point**.
9. Zoom to the first quadrant.
10. Select the endpoint of the first and second arcs, as shown.
11. Move the pointer outward and click to specify the rim point of the arc.

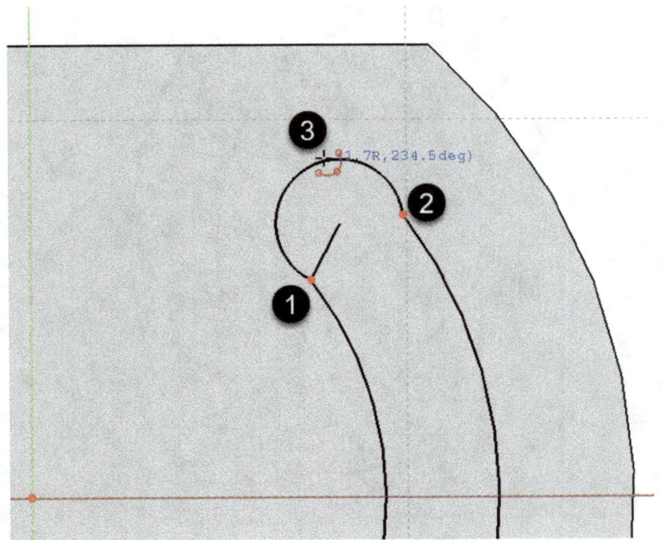

12. Use the **Constrain Coincident** tool and connect the endpoints of the small arc to the endpoints of the centerpoint arcs, if they are not correctly connected.

13. Click the **Constrain Tangent** icon on the **Sketcher constraints** toolbar.

14. Select the small arc and anyone of the centerpoint arcs; the small arc is made tangent to the centerpoint arc.

15. Likewise, make the small arc tangent to the other center point arc.

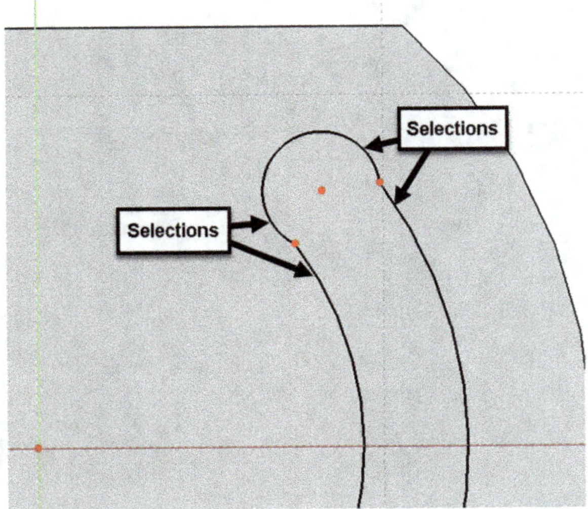

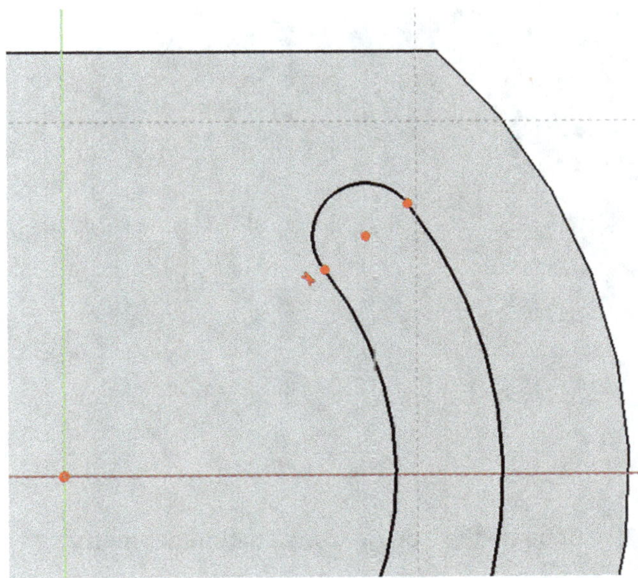

16. Likewise, create a small arc on the other ends of the centerpoint arcs.

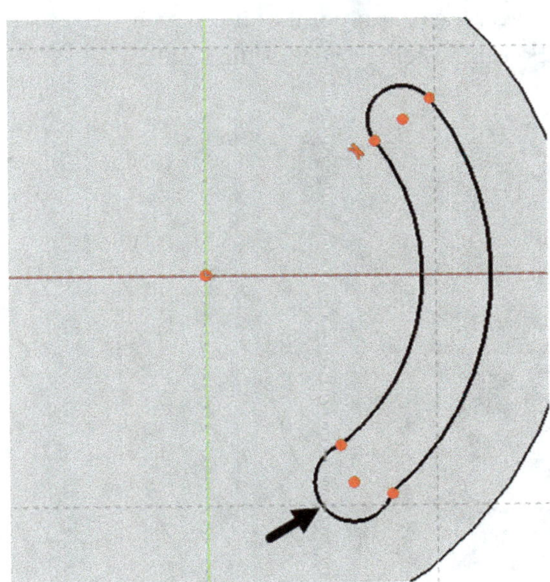

17. Use the **Constrain Coincident** tool and connect the endpoints of the small arc to the endpoints of the centerpoint arcs, if they are not correctly connected.

18. Make the small arc tangent to the centerpoint arcs.

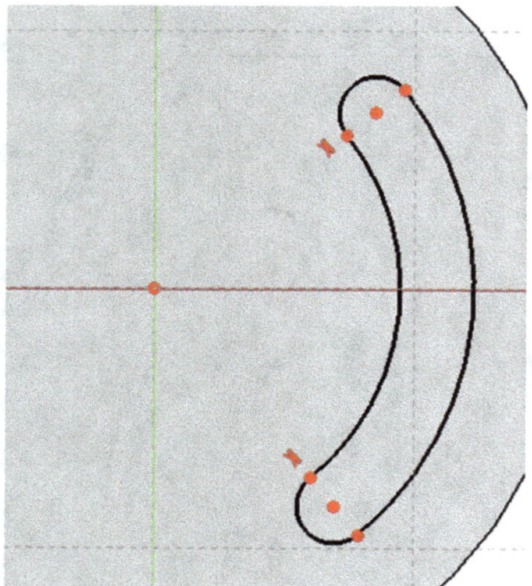

19. Activate the **Toggle Construction geometry** icon on the **Sketcher geometries** toolbar.

20. Click the **Create Line** icon on the **Sketcher geometries** toolbar.
21. Select the origin point of the sketch.
22. Select the centerpoint of the small arc.

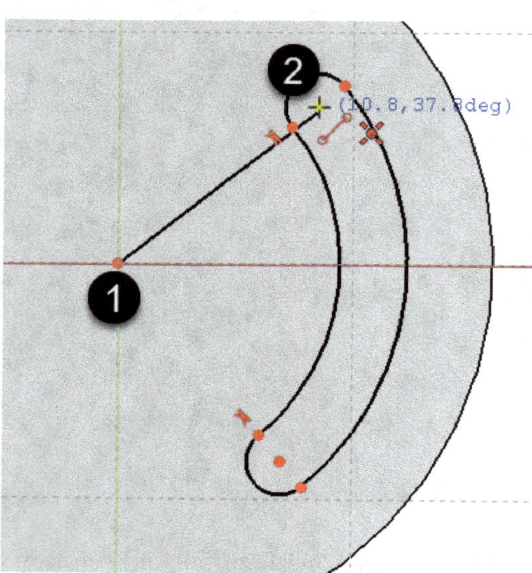

23. Likewise, create a line by selecting the origin and center point of another small arc.

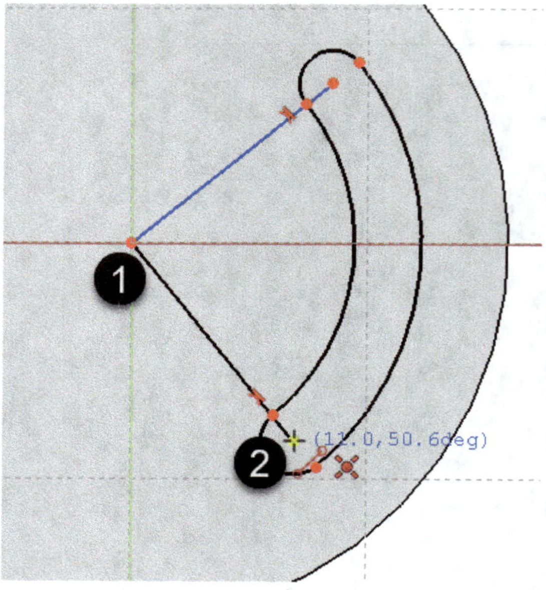

24. Use the **Constrain Coincident** tool and connect the endpoint of the line and the center point of the small arc, if not correctly connected.

25. Click the **Toggle construction geometry** icon on the **Sketcher geometries** toolbar.

26. Click the **Constrain distance** icon on the **Sketcher constraints** toolbar.
27. Select any one of the lines.
28. Type 0.512 in the **Length** box and click **OK**.

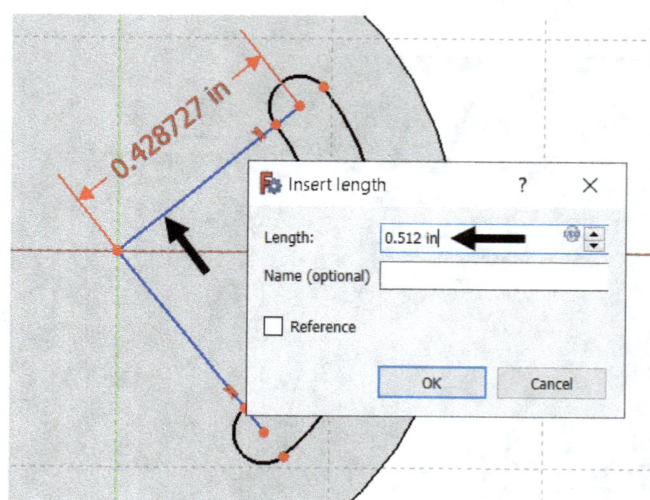

29. Click the **Constrain Radius** icon on the **Sketcher constraints** toolbar.
30. Select any one of the small arcs.

31. Type 0.039 in the **Radius** box, and then click **OK**.
32. Click the **Constrain angle** icon on the **Sketcher constraints** toolbar.
33. Select the two lines.
34. Type **30** in the **Angle** box, and then click **OK**.
35. Select the horizontal axis of the sketch and anyone of the lines.
36. Type **15** in the **Angle** box, and then click **OK**.

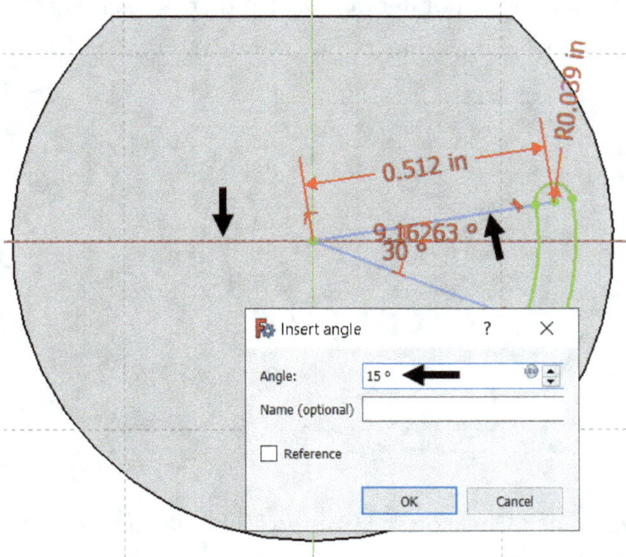

37. Click **Close** on the **Combo View** panel.
38. Click the **Pocket** icon on the **Part Design Modeling** toolbar.
39. Select **Type > Through All** from the **Pocket Parameters** dialog.
40. Click **OK**.

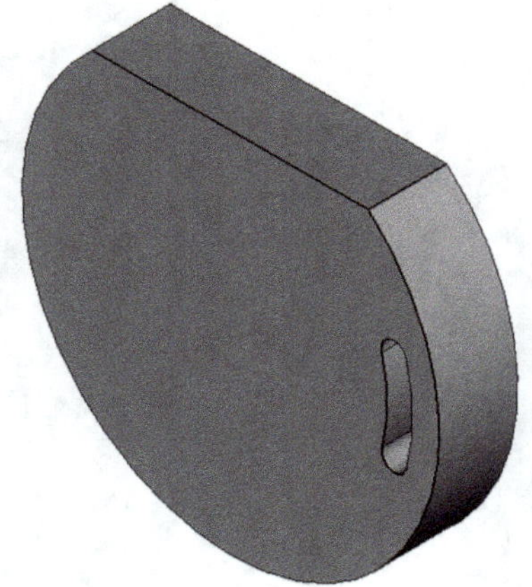

Creating a Polar Pattern

1. Click the **Polar Pattern** icon on the **Part Design Modeling** toolbar.
2. Select the **Pocket** feature from the **Select Feature** section in the **Combo View** panel.
3. Click **OK**.
4. Select **Axis > Normal sketch axis**.
5. Type **180** in the **Angle** box.
6. Type **4** in the **Occurrences** box.
7. Check the **Reverse direction** option.
8. Click **OK**.

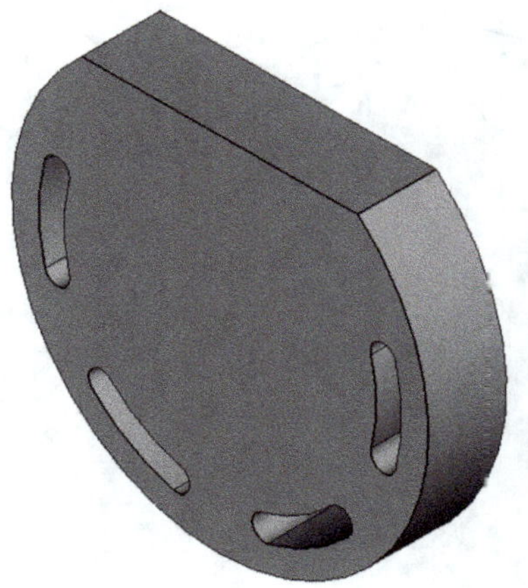

Adding the Pad feature

1. Press and hold the middle and right mouse button.
2. Drag the pointer to rotate the model.
3. Click on the back face of the model.

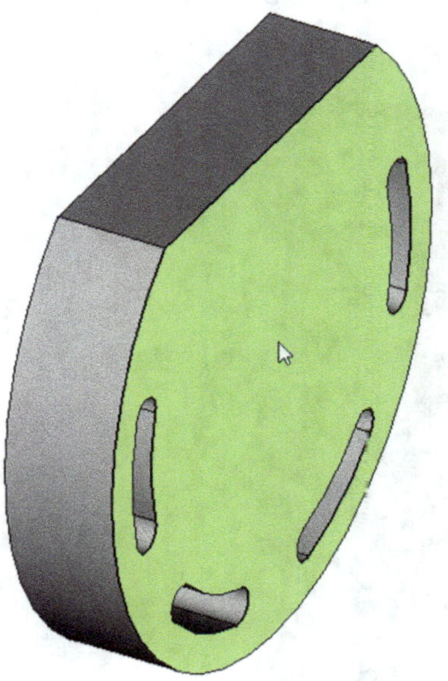

4. Click the **Create Sketch** icon on the **Part Design**

Helper toolbar.

5. Click the **Create Circle** icon on the **Sketcher geometries** toolbar.
6. Select the sketch origin.
7. Move the pointer outward and click to create the circle.
8. Click the **Constrain Radius** icon on the **Sketcher constraints** toolbar.
9. Select the circle.
10. Type **0.236** in the **Radius** box and click **OK**.

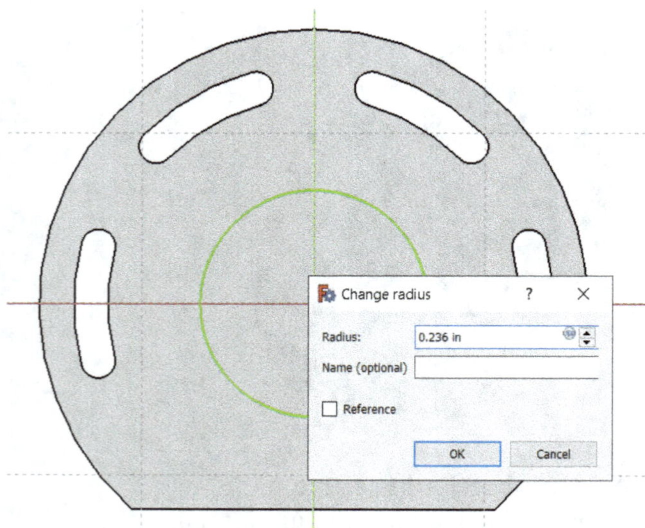

11. Click **Close** on the **Combo View** panel.
12. Click the **Pad** icon on the **Part Design Modeling** toolbar.
13. Type **0.078** in the **Length** box.
14. Click **OK**.

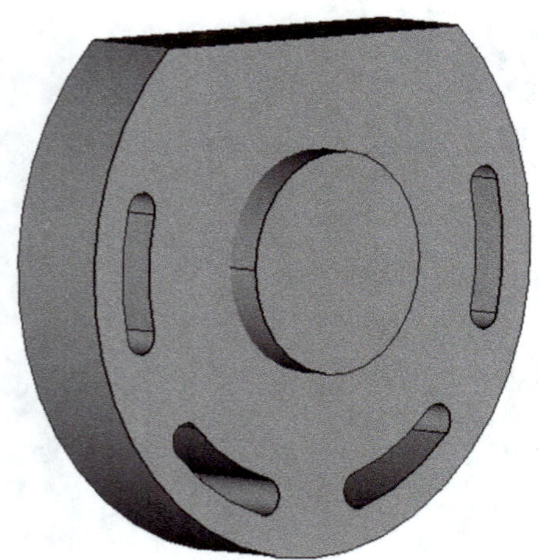

Creating a Counterbore Hole

In this section, you create a counterbore hole

concentric to the circular face.

1. Select the front face of the model.
2. Click the **Create Sketch** icon on the **Part Design Helper** toolbar.
3. Click **OK** on the **Combo View** panel.
4. Click the **Create Circle** icon on the **Sketcher geometries** toolbar.
5. Select the origin point of the sketch.
6. Move the pointer outward and click to create a circle.

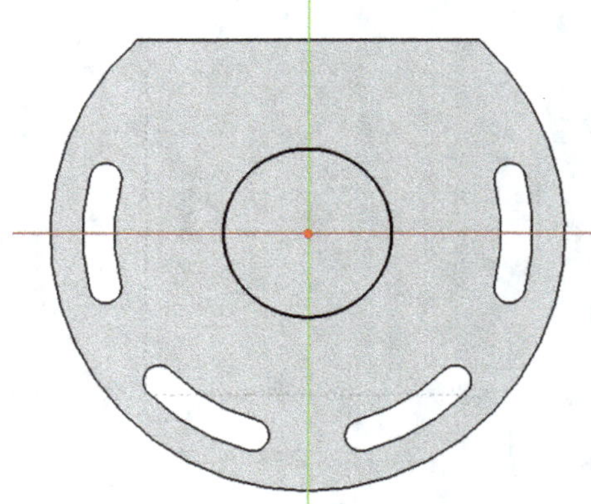

7. Click **Close** on the **Combo View** panel.
8. Click the **Hole** icon on the **Part Design Modeling** toolbar.
9. Type **0.314** in the **Diameter** box.
10. Select **Depth > Through All**.
11. On the **Hole Parameters** section, under **Hole cut**, select **Type > Counterbore**.
12. Type **0.394** in the **Diameter** box.
13. Type **0.078** in the **Depth** box.

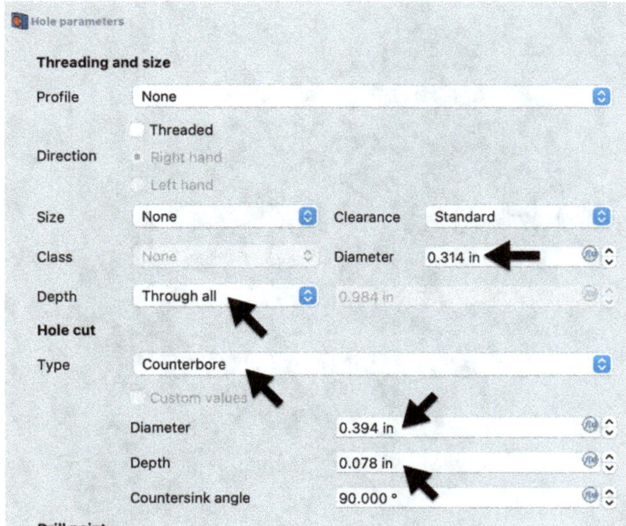

14. Click **OK** on the **Combo View** panel; the counterbore hole is created.

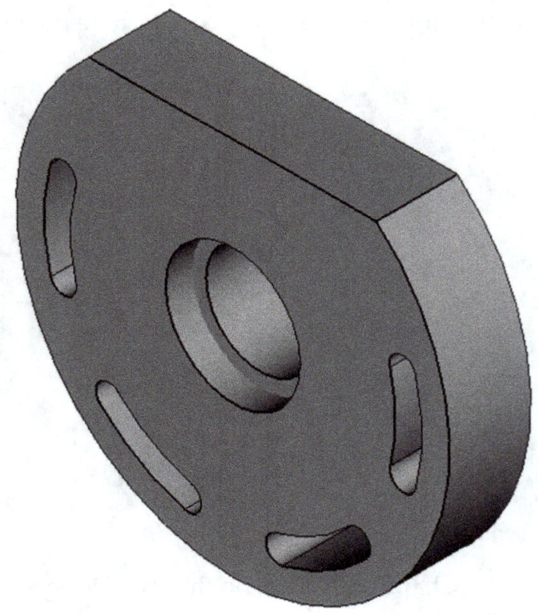

Creating Threaded holes

In this section, you create a threaded hole.

1. Click on the front face of the model.

2. Click the **Create Sketch** icon.

3. Click the **Create Circle** icon on the **Sketcher geometries** toolbar.

4. Click on the horizontal axis on the right side.

5. Move the pointer outward and click to create the circle.

6. Add the horizontal distance constraint between the centerpoint of the circle and the origin point.

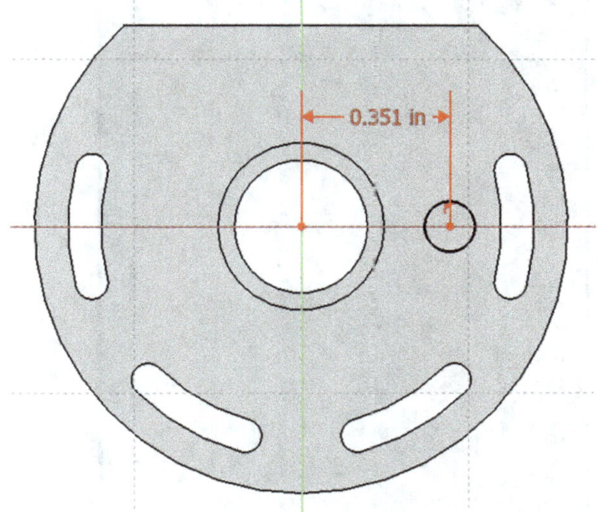

7. Click the **Close** button on the **Combo View** panel.

8. Click the **Hole** icon on the **Part Design Modeling** toolbar; the **Hole Parameters** section appears.

9. Under **Threading and size**, select **Profile > UTS coarse profile**.

10. Check the **Threaded** option.

11. Select **Direction > Right hand**.

12. Select **Size > #1**.

13. Select **Class > 2B**.

14. Select **Depth > Through all**.

15. Under **Hole cut**, select the **Counterbore** option from the **Type** drop-down.

16. Set the Counterbore **Diameter** to 0.118.

17. Set the Counterbore **Depth** to 0.039.

18. Under **Drill point**, select **Type > Flat**.

Additional Modeling Tools

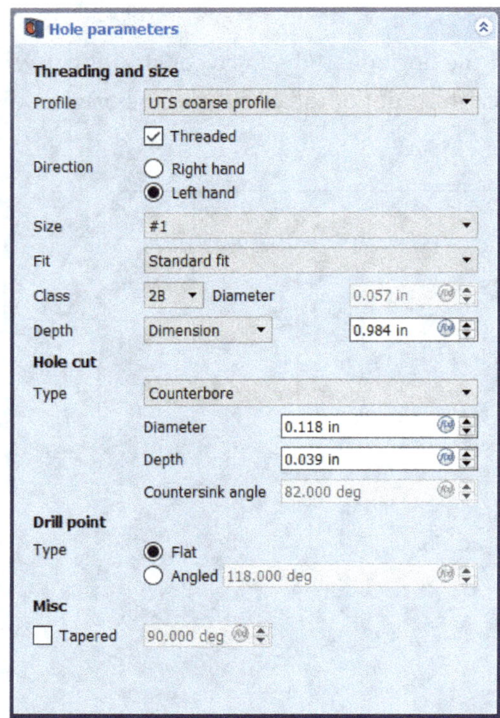

19. Click **OK** to create the hole.

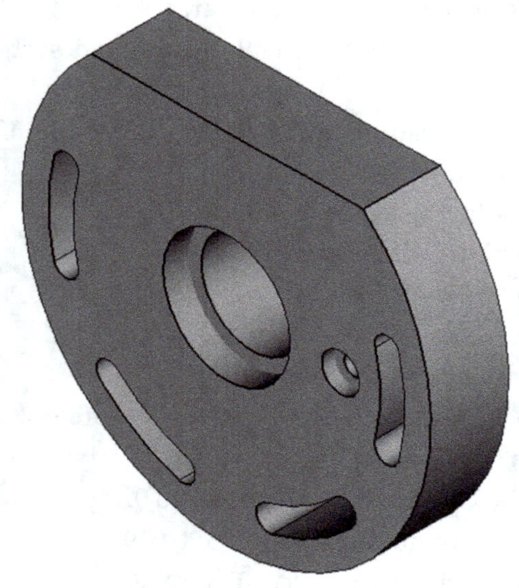

20. Click the **Polar Pattern** icon on the **Part Design Modeling** toolbar.
21. Select the **Hole** feature from the **Select Feature** section in the **Combo View** panel.
22. Click **OK**.
23. Select **Axis > Normal sketch axis**.
24. Type **360** in the **Angle** box.
25. Type **6** in the **Occurrences** box.
26. Click **OK**.

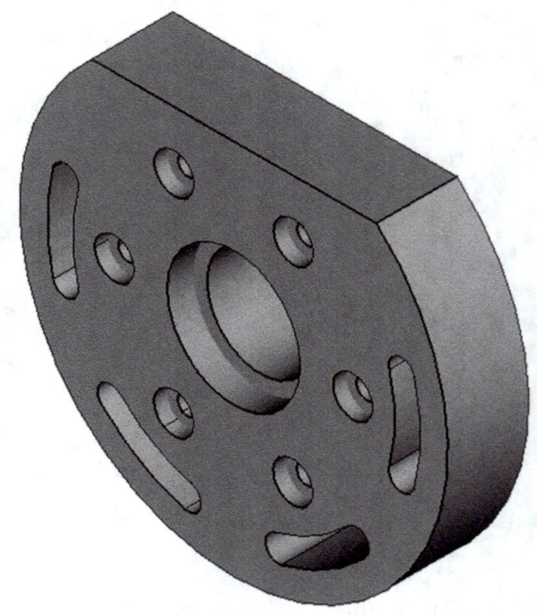

Creating Chamfers

1. Select the circular edge of the counterbore hole.

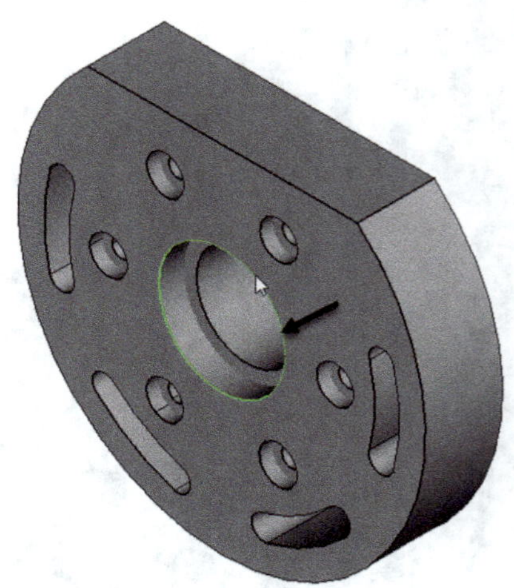

2. Click the **Chamfer** icon on the **Part Design Modeling** toolbar.
3. Enter 0.039 in the **Size** box.

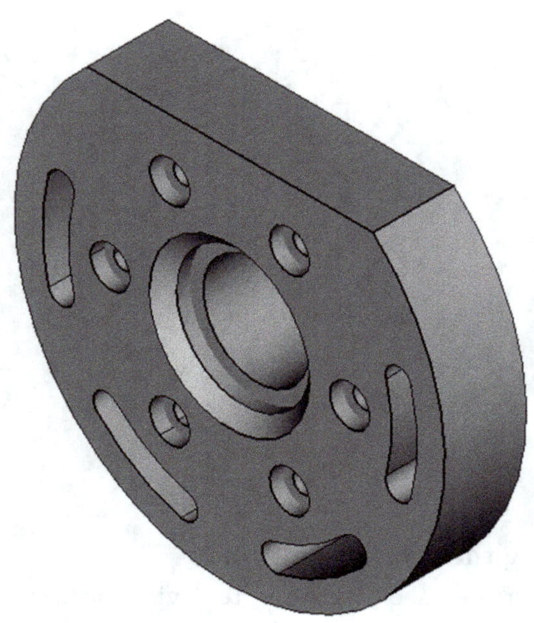

4. Click **OK** to create the chamfer.
5. Save the model and close it.

TUTORIAL 2

In this tutorial, you create the model shown in the figure.

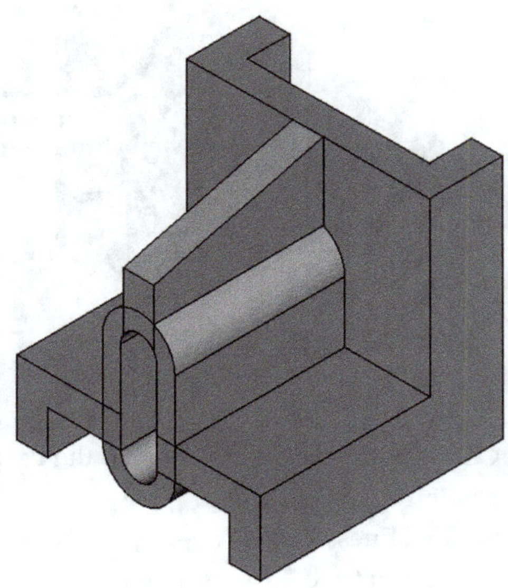

Creating the first feature

1. Open a new FreeCAD file.
2. Select the **Part Design** from the **Workbenches** drop-down.
3. Click the **Create sketch** icon on the **Part**

Design Helper toolbar, and then select the YZ Plane.

4. Click **OK** to start the sketch.

5. Draw the sketch using the **Polyline** tool, as shown.

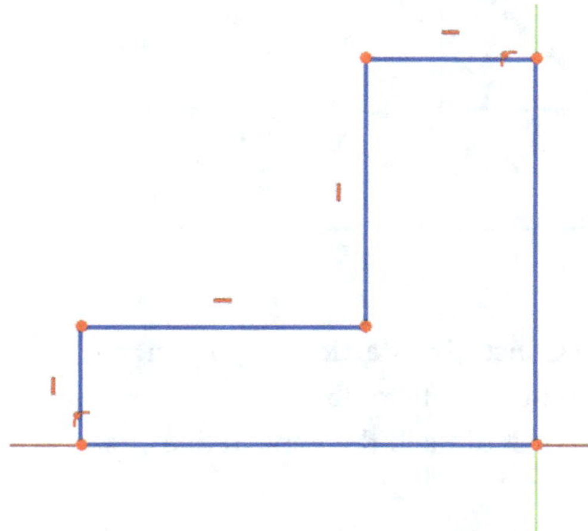

6. Click the **Constrain Equal** icon on the **Sketcher constraints** toolbar.

7. Select the vertical and horizontal lines, as shown.

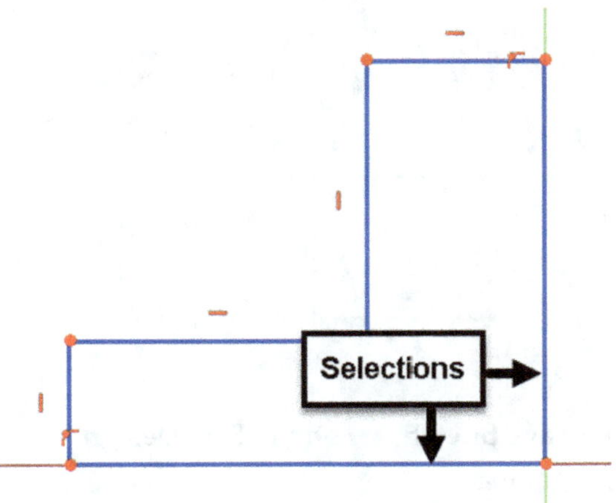

8. Select the two lines to make them equal in length.

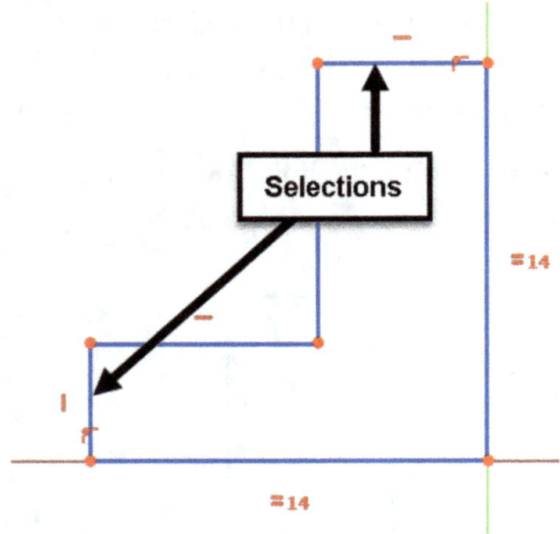

9. Click the **Constraint Vertical** icon on the **Sketcher constraints** toolbar.
10. Add the constraints to the vertical lines, as shown.

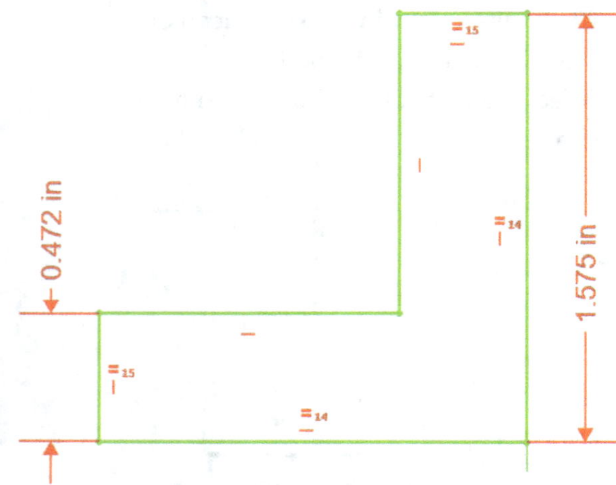

11. Click **Leave Sketch** on the **Part Design Helper** toolbar.
12. Click the **Pad** icon on the **Part Design Modeling** toolbar.
13. Select the **Symmetric plane** option from the **Pad parameters** section.
14. Set the **Length** to 1.575.
15. Click **OK** to create the first feature.

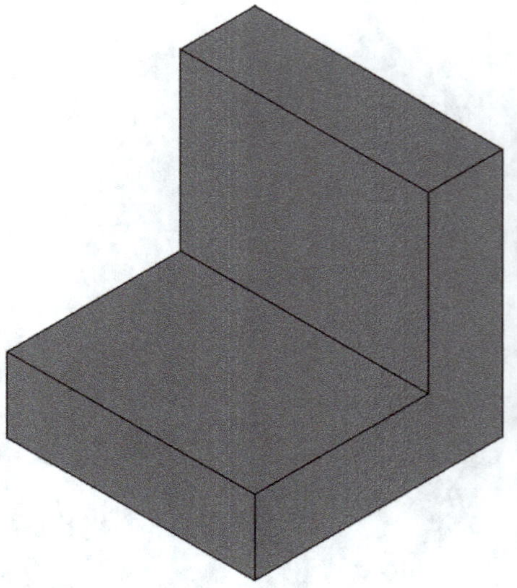

Creating the Shell feature

You can create a shell feature by removing the face of the model and applying thickness to other faces.

1. Press and hold the Ctrl key.
2. Select the top face and the back face of the model.

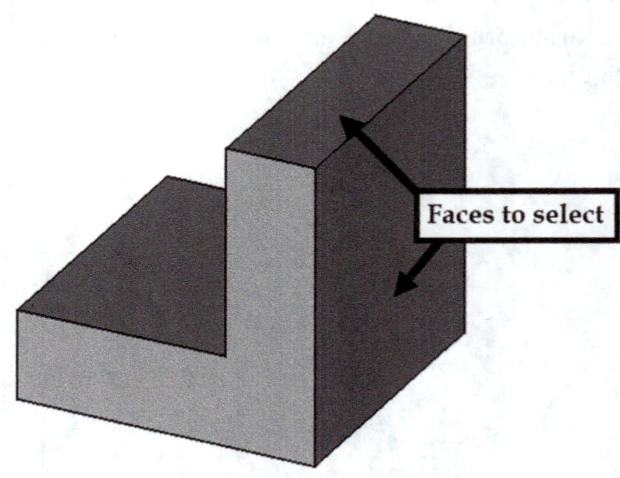

3. Click the **Thickness** icon on the **Part Design Modeling** toolbar.
4. Set **Thickness** to 0.197.
5. Select **Join type > Intersection**.
6. Check the **Make thickness inward** option.

Now, you need to select more faces.

7. Click the **Add face** button.
8. Select the front face.

9. Click the **Add face** button and the bottom face of the model.

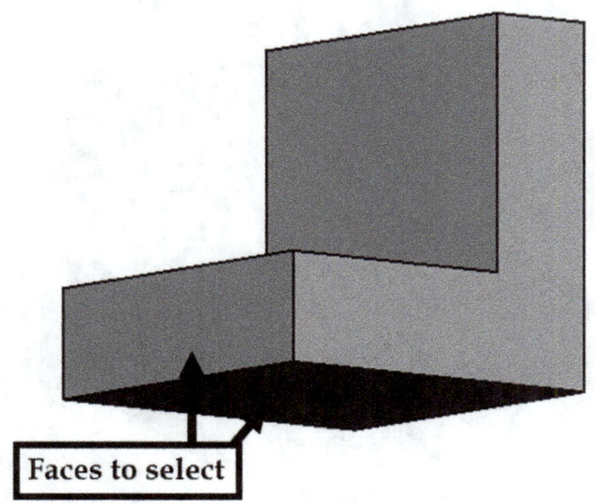

10. Click **OK** to shell the model.

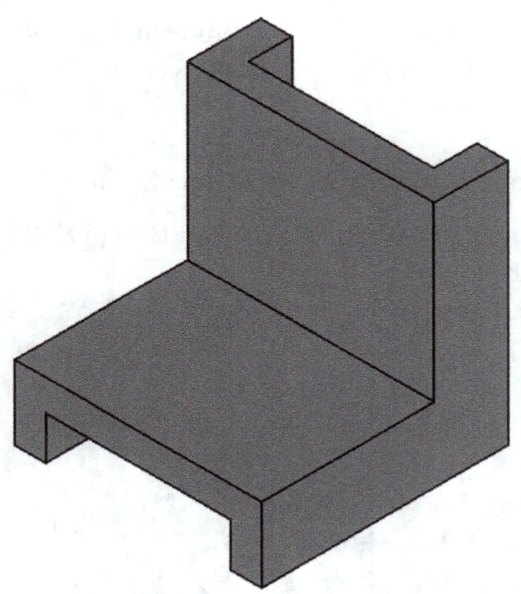

Creating the Third feature

1. Select the front face of the model.

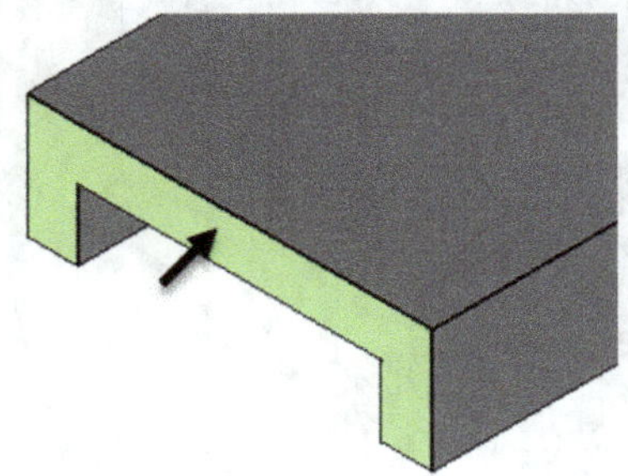

2. Click the **Create Sketch** icon on the **Part Design Helper** toolbar.

3. Click the **External geometry** icon on the **Sketcher geometries** toolbar.

4. Select the edges of the model, as shown.

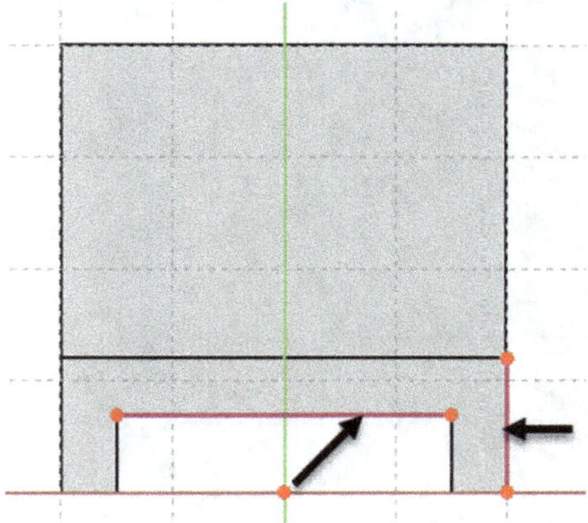

5. Click **Create Slot** on the **Sketcher geometries** toolbar.

6. Draw a slot by selecting the first and second points.

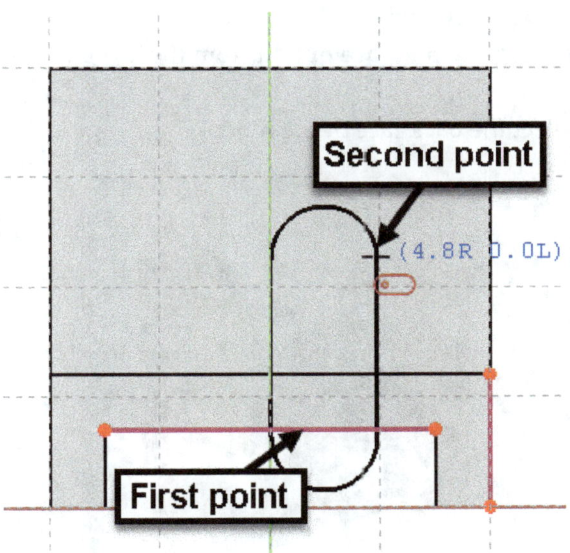

7. Add constraints to the slot.

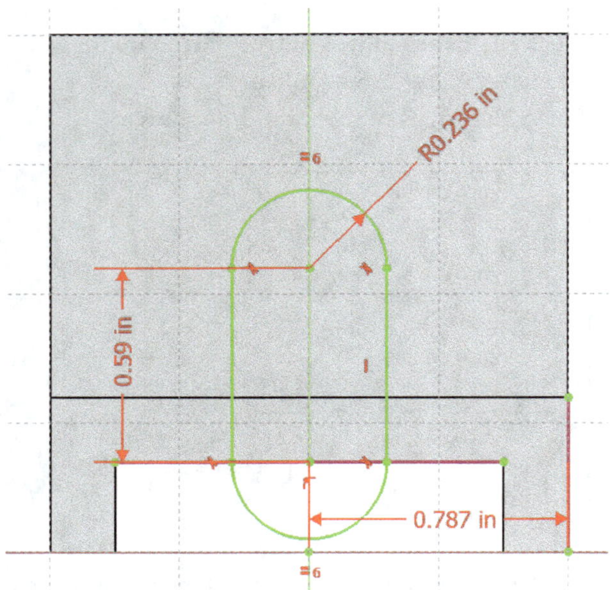

8. Click **Leave Sketch** on the **Part Design Helper** toolbar.

9. Click the **Pad** icon on the **Part Design Modeling** toolbar.

10. Select the **Up to face** option from the **Type** drop-down.

11. Select the back face of the model.

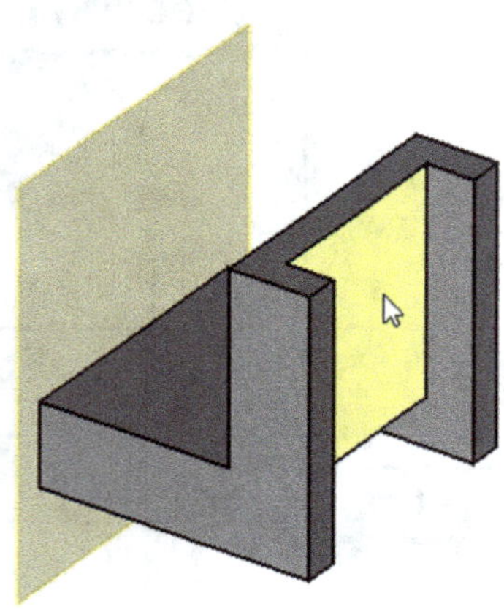

12. Click **OK** to create the feature.

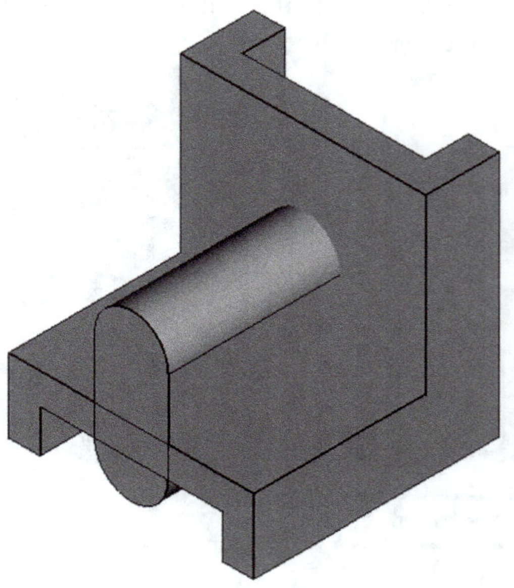

Creating the Rib Feature

In this section, you create a rib feature in the middle of the model. To do this, you must create an offset plane.

1. To create an offset plane, click the **Create a datum plane** icon on the **Part Design Helper** toolbar.

2. Select the right face of the model.

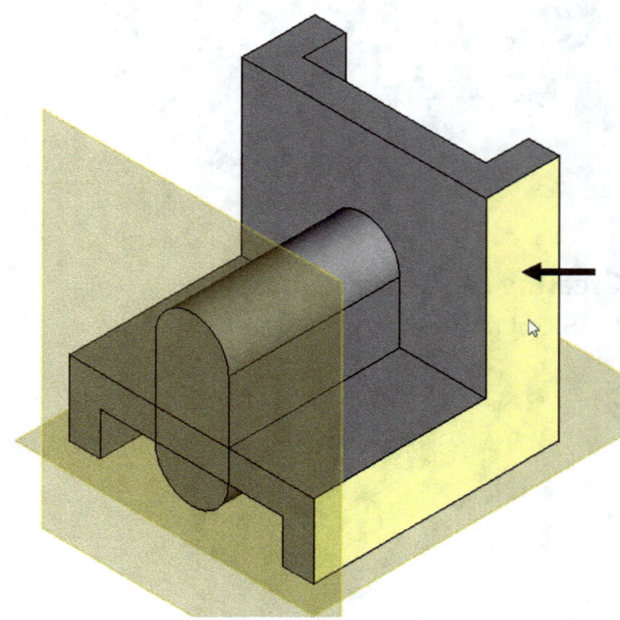

3. Type **0.7875** in the **Z** box available in the **Attachment** section.

4. Check the **Flip sides** option.

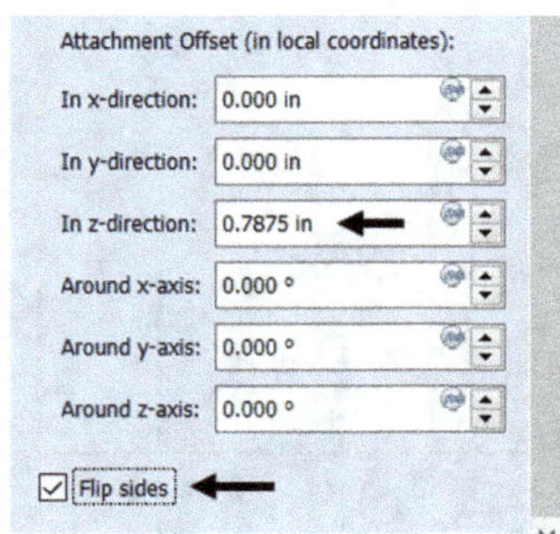

5. Click **OK** to create the plane.

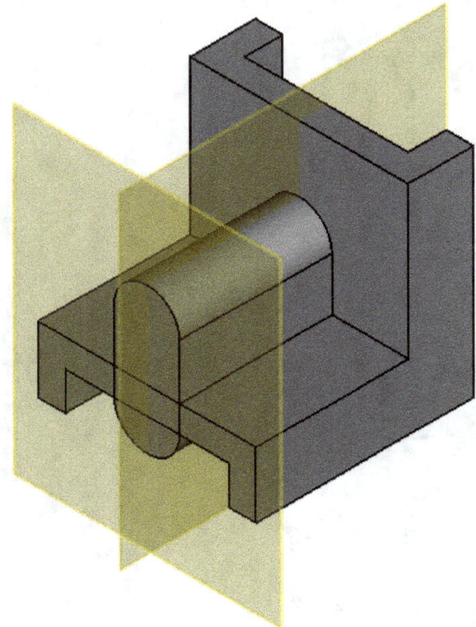

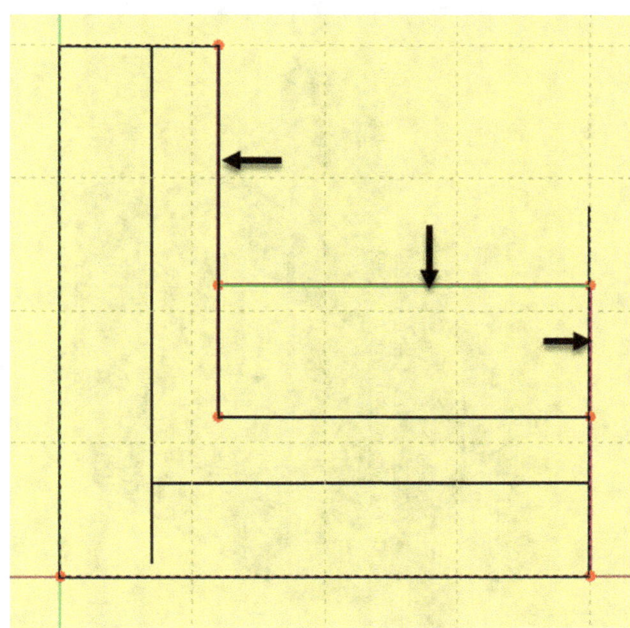

6. Click the **Create Sketch** icon on the **Part Design Helper** toolbar.
7. Select the newly created plane.
8. Click **OK**.
9. On the **View** toolbar, set the **Draw Style** to Wireframe .
10. Click the **External Geometry** icon on the **Sketcher geometries** toolbar.
11. Select the model edges, as shown.

12. Draw the sketch, as shown below.

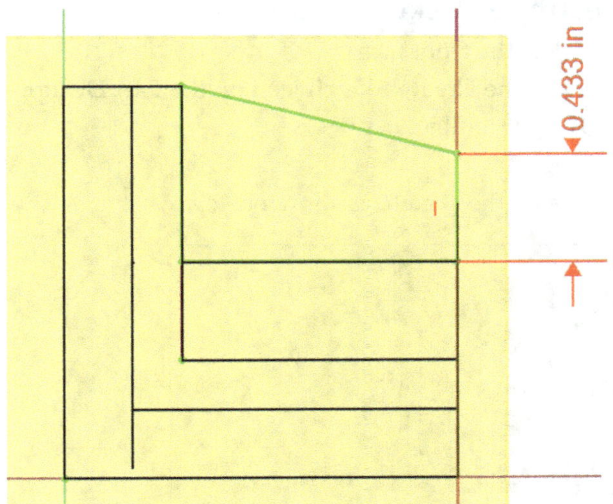

13. Click **Close** on the **Combo View** panel.
14. On the **View** toolbar, set the **Draw Style** to **Flat Lines** .
15. Click the **Pad** icon on the **Part Design Modeling** toolbar.
16. Check the **Symmetric to plane** option.
17. Type **0.197** in the **Length** box.
18. Click **OK** to create the rib feature.

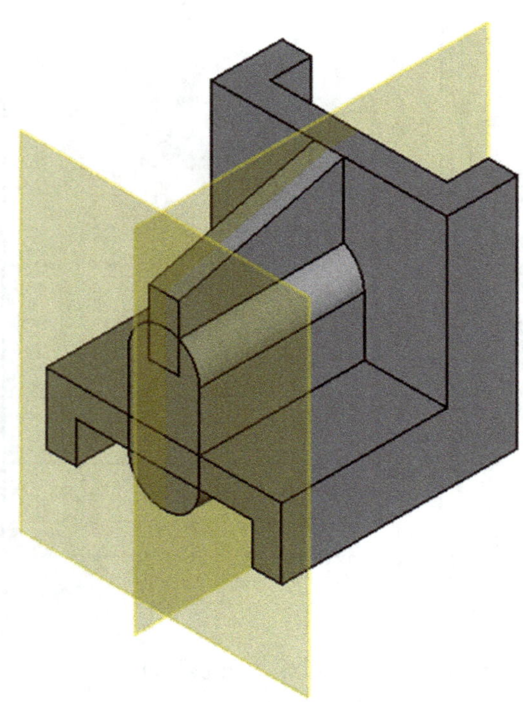

Creating a Pocket Feature

1. Select the front face.
2. Click the **Create Sketch** icon on the **Part Design Helper** toolbar.
3. Click **OK**.
4. Create the sketch, as shown below.

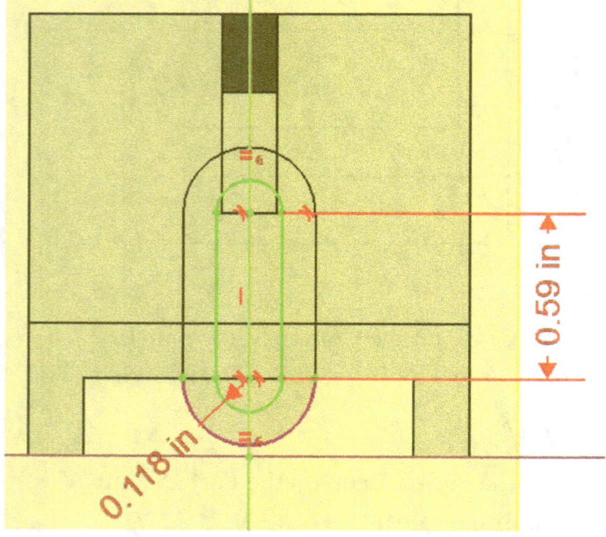

5. Click **Close** on the **Combo View** panel.
6. Click the **Pocket** icon on the **Part Design Modeling** toolbar.
7. Select the **Through All** option from the **Type** drop-down.

8. Click **OK** to create the pocket feature.

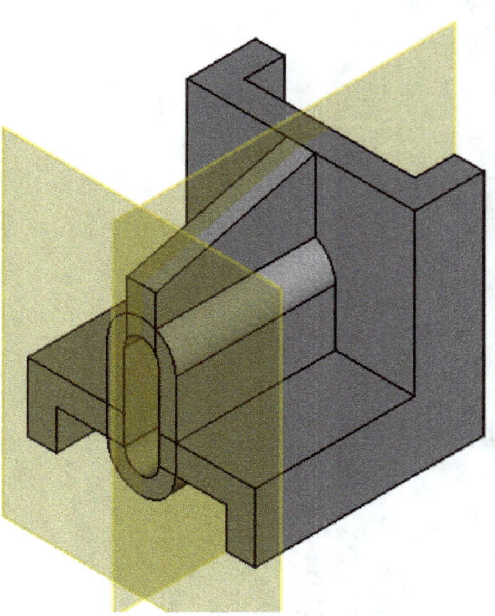

19. Save the model and close it.

TUTORIAL 3

In this tutorial, you create a helical spring.

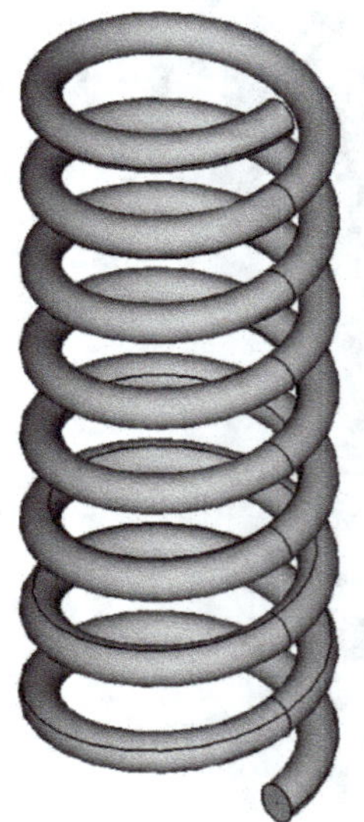

Creating the Profile

1. Open a new FreeCAD file.
2. Select **Part Design** from the **Workbenches** drop-down.
3. Click the **Create Sketch** icon on the **Part Design Helper** toolbar.
4. Select the XZ Plane from the **Combo View** panel.

5. Click **OK**.
6. Create a circle, as shown.

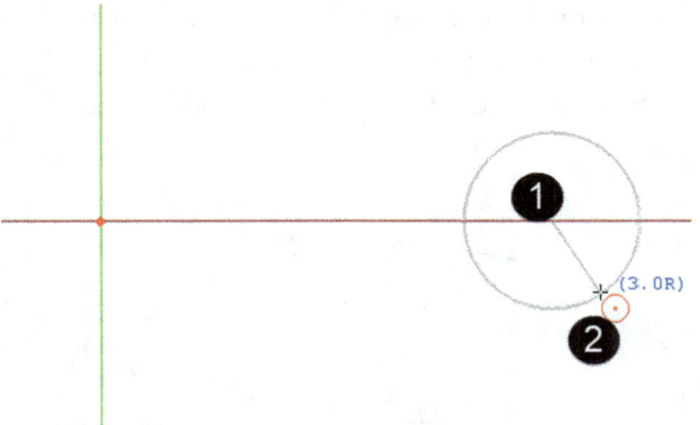

7. Add constraints to it, as shown.

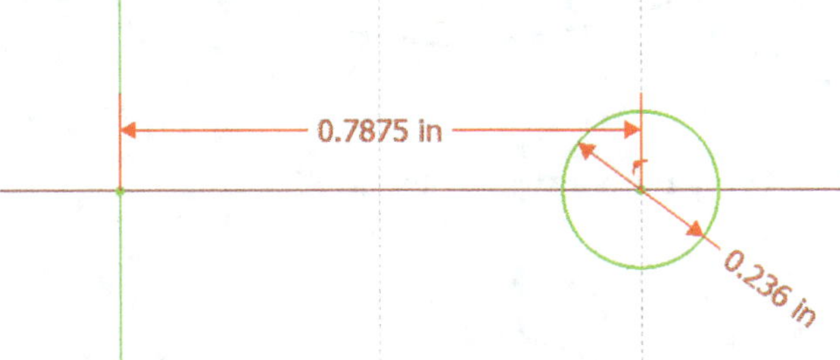

8. Click **Close** on the **Combo View** panel.

Creating the Helix

1. Select **Part** from the **Workbenches** drop-down.
2. Click the **Create primitives** icon on the **Solids** toolbar.
3. In the **Geometric Primitives** dialog, select **Helix** from the drop-down.
4. Type **0.59** in the **Pitch** box.
5. Type **4.72** in the **Height** box.
6. Type **0.7875** in the **Radius** box.
7. Select **Right-handed** from the **Coordinate system** drop-down.

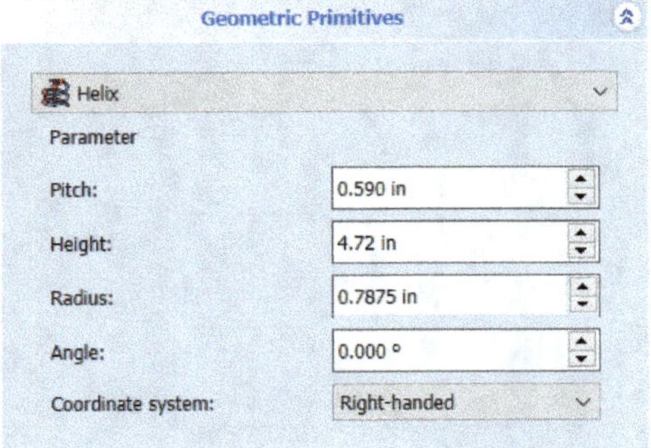

8. Expand the **Location** section.
9. Type **0** in the **X**, Y, and **Z** boxes.
10. Click the **Create** button.
11. On the **View** toolbar, click the **Isometric** icon.

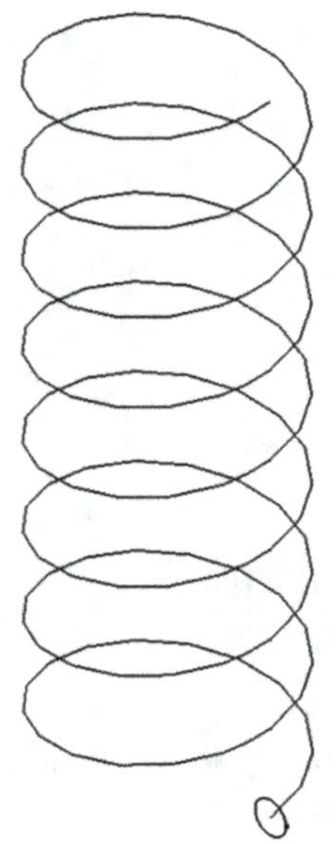

12. Click the **Close** button.

Creating the Sweep

1. Click the **Sweep** icon on the **Part tools** toolbar.
2. Select the **Sketch** from the **Available profiles** section.
3. Click the **Add** button.
4. Check the **Create solid** option.
5. Click the **Sweep Path** button.
6. Press and hold the Ctrl key and select all the elements of the helix.
7. Click **Done**.
8. Click **OK** to create the sweep.

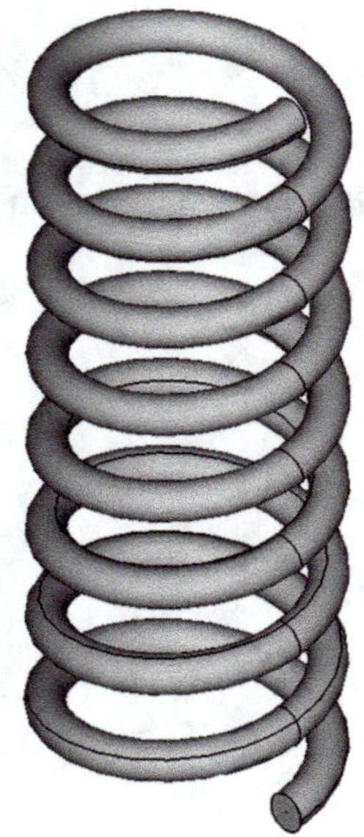

9. Save the model and close the file.

TUTORIAL 4

In this tutorial, you create a shampoo bottle using the **Loft**, **Pad**, and **Sweep** tools.

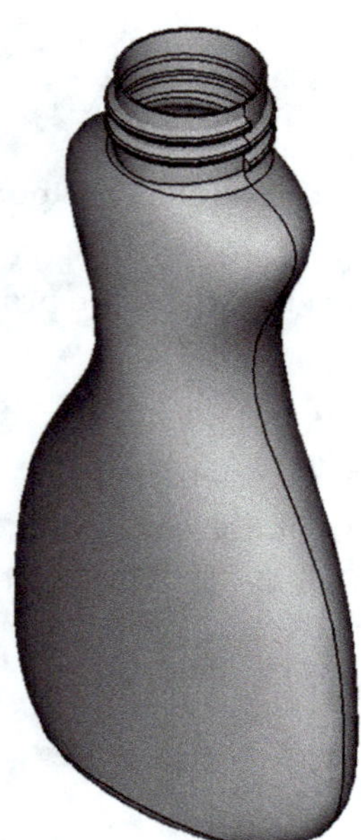

Creating the Loft feature

To create a loft feature, you need to create sections.

1. Start a new FreeCAD file.
2. Select the **Part Design** option from the **Workbenches** drop-down.
3. Click the **Create Sketches** icon on the **Part**

Design Helper toolbar.

4. Select the XY Plane and click **OK**.

5. Click the **Create ellipse by center** icon on the **Sketcher geometries** toolbar.

6. Draw the ellipse by selecting the points, as shown.

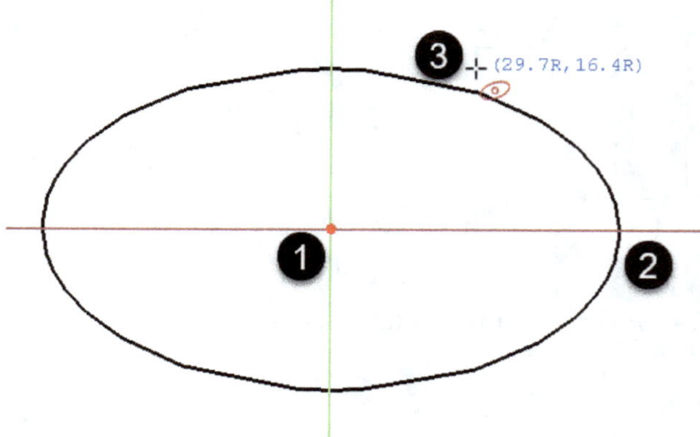

7. Apply the constraints to the ellipse.

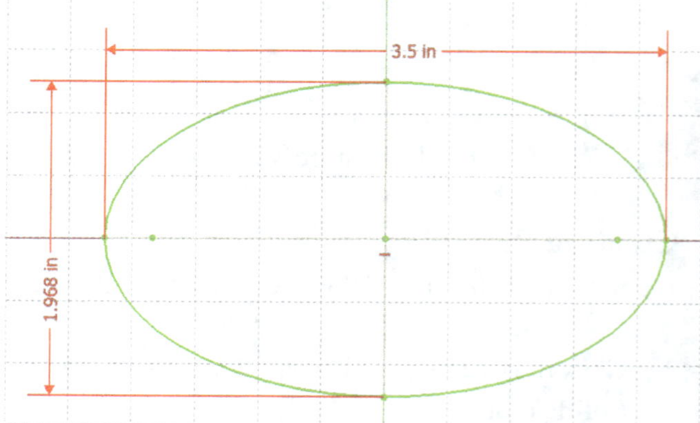

8. Click the **Close** button on the **Combo View** panel.

9. Click the **Create a datum plane** icon on the **Part Design Helper** toolbar.

10. Click on the ellipse.
11. Type 1.5 in the **Z** box.
12. Click **OK**.

13. Click the **Create a datum plane** icon on the **Part Design Helper** toolbar.
14. Click on the newly created plane.
15. Type 1.5 in the **Z** box.
16. Click **OK**.

17. Click the **Create a datum plane** icon on the **Part Design Helper** toolbar.
18. Click on the newly created plane.
19. Type 1.2 in the **Z** box.
20. Click **OK**.

21. Click the **Create a datum plane** icon on the **Part Design Helper** toolbar.
22. Click on the newly created plane.
23. Type 1.2 in the **Z** box.
24. Click **OK.**

25. Click the **Create a datum plane**  icon on the **Part Design Helper** toolbar.
26. Click on the newly created plane.
27. Type 1.5 in the **Z** box.
28. Click **OK**.

29. Click the **Create a datum plane** icon on the **Part Design Helper** toolbar.
30. Click on the newly created plane.
31. Type 1.2 in the **Z** box.
32. Click **OK**

33. Click the **Create Sketch** icon on the **Part Design Modeling** toolbar.
34. Select the first datum plane, and then click **OK**.

35. Click the **View Section** icon on the **Sketcher** toolbar.
36. Create an ellipse, as shown.

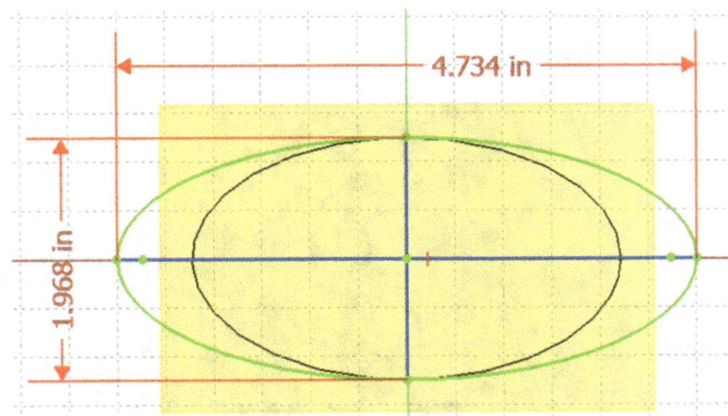

37. Click the **Close** button on the **Combo View** panel.
38. Click the **Create Sketch** icon on the **Part Design Helper** toolbar.
39. Select the second datum plane, and then click **OK**.
40. On the Menu bar, click **Sketch > View section**.
41. Create an ellipse, as shown.

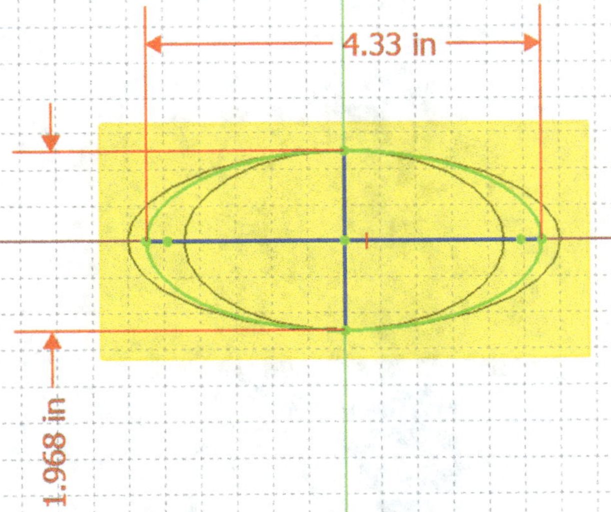

42. Click the **Close** button on the **Combo View** panel.
43. Start a sketch on the third datum plane.
44. Click the **View Section** icon on the **Sketcher** toolbar.
45. Create an ellipse, as shown.

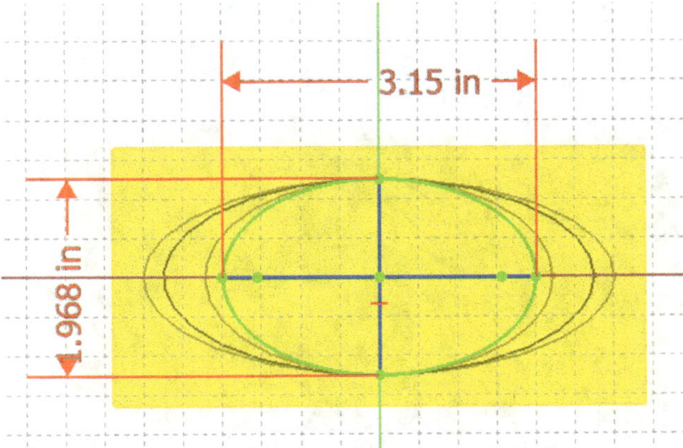

46. Click the **Close** button on the **Combo View** panel.
47. Start a sketch on the fourth datum plane, and then create an ellipse on it.

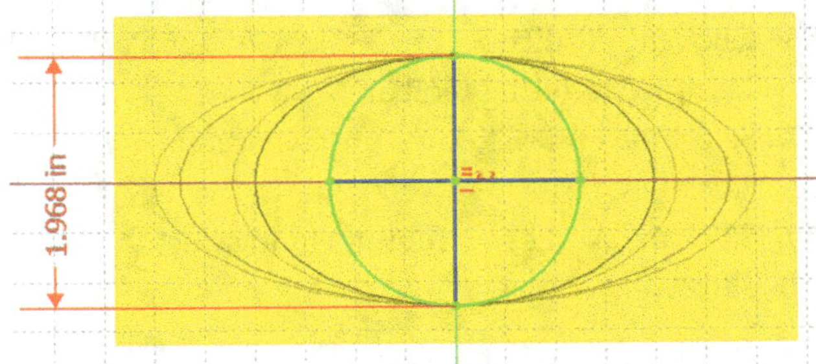

48. Click the **Close** button on the **Combo View** panel.
49. Start a new sketch on the fifth plane.
50. Create an ellipse, as shown.

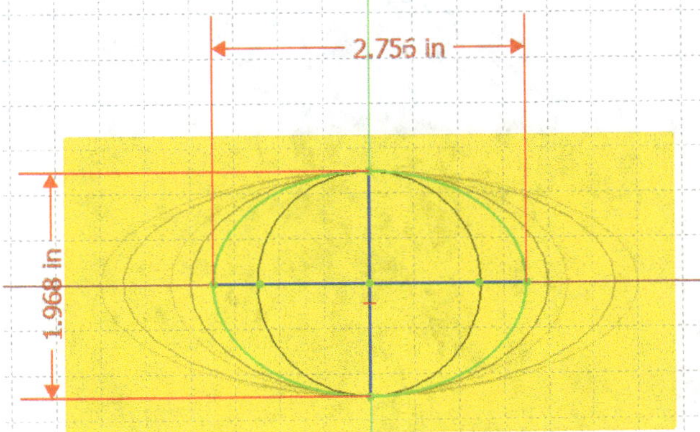

51. Click the **Close** button on the **Combo View** panel.
52. Start a new sketch on the sixth plane.
53. Create a circle, as shown.

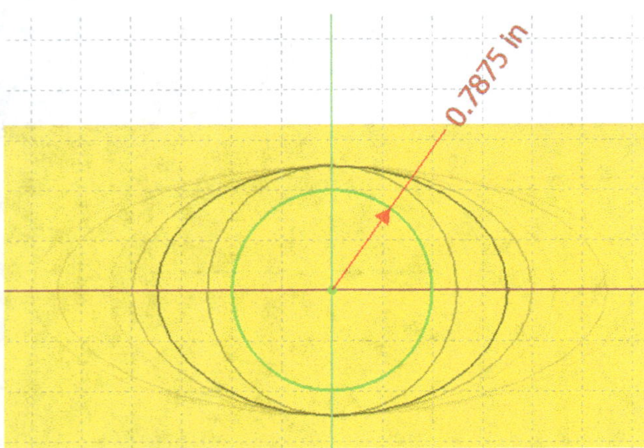

54. Click the **Close** button on the **Combo View** panel.
55. Click in the graphics window to deselect the last sketch.
56. Click the **Additive Loft** icon on the **Part Design Modeling** toolbar.
57. Select the ellipse located at the bottom.
58. Click **OK**.
59. Click the **Add section** button and select the next ellipse.

60. Likewise, select the remaining sketches in the order, as shown.

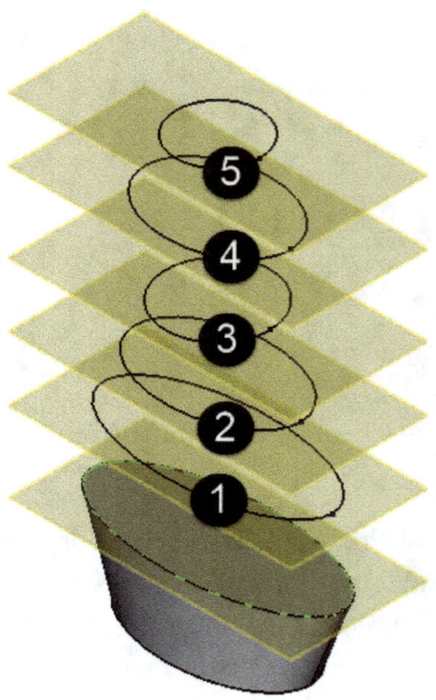

61. Click **OK** to create the loft feature.

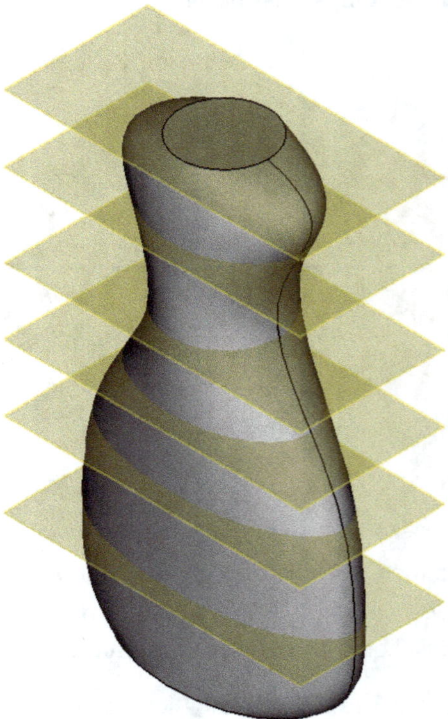

Creating the Extruded feature

1. Click the **Pad** icon on the **Part Design Modeling** toolbar.
2. Check the **Allow used features** option from the **Select Features** dialog.
3. Select the last sketch from the sketch list.

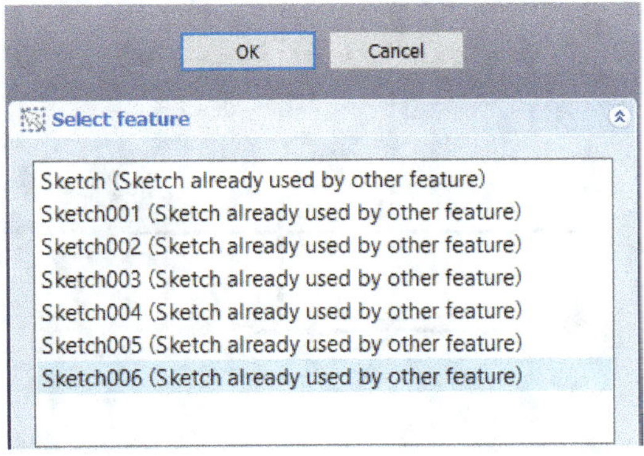

4. Click **OK**.
5. Type **1** in the **Length** box and click **OK**.

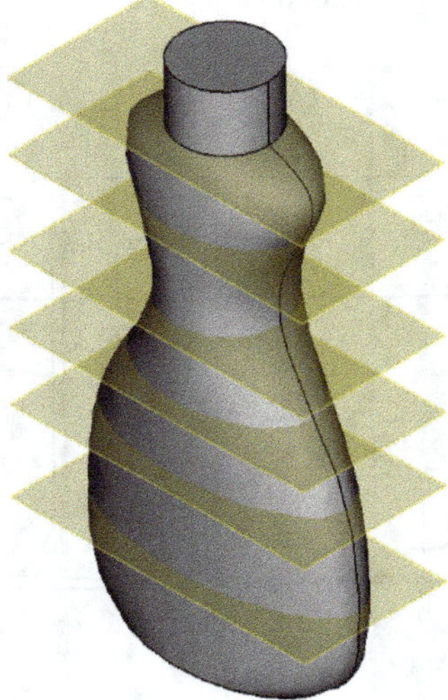

Creating Fillets

1. Press and hold the Ctrl key.
2. Click on the bottom and top edges of the swept feature.

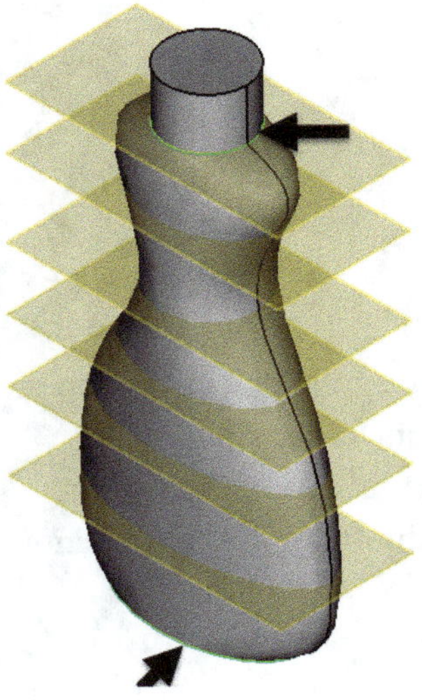

3. Click the **Fillet** icon on the **Part Design Modeling** toolbar.
4. Set **Radius** to 0.2.

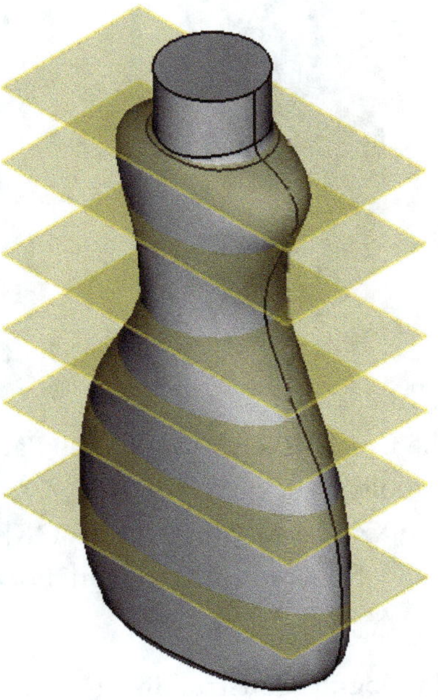

5. Click **OK**.

Shelling the Model

1. Select the top face of the cylindrical feature.

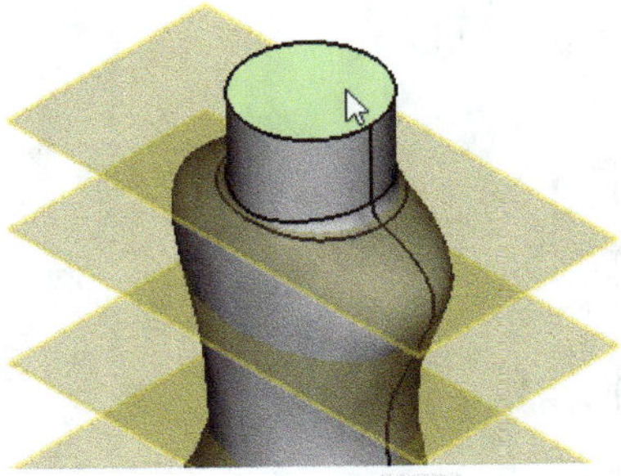

2. Click the **Thickness** icon on the **Part Design Modeling** toolbar.
3. Set **Thickness** to 0.03.
4. Click **OK** to create the shell.

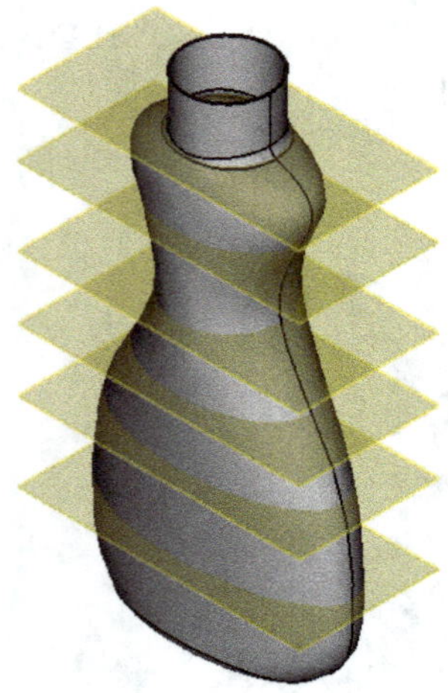

Adding Threads

1. Click the **Create Sketch** icon on the **Part Design Helper** toolbar.
2. Select the XZ Plane, and then click **OK**.
3. Click **Draw Style > Wireframe** on the **View** toolbar.
4. Click the **Toggle Construction geometry** icon on the **Sketcher geometries** toolbar.
5. Click the **Create Polyline** icon on the **Sketcher geometries** toolbar.
6. Select the origin point of the sketch, move the cursor vertically upward and click to create a vertical construction line.

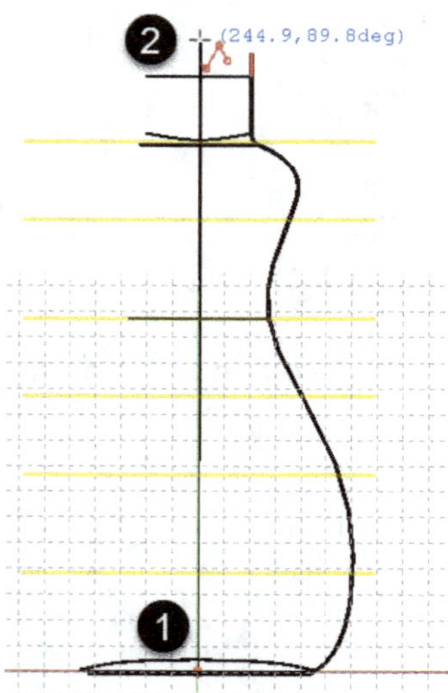

7. Right click to end the chain.
8. Create a horizontal construction line, as shown.

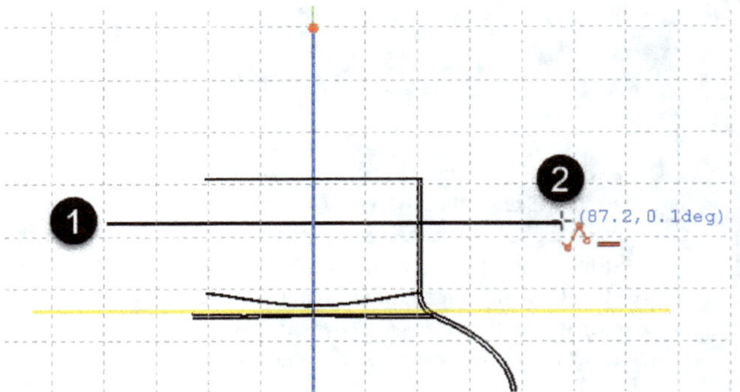

9. Click the **Toggle construction geometry** icon on the **Sketcher geometries** toolbar.
10. Create a closed profile, as shown.

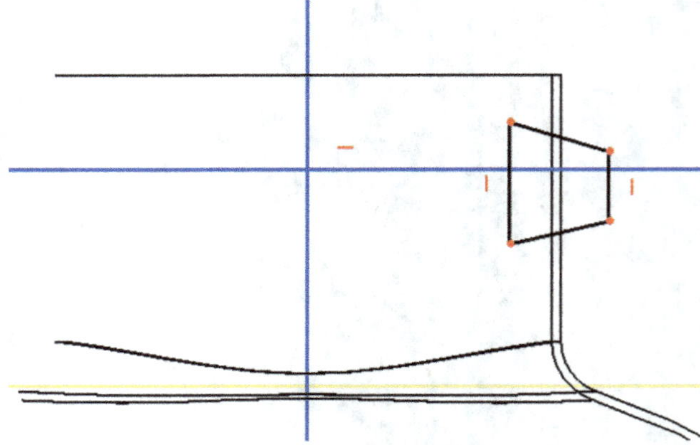

11. Press Esc to deactivate the **Create Polyline** tool.
12. Draw the thread profile.

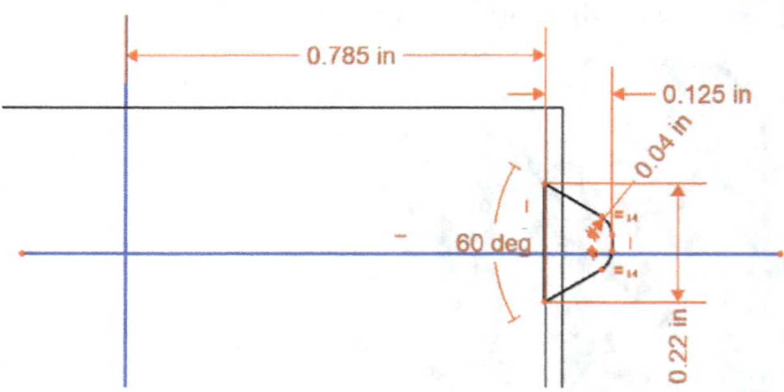

13. Click the **Constrain symmetrical** icon on the **Sketcher constraints** toolbar.
14. Select the right vertical line of the profile.
15. Select the right endpoint of the construction line.

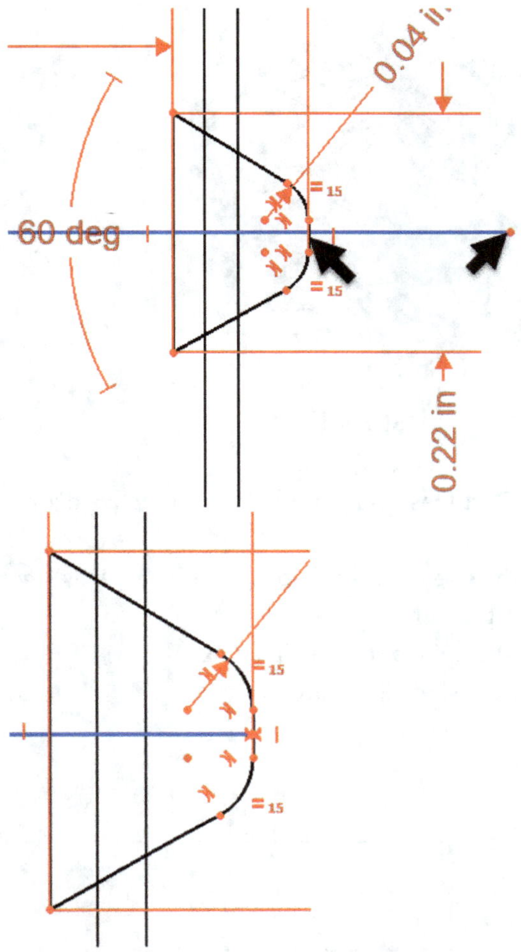

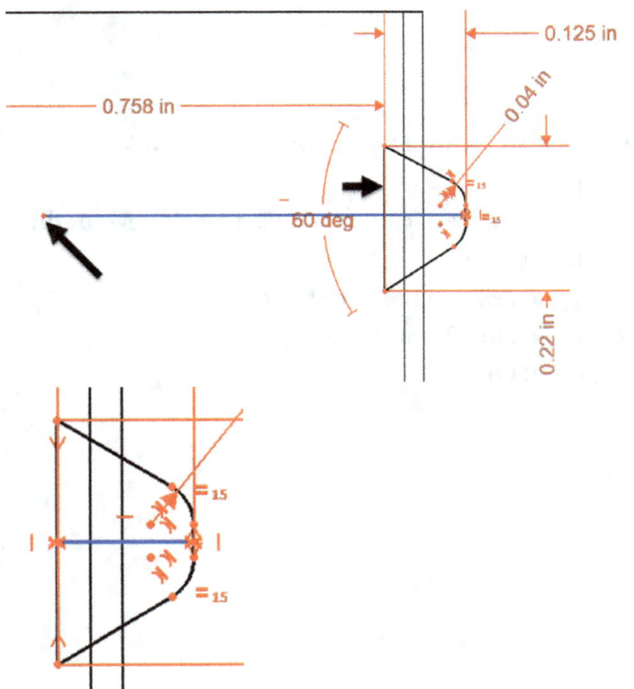

16. Select the left vertical line and the left endpoint of the horizontal construction line.

17. Create a **Vertical distance** constraint, as shown.

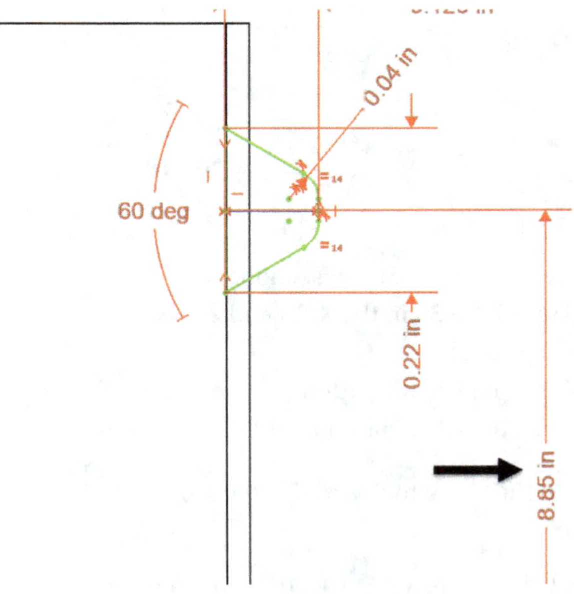

18. Click the **Close** button on the **Combo View** panel.
19. Select **Draw Style > Flat Lines** from the View toolbar.
20. Select **Part** from the **Workbenches** drop-down.

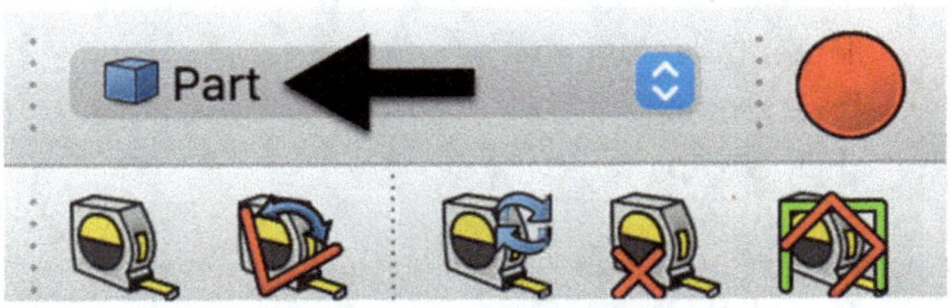

21. Click the **Create primitives** icon on the **Solids** toolbar.
22. In the **Geometric Primitives** dialog, select **Helix** from the drop-down.
23. Type **0.27** in the **Pitch** box.
24. Type **0.55** in the **Height** box.
25. Type **0.785** in the **Radius** box.
26. Type **90** in the **Angle** box.
27. Select **Right-handed** from the **Coordinate system** drop-down.

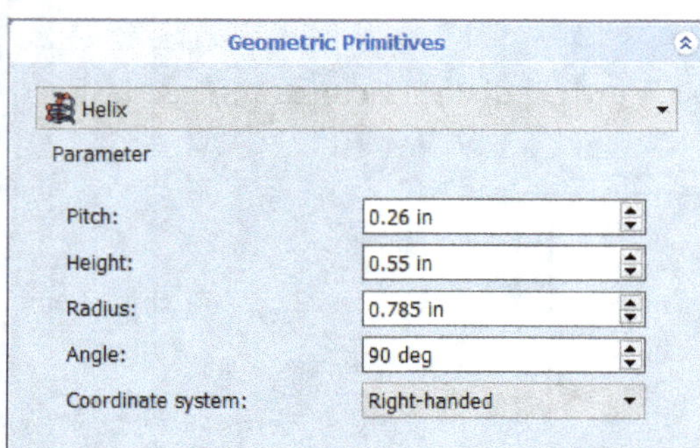

28. Expand the **Location** section.
29. Type **0,0, 8.35** in the **X**, **Y**, and **Z** boxes, respectively.
30. Click the **Create** button.
31. Click the **Close** button.
32. On the **View** toolbar, click the **Isometric**  icon.
33. Click the **Sweep** icon on the **Part tools** toolbar.
34. Select the last sketch from the **Available profiles** section.
35. Click the **Add** button.
36. Check the **Create solid** and **Frenet** options.
37. Click the **Sweep Path** button.
38. Press and hold the Ctrl key and select all the elements of the helix.
39. Click **Done**.
40. Click **OK** to create the sweep.

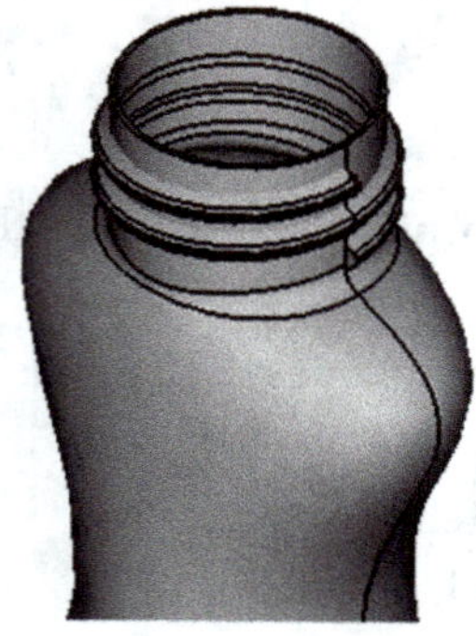

41. Save the model.

TUTORIAL 5

In this tutorial, you create the model, as shown.

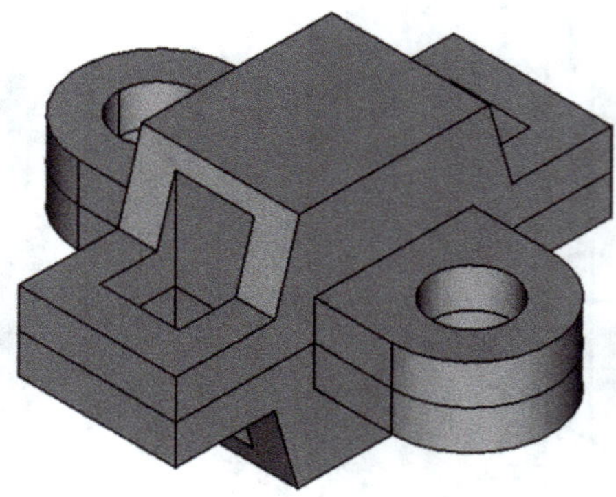

Creating the First feature

1. Open a new FreeCAD file.
2. Select **Part Design** from the **Workbenches** drop-down.
3. Click the **Create Sketch** icon on the **Part Design Helper** toolbar.
4. Select the YZ Plane and click **OK**.
5. Create the sketch, as shown.

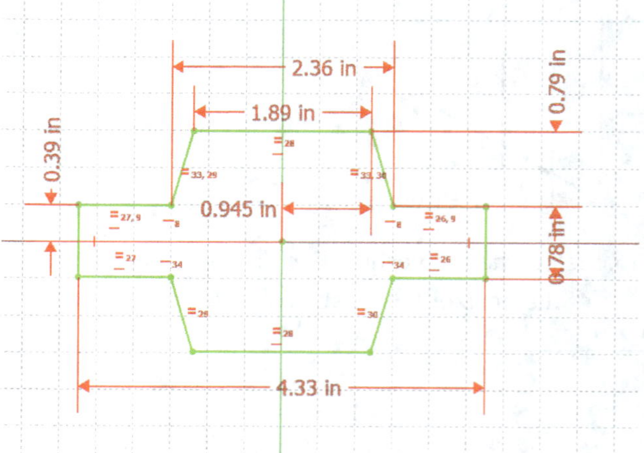

6. Click the **Close** button on the **Combo View** panel.
7. Click the **Pad** icon on the **Part Design Modeling** toolbar.
8. Type **1.575** in the **Length** box.
9. Check the **Symmetric to plane** option.
10. Click **OK**.

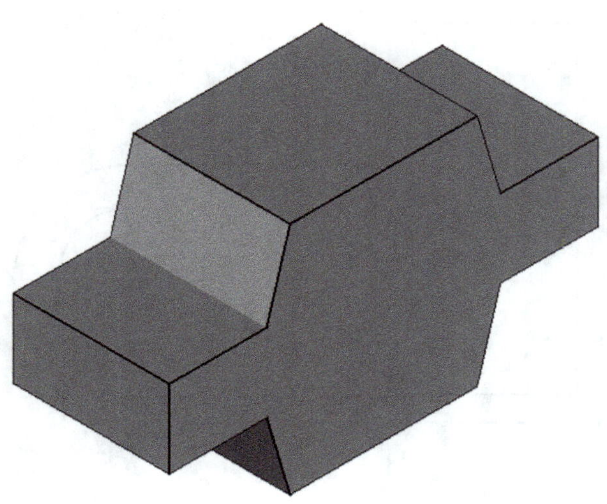

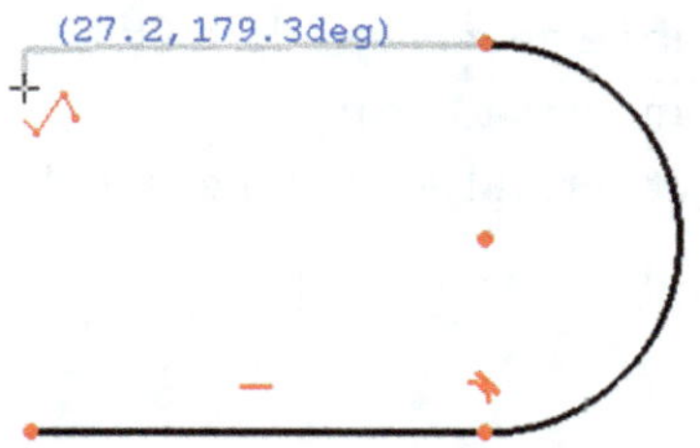

9. Select the start point of the polyline.

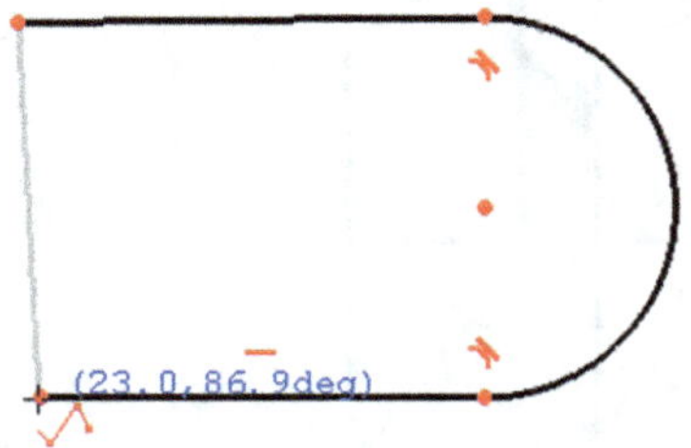

Creating the Second feature

1. Click the **Create Sketch** icon on the **Part Design Helper** toolbar.
2. Select the XY Plane and click **OK**.
3. Select **Draw Style > Wireframe** from the **View** toolbar.
4. Click the **Create Polyline** icon on the **Sketcher geometries** toolbar.
5. Create a horizontal line, as shown.

6. Press the M key thrice; the Arc tool is activated.
7. Move the pointer upward and click to create a tangent arc.

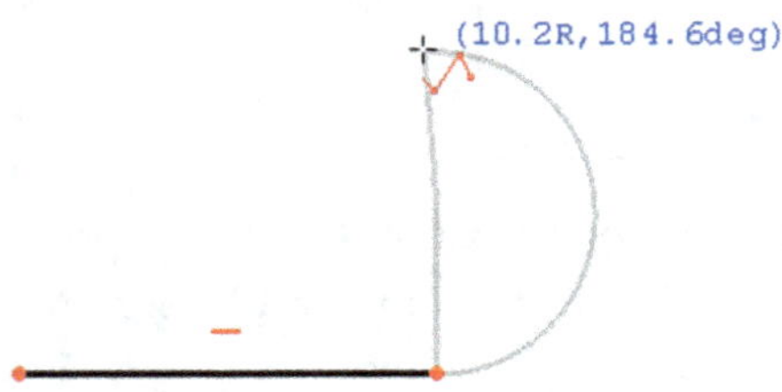

8. Move the pointer toward the left and click to create a line.

10. Apply the **Horizontal** and **Vertical** constraints to the lines, as shown.

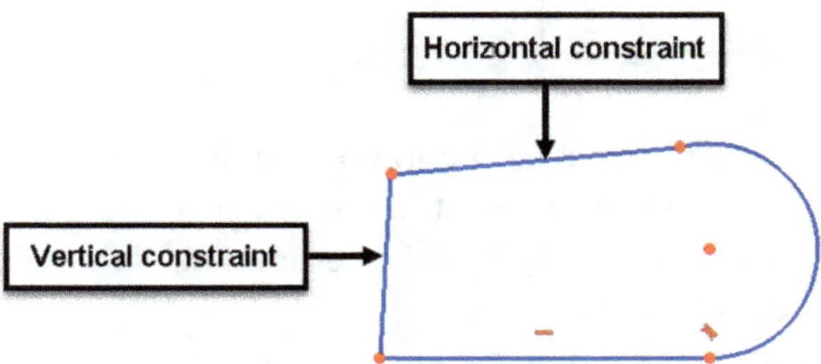

11. Click the **Constrain point onto object** icon on the **Sketcher constraints** toolbar.
12. Select the centerpoint of the arc.
13. Select the horizontal axis of the sketch.

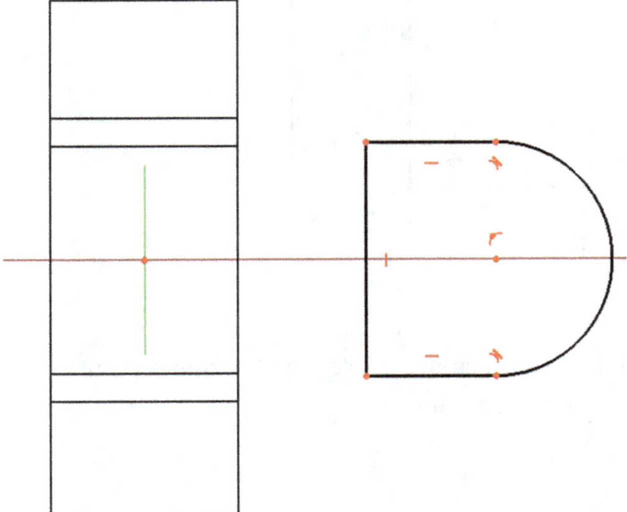

14. Click the **External geometry** icon on the **Sketcher geometries** toolbar.
15. Select the right vertical edge of the model, as shown.

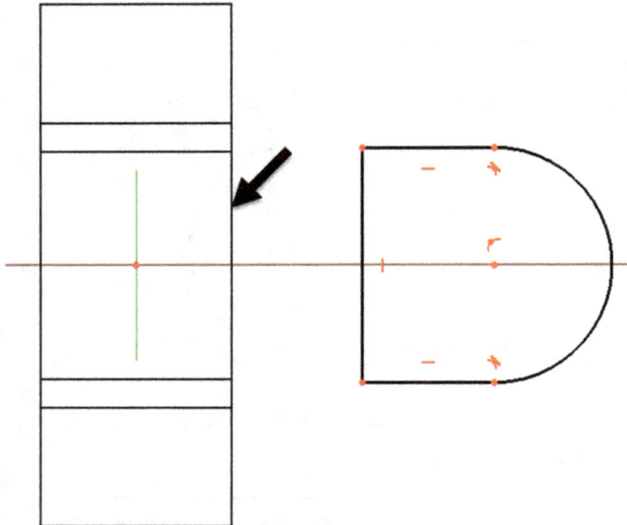

16. Click the **Constrain point onto object** icon on the **Sketcher constraints** toolbar.
17. Select the endpoint of the vertical line of the sketch, as shown.
18. Select the external geometry element.

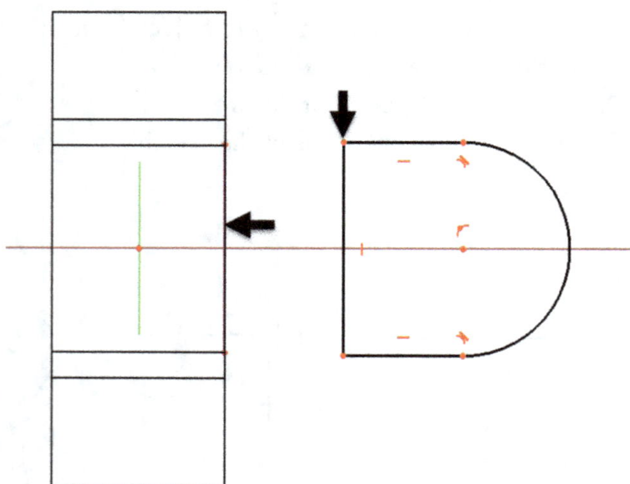

19. Create a circle by selecting the center point of the arc, as shown.

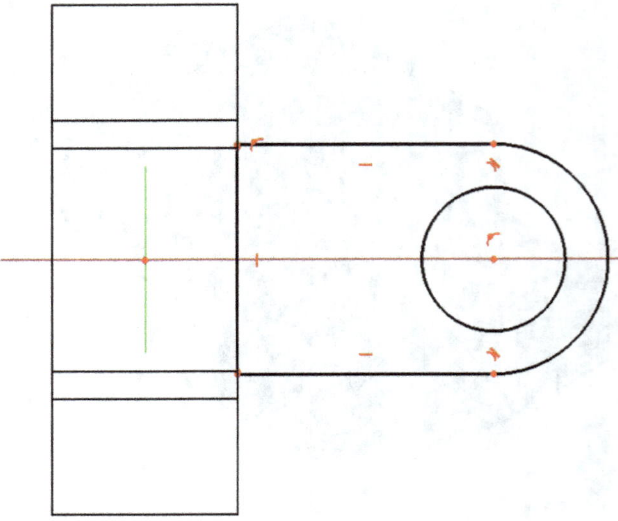

20. Add remaining constraints to the sketch, as shown.

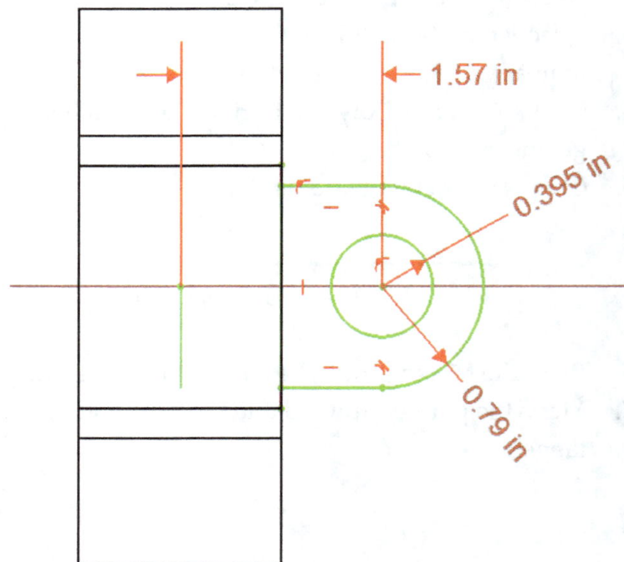

21. Click **Close** on the **Combo View** panel.
22. Click the **Pad** icon on the **Part Design Modeling** toolbar.
23. Type **0.78** in the **Length** box.
24. Click **OK**.
25. Select **Draw Style > Flat Lines** from the **View** toolbar.

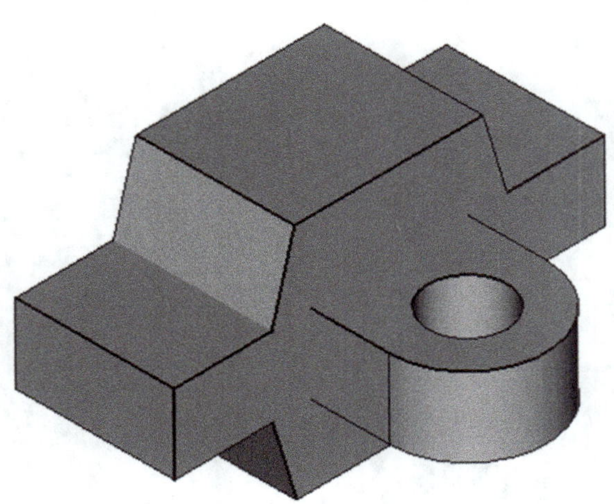

Creating the Mirrored feature

1. Click the **Mirrored** icon on the **Part Design Modeling** toolbar.
2. Select the **Pad001** feature from the **Select feature** list.
3. Click **OK**.
4. Select the **Base YZ plane** from the **Plane** drop-down.
5. Click **OK**.

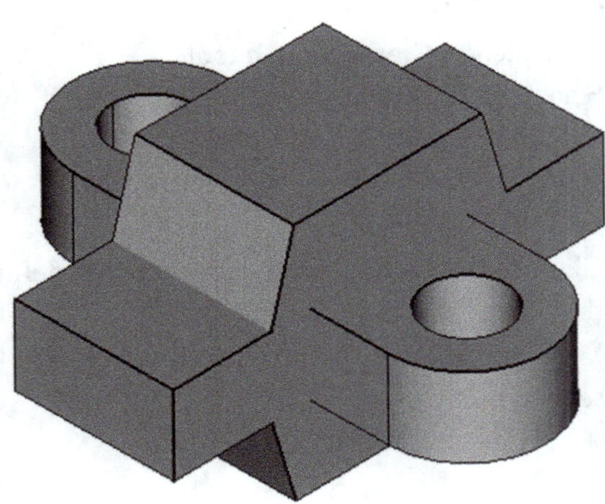

Creating the Pocket Feature

1. Click the **Create Sketch** icon on the **Part Design Helper** toolbar.
2. Select the XY Plane and click **OK**.
3. Change the **Draw Style** to **Wireframe**.
4. Create a rectangle and add constraints to it, as shown.

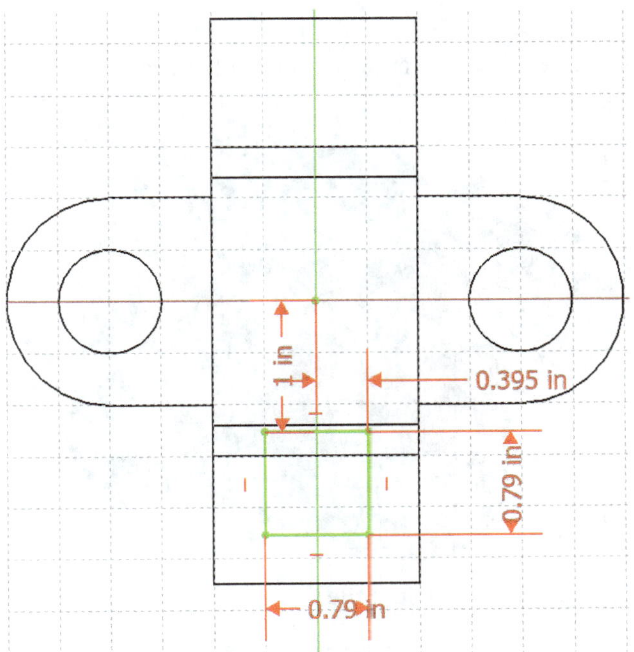

5. Click **Close** on the **Combo View** panel.
6. Click the **Pocket** icon on the **Part Design Modeling** toolbar.
7. Select **Type > Through All**.
8. Check the **Symmetric to plane** option.
9. Click **OK**.
10. Select **Draw Style > Flat Lines** from the **View** toolbar.

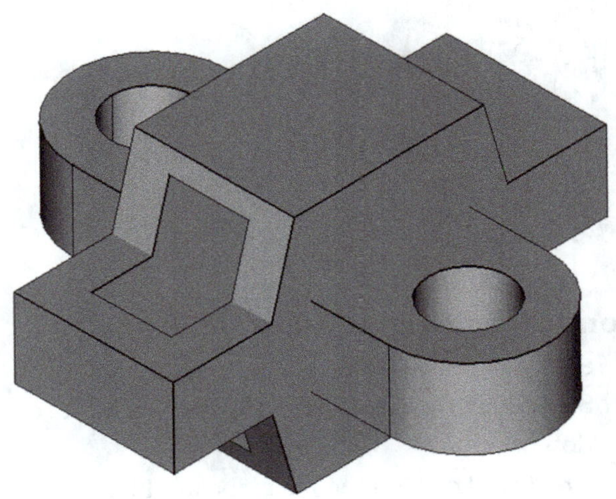

6. Click the **Mirrored** icon on the **Part Design Modeling** toolbar.
7. Select the **Pocket** feature from the **Select feature** list, and then click **OK**.
8. Select the **Base XZ plane** from the **Plane** drop-

down.

9. Click **OK** to mirror the pocket feature.

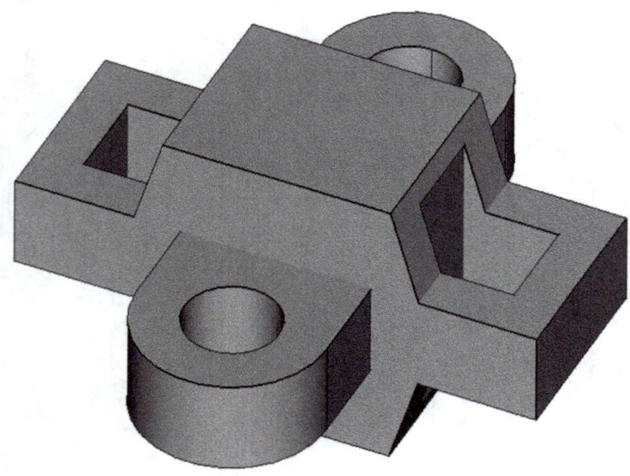

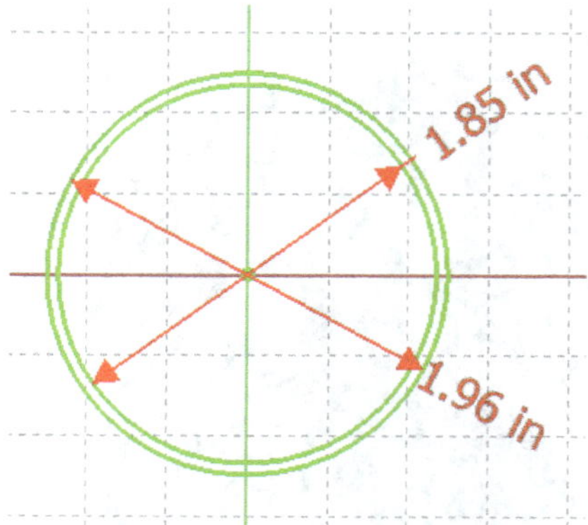

4. Extrude the sketch up to 3.93 depth.

10. Save and close the file.

TUTORIAL 6

In this tutorial, you construct a patterned cylindrical shell.

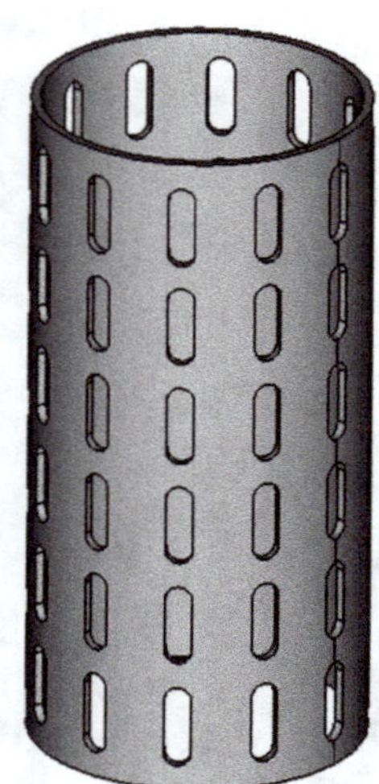

Constructing a cylindrical shell

1. Start a new FreeCAD file.
2. Select **Part Design** from the **Workbenches** drop-down.
3. Create a sketch on the XY plane (add Diameter constraints to the circles).

Adding a Slot

1. Activate the **Create Sketch** tool.
2. Select the **XZ Plane** and click **OK**.
3. Set the **Draw Style** to **Wireframe**.
4. Click the **Create Slot** icon on the **Sketcher geometries** toolbar.
5. Click on the vertical axis of the sketch to define the first point of the slot.
6. Move the pointer up and click to define the second point.

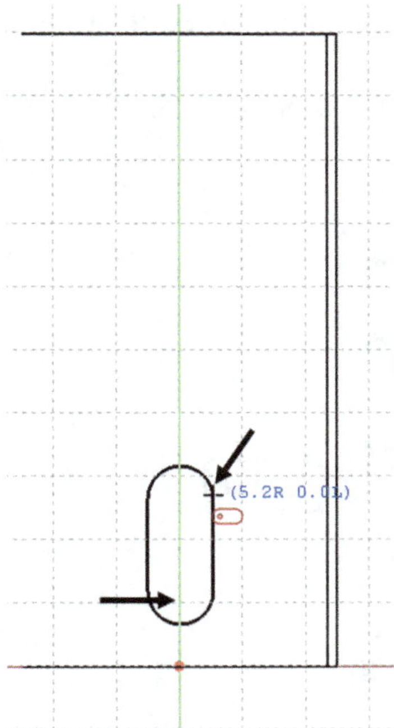

7. Add constraints to the slot.

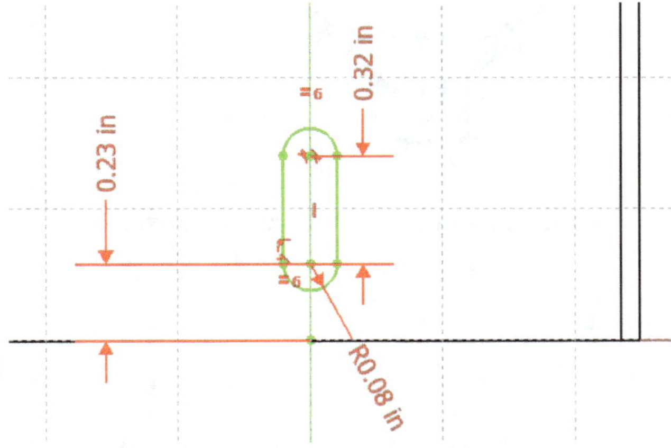

8. Click the **Leave Sketch** icon on the **Part Design Helper** toolbar.
9. Set the **Draw Style** to **Flat Lines**.
10. Click the **Pocket** icon on the **Part Design Modeling** toolbar.
11. On the **Pocker Parameters** section, select **Type > Through All**.
12. Check the **Reversed** option.
13. Click **OK**.

Constructing the Linear and Circular patterns using the MultiTransform tool

1. Click the **MultiTransform** icon on the **Part Design Modeling** toolbar.
2. Select the **Pocket** feature from the **Select feature** list, and then click **OK**.
3. Right-click in the **Transformations** section and select **Add linear pattern**.
4. Select **Direction > Base Z axis**.
5. Type **3.145** in the **Length** box.
6. Type **6** in the **Occurrences** box.
7. Right-click in the **Transformations** section and select **Add polar pattern**.
8. Select the **Base Z axis** from the **Axis** drop-down.
9. Type **360** in the **Angle** box.
10. Type-in **12** in the **Occurrences** box.
11. Click **OK** to create the circular pattern.

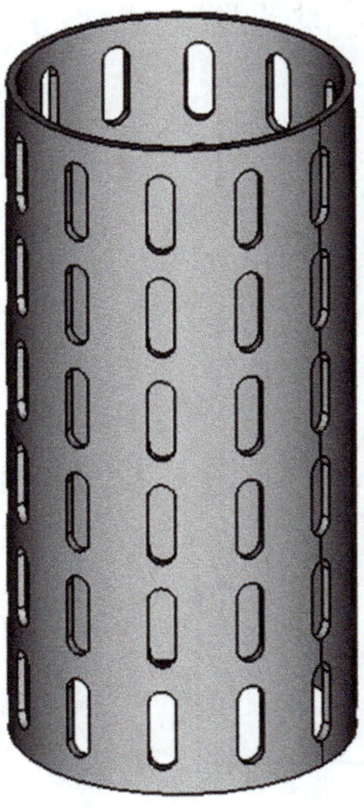

11. Save and close the model.

TUTORIAL 7

In this tutorial, you construct a pulley wheel using the **Revolution** and **Groove** tools.

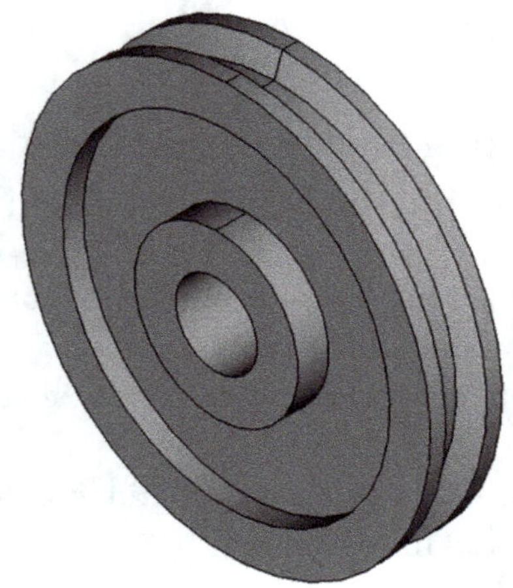

1. Open a new FreeCAD file.
2. Select **Part Design** from the **Workbenches** drop-down.
3. Click the **Create Sketch** icon on the **Part Design Helper** toolbar.
4. Select the YZ plane and click **OK**.
5. Click the **Create Polyline** icon on the **Sketcher geometries** toolbar.
6. Create a closed sketch, as shown.

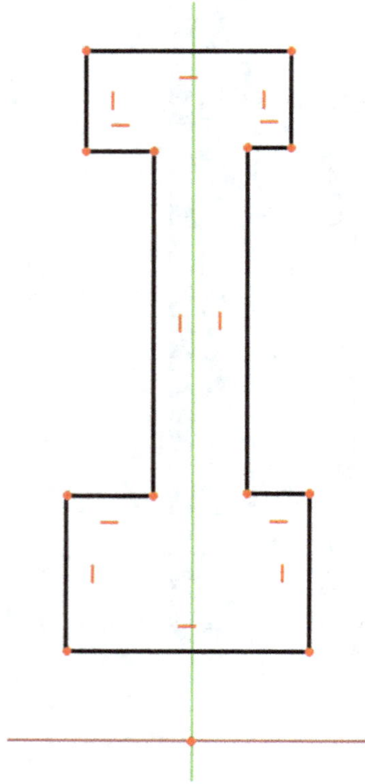

7. Click the **Constrain Equal** icon on the **Sketcher constraints** toolbar.
8. Make the entities of the sketch equal in length, as shown.

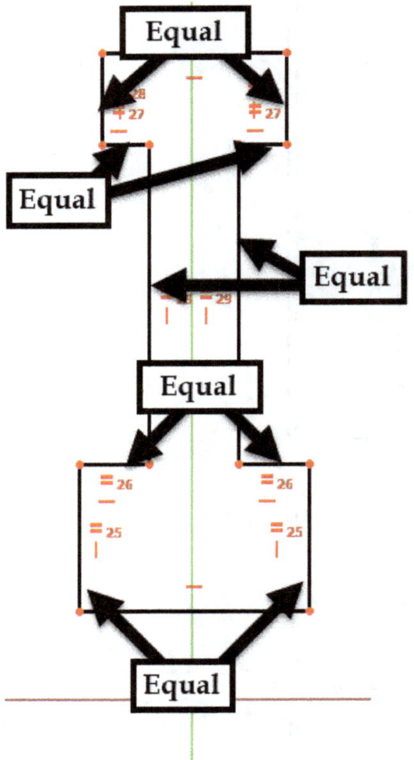

9. Create remaining constraints, as shown.

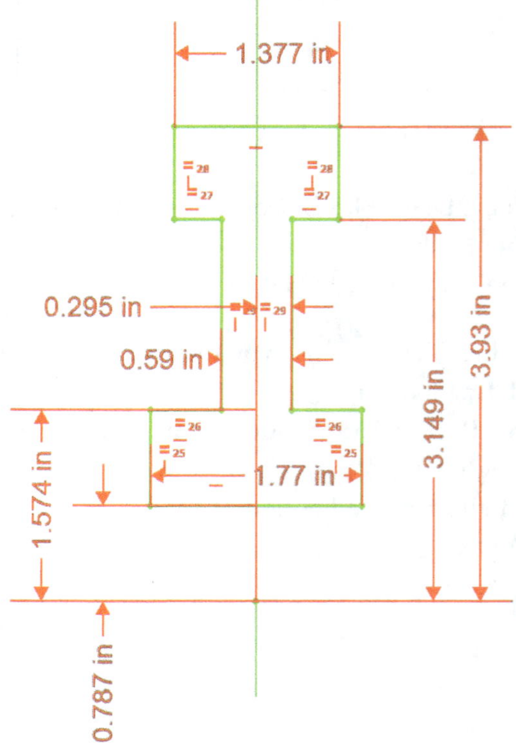

10. Click the **Close** button on the **Combo View** panel.
11. Click the **Revolution** icon on the **Part Design Modeling** toolbar; the sketch is selected automatically.
12. Select the Y axis from the graphics window.
13. Type 360 in the **Angle** box.
14. Click **OK** to construct the revolved feature.

Constructing the Groove feature

1. Click the **Create Sketch** icon on the **Part Design Helper** toolbar.
2. Select the YZ Plane and click **OK**.
3. Set the **Draw Style** to **Wireframe**.
4. Create the sketch, as shown.

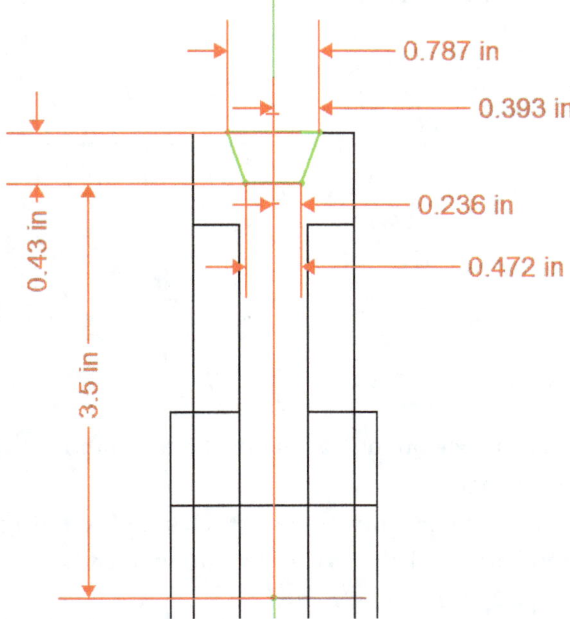

5. Click the **Close** button on the **Combo View** panel.
6. Set the **Draw Style** to **Flat Lines**.
7. Click the **Groove** icon on the **Part Design geometries** toolbar.
8. Select the Y-axis from the graphics window.
9. Type 360 in the **Angle** box.
10. Click **OK**.

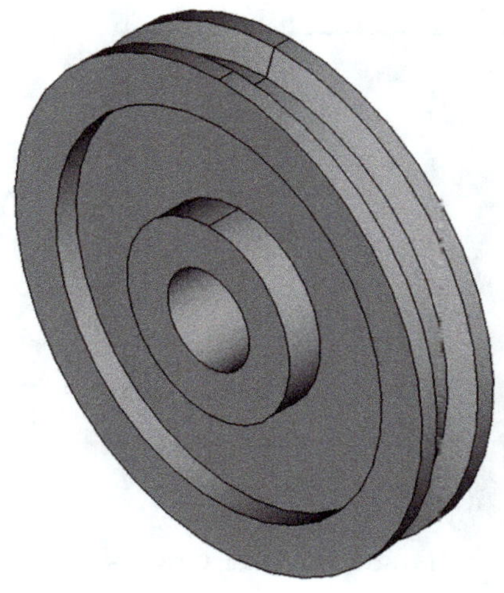

11. Save and close the model.

TUTORIAL 8

In this tutorial, you construct the model shown in the figure.

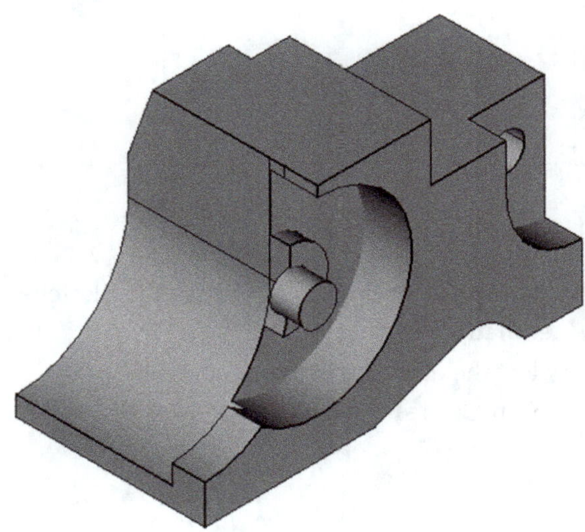

Creating the Base Feature

1. Open a new FreeCAD file.
2. Select **Part Design** from the **Workbenches** drop-down.

3. Click the **Create Sketch** icon on the **Part Design Helper** toolbar.
4. Select the YZ plane and click **OK**.
5. Click the **Create Rectangle** icon on the **Sketcher geometries** toolbar.
6. Specify the first and second corners of the rectangle, as shown.

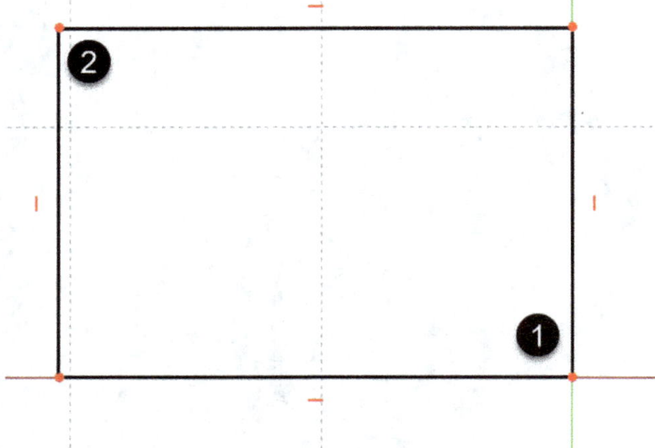

7. Create another rectangle by specifying its first and second corners, as shown.

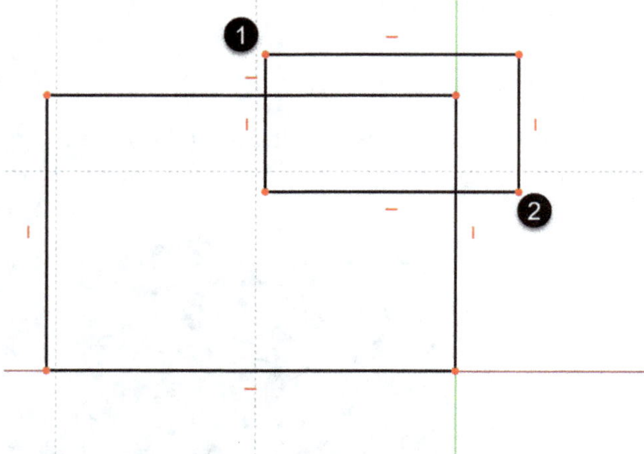

8. Click the **Trim Edge** icon on the **Sketcher geometries** toolbar.
9. Select the elements of the rectangles to be trimmed, as shown.

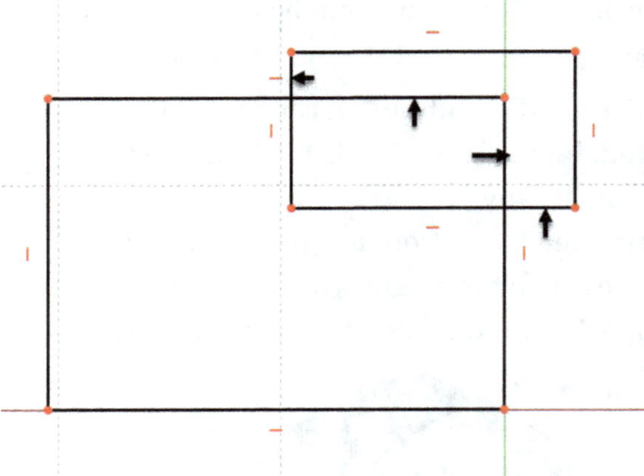

10. Press Esc to deactivate the **Trim Edge** tool.
11. Select the lines, as shown.
12. Press Delete.

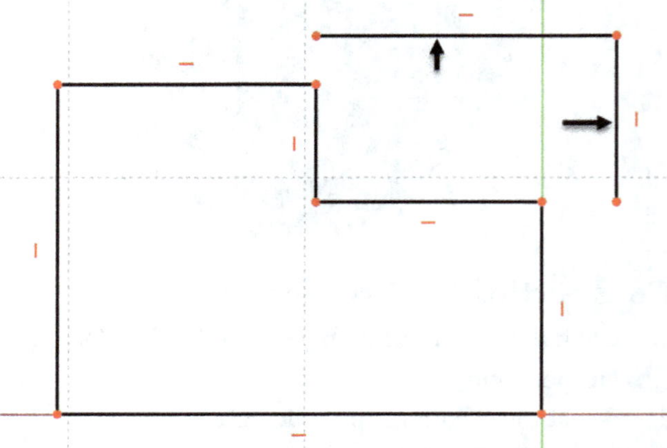

13. Add vertical and horizontal distance constraints to the sketch, as shown.

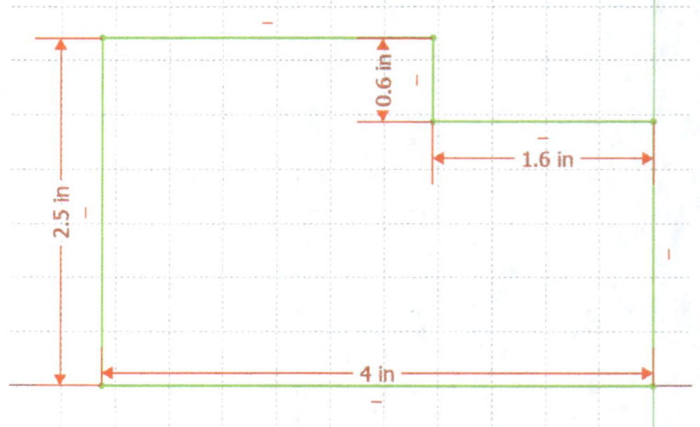

14. Click **Close** on the **Tasks** tab of the **Combo View** panel.
15. Click the **Pad** icon on the **Part Design Modeling** toolbar; the sketch is selected automatically.
16. Type 2 in the **Length** box.
17. Check the **Symmetric to Plane** option.

18. Click **OK**.

Creating the Pocket Features

1. Click the **Create Sketch** icon on the **Part Design Helper** toolbar.
2. Select the YZ plane and click **OK**.
3. Click the **Create Polyline** icon on the **Sketcher geometries** toolbar.
4. Specify the endpoints of the polyline, as shown.

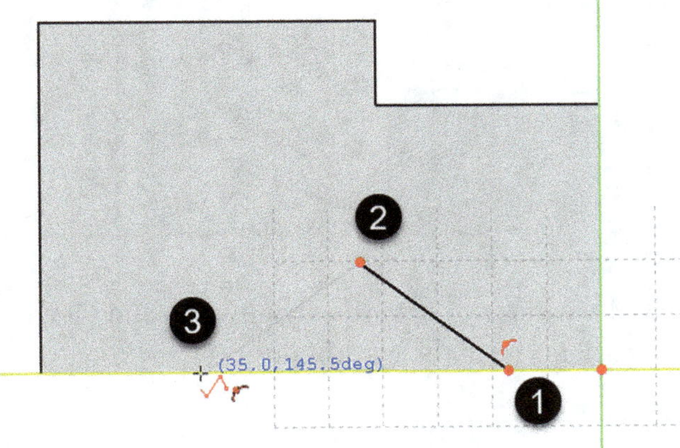

5. Press Esc.
6. Click the **Create Fillet** icon on the **Sketcher geometries** toolbar.
7. Select the corner point of the sketch, as shown.

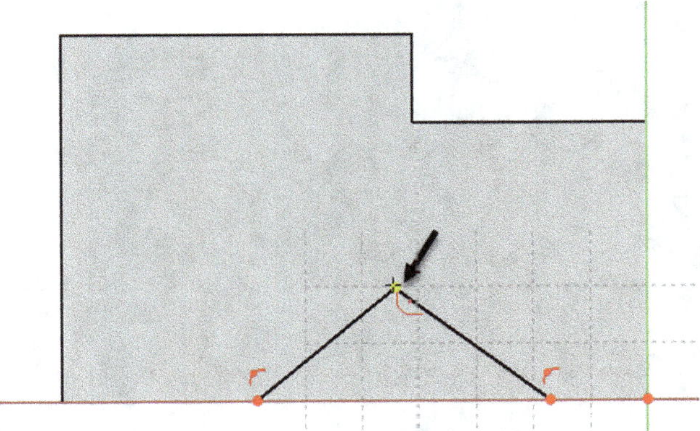

8. Click the **Constrain Angle** icon on the **Sketcher constraints** toolbar.
9. Select the inclined line and the horizontal axis of the sketch.

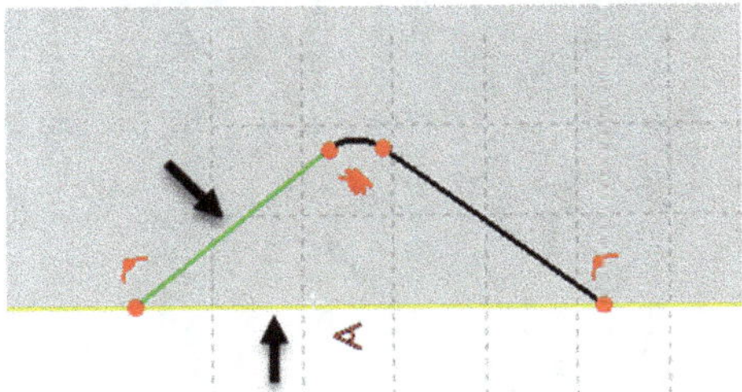

10. Type **20** in the **Angle** box and click **OK**.
11. Select the other inclined line and the horizontal axis of the sketch, as shown.

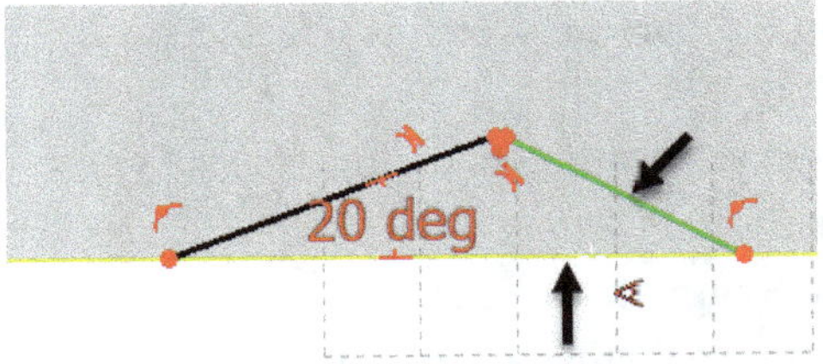

12. Type **135** in the **Angle** box and click **OK**.

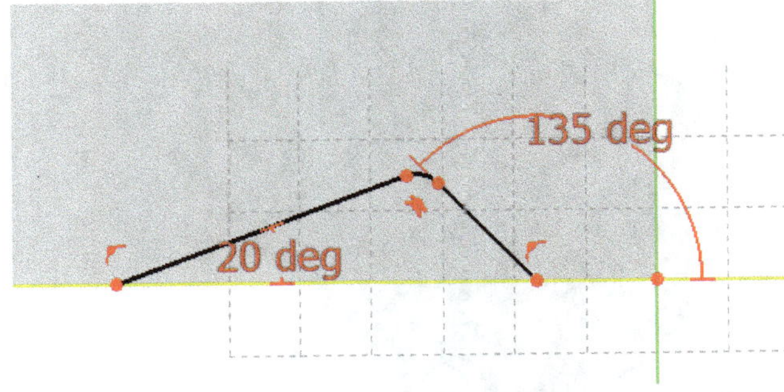

13. Add vertical and horizontal distance constraints to the sketch, as shown.
14. Add the radius constraint to the fillet.

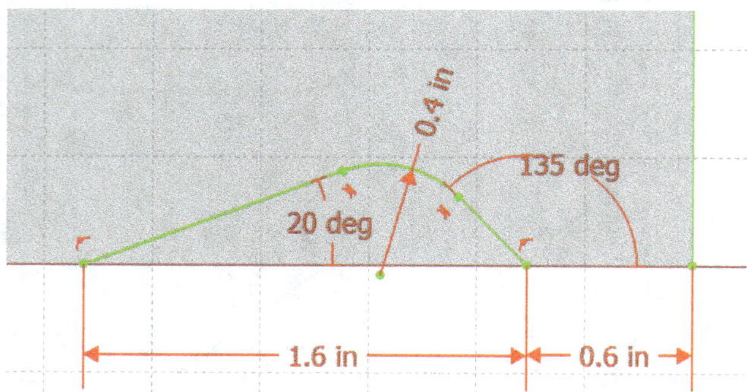

15. Click the **Create Line** icon on the **Sketcher geometries** toolbar.
16. Select the endpoints of the sketch, as shown.

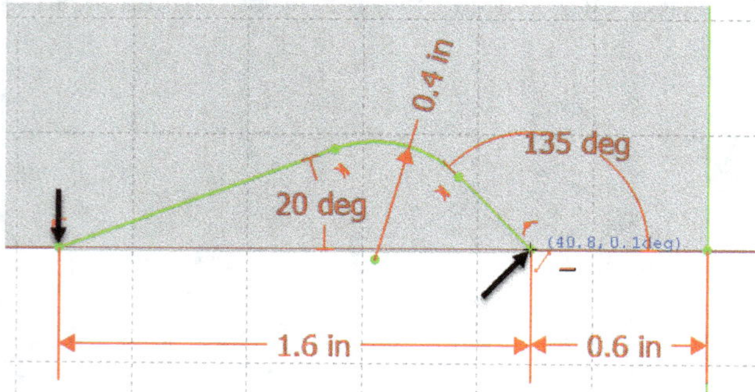

17. Click **Close** on the **Tasks** tab of the **Combo View** panel.

18. Click the **Pocket** icon on the **Part Design Modeling** toolbar; the sketch is selected automatically.
19. On the **Pocket parameters** dialog, select **Type > Through all**.
20. Check the **Symmetric to plane**.
21. Click **OK** to create the pocket feature.

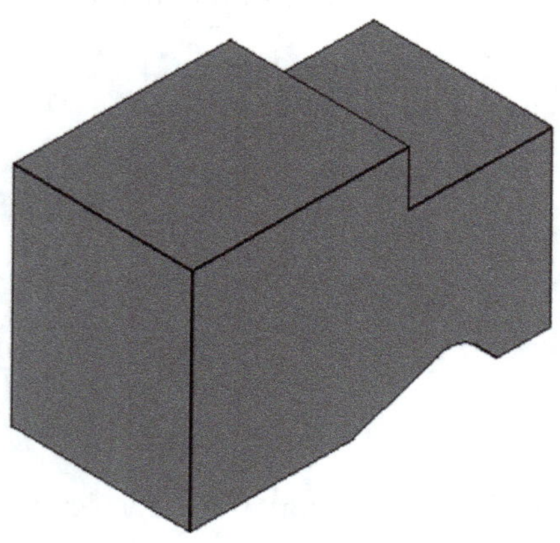

22. Click on the right side face of the model.

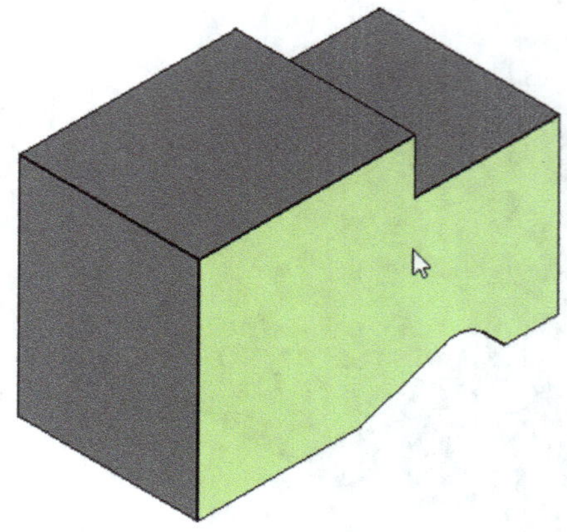

23. Click the **Create Sketch** icon on the **Part Design Helper** toolbar.
24. Click the **Create Polyline** icon on the **Sketcher geometries** toolbar.
25. Click on the vertical axis of the sketch to define the start point.

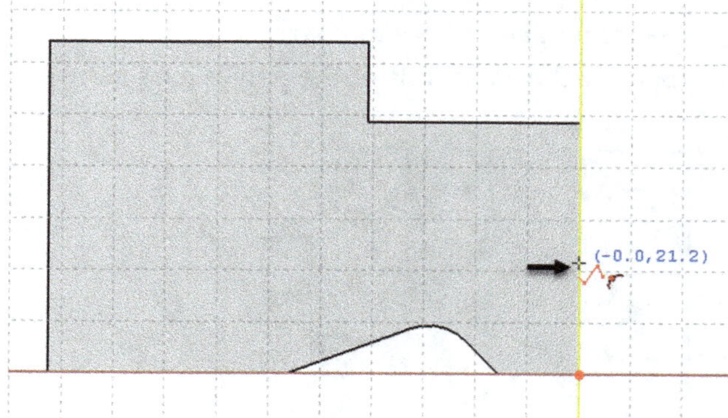

26. Move the pointer vertically upward, and then click to create the vertical line.

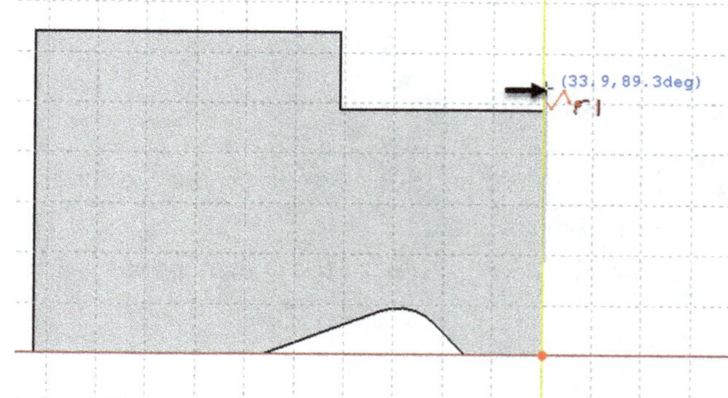

27. Move the pointer horizontally toward left, and then click.

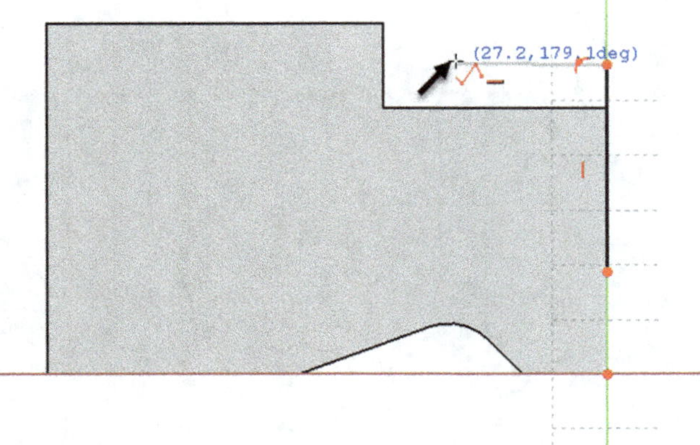

28. Move the vertically downward and click.

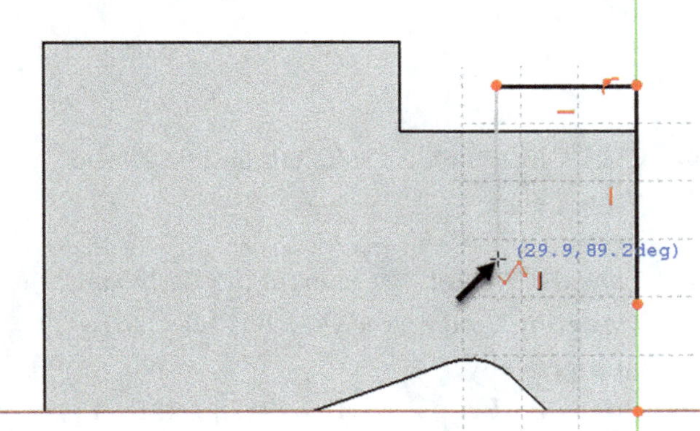

29. Press Esc.
30. Click the **Arc** drop-down > **End points and rim point** on the **Sketcher geometries** toolbar.
31. Select the endpoints of the two vertical lines.

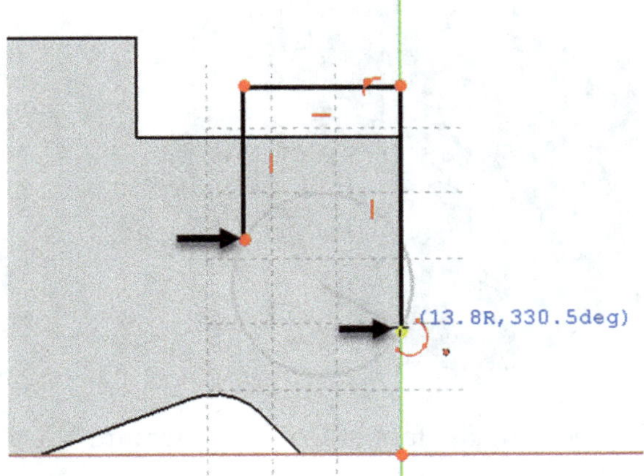

32. Move the pointer outward and click to create the arc.

33. Click the **Constrain Tangent** 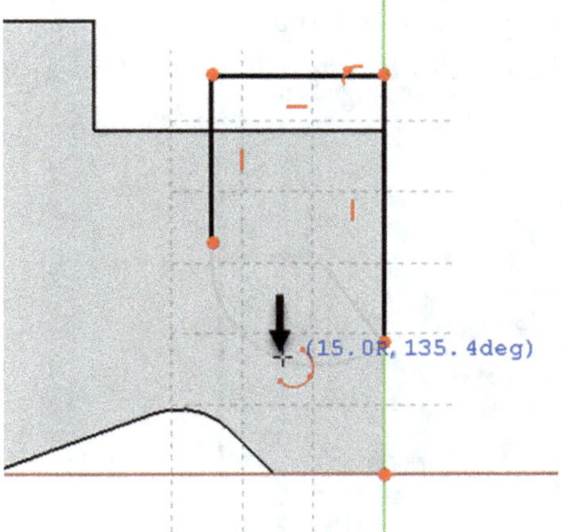 icon on the **Sketcher constraints** toolbar.
34. Select the left vertical line and the arc.

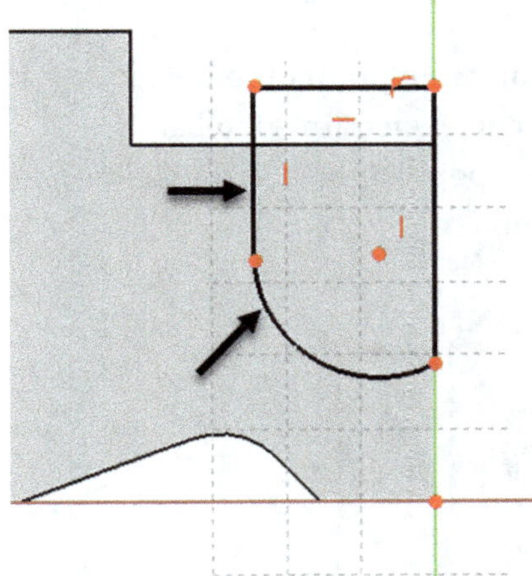

35. Click the **Constrain point onto object** icon on the **Sketcher constraints** toolbar.
36. Select the center point of the circle and the right vertical line.

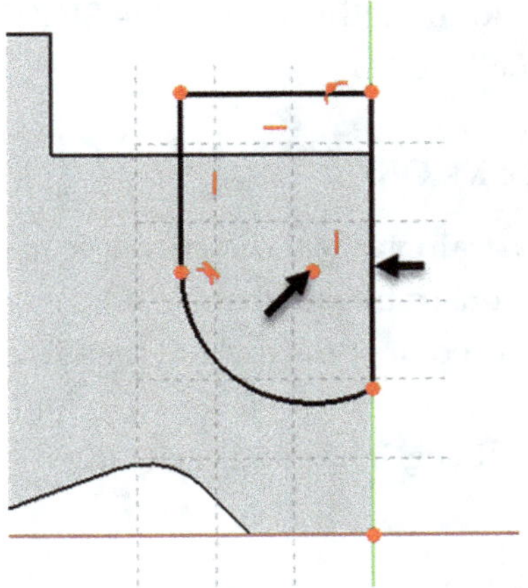

37. Click the **External geometry** icon on the

Sketcher geometries toolbar.

38. Select the horizontal edge of the model, as shown.

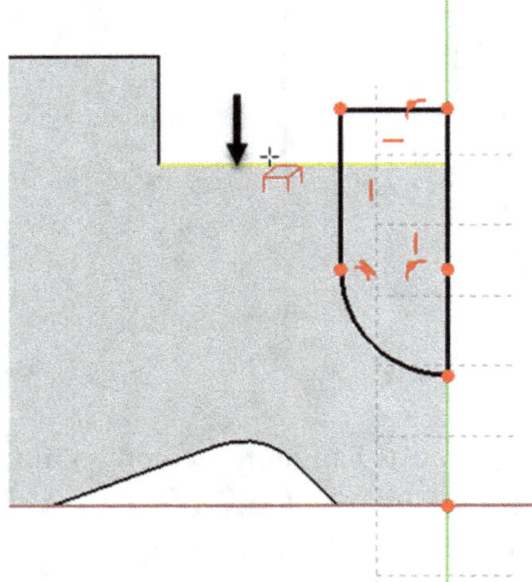

39. Click the **Constrain point onto object** icon on the **Sketcher constraints** toolbar.
40. Select the endpoint of the horizontal line and the external geometry.

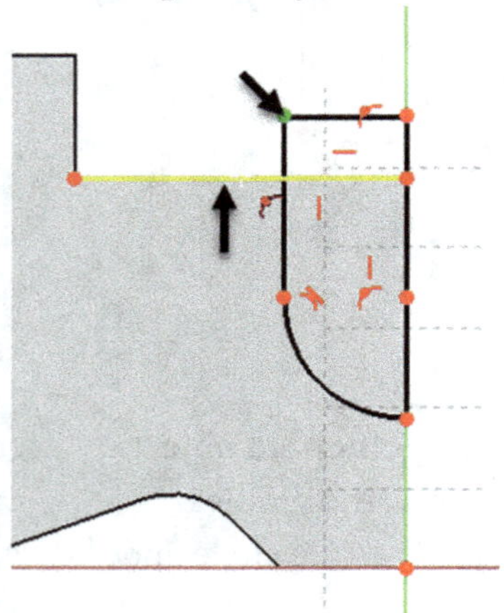

41. Click the **Constrain radius** icon on the **Sketcher constraints** toolbar.
42. Select the arc.
43. Type **0.8** and click **OK**.
44. Click the **Constrain vertical distance** icon on the **Sketcher constraints** toolbar.
45. Select the centerpoint of the arc and the sketch origin.
46. Type 1.4 in the **Length** box and click **OK**.

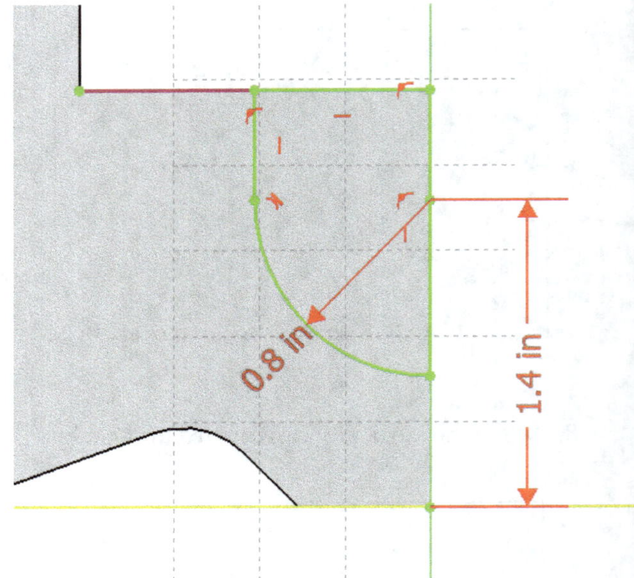

47. Click **Close** on the **Tasks** tab of the **Combo View** panel.
48. Click the **Pocket** icon on the **Part Design Modeling** toolbar; the sketch is selected automatically.
49. On the **Pocket parameters** dialog, select **Type > Dimension**.
50. Type **0.4** in the **Length** box.
51. Click **OK**.

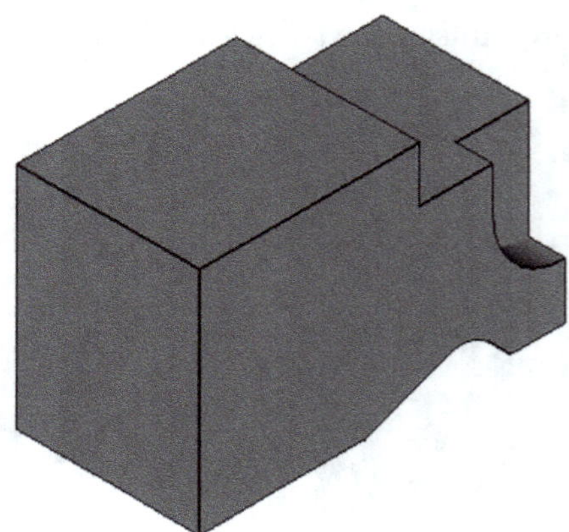

52. Select the flat face of the pocket feature.
53. Click the **Create Sketch** icon on the **Part Design Helper** toolbar.
54. Create a circle.
55. Click the **External geometry** icon on the **Sketcher geometries** toolbar.
56. Select the curved edge of the model, as shown.

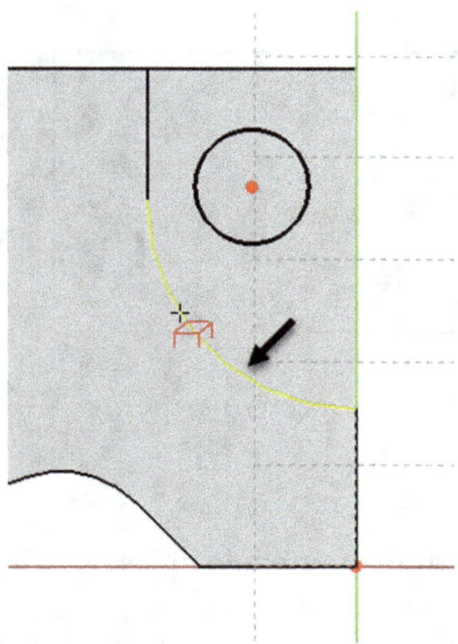

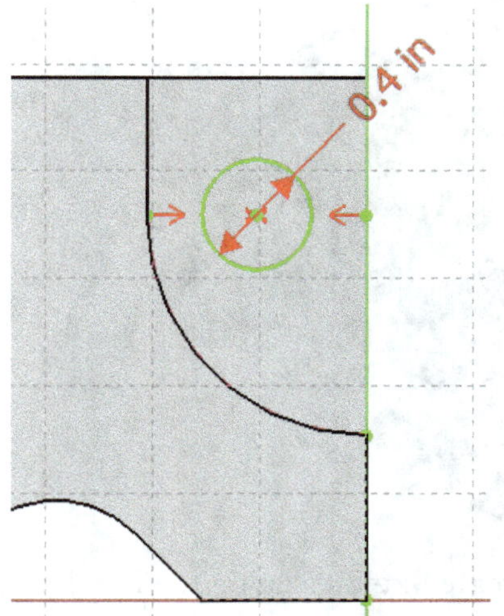

57. Click the **Constrain symmetrical** ⟩⟨ icon on the **Sketcher constraints** toolbar.
58. Select the centerpoint of the curved edge.
59. Select the centerpoint of the circle.
60. Select the endpoint of the curved edge.

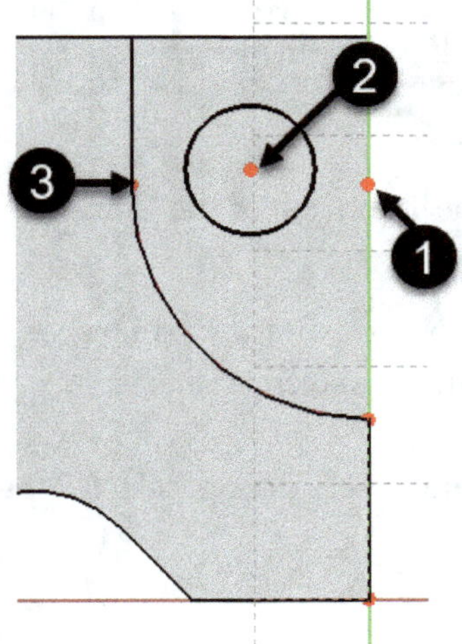

61. Add the diameter constraint to the circle.

62. Click **Close** on the **Tasks** tab of the **Combo View** panel.
63. Click the **Pocket** icon or the **Part Design Modeling** toolbar; the sketch is selected automatically.
64. On the **Pocket parameters** dialog, select **Type > Through all**.
65. Click **OK**.

Creating the Pocket Feature on the left side

1. Click on the top face of the model.

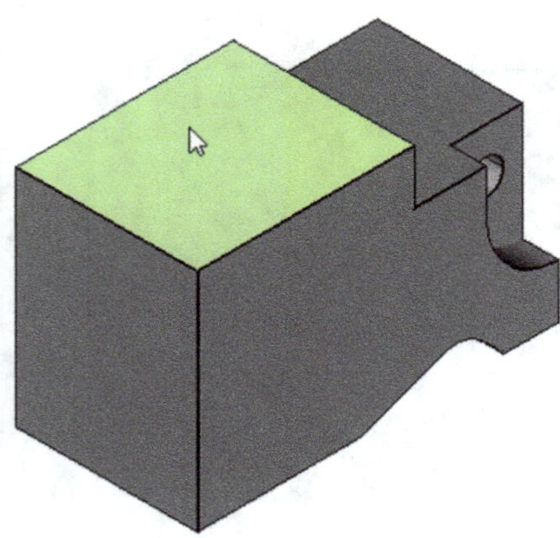

2. Click the **Create Sketch** icon on the **Part Design Helper** toolbar.

3. Create a rectangle, as shown.

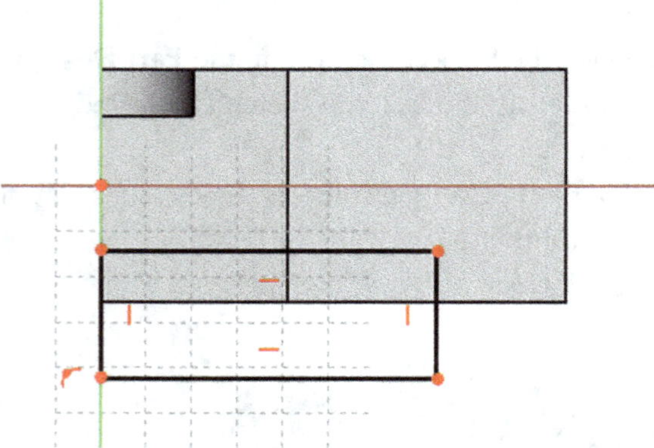

4. Create horizontal and vertical distance constraints, as shown.

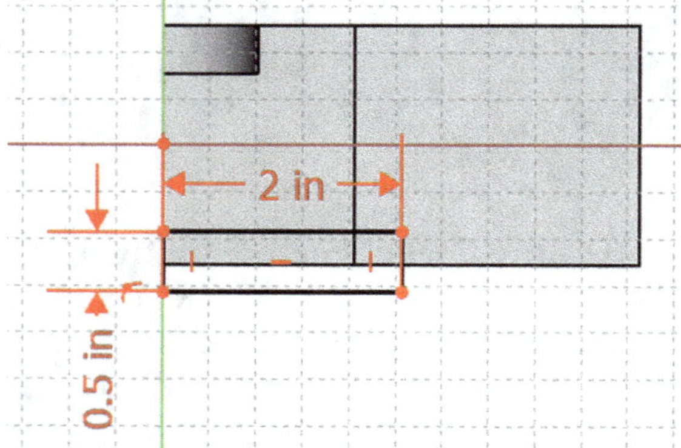

5. Click the **External geometry** icon on the **Sketcher geometries** toolbar.

6. Select the horizontal edge of the model, as shown.

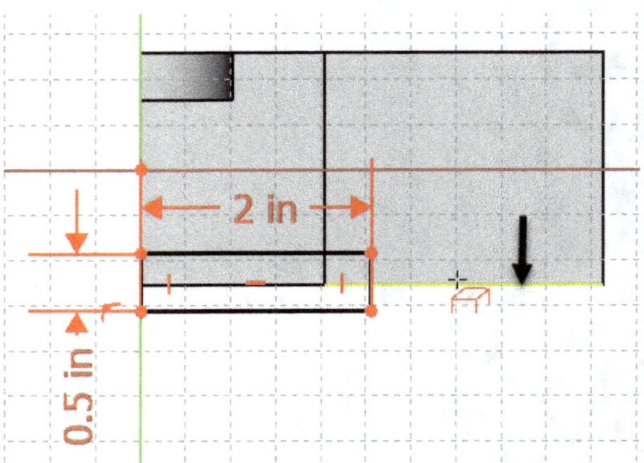

7. Click the **Constrain point onto object** icon on the **Sketcher constraints** toolbar.

8. Select the endpoint of the horizontal line and the external geometry.

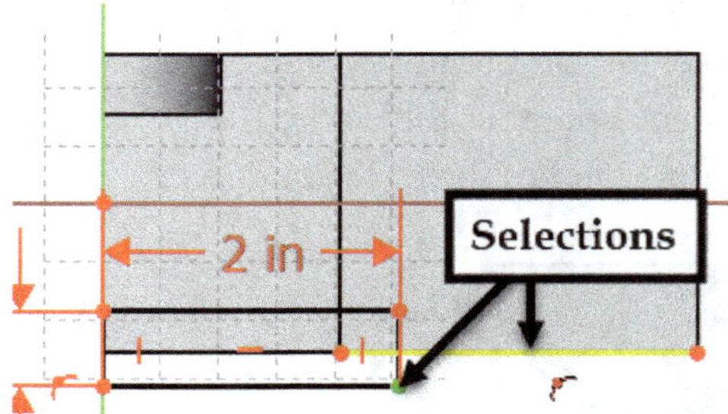

66. Click **Close** on the **Tasks** tab of the **Combo View** panel.

67. Click the **Pocket** icon on the **Part Design Modeling** toolbar; the sketch is selected automatically.

68. On the **Pocket parameters** dialog, select **Type > Through all**.

69. Click **OK**.

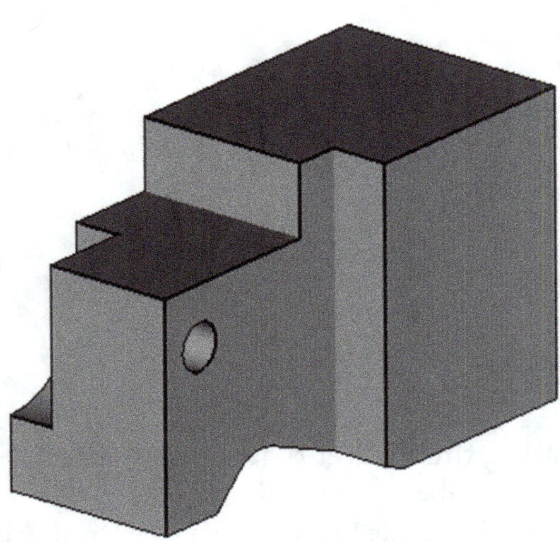

Creating the Angled Cut

1. Click on the front face of the model.

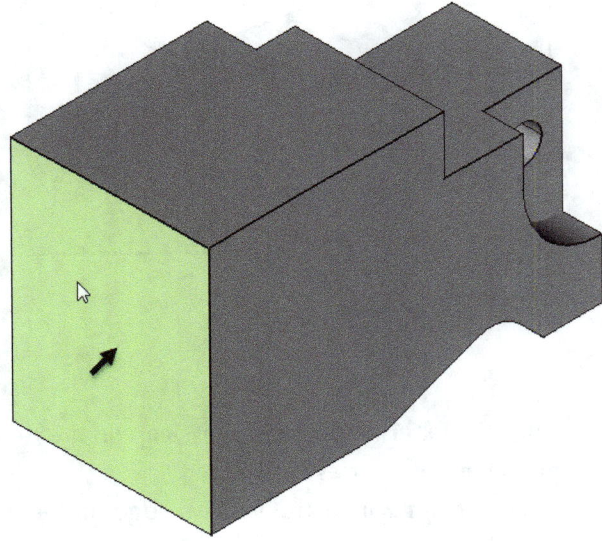

2. Click the **Create Sketch** icon on the **Part Design Helper** toolbar.

3. Create a line, as shown.

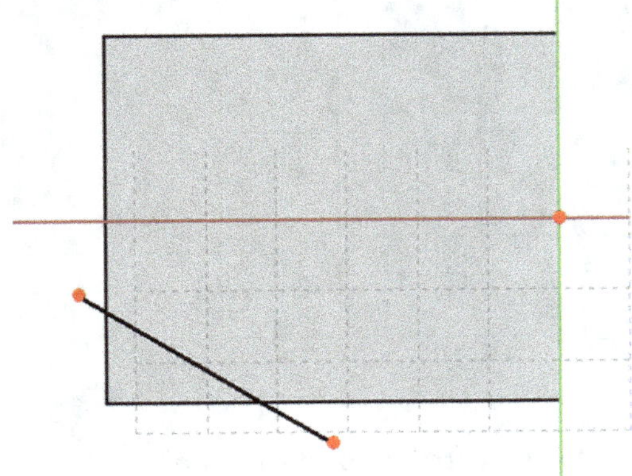

4. Click the **External geometry** icon on the **Sketcher geometries** toolbar.

5. Select the horizontal and vertical edges of the model, as shown.

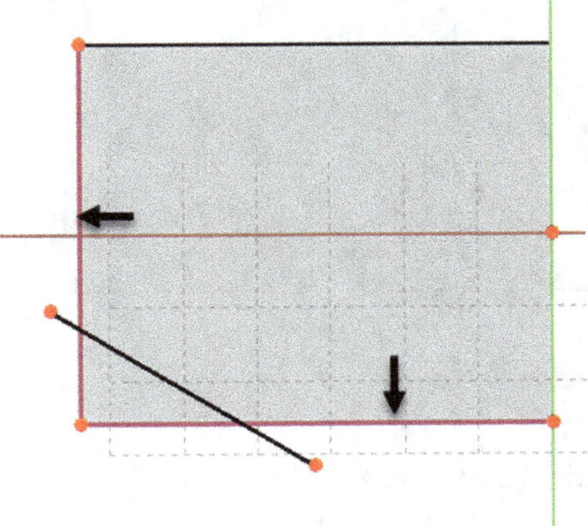

6. Click the **Constrain point onto object** icon on the **Sketcher constraints** toolbar.

7. Select the endpoint of the line and the vertical edge.

8. Select the endpoint of the line and the horizontal edge.

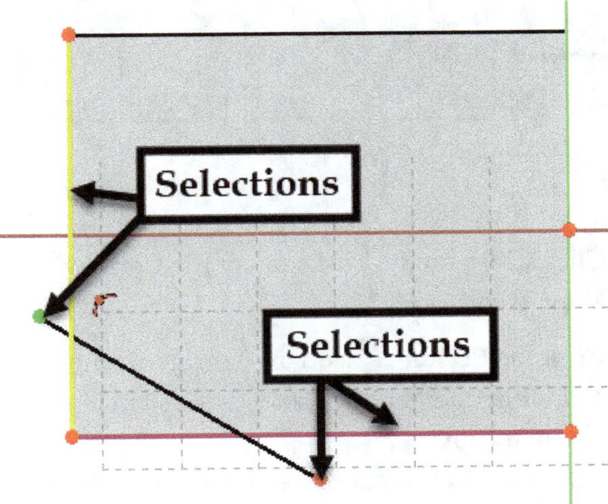

9. Create horizontal distance and angle constraints, as shown.

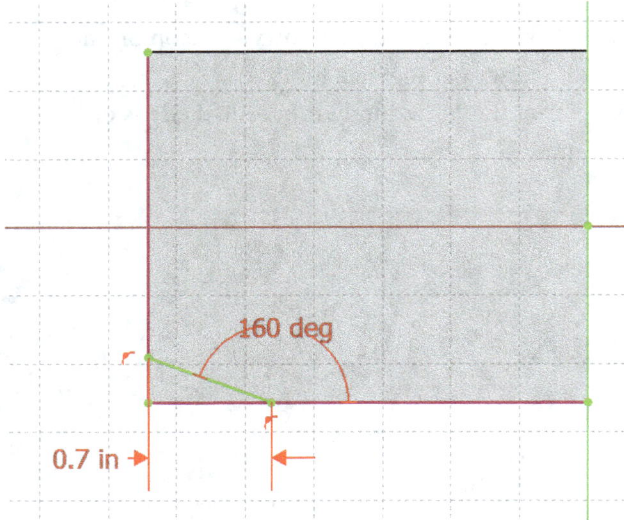

10. Create vertical and horizontal lines coincident with the extracted edges.

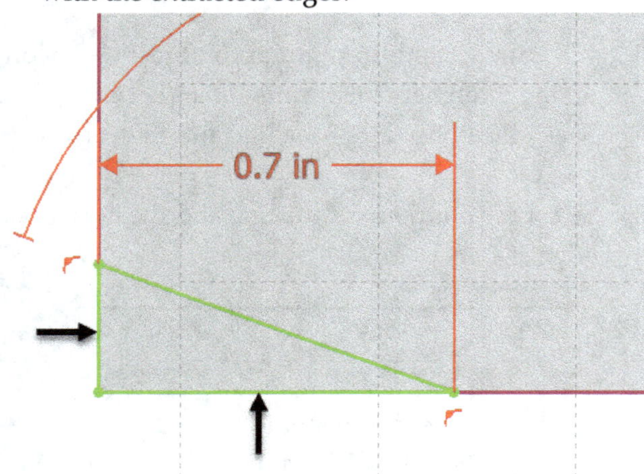

11. Click **Close** on the **Tasks** tab of the **Combo View** panel.

12. Click the **Pocket** icon on the **Part Design Modeling** toolbar; the sketch is selected automatically.

13. On the **Pocket parameters** dialog, select **Type > Through all**.

14. Click **OK**.

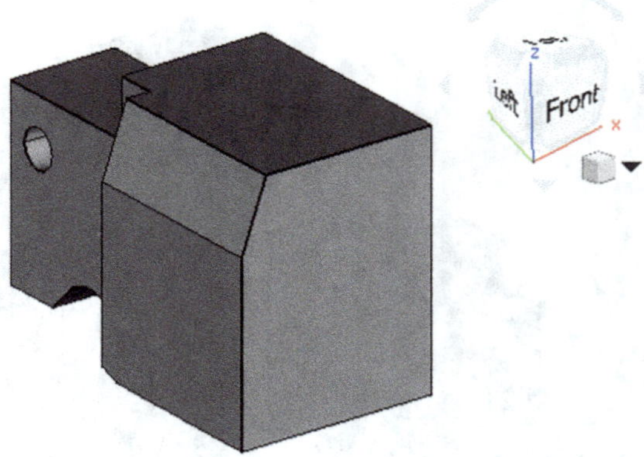

Creating the Pocket feature on the left

1. Click on the left face of the model.

2. Click the **Create Sketch** icon on the **Part Design Helper** toolbar.

3. Create a line and arc, as shown.

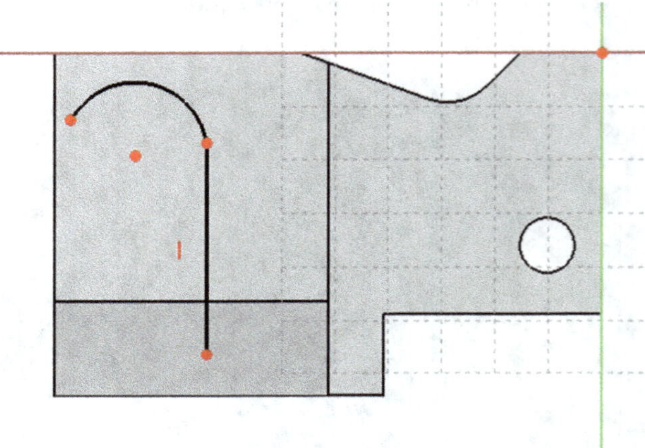

4. Click the **External geometry** icon on the **Sketcher geometries** toolbar.

5. Select the horizontal and vertical edges of the model, as shown.

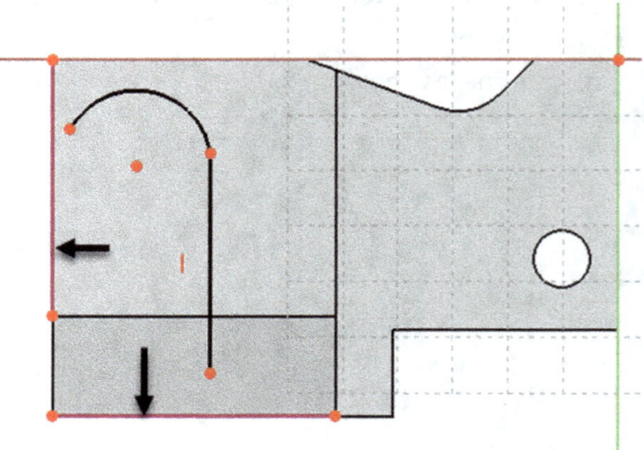

6. Click the **Constrain point onto object**  icon

on the **Sketcher constraints** toolbar.

7. Select the endpoint of the arc and the vertical edge.

8. Select the endpoint of the line and the horizontal edge.

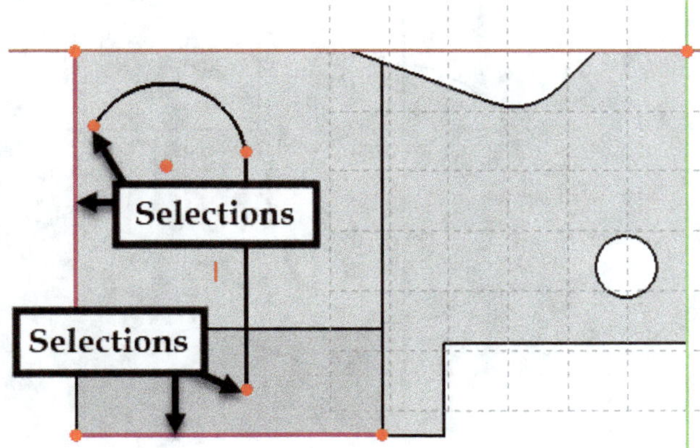

9. Click the **Constrain Tangent** icon on the **Sketcher constraints** toolbar.

10. Select the vertical line and the arc.

11. Create vertical and horizontal lines, as shown.

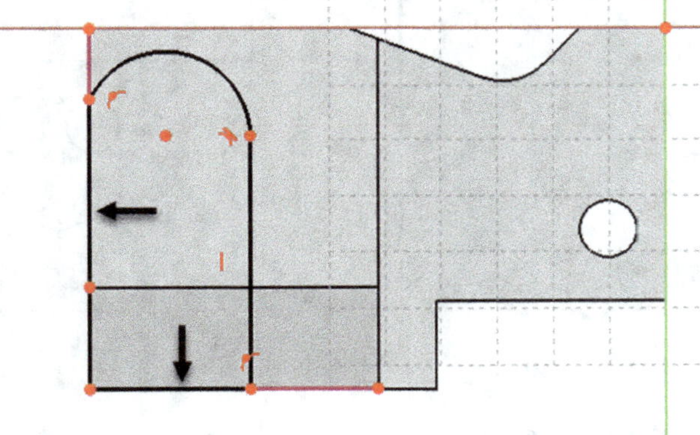

12. Click the **Constrain point onto object** icon on the **Sketcher constraints** toolbar.

13. Select the centerpoint of the arc and the vertical edge.

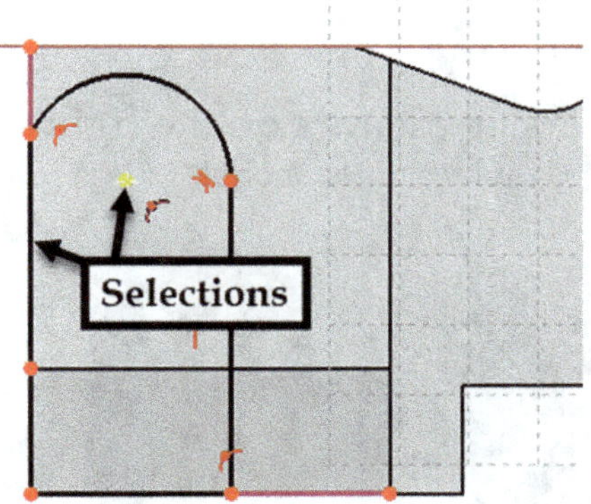

14. Create the radius and vertical distance constraints, as shown.

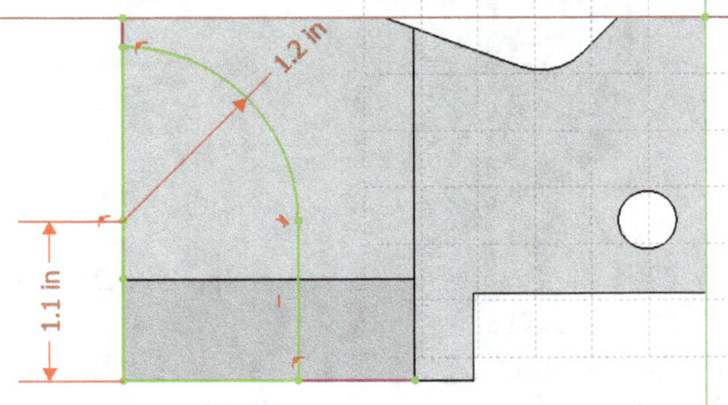

15. Click **Close** on the **Tasks** tab of the **Combo View** panel.

16. Click the **Pocket** icon on the **Part Design Modeling** toolbar; the sketch is selected automatically.

17. On the **Pocket parameters** dialog, select **Type > Dimension**.

18. Type **1.65** in the **Length** box.

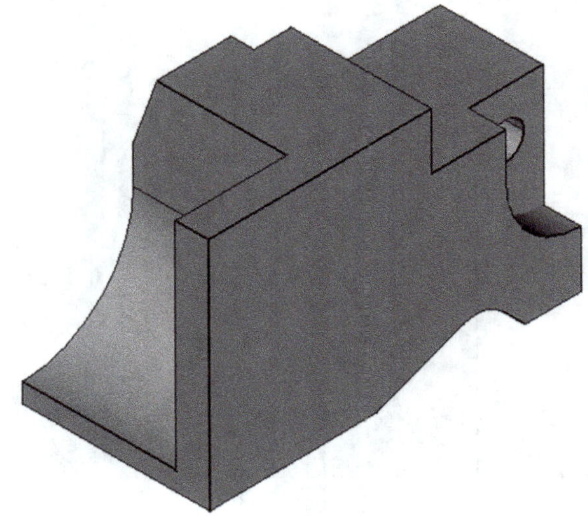

19. Click **OK**.

Creating the Pocket feature on the right

1. Click on the right face of the model.

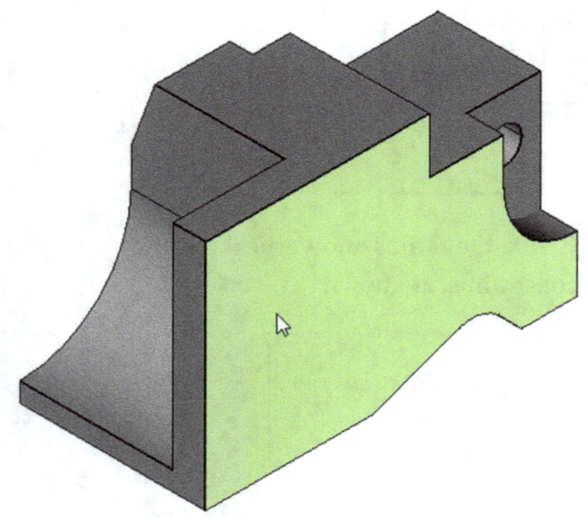

2. Click the **Create Sketch** icon on the **Part Design Helper** toolbar.
3. Create a circle.
4. Add the diameter and vertical distance constraint, as shown.

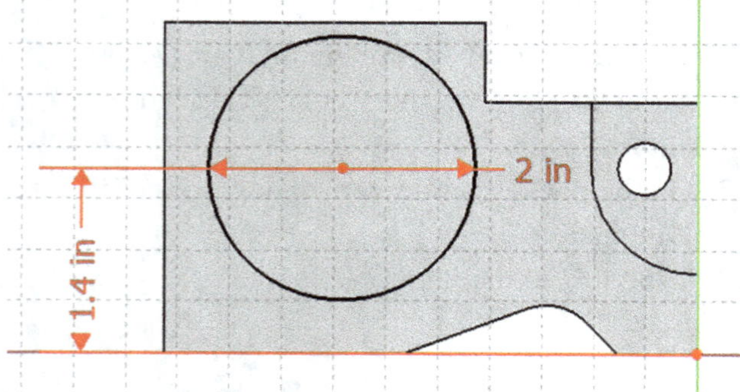

5. Create a vertical line, as shown.

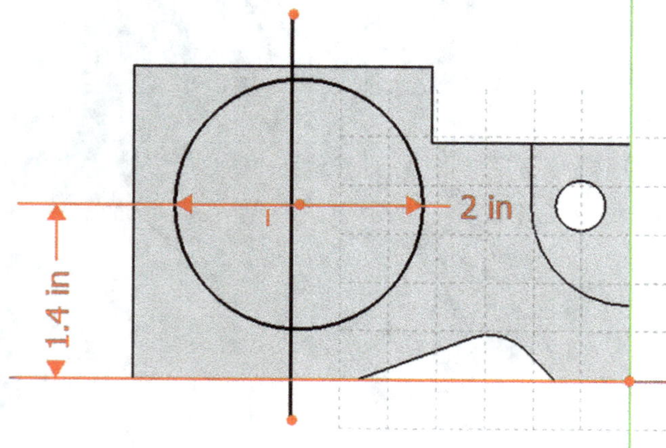

6. Click the **External geometry** icon on the **Sketcher geometries** toolbar.
7. Select the vertical and horizontal edges of the model, as shown.

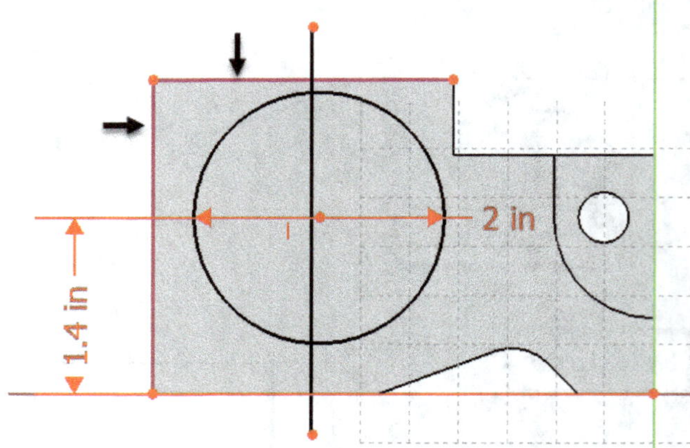

15. Click the **Trim Edge** icon on the **Sketcher geometries** toolbar.
16. Select the left side portion of the circle.

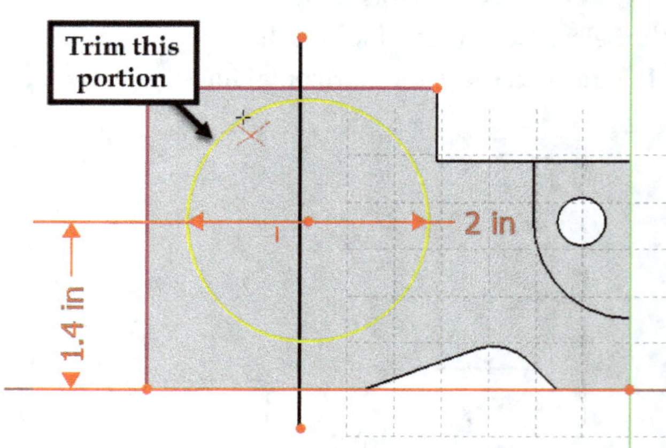

17. Click the **Constrain point onto object** icon on the **Sketcher constraints** toolbar.
18. Select endpoint the vertical line and the horizontal edge.

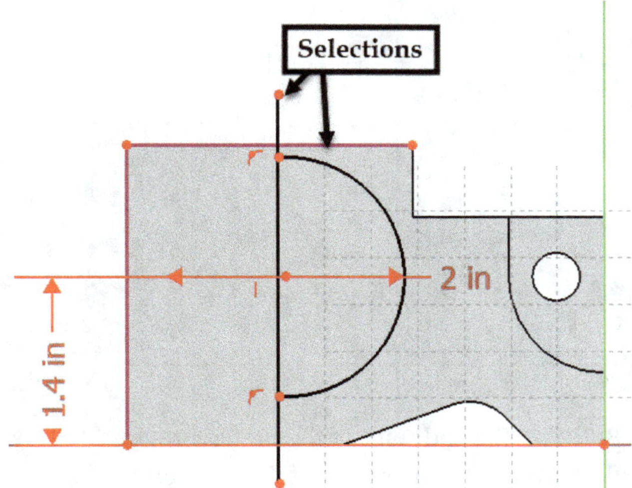

19. Trim the bottom and middle portions of the vertical line.

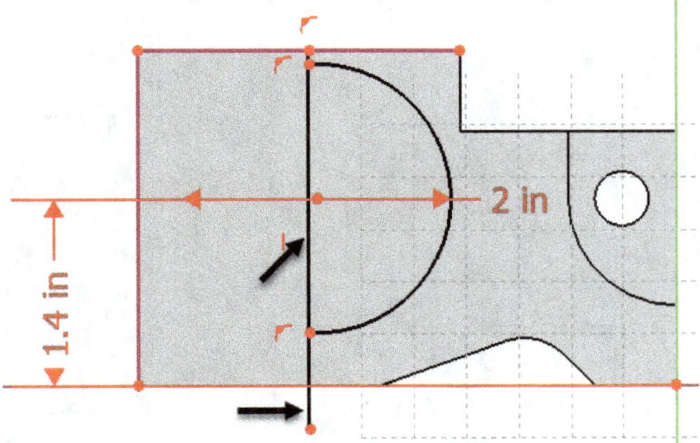

20. Click the **Arc** drop-down > **End points and rim point** on the **Sketcher geometries** toolbar.
21. Select the endpoint of the arc.
22. Move the pointer toward the left and click on the extracted edge.

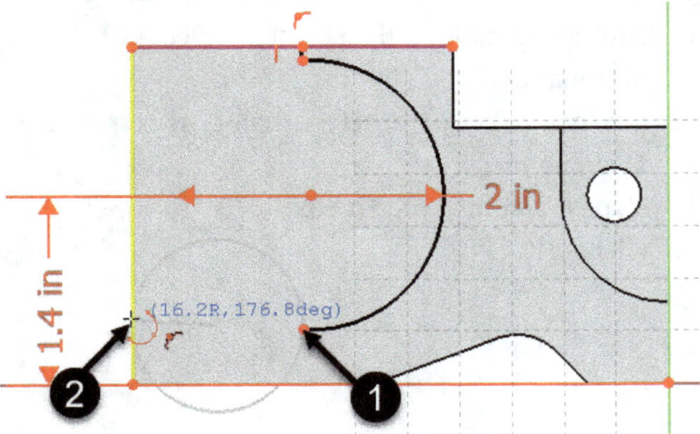

23. Move the pointer downward and click to create the arc.

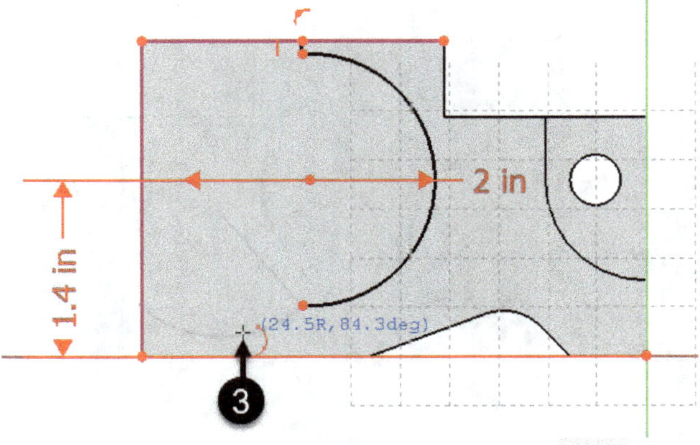

24. Click the **Constrain point onto object** icon on the **Sketcher constraints** toolbar.
25. Select the centerpoint of the new arc.
26. Select the extracted vertical edge.

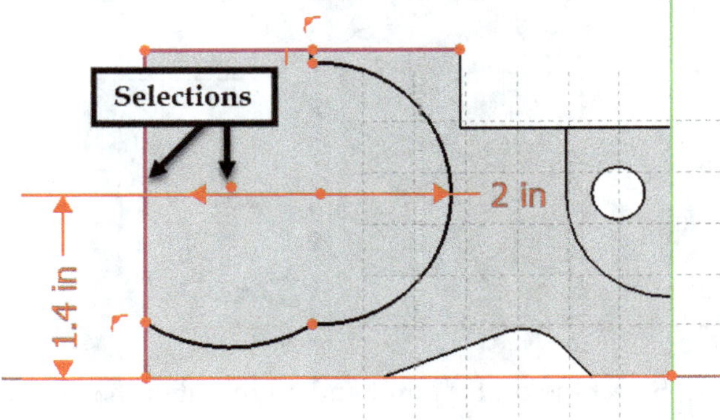

27. Press Esc.
28. Select the centerpoints of the two arcs.

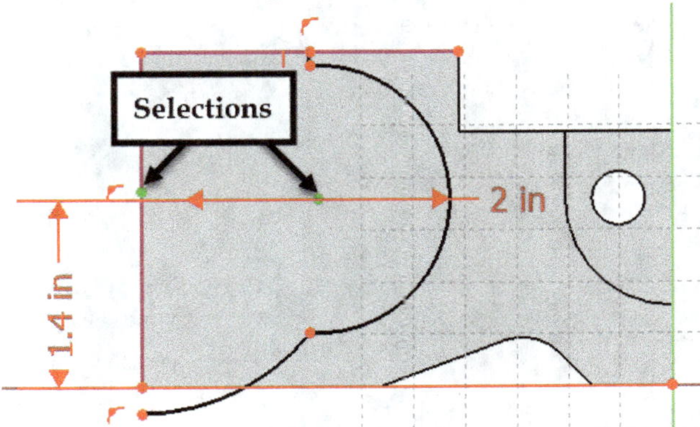

29. Click the **Constrain horizontal** icon on the **Sketcher constraints** toolbar.
30. Click the **Constrain equal** icon on the **Sketcher constraints** toolbar.
31. Select the two arcs to make their radius equal.

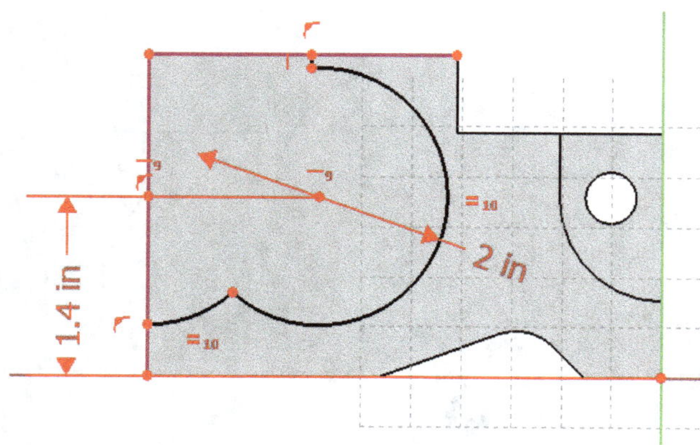

32. Create a horizontal distance constraint, as shown.

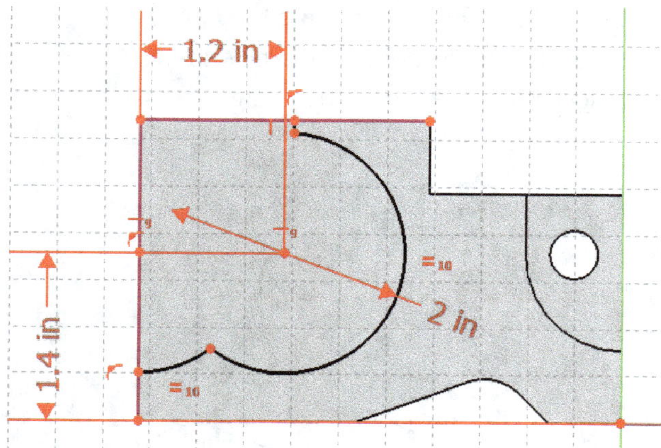

33. Select the center point and endpoint of the arc, as shown.

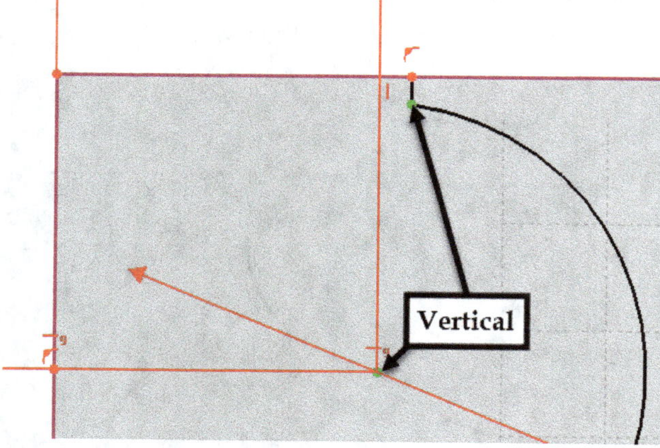

34. Click the **Constrain vertical** icon on the **Sketcher constraints** toolbar.
35. Click the **Create line** icon on the **Sketcher geometries** toolbar.
36. Select the endpoint of the small arc.
37. Move the pointer vertically upward and select the endpoint of the vertical edge.

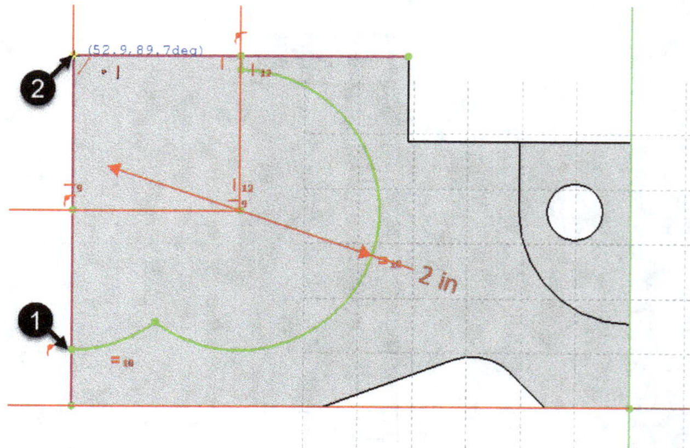

38. Select the endpoint of the vertical edge.
39. Move the pointer toward the right and select the endpoint of the vertical line.

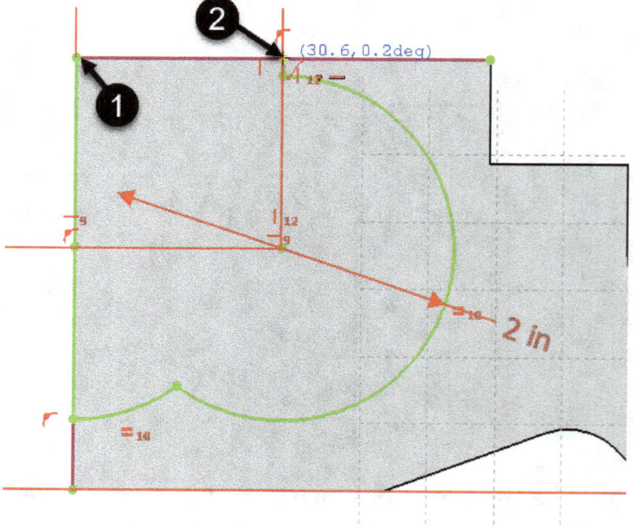

40. Click **Close** on the **Tasks** tab of the **Combo View** panel.
41. Click the **Pocket** icon on the **Part Design Modeling** toolbar; the sketch is selected automatically.
42. On the **Pocket parameters** dialog, select **Type > Dimension**.
43. Type **0.5** in the **Length** box.
44. Click **OK**.

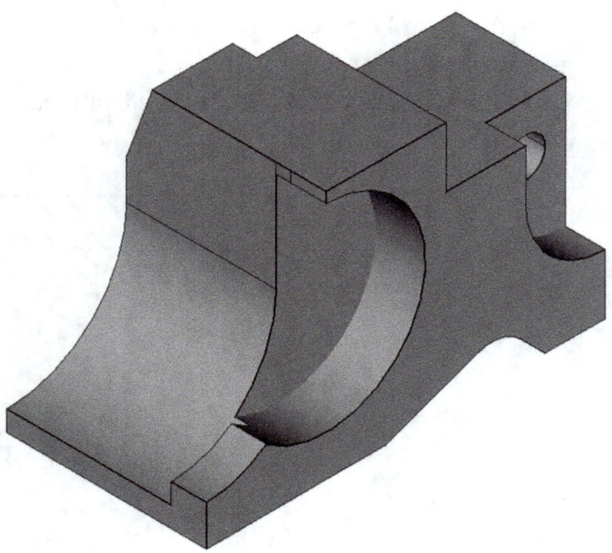

Adding the Pad Features

1. Click on the flat face of the pocket feature.

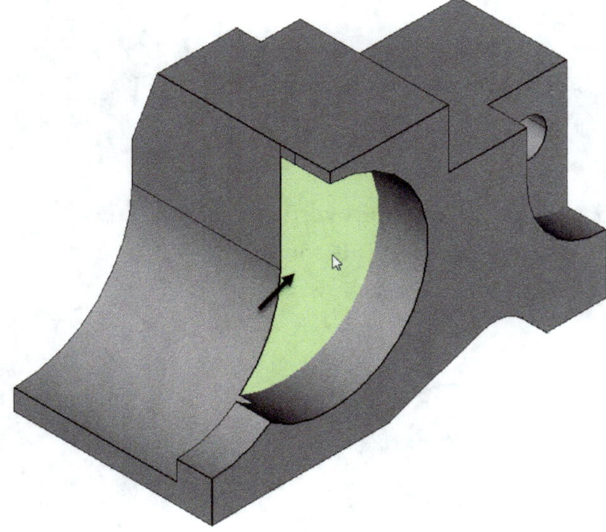

2. Click the **Create Sketch** icon on the **Part Design Helper** toolbar.
3. Create a circle and add the diameter constraint to it.

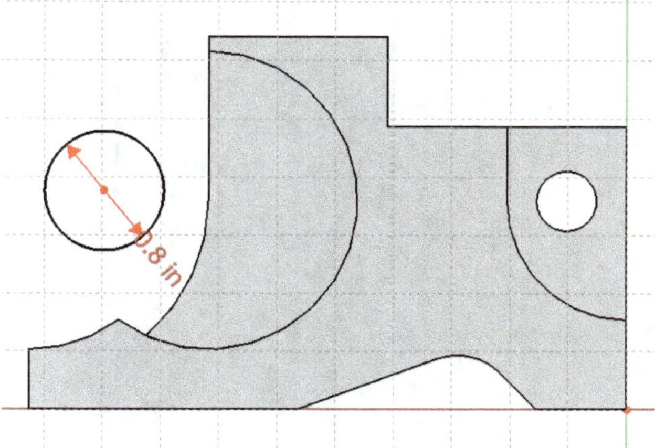

4. Click the **External geometry** icon on the **Sketcher geometries** toolbar.
5. Select the circular edge of the model.
6. Select the vertical and circular edge, as shown.

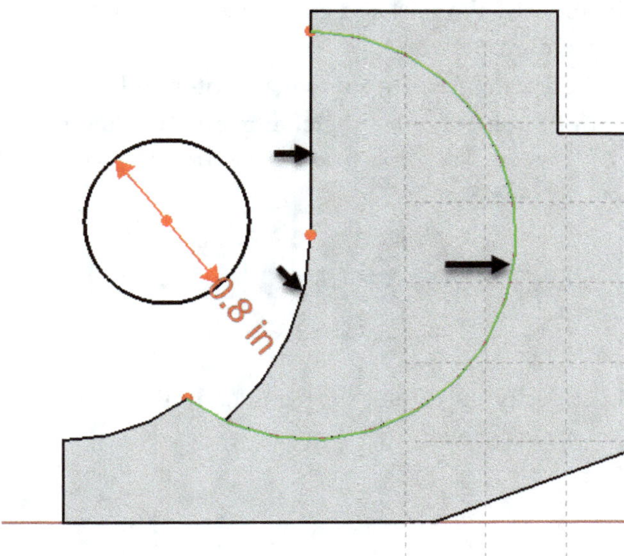

7. Click the **Constrain coincident** icon on the **Sketcher constraints** toolbar.
8. Select the centerpoint of the circle and the curved edge.

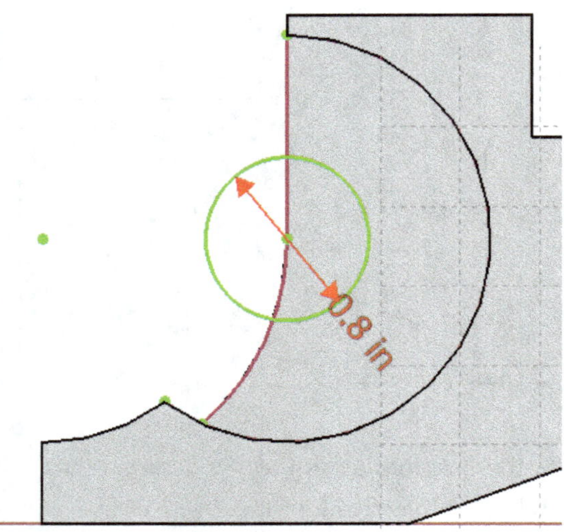

9. Click the **Create Line** icon on the **Sketcher geometries** toolbar.
10. Specify the start and endpoint of the line, as shown.
11. Click the **Arc** drop-down > **Center and endpoints** on the **Sketcher geometries** toolbar.

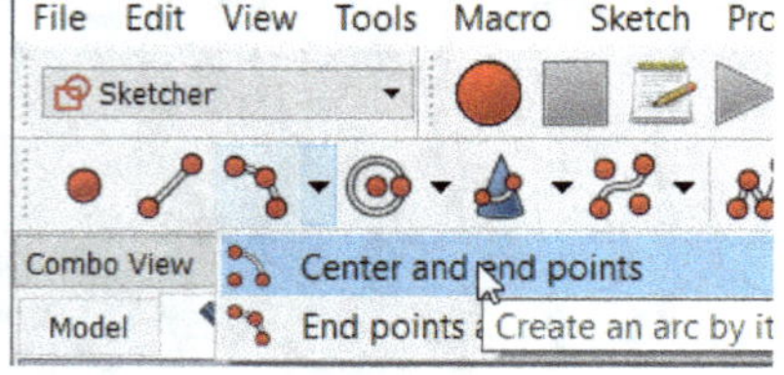

12. Specify the center, start, and endpoints of the arc, as shown.

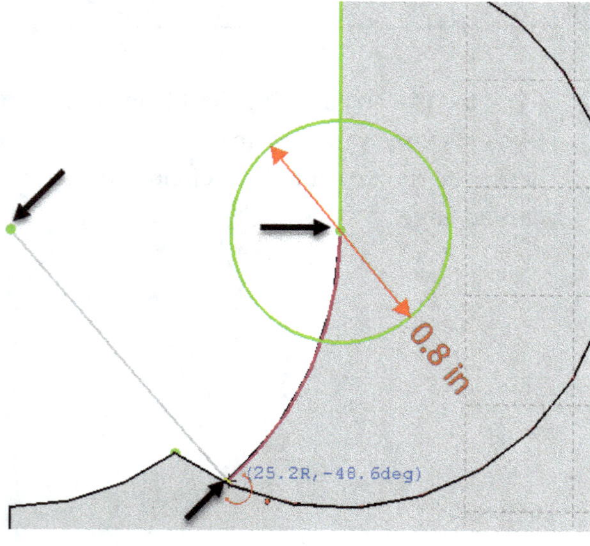

13. Click the **Trim Edge** icon on the **Sketcher geometries** toolbar.
14. Select the portions of the sketch to be trimmed, as shown.

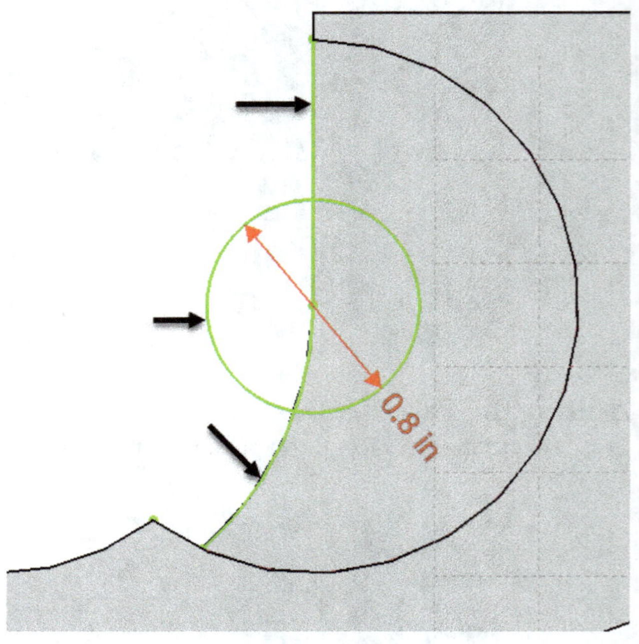

15. Click the **Constrain vertical** icon on the **Sketcher constraints** toolbar.
16. Select the line, as shown.

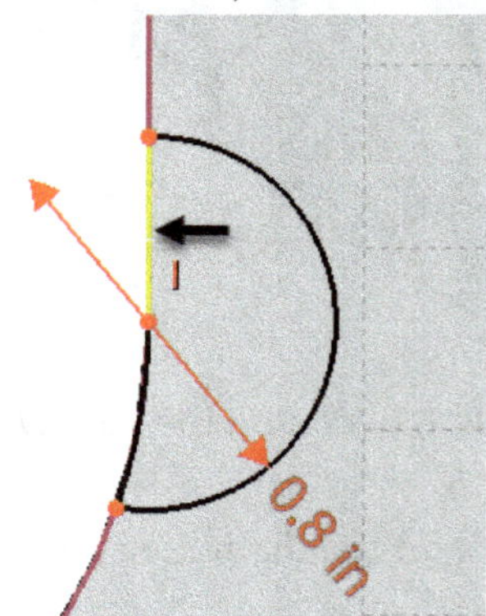

17. Click **Close** on the **Tasks** tab of the **Combo View** panel.
18. Click the **Pad** icon on the **Part Design Modeling** toolbar; the sketch is selected automatically.
19. Type 0.2 in the **Length** box.
20. Click **OK**.

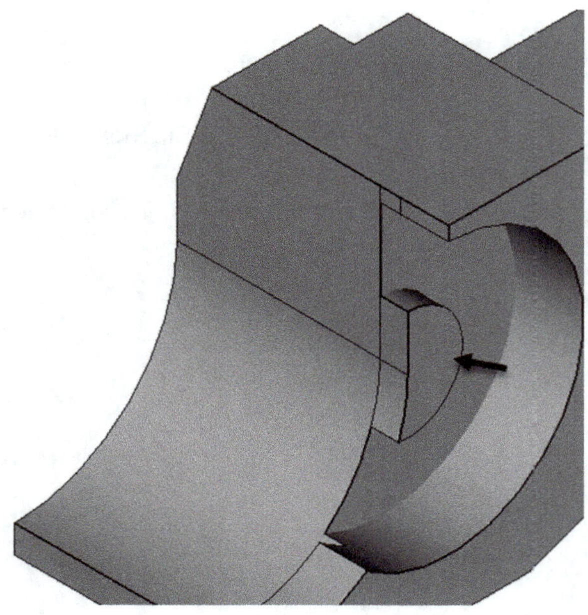

21. Click on the face of the pad feature, as shown.

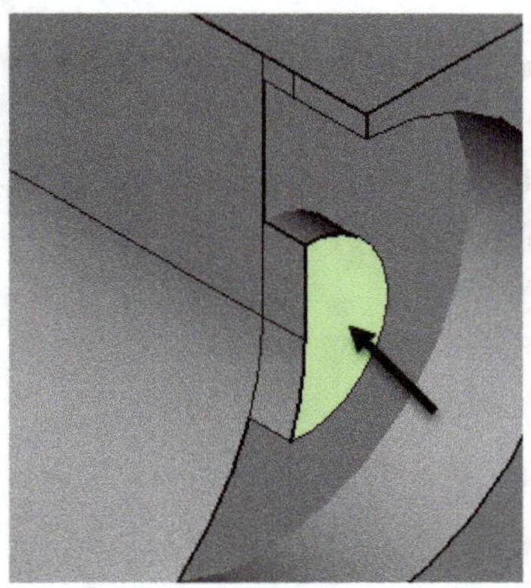

22. Click the **Create Sketch** icon on the **Part Design Helper** toolbar.
23. Create a circle and add the diameter constraint to it.
24. Click the **External geometry** icon on the **Sketcher geometries** toolbar.
25. Select the circular edge of the model, as shown.

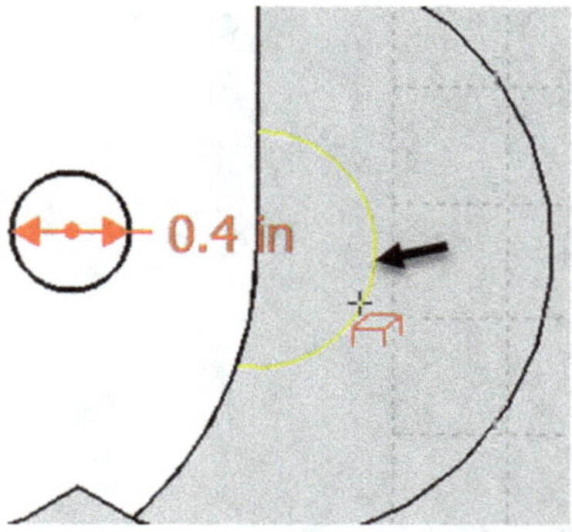

26. Click the **Constrain coincident** icon on the **Sketcher constraints** toolbar.
27. Select the centerpoint of the circle and the curved edge.
28. Click **Close** on the **Tasks** tab of the **Combo View** panel.
29. Click the **Pad** icon on the **Part Design Modeling** toolbar; the sketch is selected automatically.
30. On the **Padparameters** dialog, select **Type > Up To face**.
31. Select the right face of the model, as shown.

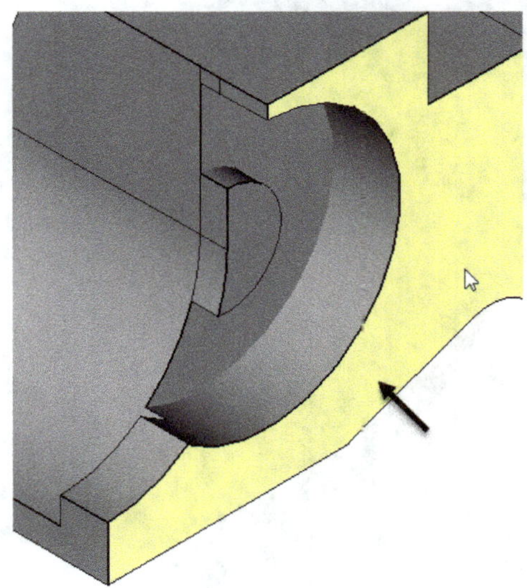

32. Click **OK**.

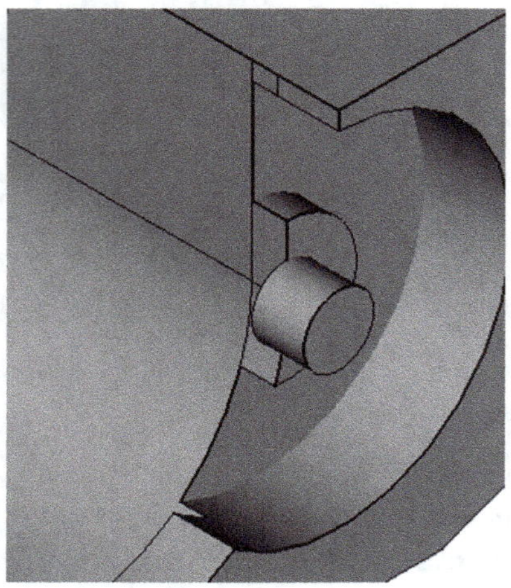

33. Save and close the model.

TUTORIAL 9

In this tutorial, you construct the model shown in the figure.

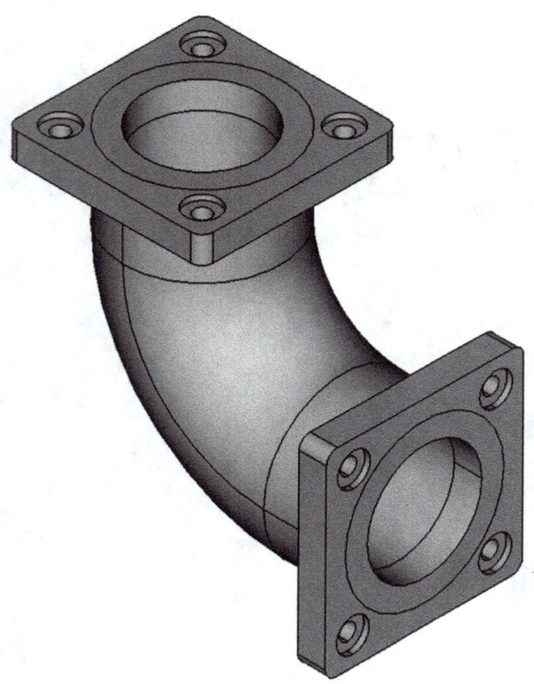

Creating the first feature

1. Open the FreeCAD application.
2. Click **File > New** on the Menu bar.
3. Select the **Part Design** option from the **Workbenches** drop-down.
4. Click the **Create sketch** icon on the **Part Design Helper** toolbar, and then select the XZ

Plane.

5. Click **OK** to start the sketch.
6. Click the **Polyline** icon on the **Sketcher geometries** toolbar.
7. Create a vertical and horizontal lines connected to each other, as shown.

8. Click the **Fillet** drop-down > **Sketch Fillet** on the **Sketcher geometries** toolbar.
9. Select the vertical and horizontal lines; a fillet created at the intersection of the two lines.

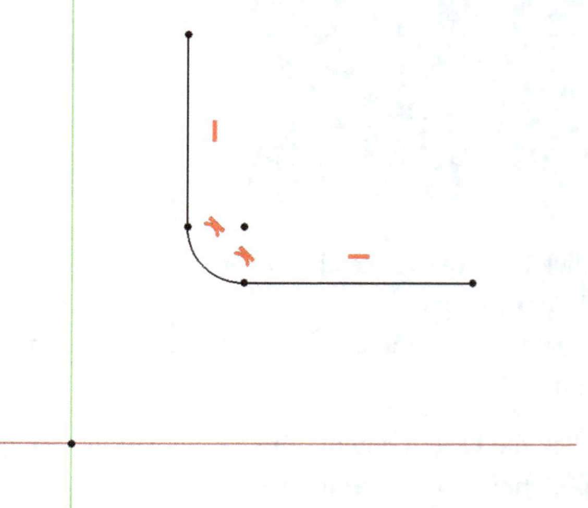

10. Click **Sketcher constraints** toolbar > **Constrain vertical distance** (or) click **Sketch > Sketcher constraints > Constrain vertical distance** on the menu bar.
11. Select the vertical line.
12. Enter **5.9** in the **Length** box of the **Insert Length** dialog and click **OK**.

13. Click **Sketcher constraints** toolbar > **Constrain horizontal distance** 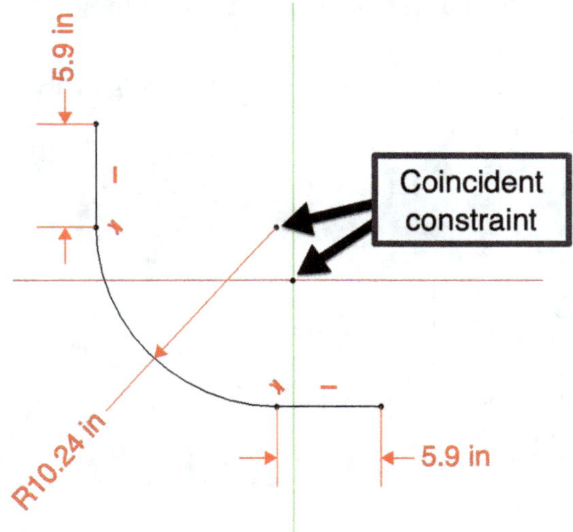 (or) click **Sketch > Sketcher constraints > Constrain horizontal distance** on the menu bar.
14. Select the horizontal line.
15. Enter **5.9** in the **Length** box of the **Insert Length** dialog and click the **OK** button.
16. On the **Sketcher constraints** toolbar, click the **Constrain radius** icon.
17. Select the circle and type **10.24** in the **Radius** box of the **Change Radius** dialog.
18. Click **OK**.
19. Click the **Constrain Coincident** icon on the **Sketcher constraints** toolbar.
20. Select the origin point of the sketch
21. Select the center point of the fillet.

22. Click **Close** on the **Tasks** tab of the **Combo View** panel.

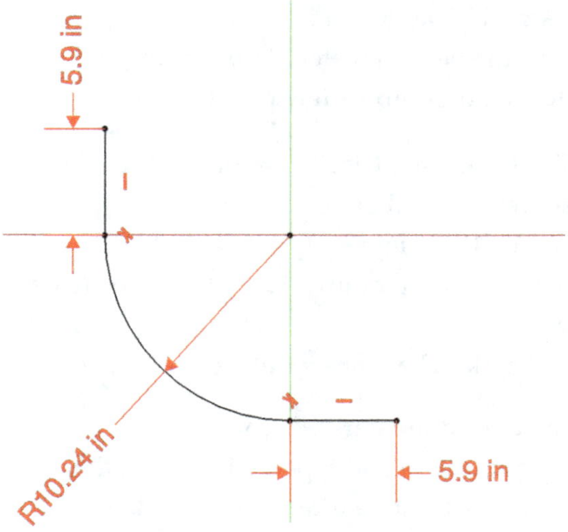

23. On the **Part Design Helper** toolbar, click the **Create a new datum plane** icon.
24. Select the horizontal line of the sketch.
25. Select the endpoint of the horizontal line.
26. Select the **Normal to edge** option from the **Attachment mode** section of the **Combo View** panel.
27. Click **OK**.

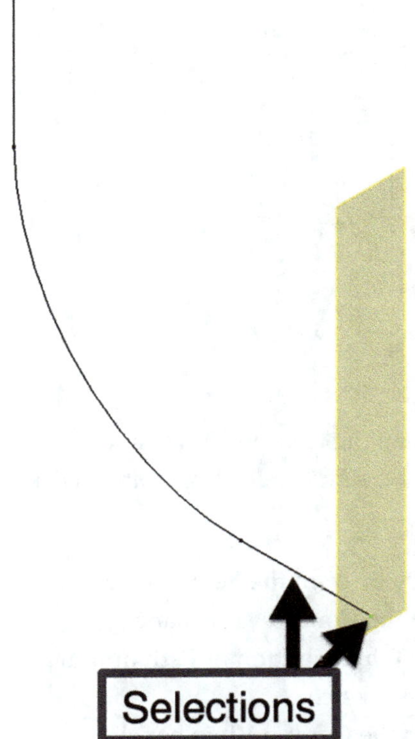

28. Click the **Create a new Sketch** icon the **Part**

Design Helper toolbar.

29. Select the newly created datum plane and click **OK** on the **Combo View** panel.

30. Click the **Create Circle** on the **Sketcher geometries** toolbar.

31. Click on the origin.

32. Move the pointer outward and click to create a circle.

33. On the **Sketcher constraints** toolbar, click the **Constrain diameter** icon.

34. Select the circle and type **11.41** in the **Diameter** box on the **Change diameter** dialog.

35. Make sure that the center of the circle and origin point are coincident.

36. Click **OK**.

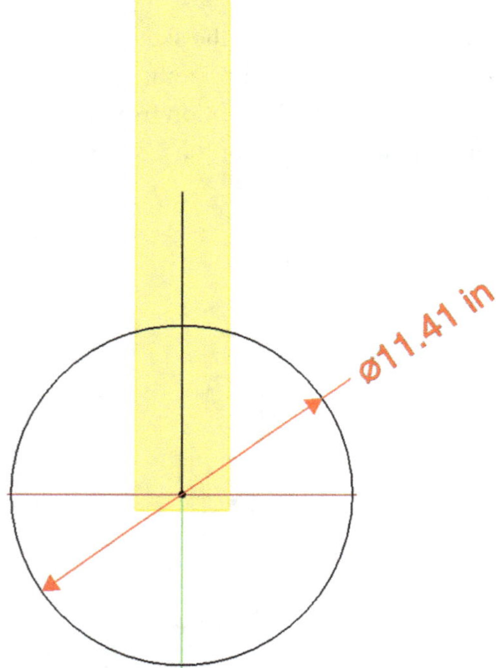

37. Click **Close** on the **Combo View** panel.

38. On the **Part Design Modelling** toolbar, click the **Sweep** icon.

39. Select Sketch001 from the **Select feature** and click **OK** on the **Combo View** panel.

40. Click on the **Object** button of **Path** option and select the first sketch.

41. Click **OK** on the **Combo View** panel.

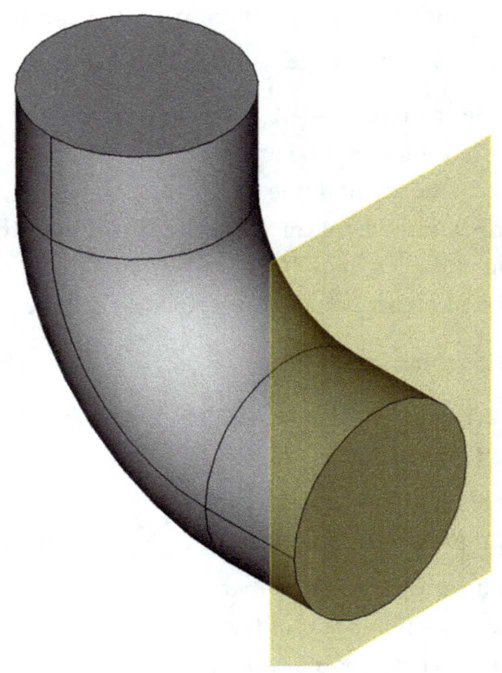

42. Select the datum plane from the graphics window.

43. On the **Combo View** panel, set the **Visibility** value to **false**.

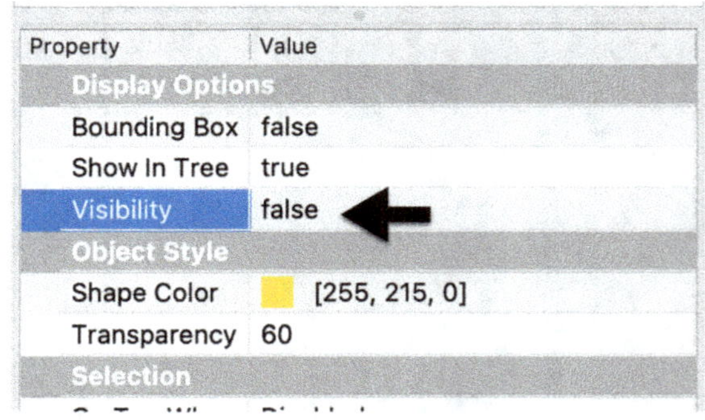

Property	Value
Display Options	
Bounding Box	false
Show In Tree	true
Visibility	false
Object Style	
Shape Color	[255, 215, 0]
Transparency	60
Selection	

44. Click in the graphics window to deselect the datum plane.

Creating the Shell feature

1. Press **Ctrl** and select the faces as shown.

2. Click the **Thickness** tool on the **Part Design Modeling** toolbar.

3. Enter **1.575** in the **Thickness** box under the **Thickness Parameter** section.

4. Check **Make thickness inwards** option.

5. Click **OK** on the **Combo View** panel.

6. Select the flat face of the AdditivePipe, as

shown.

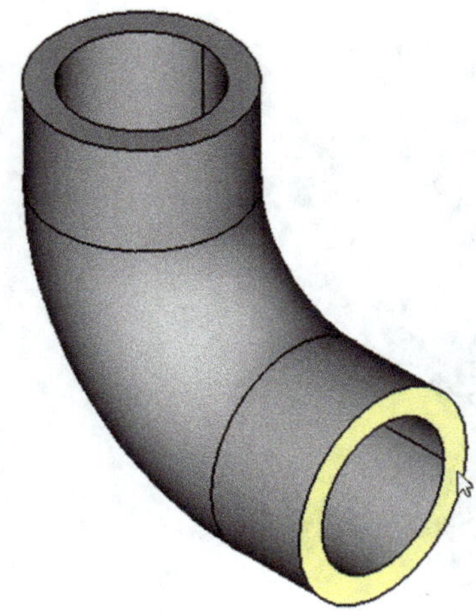

Creating the Flanges

1. Click **Create new Sketch** 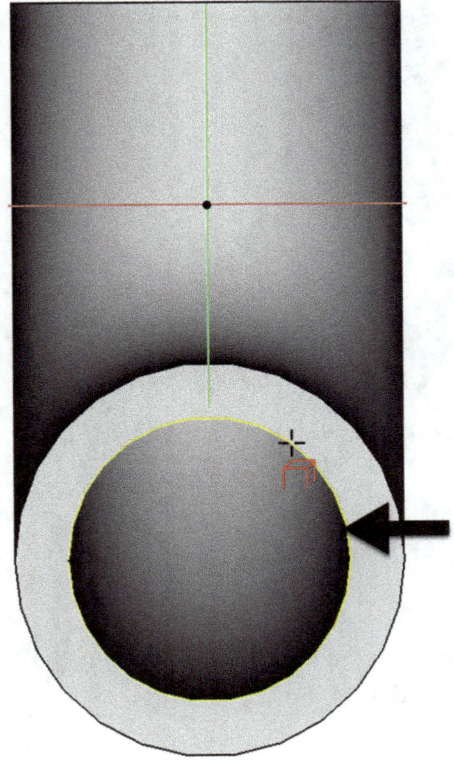 icon on the **Part Design Helper toolbar**.

2. Click the **External Geometry** icon on the **Sketcher geometries** toolbar.

3. Select the inner circular edge of the model, as shown.

4. Expand the **Sketcher geometries** toolbar and click the **Polygon** drop-down > **Square**.

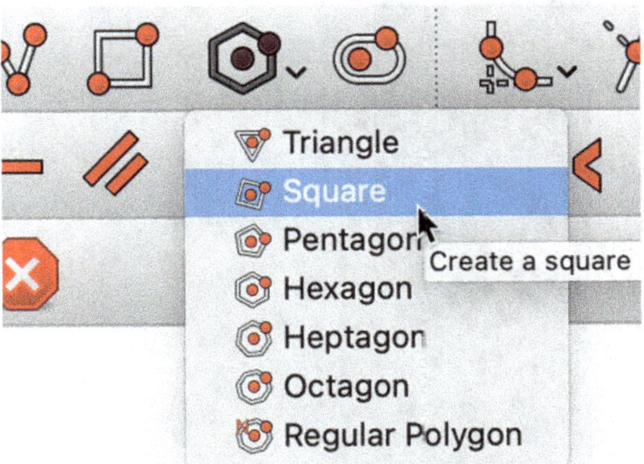

5. Select the centerpoint of the circular edge.

6. Move the pointer outward and click to create a square. Next, Press **Esc**.

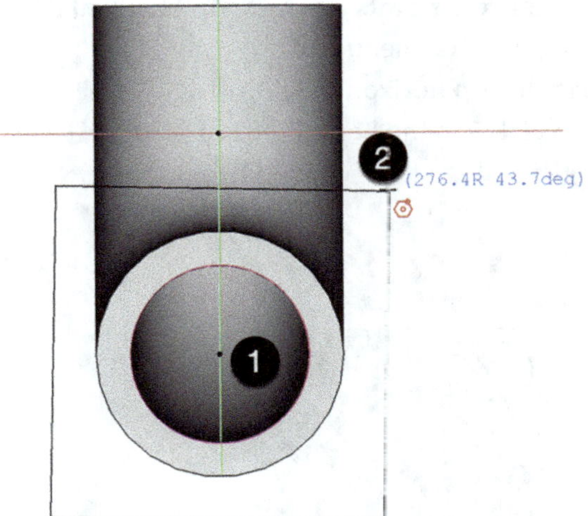

7. On the **Sketcher constraints** toolbar, click the **Horizontal constraint** icon.

8. Select the top horizontal line, as shown.

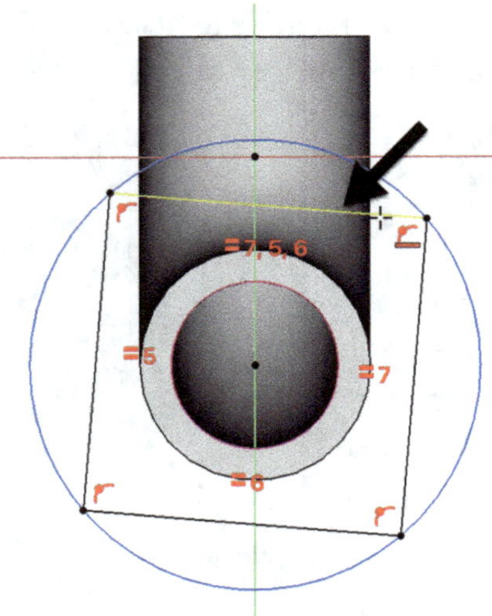

9. Click **Sketcher constraints** toolbar > **Constrain horizontal distance** (or) click **Sketch > Sketcher constraints > Constrain horizontal distance** on the menu bar.

10. Select the top horizontal line.

11. Enter **14.173** in the **Length** box of the **Insert Length** dialog and click the **OK** button.

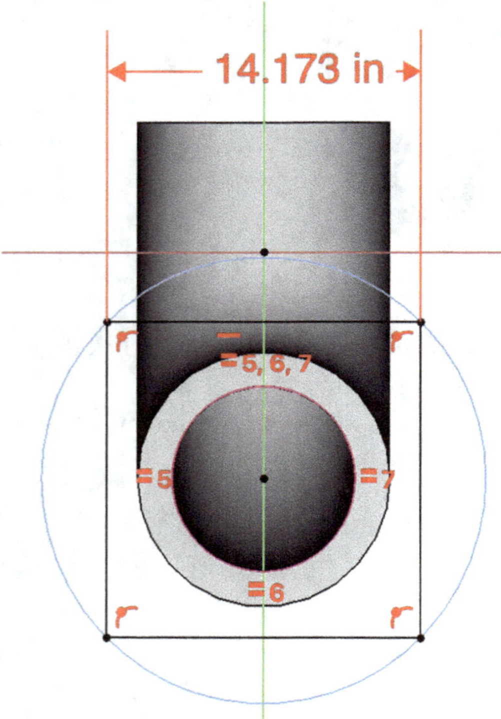

12. Click the **Create Circle** on the **Sketcher geometries** toolbar.

13. Select the centerpoint of the circular edge.

14. Move the pointer outward and click on the inner circular edge.

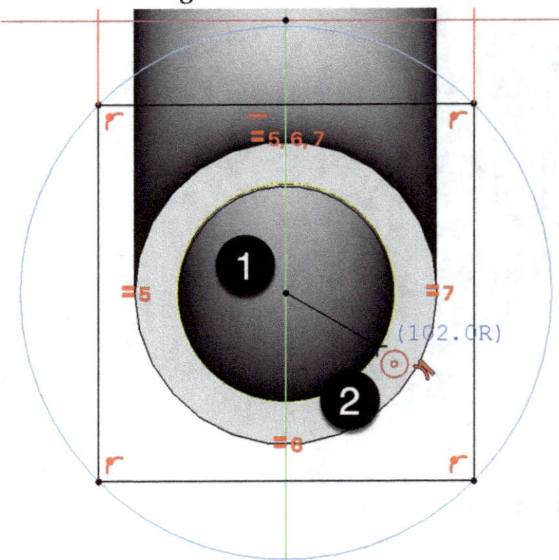

15. Click **Close** on the **Combo View** panel.

16. On the **Part Design Modeling** toolbar, click the **Pad** icon.

17. Type **1.969** in the **Length** box of the **Pad Parameters** dialog.

18. Check the **Reversed** option and click **OK**.

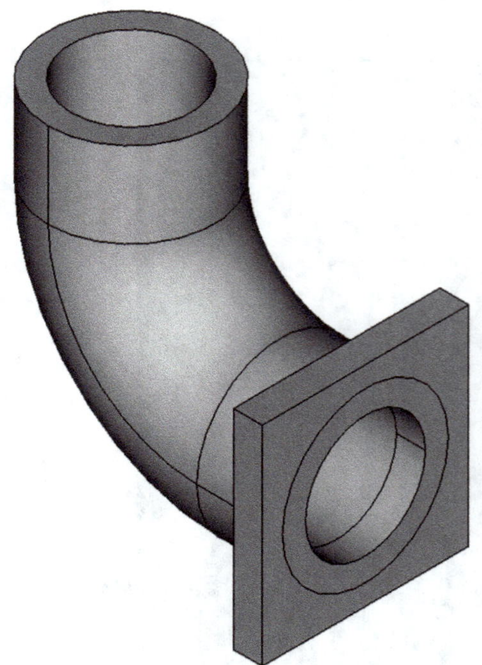

19. Press and hold the Ctrl key and select the edges of the model, as shown.

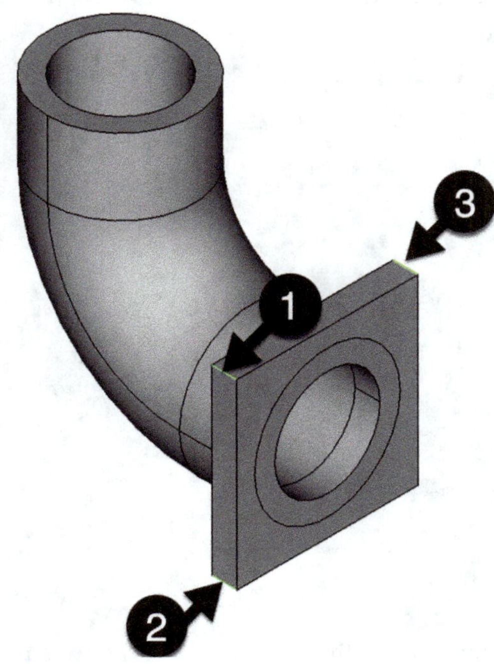

20. On the **Part Design Modeling** toolbar, click the
    Fillet icon.
21. Click the **Add** button on the **Fillet Parameters**
    dialog.
22. Press and hold the middle and right mouse
    buttons, and then drag the pointer; the model is
    rotated.
23. Select the edge of the model, as shown.

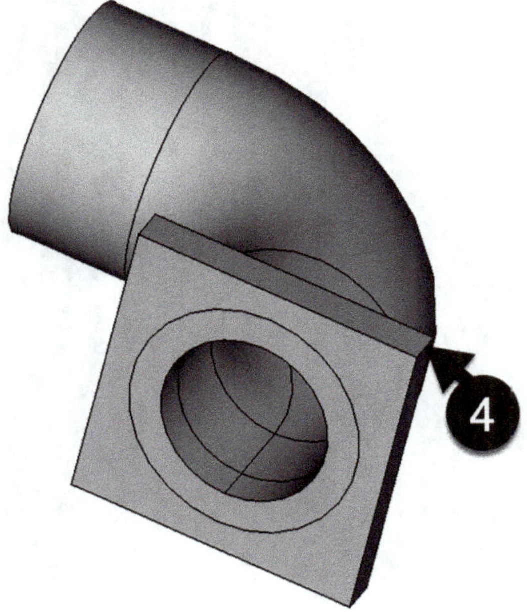

24. Type **0.787** in the **Radius** box.
25. Click **OK**.
26. Click the **ViewCube** drop-down, and then select
    the **Isometric** option.

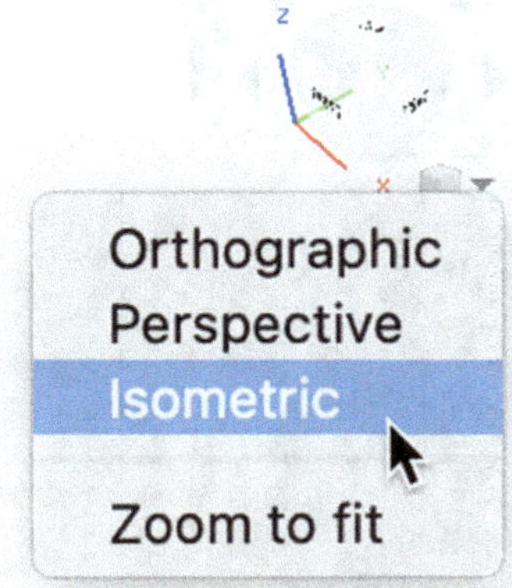

27. Select the flat face of the **Pad** feature, as shown.

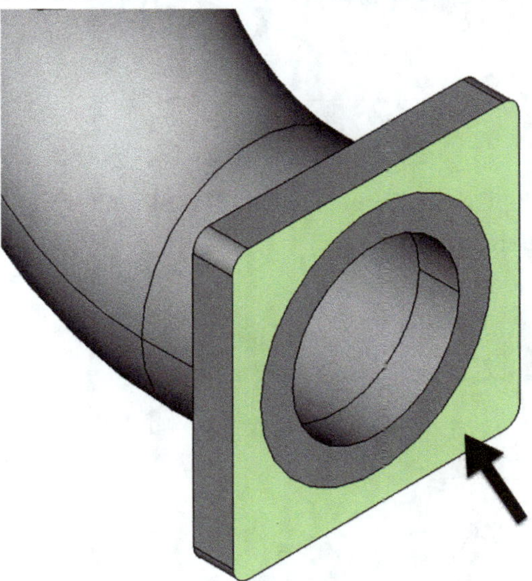

28. Click **Create new Sketch** icon on the **Part
    Design Helper toolbar**.
29. Click the **External Geometry** icon on the
    Sketcher geometries toolbar.
30. Select the horizontal and vertical edges, as
    shown.

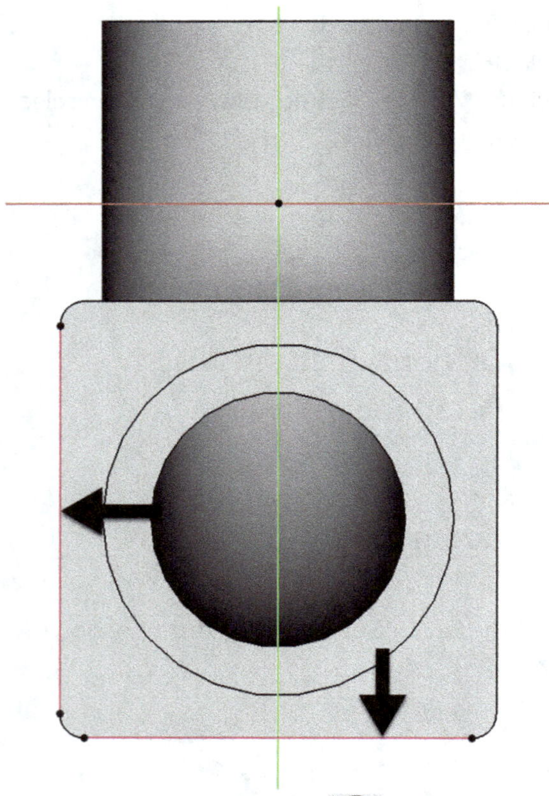

31. Click the **Create Circle** on the **Sketcher geometries** toolbar.
32. Create a circle, as shown.

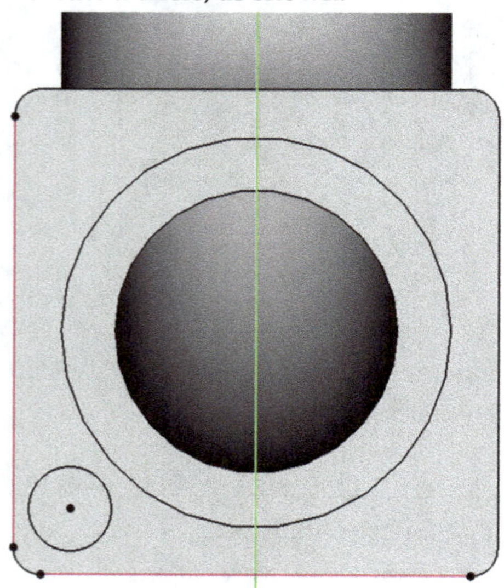

33. Click **Sketcher constraints** toolbar > **Constrain vertical distance** (or) click **Sketch > Sketcher constraints > Constrain vertical distance** on the menu bar.
34. Select the centerpoint of the circle.

35. Select the left endpoint of the horizontal edge, as shown.

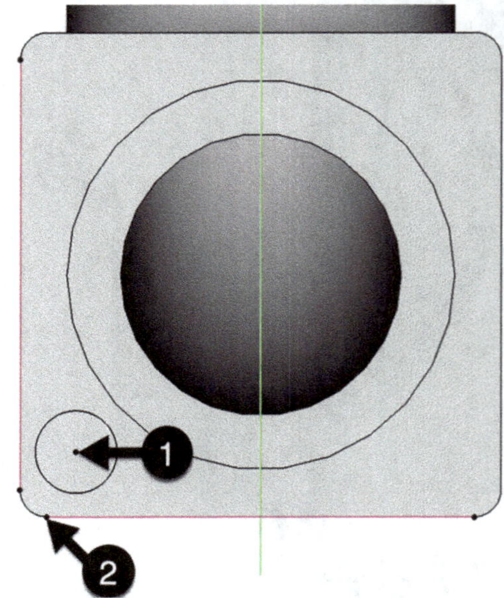

36. Enter **1.969** in the **Length** box of the **Insert Length** dialog and click **OK**.
37. Click **Sketcher constraints** toolbar > **Constrain horizontal distance** (or) click **Sketch > Sketcher constraints > Constrain horizontal distance** on the menu bar.
38. Select the centerpoint of the circle.
39. Select the lower endpoint of the vertical edge, as shown.
40. Enter **1.969** in the **Length** box of the **Insert Length** dialog and click the **OK** button.

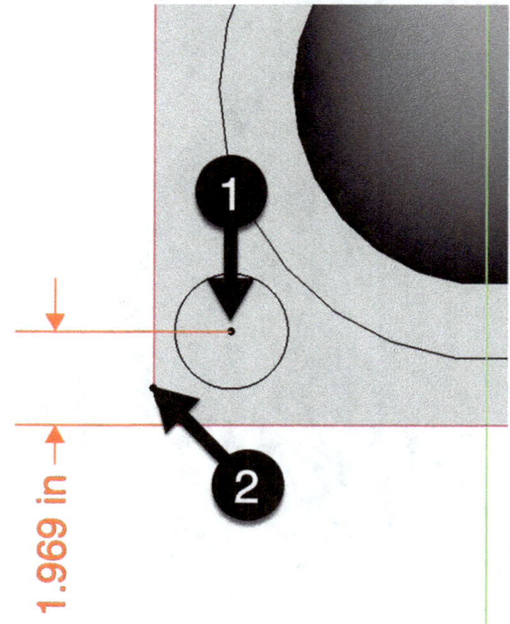

41. Click **Close** on the **Combo View** panel.
42. Click the **Hole** icon on the **Part Design Modeling** toolbar.
43. Type **1.181 in** in the **Diameter** box.
44. Select **Depth > Dimension**.
45. Type 1.969 in the **Depth** box located next to the **Depth** drop-down.
46. On the **Hole Parameters** section, under **Hole cut**, select **Type > Counterbore**.
47. Type **2.362** in the **Diameter** box.
48. Type **0.394** in the **Depth** box.
49. Under **Drill point**, select **Type > Flat**.

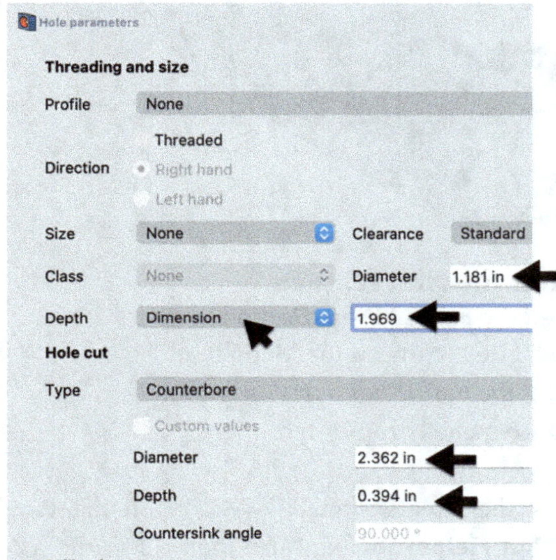

50. Click **OK** on the **Combo View** panel; the counterbore hole is created.

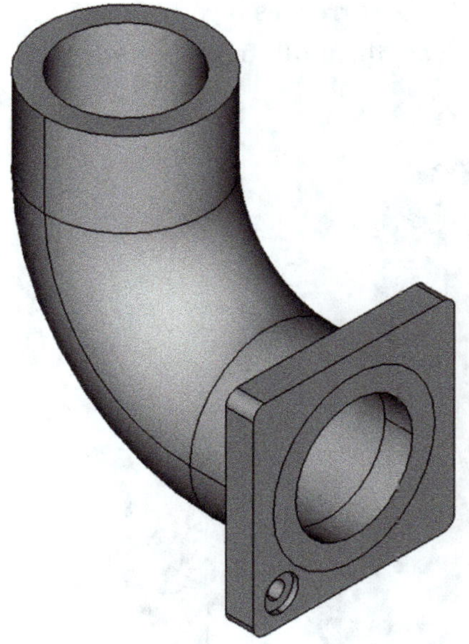

51. Select the **Hole** feature from the **Model** tab of the **Combo View** panel.

52. Click the **MultiTransform** tool on the **Part Design Modeling** toolbar.
53. In the **MultiTransform parameters** section, right click in the **Transformations** section, and then select **Add linear pattern**.

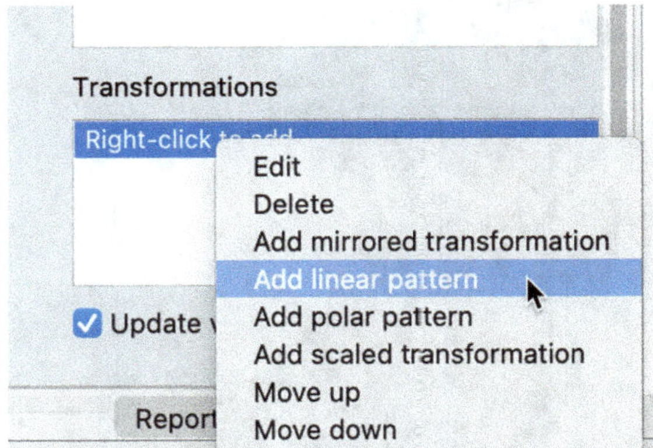

54. Select the **Horizontal sketch axis** from the **Direction** drop-down.
55. Type **10.235** in the **Length** box.
56. Type-in **2** in the **Occurrences** box.
57. Right click in the **Transformations** section, and then select **Add linear pattern**.
58. Select the **Vertical sketch axis** from the **Direction** drop-down.
59. Type **10.235** in the **Length** box.

60. Type-in **2** in the **Occurrences** box.
61. Click **OK** to create the multi transformation pattern.

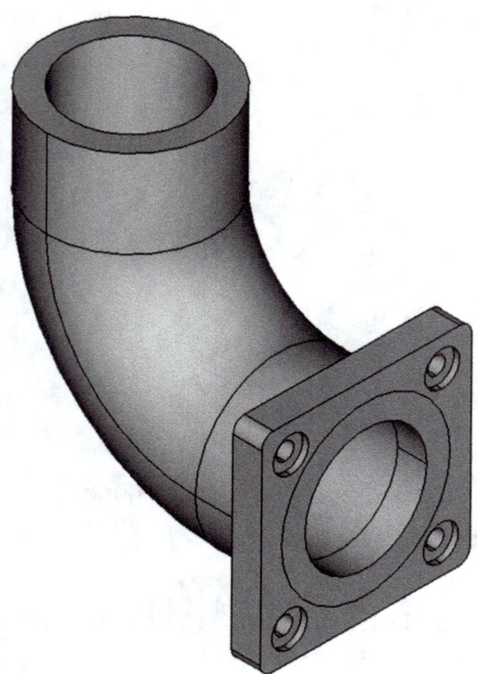

62. Likewise, create another flange on the other end of the AdditivePipe, as shown.

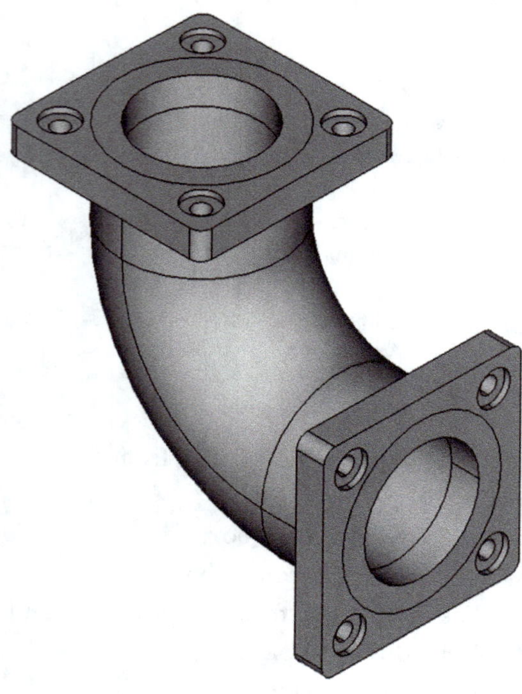

TUTORIAL 10

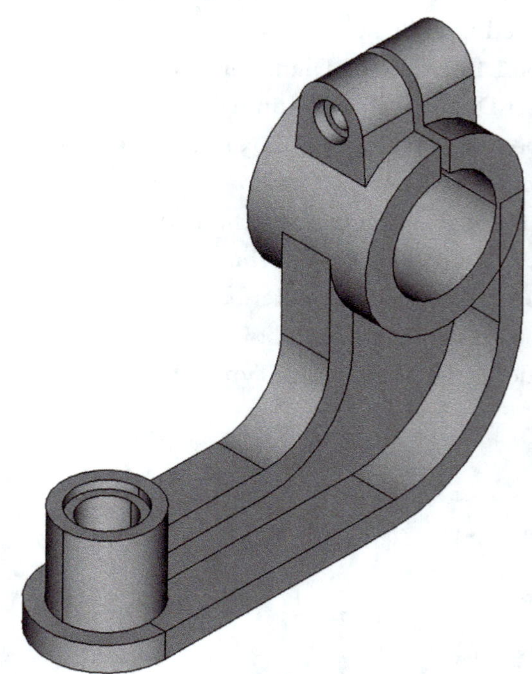

Creating the first feature

1. Open the FreeCAD application.
2. Click **File > New** on the Menu bar.
3. Select the **Part Design** option from the **Workbenches** drop-down.
4. Click the **Create sketch** icon on the **Part Design Helper** toolbar, and then select the YZ Plane.
5. Click **OK** to start the sketch.
6. Click the **Create circle** icon on the **Sketcher geometries** toolbar.
7. On the **Sketcher constrain** toolbar, click the **Constrain Diameter** icon.
8. Select the circle and type in **3.937** in the **Diameter** box on the **Change diameter** dialog.
9. Click **OK**.

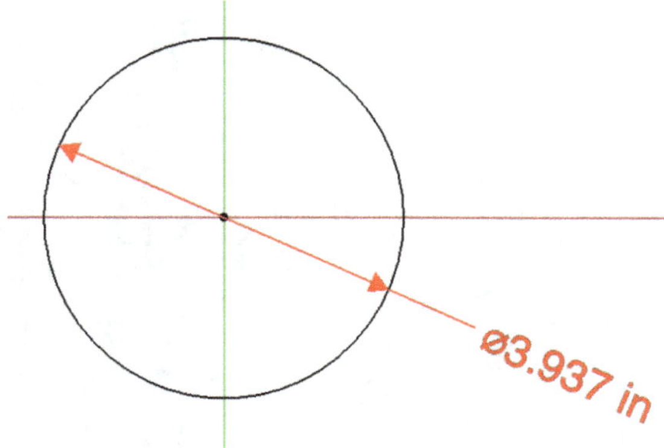

10. Click the **Leave Sketch** icon on the **Part Design Helper toolbar**.
11. On the **Part Design Modelling** toolbar, click **Pad** icon.
12. Type-in **2.953** in the **Length** box.
13. Check the **Symmetric to plane** option and click **OK**.

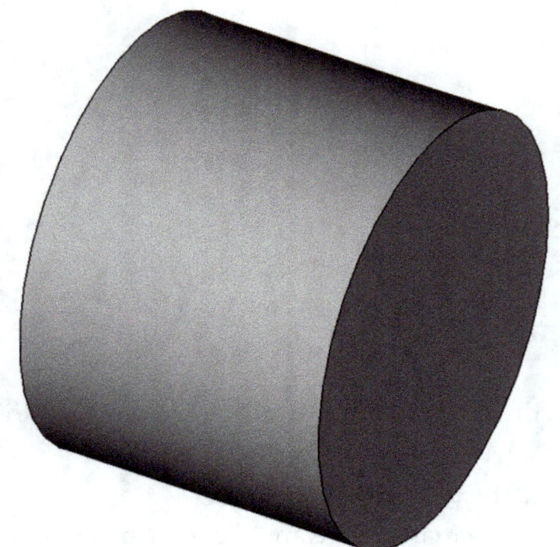

Creating the Second feature

1. Click the **Create sketch** icon on the **Part Design Helper** toolbar, and then select the YZ Plane.
2. Click **OK** on the **Combo View** panel.
3. Create a sketch using the **Polyline** and **Fillet** tools, as shown.

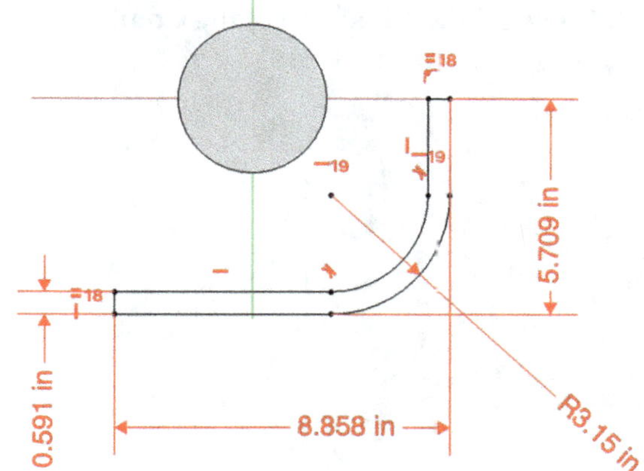

4. Click the **External Geometry** icon on the **Sketcher geometries** toolbar.
5. Select the circular edge of the model, as shown.

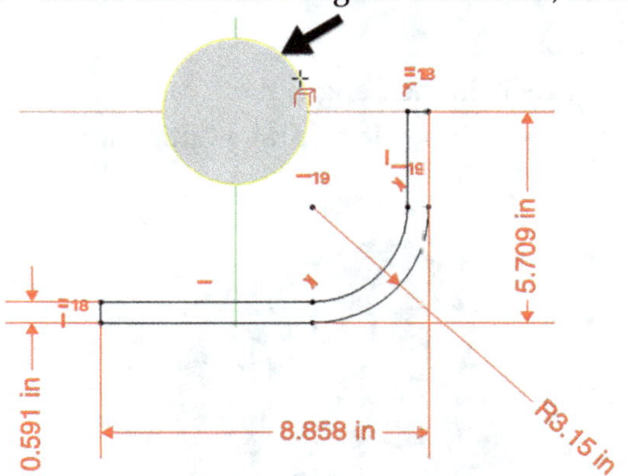

6. On the **Sketcher constrain** toolbar, click the **Tangent Constraint** icon.
7. Select the circular edge and the right vertical line.

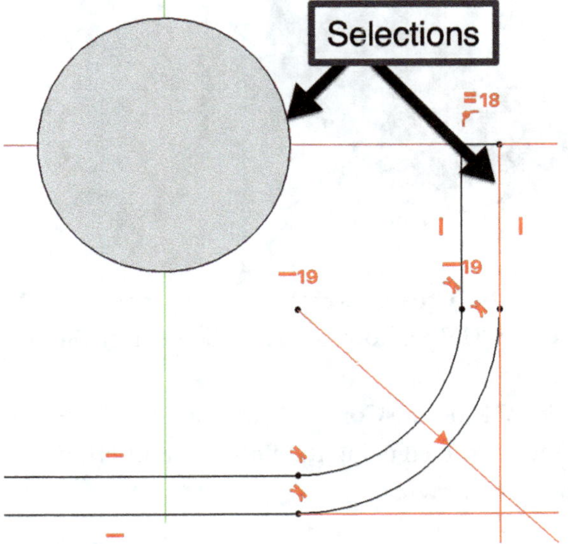

8. Click **Close** on the **Tasks** tab of the **Combo View** panel.

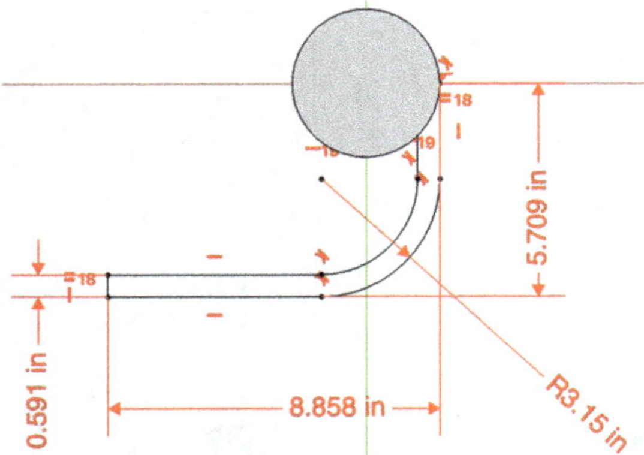

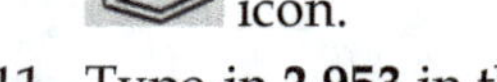

9. Click **Model** tab on the **Combo View** panel.
10. On the **Part Design Modelling** toolbar, click **Pad** icon.
11. Type-in **2.953** in the **Length** box.
12. Check the **Symmetric to plane** option and click **OK**.

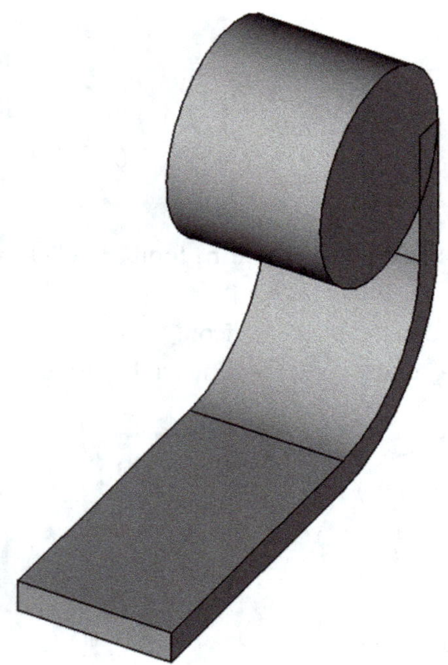

13. Click the **Create sketch** icon on the **Part Design Helper** toolbar, and then select the YZ Plane.
14. Click **OK** on the **Combo View** panel.
15. Create a sketch using the **Polyline** and **Fillet** tools, as shown.

16. Click the **External Geometry** icon on the **Sketcher geometries** toolbar.
17. Select the circular, horizontal and vertical edges of the model, as shown.

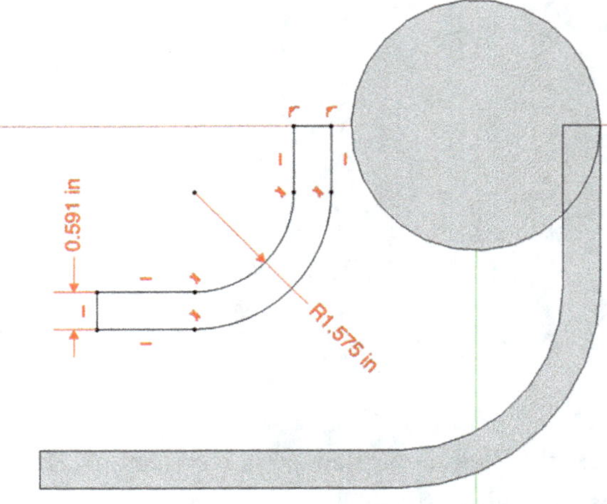

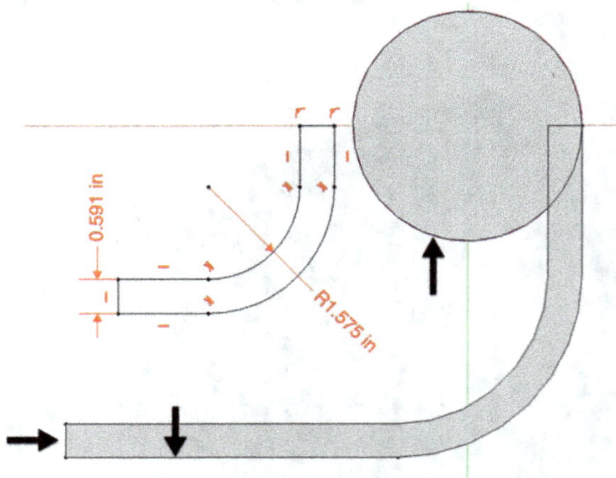

18. On the **Sketcher constrain** toolbar, click the **Tangent Constraint** icon.
19. Select the circular edge and the left vertical line.

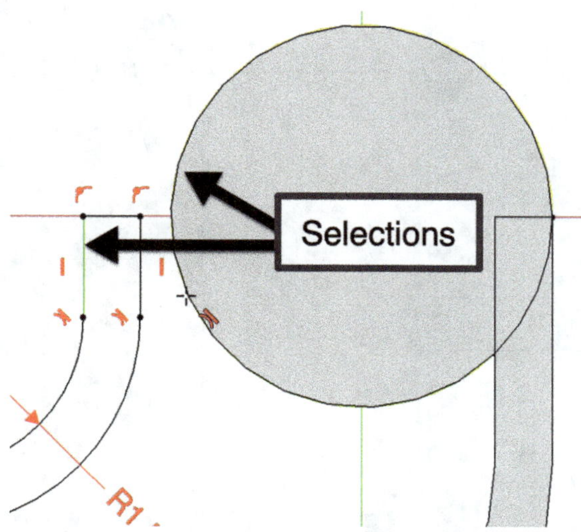

20. On the **Sketcher constrain** toolbar, click the **Vertical Constraint** icon.
21. Select the lower end point of the vertical line, as shown.
22. Select anyone of the vertices of the vertical edge, as shown.

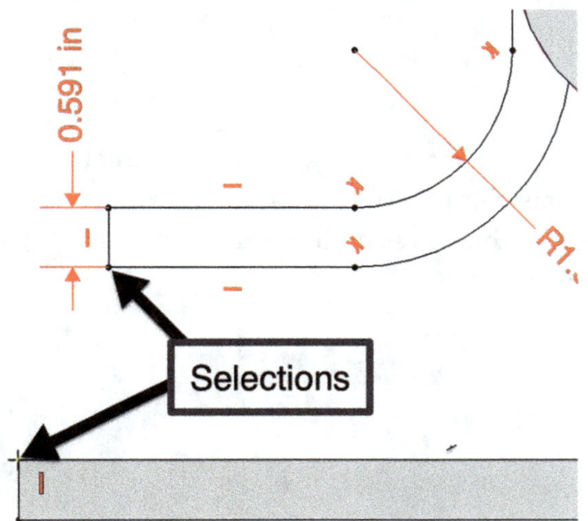

23. Click **Sketcher constraints** toolbar > **Constrain vertical distance** (or) click **Sketch >**
Sketcher constraints > Constrain vertical distance on the menu bar.
24. Select the top endpoint of the vertical line, as shown
25. Select the left endpoint of the horizontal edge, as shown.

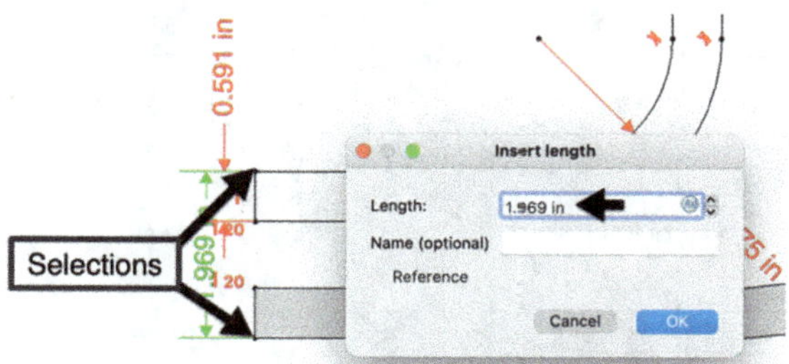

26. Type **1.969** in the **Length** box and click **OK**.
27. Click **Close** on the **Combo View** panel.
28. On the **Part Design Modeling** toolbar, click the **Pad** icon.
29. Type **1.181** in the **Length** box of the **Pad Parameters** dialog.
30. Check the **Symmetric to plane** option and click **OK**.

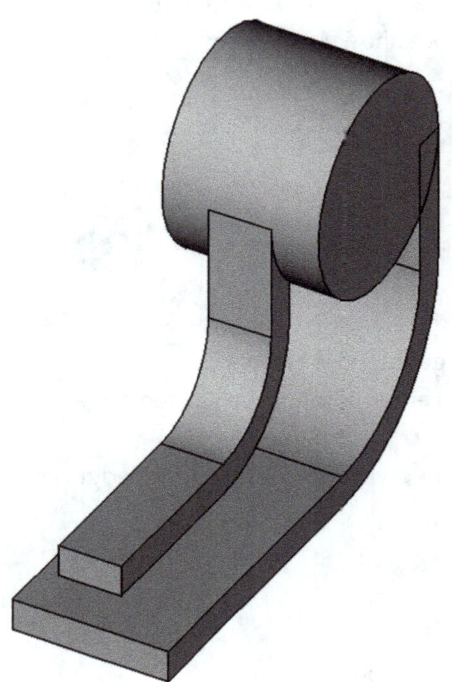

31. Click the **Create sketch** icon on the **Part Design Helper** toolbar, and then select the YZ Plane.
32. Click **OK** on the **Combo View** panel.
33. Click the **External Geometry** icon on the **Sketcher geometries** toolbar.
34. Select the edges of the model, as shown.

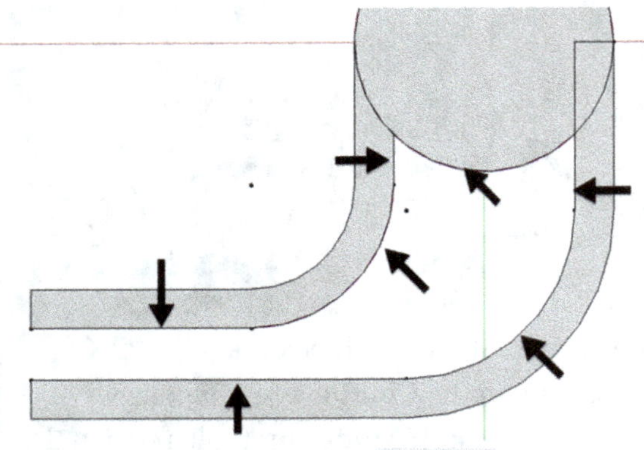

35. Click the **View section** icon on the **Part Design Helper** toolbar.

36. Click the **Create Polyline** icon on the Sketcher geometries toolbar.

37. Select the vertices of the external geometry in the sequence shown in figure.

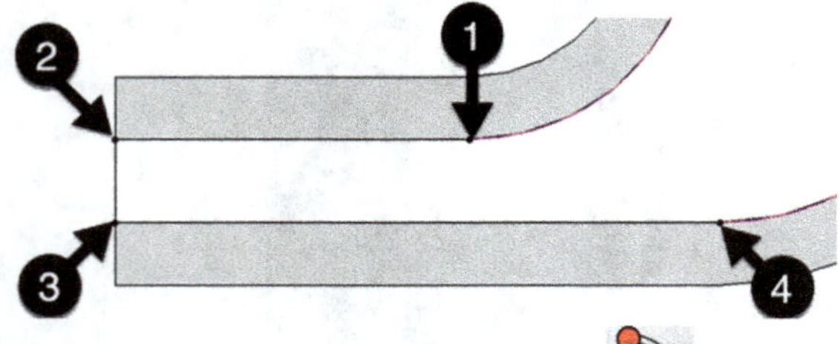

38. Click the **Create arc by center** icon on the **Sketcher geometries** toolbar.

39. Select the center point of the curved edge, as shown.

40. Select the two vertices of the curved edge, as shown.

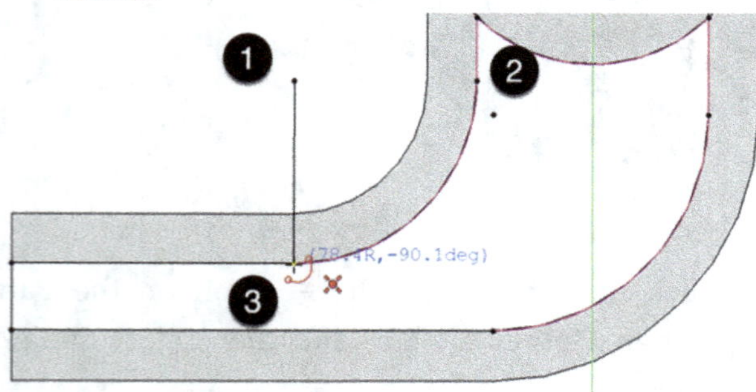

41. Likewise, create two more arcs by specifying the center, start, and end points, as shown.

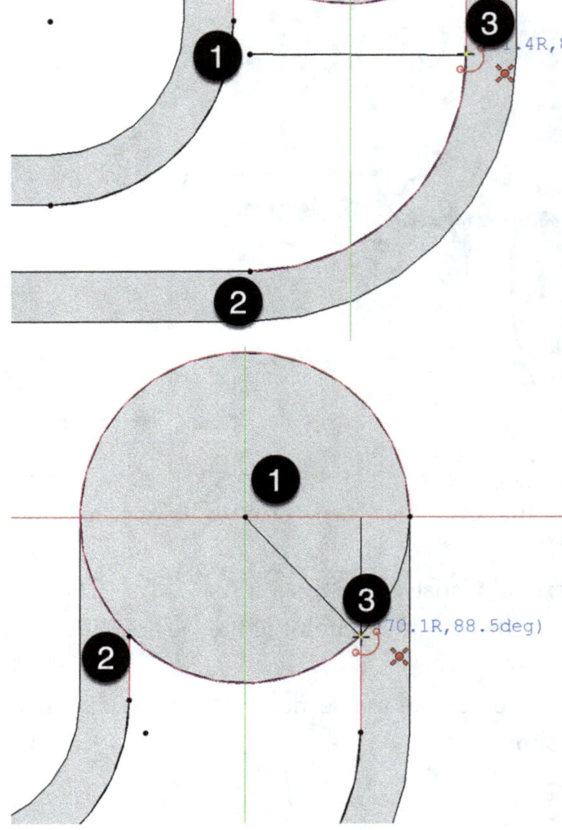

42. Click the **Create line** icon on the **Sketcher geometries** toolbar.

43. Select the vertices of the vertical edges, as shown.

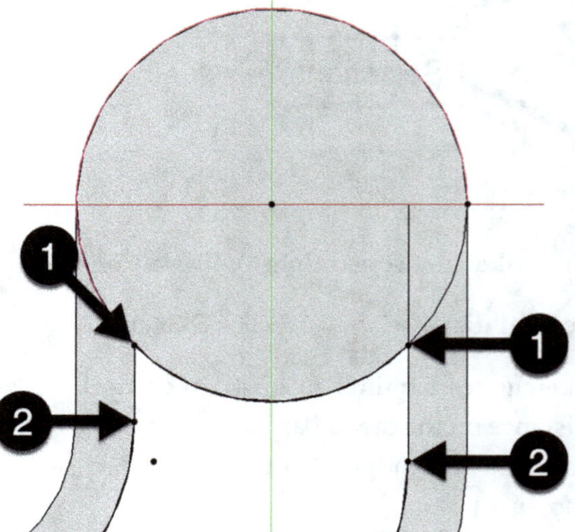

44. Click **Close** on the **Combo View** panel.

45. On the **Part Design Modeling** toolbar, click the **Pad** icon.

46. Type **0.787** in the **Length** box of the **Pad Parameters** dialog.

47. Check the **Symmetric to plane** option and click **OK**.

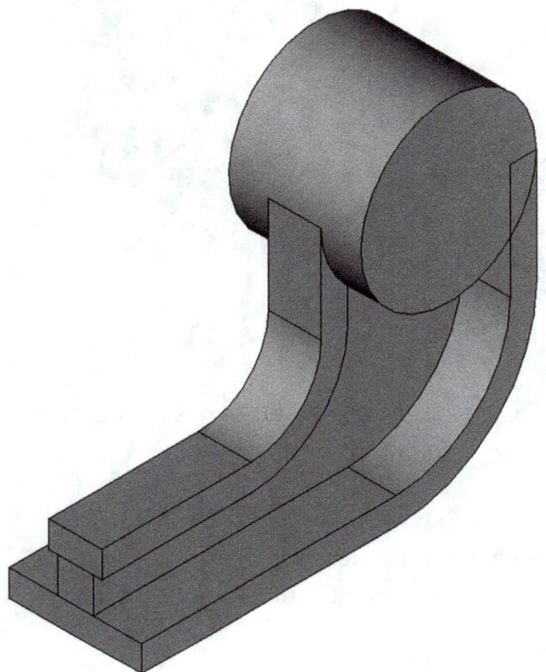

48. Press and hold the right and middle mouse button and drag the pointer upward.

49. Select the bottom flat face.

53. Click the **Create arc by three points** icon on the **Sketcher geometries** toolbar.

54. Select the two vertices of the edge, as shown.

55. Move the pointer towards left and click.

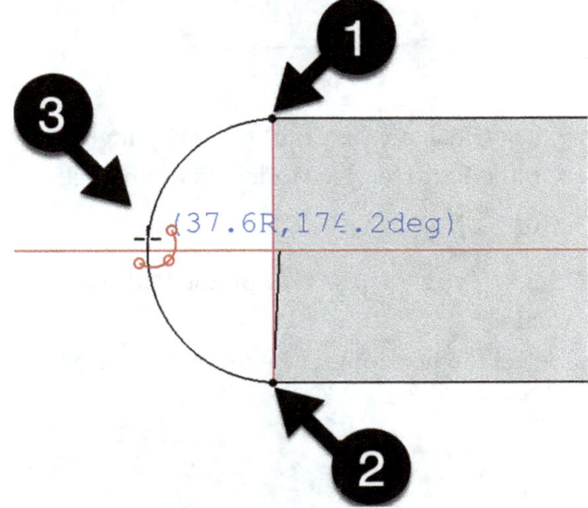

56. Click the **Create line** icon on the **Sketcher geometries** toolbar.

57. Select the vertices of the vertical edge, as shown.

50. Click **Create new Sketch** icon on the **Part Design Helper toolbar.**

51. Click the **External Geometry** icon on the **Sketcher geometries** toolbar.

52. Select the edge of the model, as shown.

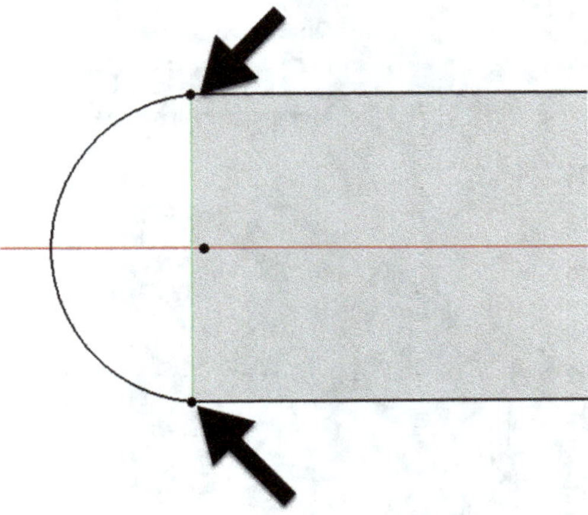

58. On the **Sketcher constrain** toolbar, click the **Constrain point onto object** icon.

59. Select the centerpoint of the arc and the vertical line, as shown.

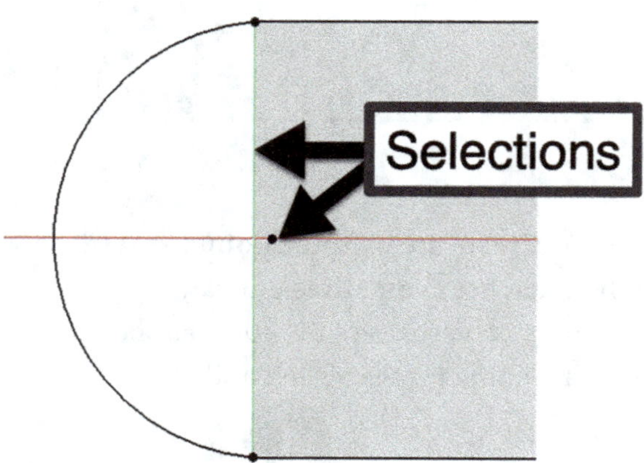

60. Click **Close** on the **Combo View** panel.
61. On the **Part Design Modeling** toolbar, click the **Pad** icon.
62. Select **Type > Up to face** on the Pad parameters dialog.
63. Select the horizontal face of the model, as shown.

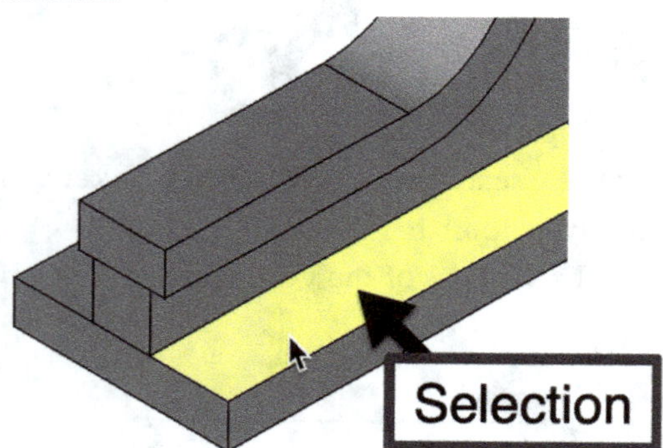

64. Click **OK**.

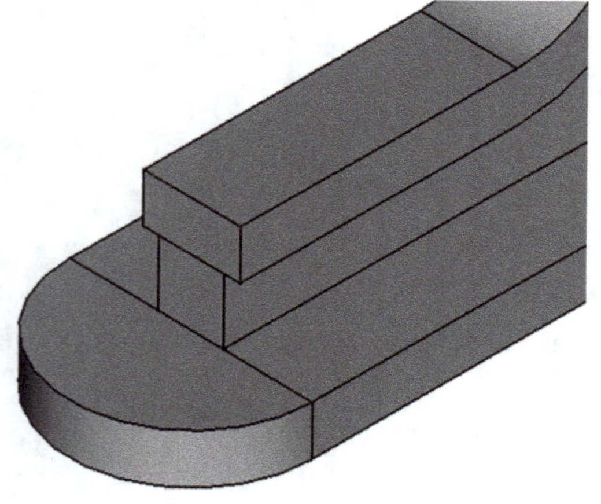

Creating the third feature

1. Select the horizontal face of the model, as shown.

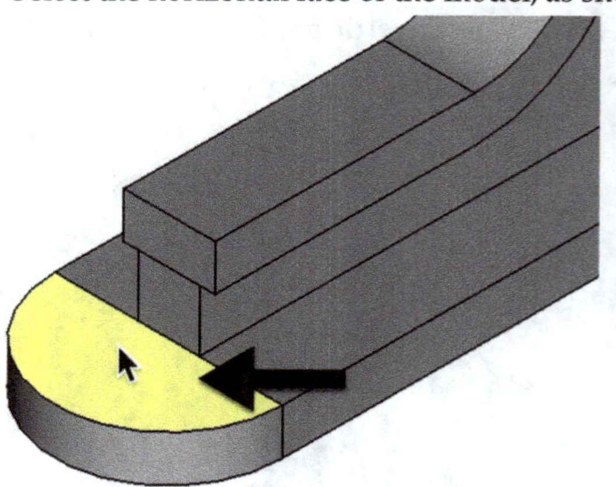

2. Click **Create new Sketch** icon on the **Part Design Helper toolbar**.

3. Click the **External Geometry** icon on the **Sketcher geometries** toolbar.
4. Select the circular edge of the model, **as shown**.

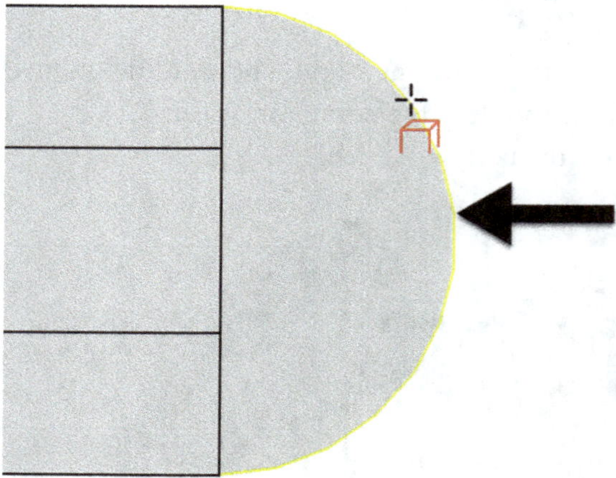

5. Click the **Create circle** icon on the **Sketcher geometry** toolbar.
6. Click on the centerpoint of the curved edge.
7. Move the pointer outward and click to create the circle.

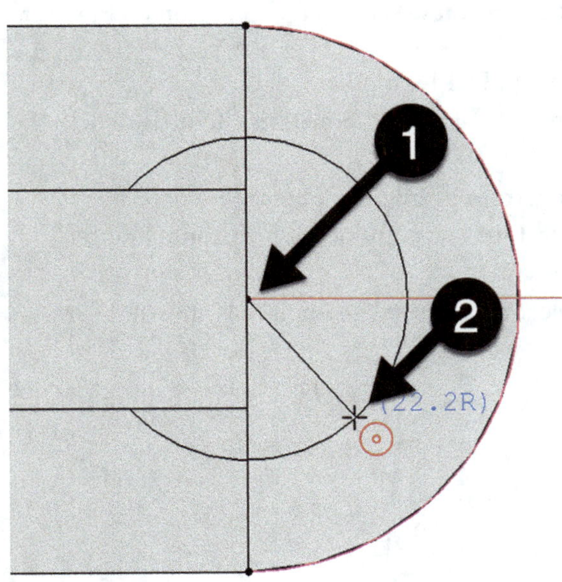

8. On the **Sketcher constraints** toolbar, click the **Constrain radius** drop-down and select **Constrain diameter** .

9. Select the circle and type-in **2.165** in the **Diameter** box on the **Change Diameter** dialog.

10. Click **OK**.

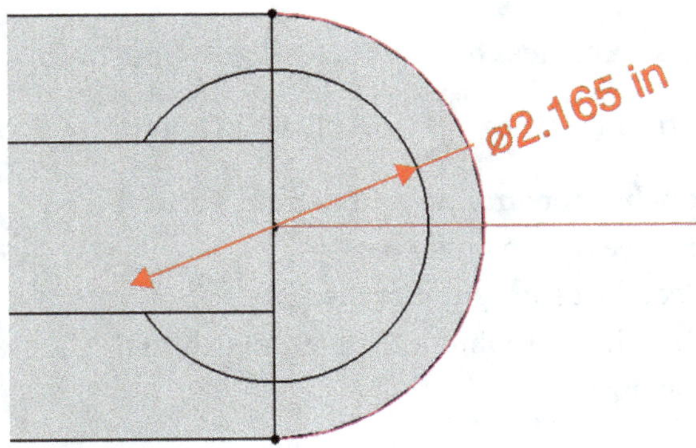

11. Click **Close** on the **Combo View** panel.

12. On the **Part Design Modeling** toolbar, click the **Pad** icon.

13. Type **1.969** in the **Length** box of the **Pad Parameters** dialog.

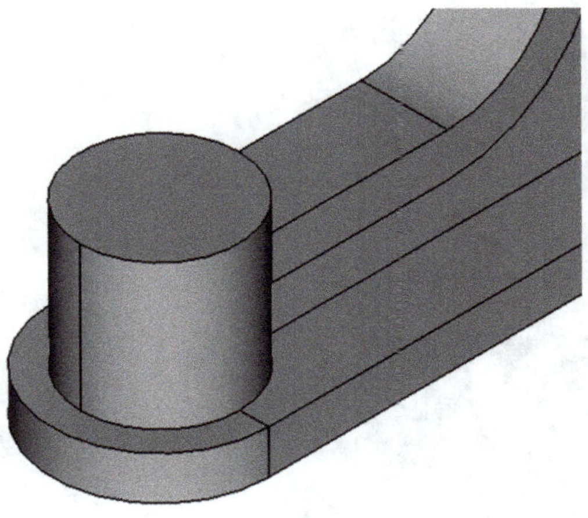

Creating the fourth feature

1. Click the **Create sketch** icon on the **Part Design Helper** toolbar, and then select the XZ Plane.

2. Click **OK** to start the sketch.

3. Create the sketch, as shown.

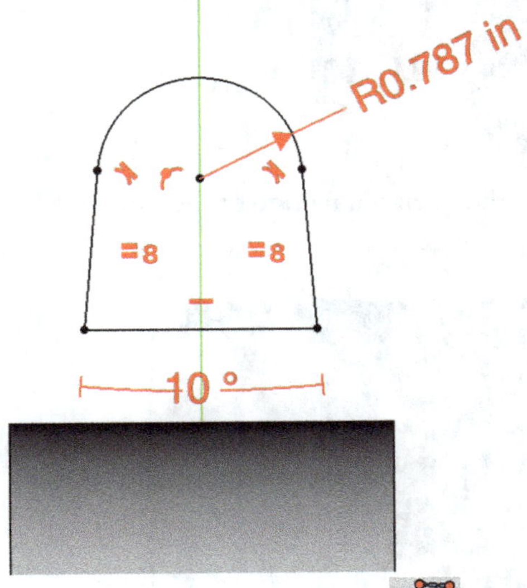

4. Click the **External Geometry** icon on the **Sketcher geometries** toolbar.

5. Select the bottom horizontal edge of the model, as shown.

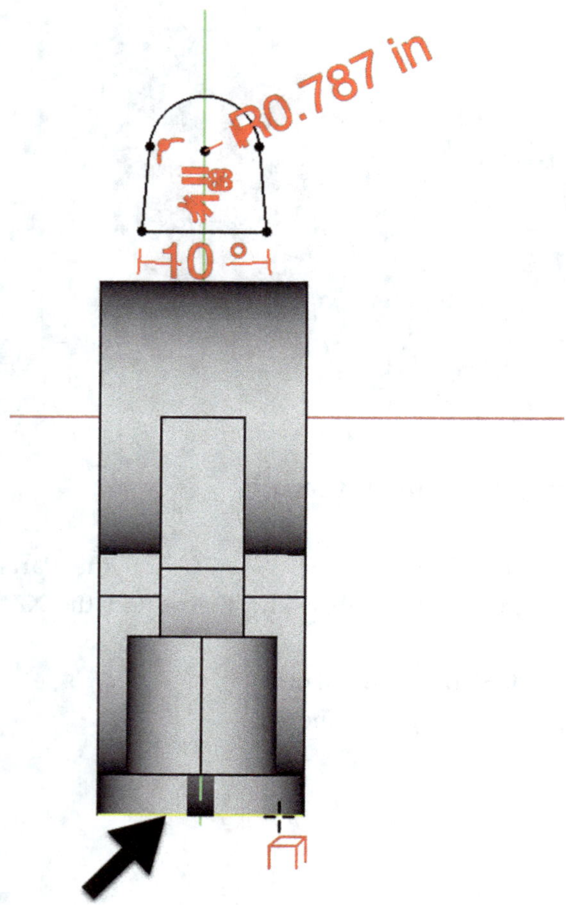

6. Select the horizontal edge of the model, as shown.

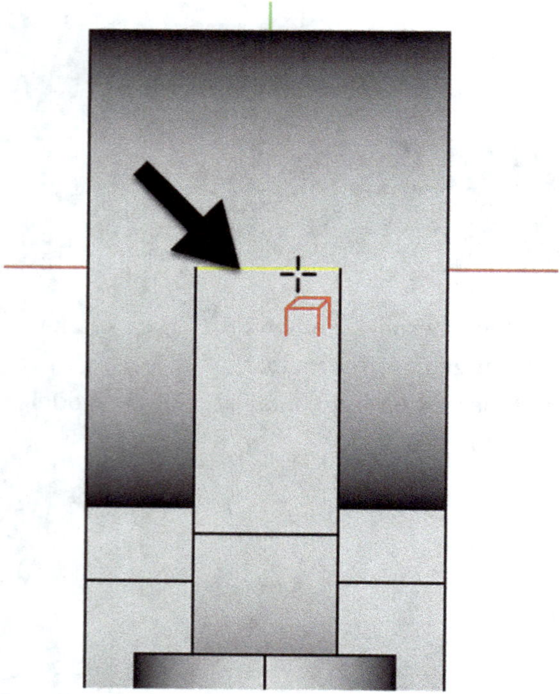

7. Click the **View section**  icon on the **Part Design Helper** toolbar.

8. On the **Sketcher constrain** toolbar, click the **Constrain point onto object** icon.

9. Select the endpoint of the horizontal line, as shown.

10. Select the external geometry, as shown.

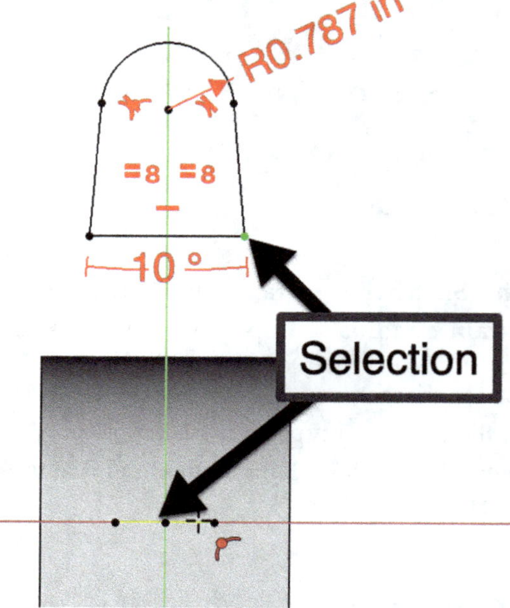

11. Click **Sketcher constraints** toolbar > **Constrain vertical distance** (or) click **Sketch >
Sketcher constraints > Constrain vertical distance** on the menu bar.

12. Select the centerpoint of the arc.

13. Select the endpoint of the bottom external geometry.

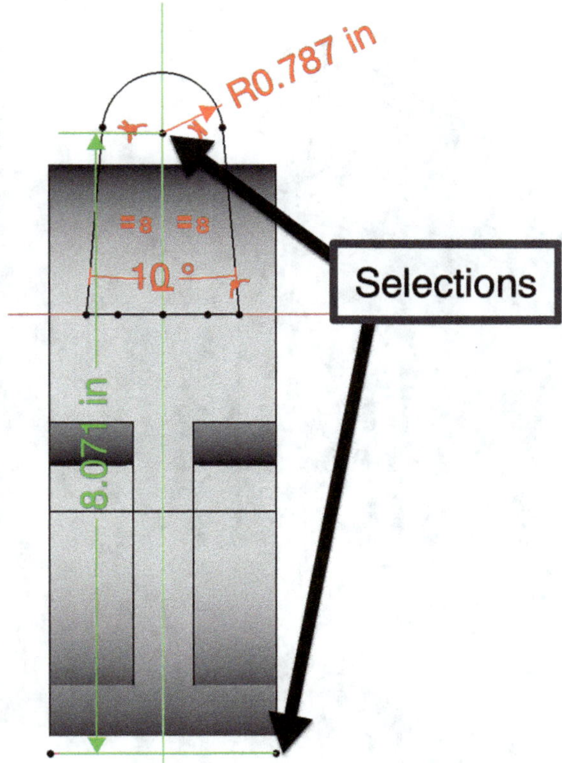

14. Enter **8.071** in the **Length** box of the **Insert Length** dialog and click **OK**.
15. Click **Close** on the **Combo View** panel.
16. On the **Part Design Modeling** toolbar, click the **Pad** icon.
17. Type **2.756** in the **Length** box of the **Pad Parameters** dialog.
18. Check the **Symmetric to plane** option and click **OK**.

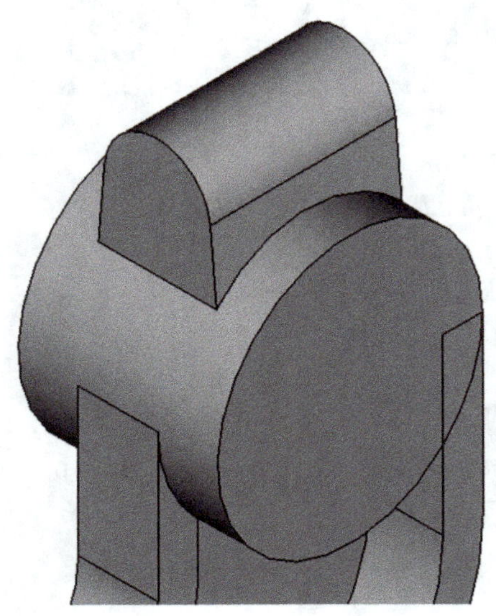

Creating Holes

1. Select the horizontal face of the model, as shown.

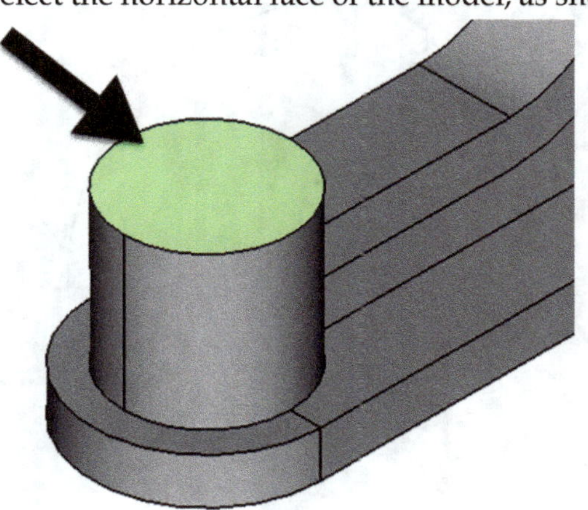

2. Click **Create new Sketch** icon on the **Part Design Helper toolbar**.

3. Click the **External Geometry** icon on the **Sketcher geometries** toolbar.

4. Select the circular edge of the model, as shown.

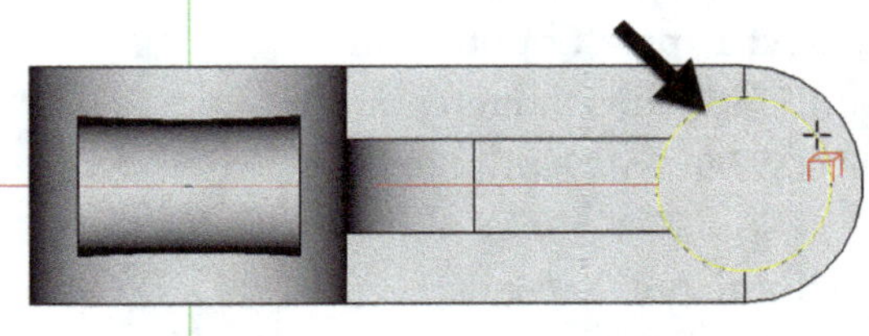

5. Click the **Create circle** icon on the **Sketcher geometry** toolbar.
6. Click on the centerpoint of the curved edge.
7. Move the pointer outward and click to create the circle.

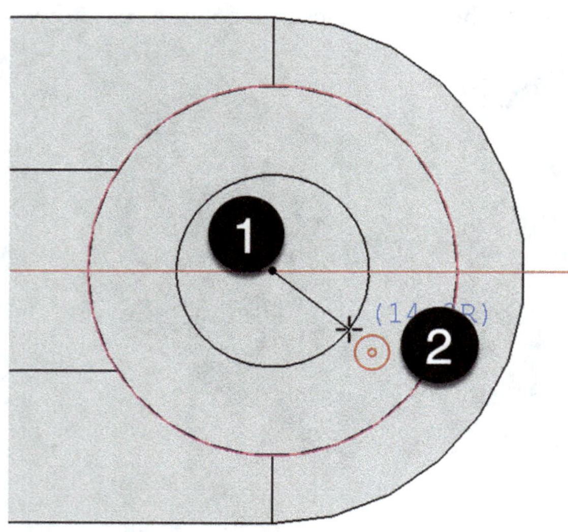

8. Click **Close** on the **Combo View** panel.
9. Click the **Hole** icon on the **Part Design Modeling** toolbar.
10. Type **1.181** in the **Diameter** box.
11. Select **Depth > Through All**.
12. On the **Hole Parameters** section, under **Hole cut**, select **Type > Counterbore**.
13. Type **1.575** in the **Diameter** box.
14. Type **0.197** in the **Depth** box.
15. Click **OK** on the **Combo View** panel; the counterbore hole is created.

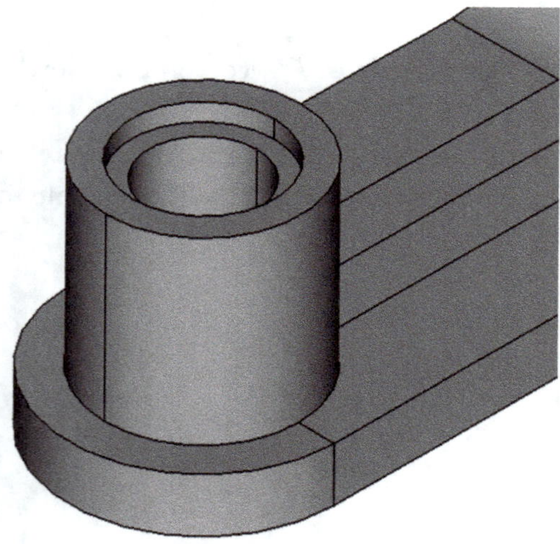

16. Likewise, create a simple and counterbored hole, as shown.

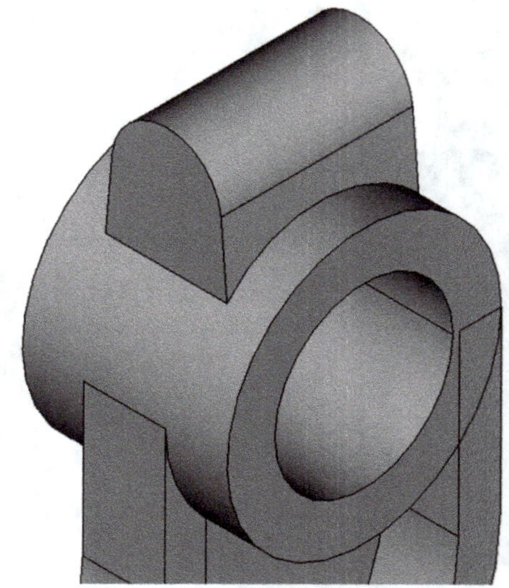

Hole diameter: 2.559 in
Depth: Through all

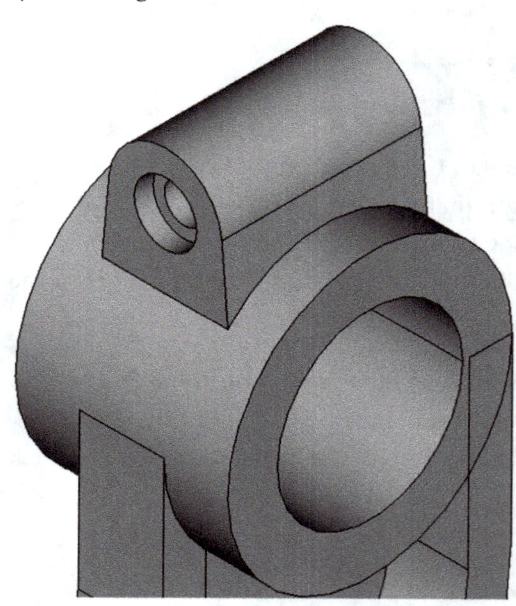

Diameter: 0.551 in
Depth: Through all
Type: Counterbore
Counterbore Diameter: 0.866 in
Depth: 0.260 in

Creating the Pocket feature

1. Select the flat face of the model, as shown.

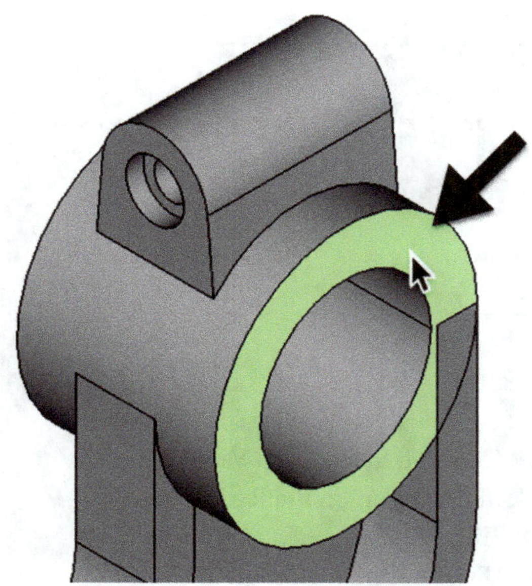

2. Click **Create new Sketch** icon on the **Part Design Helper toolbar**.

3. Create a rectangle and dimensions to it, as shown.

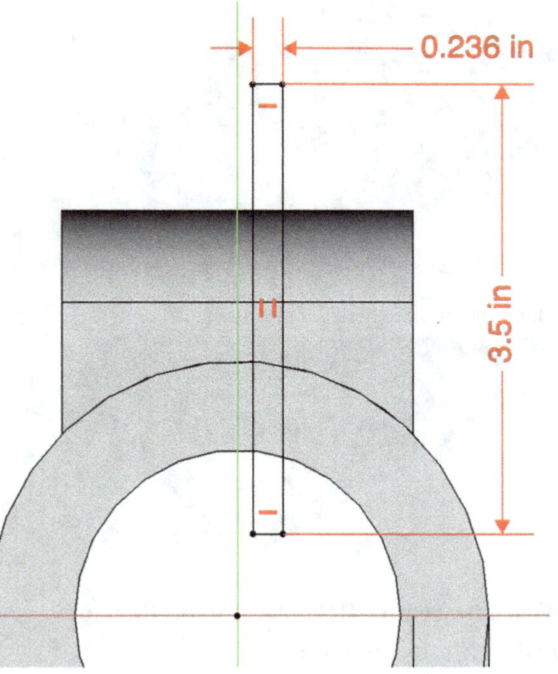

4. On the **Sketcher constrain** toolbar, click the **Constrain symmetrical** icon.

5. Select the endpoints of the horizontal line, as shown.

6. Select the sketch origin.

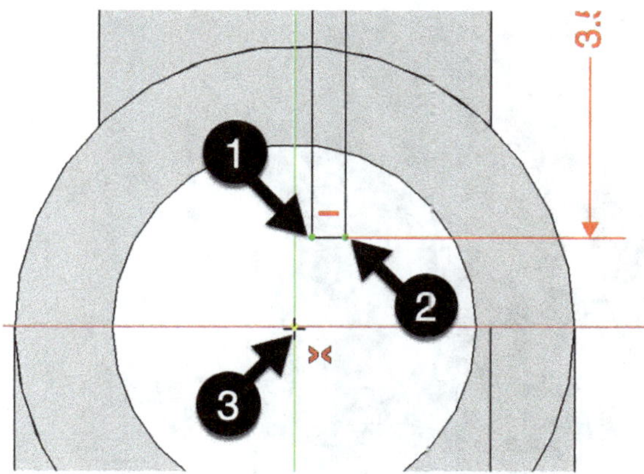

7. Click **Close** on the **Combo View** panel.

8. On the **Part Design Modeling** toolbar, click the **Pocket** icon.

9. Select **Type > Through all**, and then click **OK**.

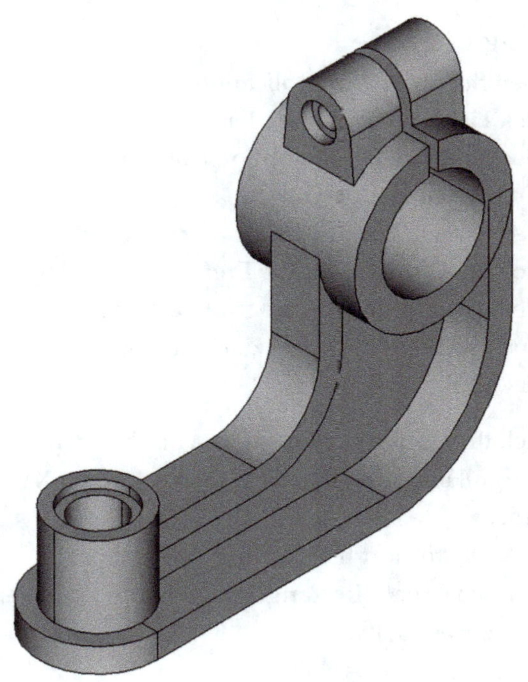

TUTORIAL 11

In this tutorial, you create the model shown in the figure:

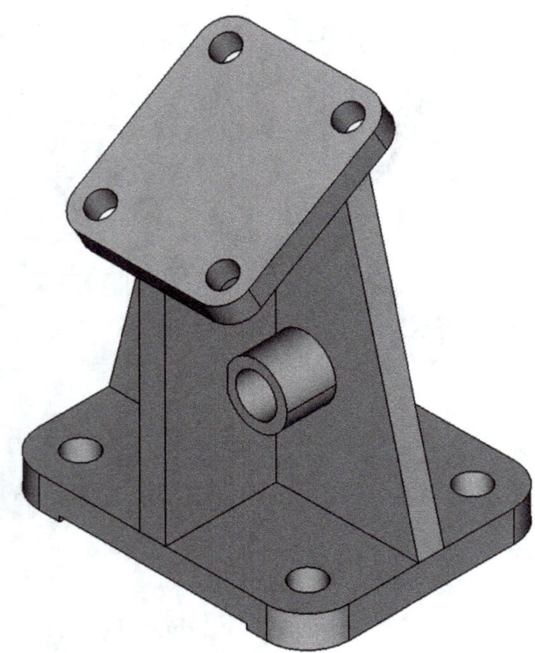

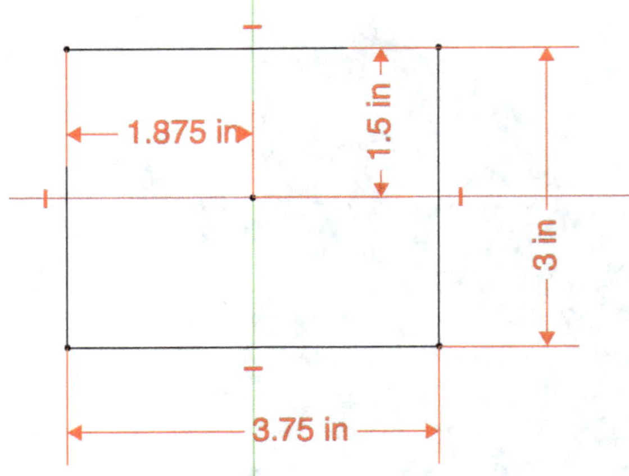

Creating the Base

1. Open the FreeCAD application.
2. Click **File > New** on the Menu bar.
3. Select the **Part Design** option from the **Workbenches** drop-down.
4. On the Menu bar, click **Edit > Preferences**.
5. Click the **Units** tab on the **Preferences** dialog.
6. Select **User system > Imperial decimal**.
7. Type **3** in the **Number of decimals** box.
8. Click **OK**.
9. Click the **Create sketch** icon on the **Part Design Helper** toolbar, and then select the XY Plane.
10. Click **OK** to start the sketch.
11. Click the **Create Rectangle** icon on the **Sketcher geometries** toolbar.
12. Create a sketch, as shown.

13. Click **Close** on the **Combo View** panel.
14. Click the **Pad** icon on the **Part Design Modelling** toolbar.
15. Select **Type > Dimension** on the **Pad parameters** section.
16. Type-in **0.38** in in the **Length** box.
17. Click **OK** on the **Combo View** panel.

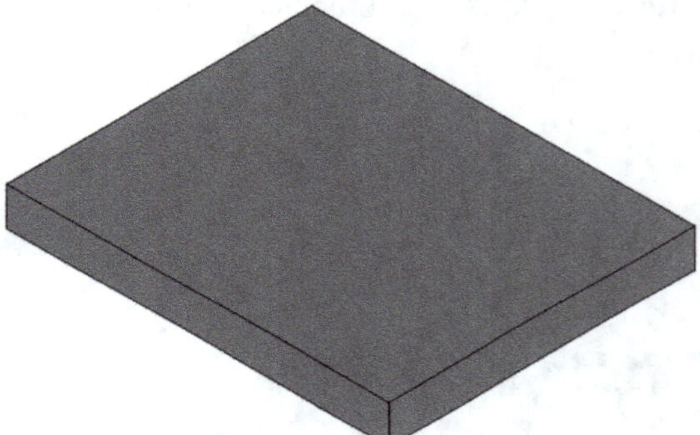

18. Select the front right edge, as shown.

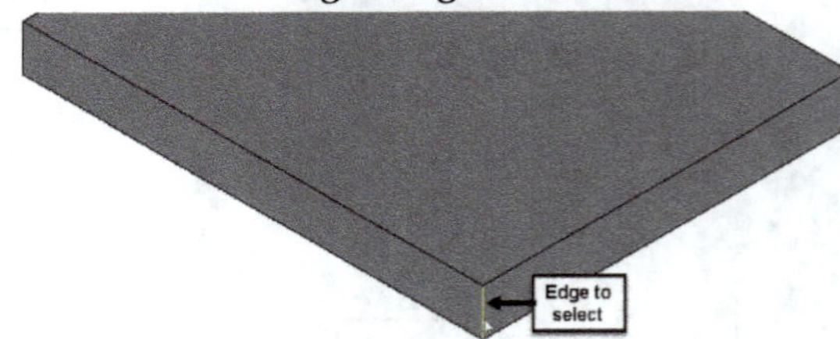

19. Click the **Create fillet** icon on the **Part Design Modeling** toolbar.
20. Click the **Add** button on the **Fillet parameters** section.
21. Select the front left edge.
22. Likewise, select the back vertical edges of the pad features.
23. Type-in **0.50** in in the **Radius** box.
24. Click **OK** on the **Combo View** panel.

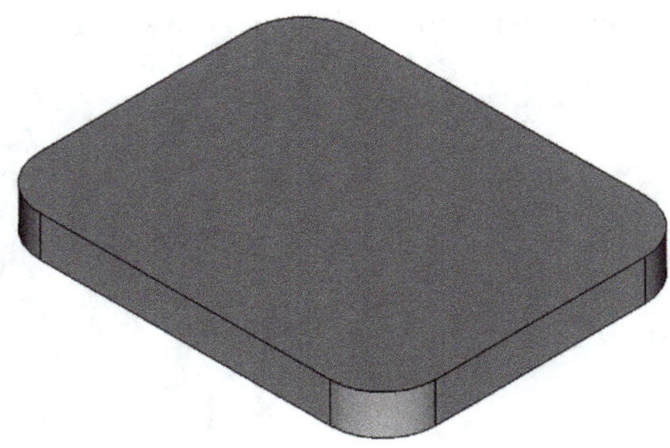

25. Click on the top face of the **Pad** feature and click **Create Sketch** on the **Part Design Helper** **toolbar**.

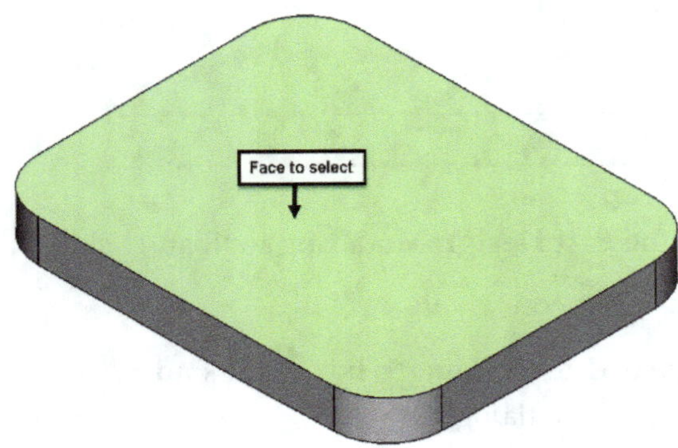

26. Click the **External geometry** icon on the **Sketcher geometries** toolbar.
27. Select the top right arc of the Pad feature, as shown.
28. Likewise, select the remaining arcs of the pad feature, as shown.

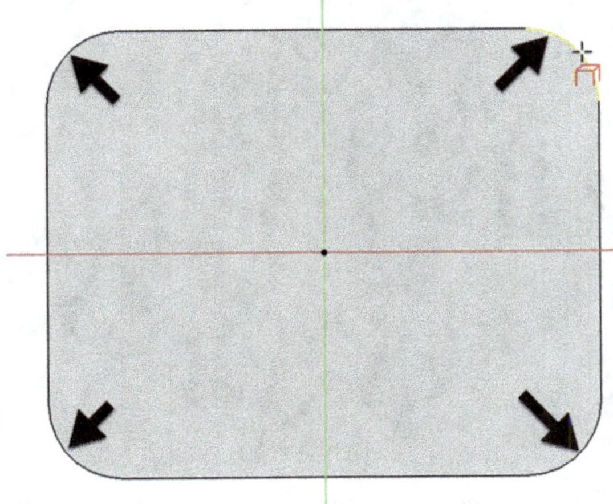

29. Press **Esc** to deactivate the tool.
30. On the **Sketcher geometries** toolbar, click the **Create circle** icon.

31. Select the centerpoint of the circular edge.
32. Move the pointer outward and click.

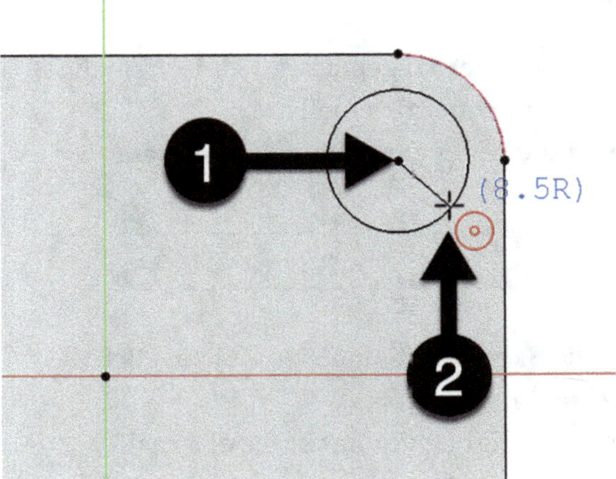

33. Likewise, create three more circles, as shown.

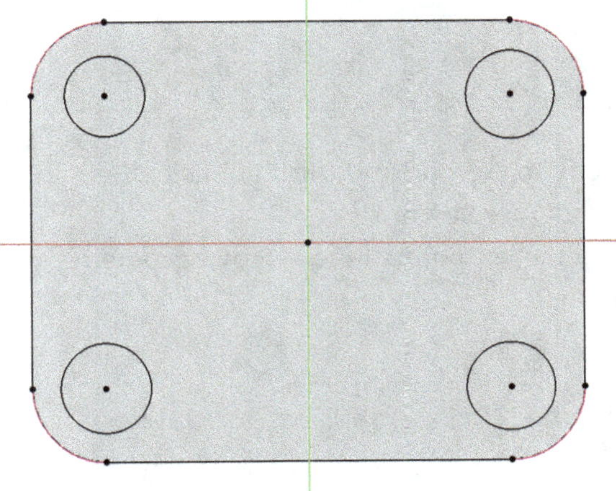

34. Click **Close** on the **Combo View** panel.
35. On the **Part Design Modelling** toolbar, click the **Hole** icon.
36. Select **Depth > Through all**.
37. Type **0.38** in the **Diameter** box.
38. Click **OK** on the **Combo View** panel.

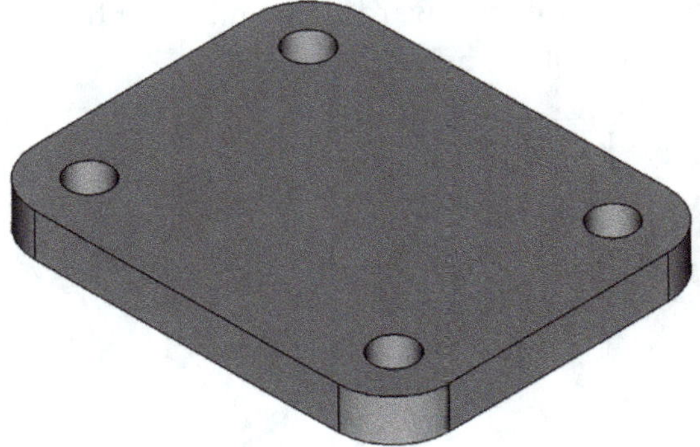

Creating the Rib

1. On the **Part Design Helper toolbar**, click the

Create Sketch icon.

2. Select **XZ-Plane** on the **Select feature** and click **OK**.

3. Click the **External geometry** icon on the **Sketcher geometries** toolbar.

4. Select the edges of the model, as shown.

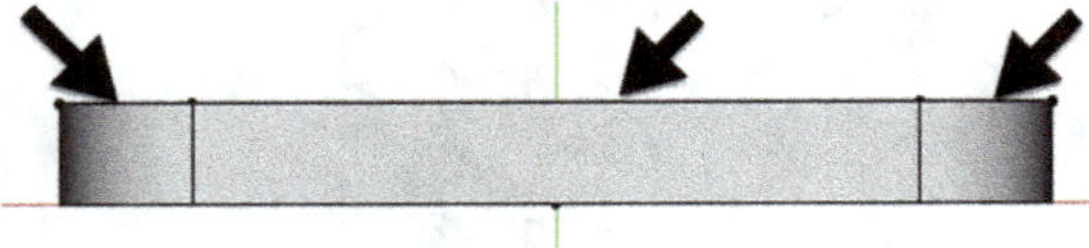

5. On the **Sketcher geometries** toolbar, click the **Create Polyline** icon.

6. Select the right endpoint of the external geometry, as shown.

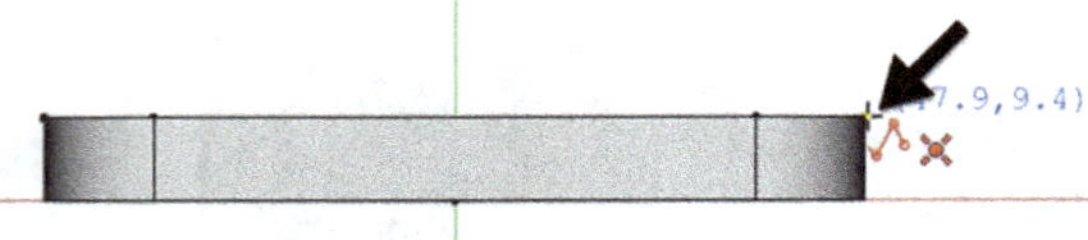

7. Specify the second and third points of the polyline, as shown.

8. Select the left point of the external geometry, as shown.

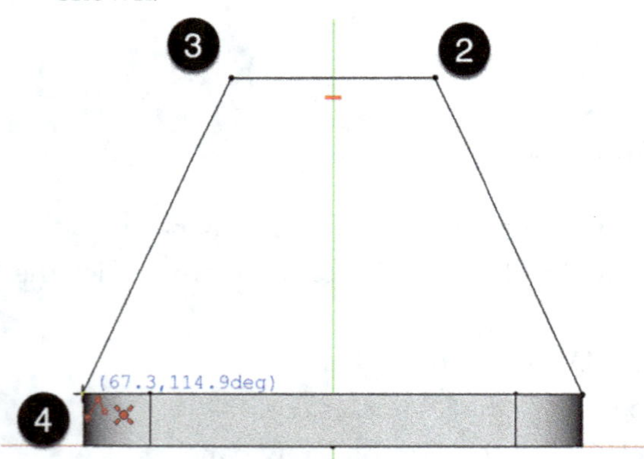

9. Move the pointer toward right and select the start point of the polyline.

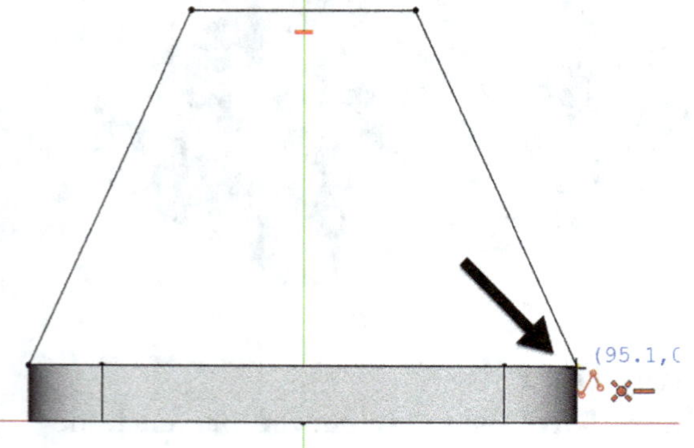

10. Add dimensional constraints to the sketch, and then click **Leave Sketch**.

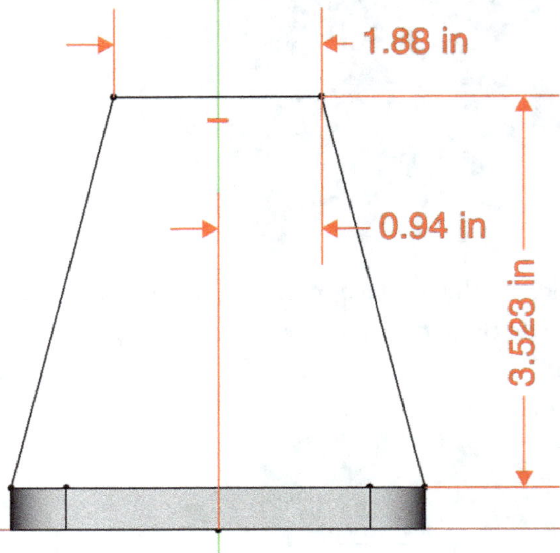

11. On the **Part Design Modeling** toolbar, click the **Pad** icon.

12. Type **0.31** in the **Length** box of the **Pad Parameters** dialog.

13. Check the **Symmetric to plane** option and click **OK**.

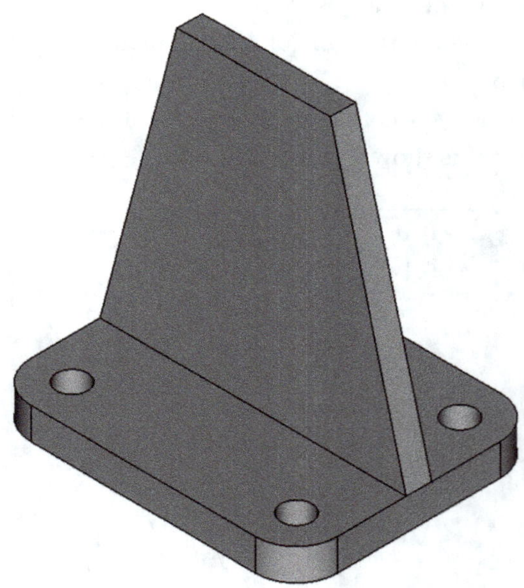

14. Click on the horizontal face of the model, as shown.

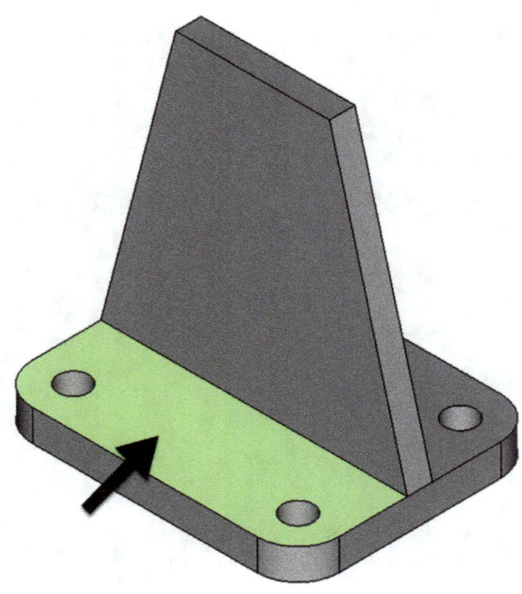

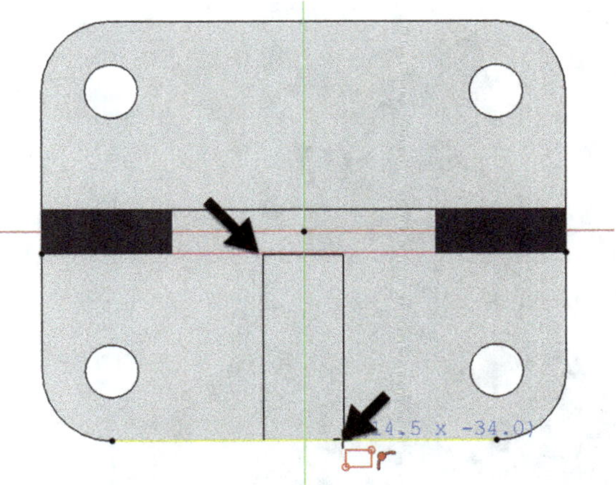

15. Click **Create Sketch** on the **Part Design Helper** toolbar.

16. Click the **External geometry** icon on the **Sketcher geometries** toolbar.

17. Select the horizontal edges of the model, as shown.

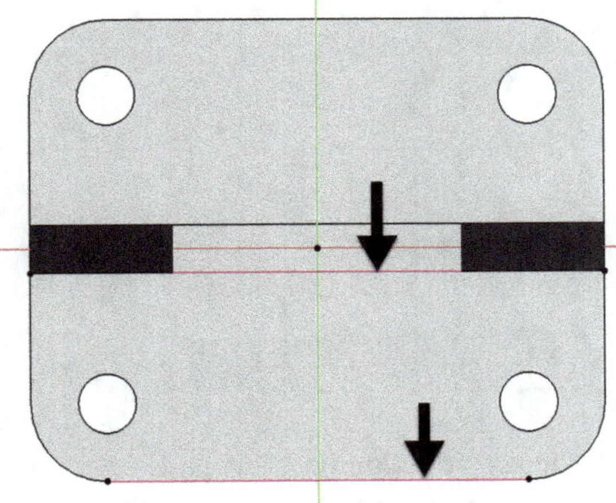

18. Specify the first and second corners of the rectangle of the two external geometries, as shown.

19. Add dimensional constraints to the rectangle, and then click **Leave Sketch** .

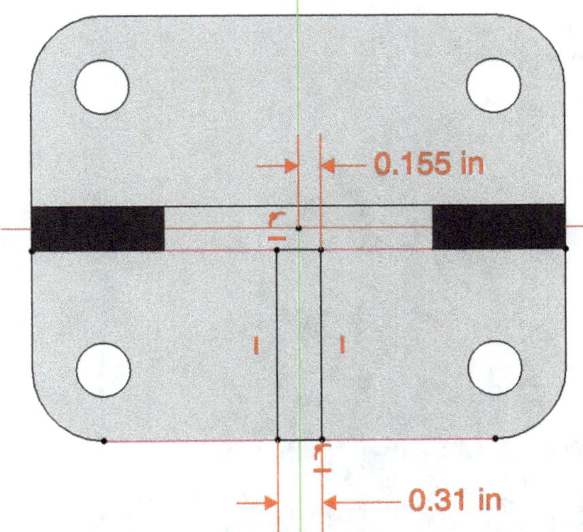

20. On the **Part Design Modeling** toolbar, click the **Pad** icon.

21. Select **Type > Up to face** on the Pad parameters dialog.

22. Select the horizontal face of the model, as shown.

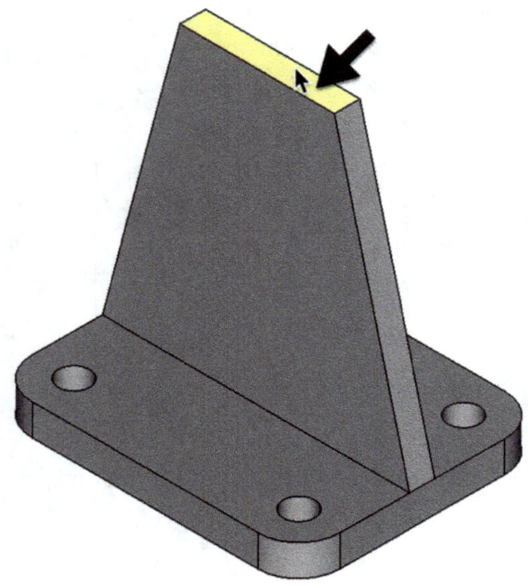

23. Click **OK**.

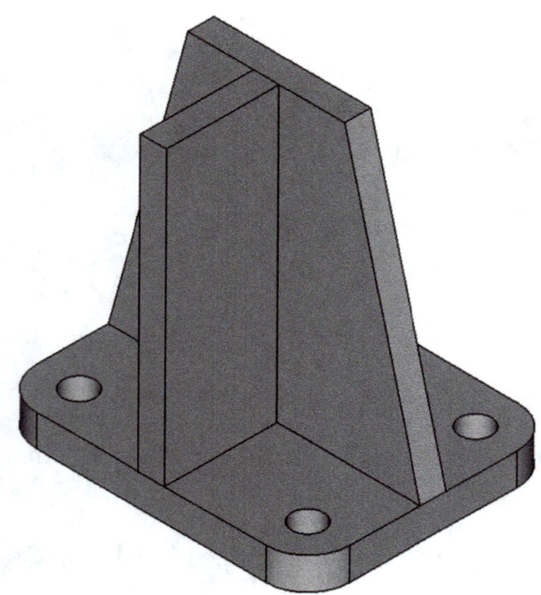

24. On the **Part Design Helper** toolbar, click the **Create Sketch** icon.
25. Select **YZ-Plane** on the **Select feature** and click **OK**.
26. Click the **View section** icon on the **Part Design Helper** toolbar.
27. On the **Sketcher geometries** toolbar, click the **Create Polyline** icon.
28. Create a closed sketch, as shown.

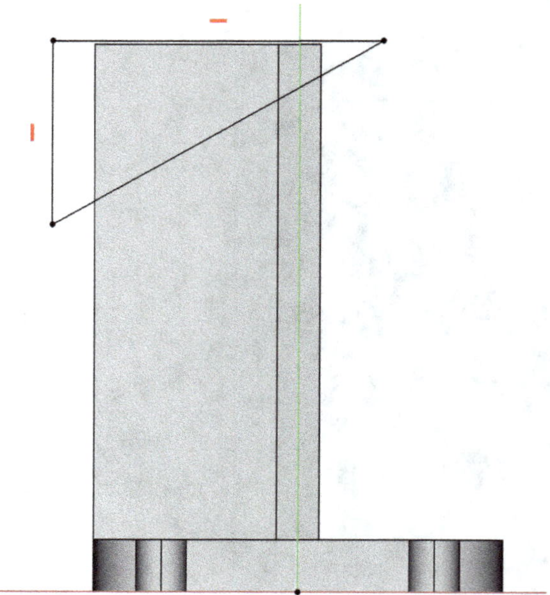

29. Add dimensions to the sketch, as shown.

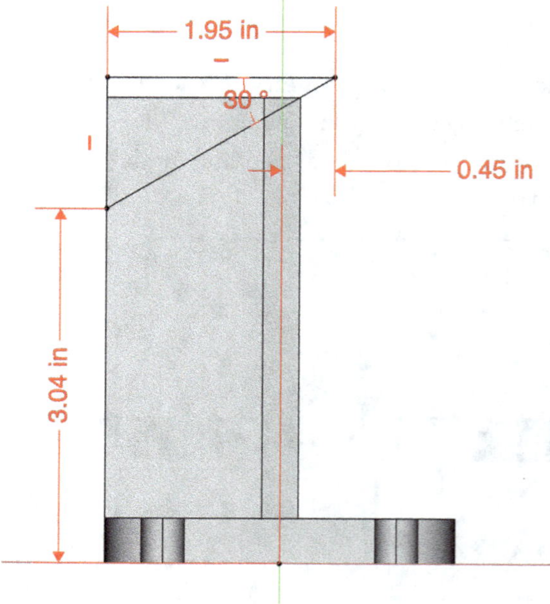

30. Click **Close** on the **Combo View** panel.
31. On the **Part Design Modelling** toolbar, click the **Pocket** icon.
32. Select **Type > Through all** under the **Pad parameters** section.
33. Check the **Symmetric to plane** option.
34. Click **OK** on the **Combo View** panel.

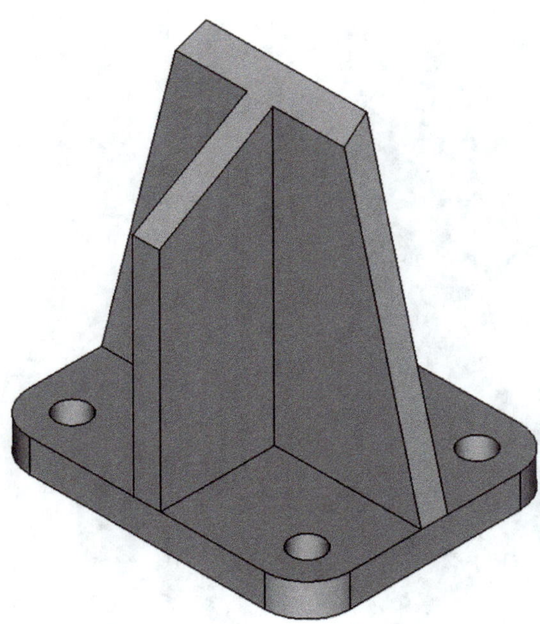

Creating the Third feature

1. Click on the inclined face of the model, as shown.

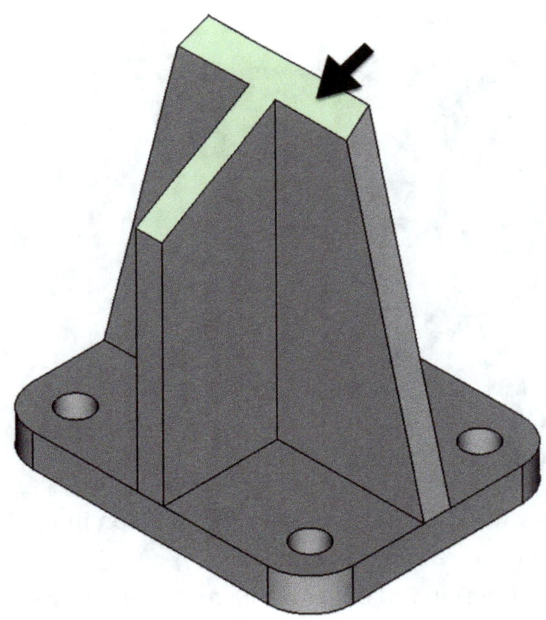

2. On the **Part Design Helper** toolbar, click the **Create Sketch** icon.

3. Create the rectangle and add dimensions to it, as shown.

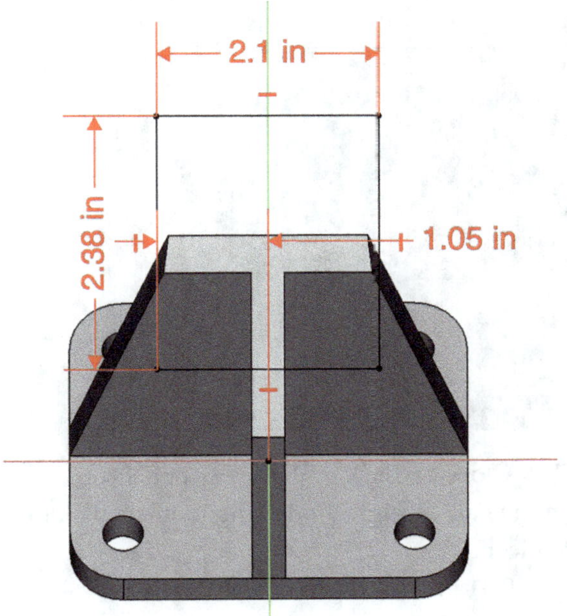

4. Click the **External geometry** icon on the **Sketcher geometries** toolbar.

5. Select the horizontal edges of the model, as shown.

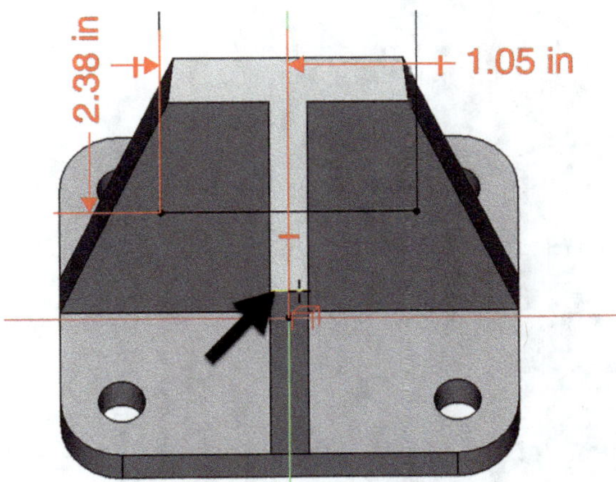

6. On the **Sketcher constrain** toolbar, click the **Constrain point onto object** icon.

7. Select the endpoint of the external geometry and the horizontal line, as shown.

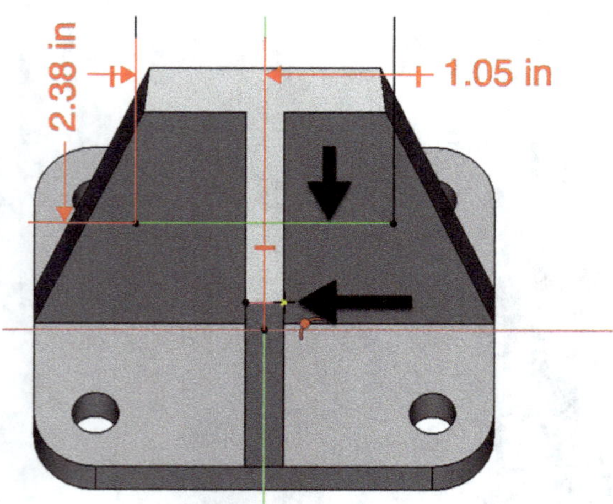

8. Click **Close** on the **Combo View** panel.
9. On the **Part Design Modelling** toolbar, click the **Pad** icon.
10. Type **0.31** in the **Length** box of the **Pad Parameters** dialog.
11. Click **OK**.

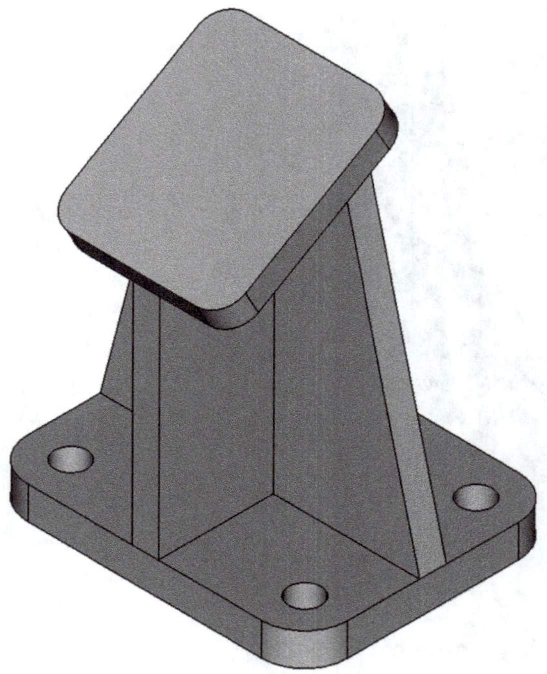

13. Click on the inclined face, as shown.

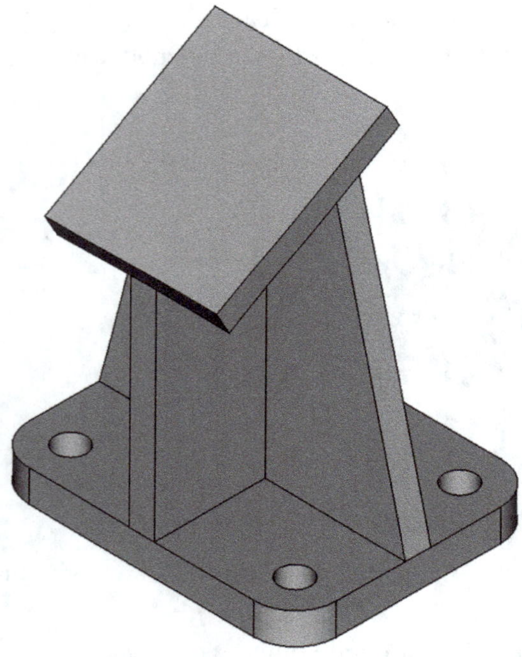

14. On the **Part Design Helper** toolbar, click the **Create Sketch** icon.

15. Click the **External geometry** icon on the **Sketcher geometries** toolbar.

16. Select the curved edges of the model, as shown.

12. Add fillets of 0.31 in radius, as shown.

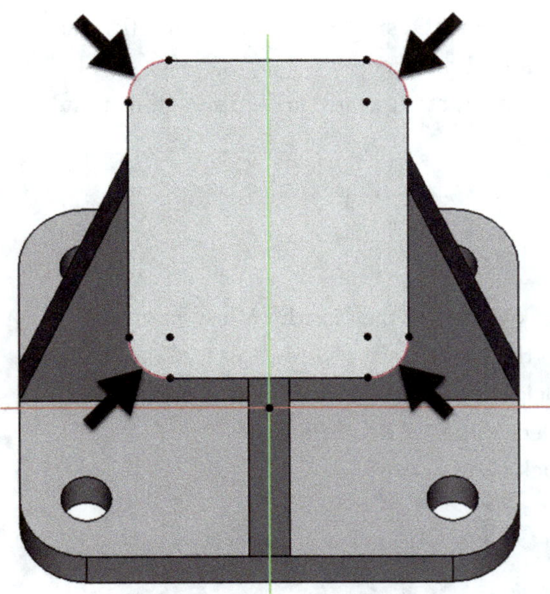

17. Click the **Create Circle** on the **Sketcher geometries** toolbar.
18. Create circles, as shown.

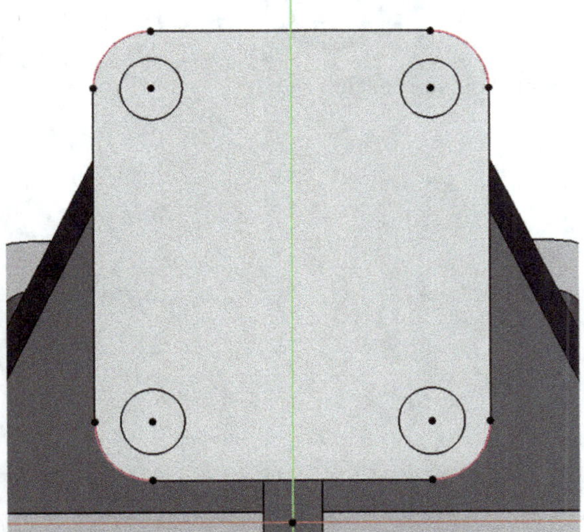

19. Click **Close** on the **Combo View** panel.
20. Click the **Hole** icon on the **Part Design Modeling** toolbar.
21. Type **0.31** in the **Diameter** box.
22. Select **Depth > Dimension**.
23. Type **0.31** in the **Depth** box.
24. Click **OK** on the **Combo View** panel; the holes are created.

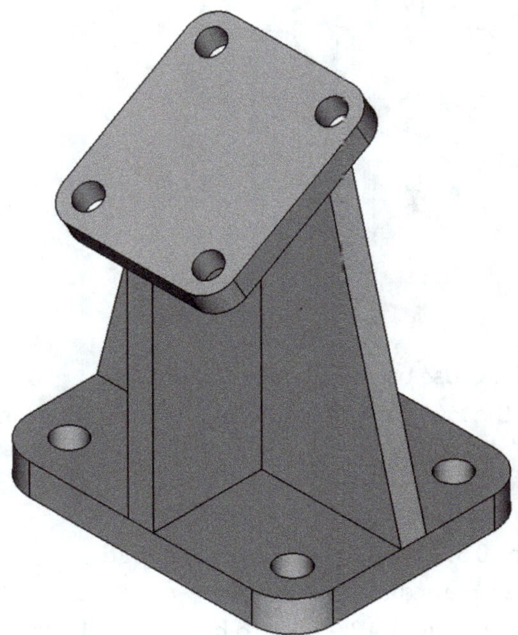

25. Click on the vertical face, as shown.

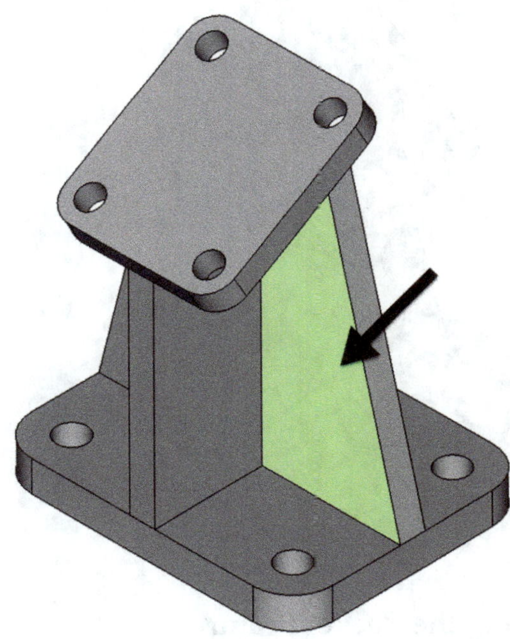

26. On the **Part Design Helper** toolbar, click the **Create Sketch** icon.
27. Create two circles and add dimensions to it, as shown.

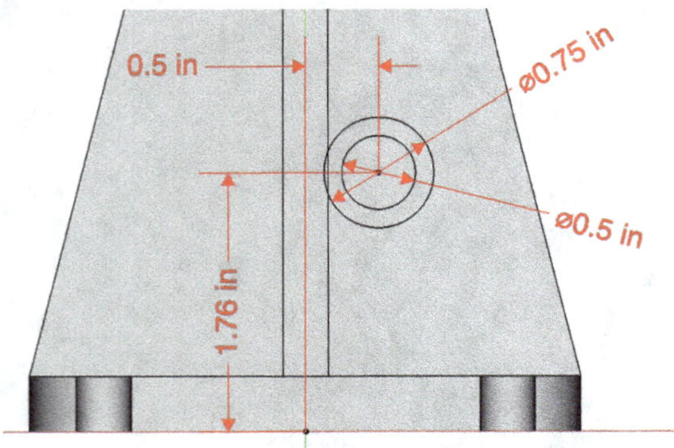

28. Click **Close** on the **Combo View** panel.
29. On the **Part Design Modeling** toolbar, click the **Pad** icon.
30. Select **Type > Two dimensions**.
31. Type **0.59** in the **Length** box of the **Pad Parameters** dialog.
32. Type **0.79** in the **2nd Length** box and click **OK**.

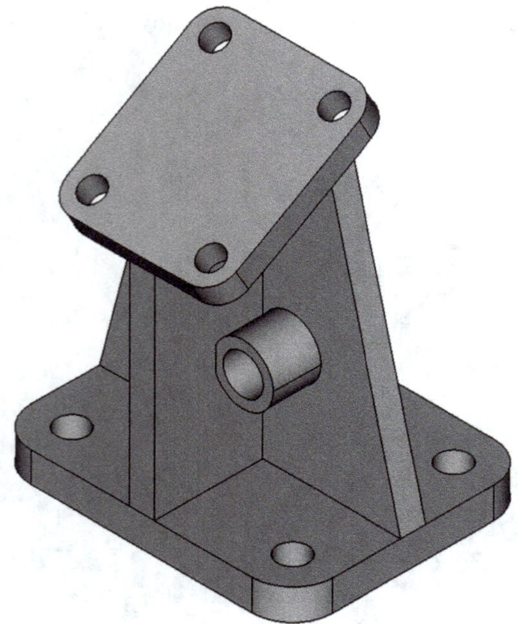

Creating the Pocket Feature

1. Click on the vertical face, as shown.

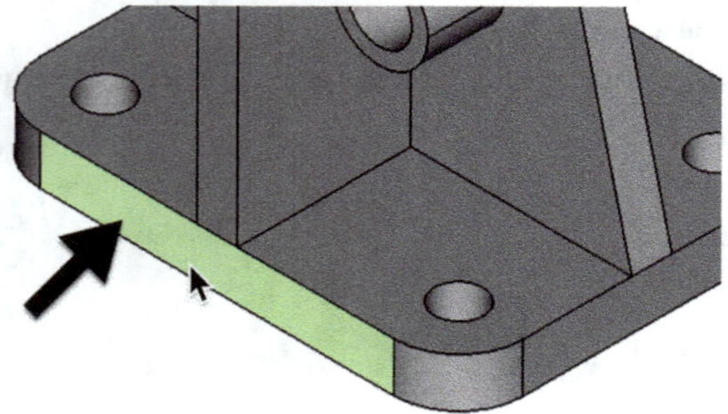

2. On the **Part Design Helper** toolbar, click the **Create Sketch** icon.
3. Create a rectangle and add dimensions to it.

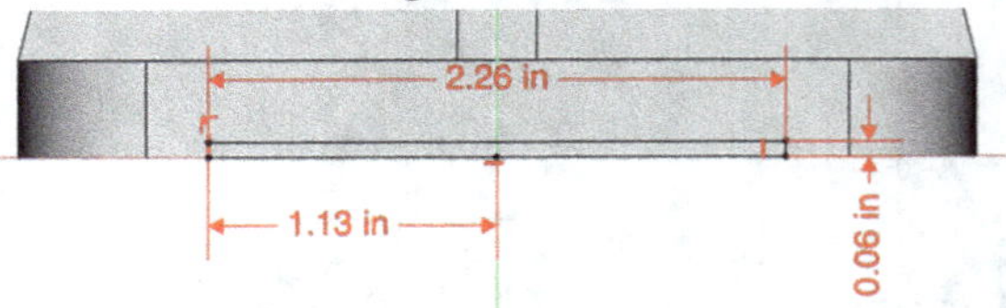

4. Click **Close** on the **Combo View** panel.
5. On the **Part Design Modeling** toolbar, click the **Pocket** icon.
6. Select **Type > Through all**.
7. Click **OK**.

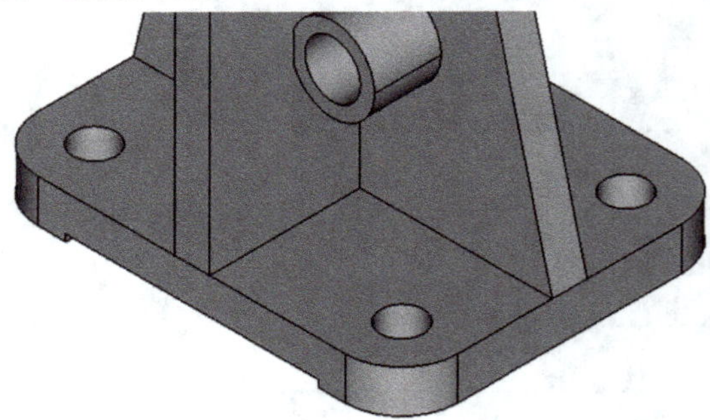

8. Save and close the file.

Chapter 6: Creating Drawings

In this chapter, you generate 2D drawings of the parts. You learn to:

- Insert standard views of a part model
- Add dimensions

TUTORIAL 1

In this tutorial, you create the drawing of the Tutorial 7 file created in the fourth chapter.

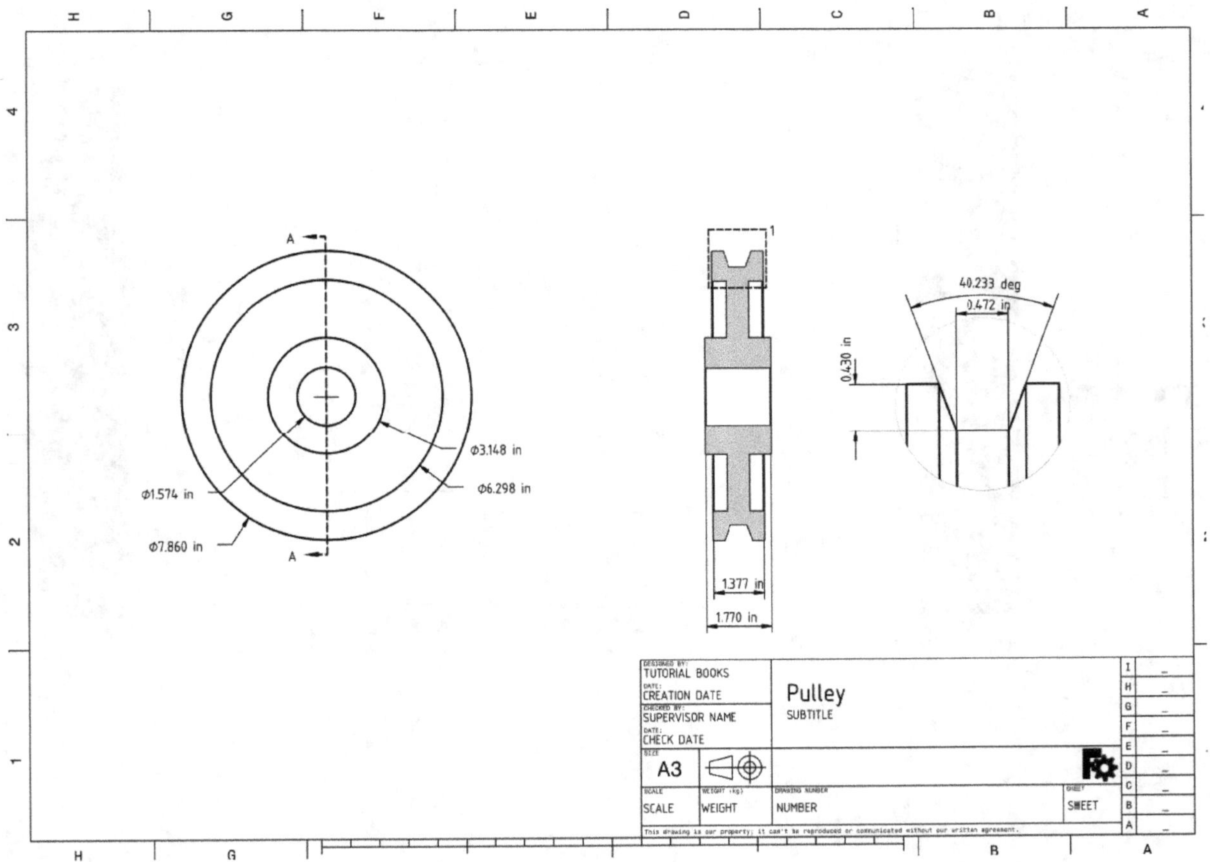

Starting a New Drawing File

1. Click **File > Open** on the Menu bar.

2. Go to the location of the Tutorial 7 file of Chapter 5.

3. Select the Tutorial 7 file and click the **Open** button.

4. Select **TechDraw** from the **Workbenches** drop-down.

5. Click the **Insert new drawing page from template** 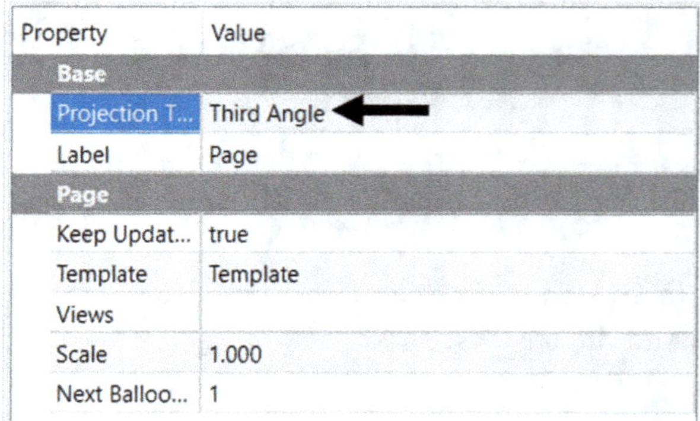 icon on the **TechDraw Pages** toolbar.
6. Select the **A3_LandscapeTD** template.
7. Click **Open**.
8. In the **Combo View** panel, select the **Page** from the **Model** tab.
9. In the **Properties** section of the **Combo View** panel, select **Projection Type > Third Angle**.

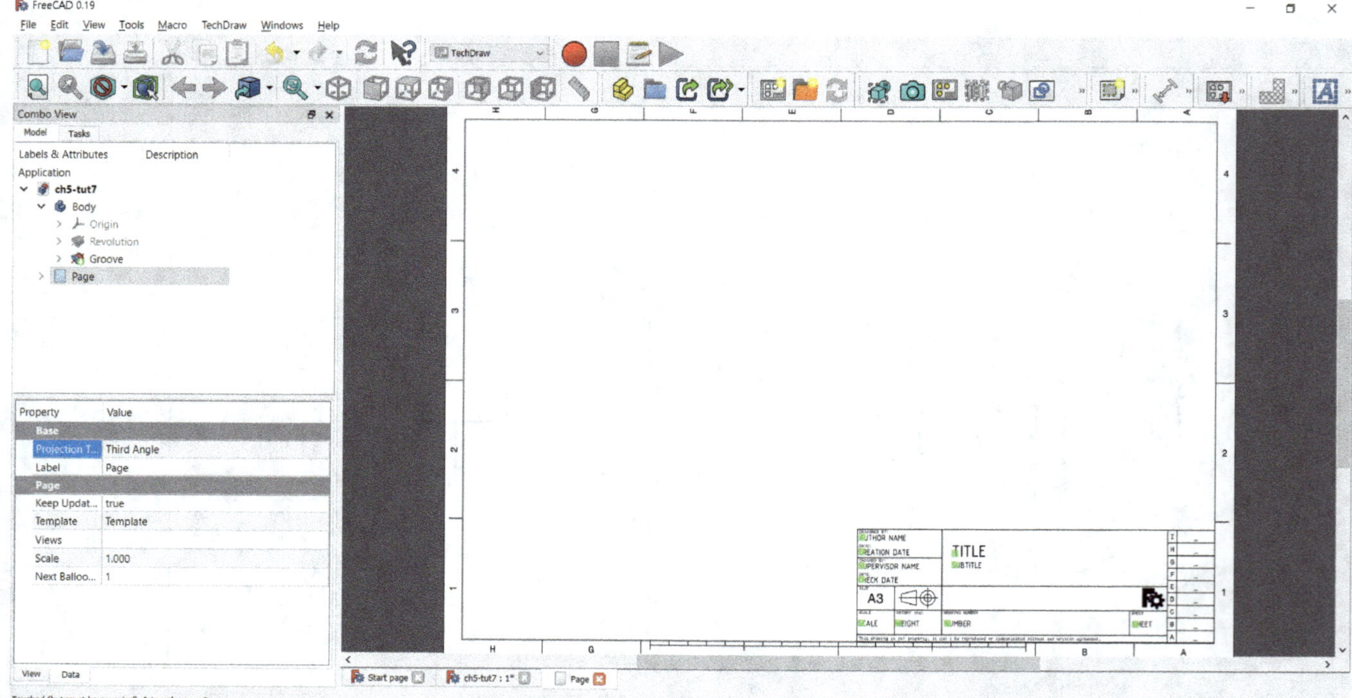

Generating the Base View

1. Click the **Tutorial 7** tab on the bottom of the window.

2. Select the Front face of the ViewCube.

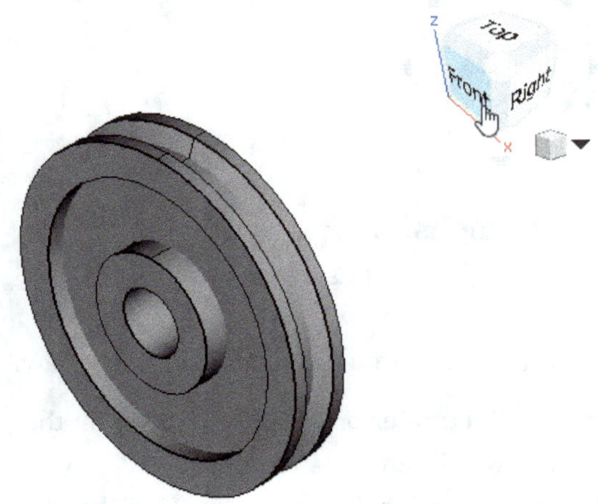

3. Click the **Page** tab on the bottom of the window.

4. To generate the base view, click the **Insert Projection Group** icon on the **TechDraw Views** toolbar.

5. On the **Projection Group** section, select **Scale > Custom**.

6. Type **1** and **2** in the **Scale Numerator** and **Scale Denominator** boxes located next to **Custom Scale**.

7. Click **OK** on the **Combo View** panel.

8. Click on the dotted borderline of the view.

9. Press and hold the left mouse and drag the view to left.

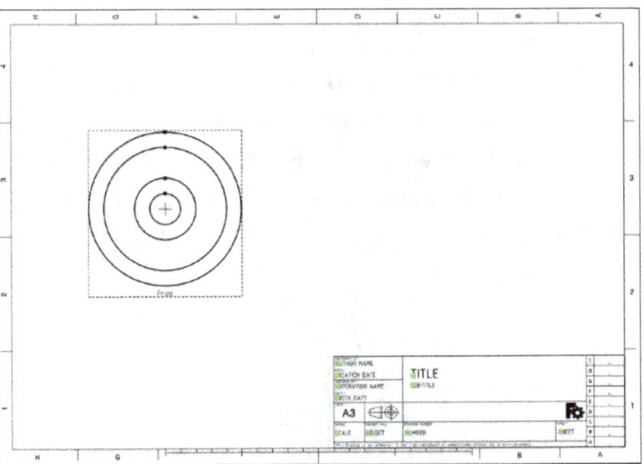

Generating the Section View

1. Select the base view.

2. Click the **Insert section view in drawing** icon on the **TechDraw Views** toolbar.

3. Click the **Looking left** icon on the **Quick Section Parameters** section.

4. Type **0** in the **X**, **Y**, and **Z** boxes, respectively. These values define the location of the section plane.

5. Click **OK** to create the section view.

6. Drag the section view and position it correctly. Make sure that it is horizontally in-line with the base view.

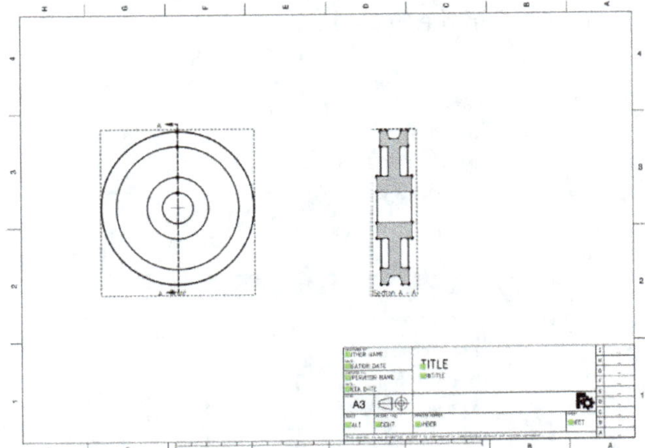

Creating the Detailed View

Now, you have to create the detailed view of the groove, which is displayed, in the section view.

1. Select the section view.

2. Click the **Insert detail view in drawing** 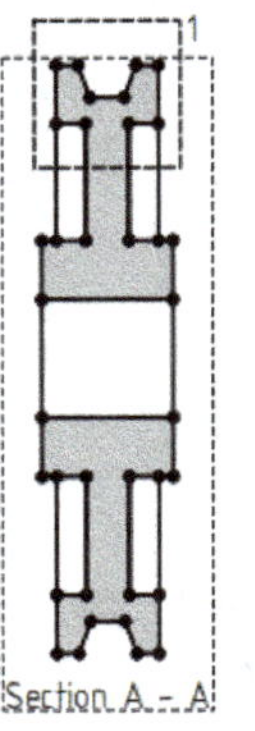 icon on the **TechDraw Views** toolbar.
   The detailed view is generated, as shown. Now, you need to specify the portion of the section view to be displayed in the detailed view.

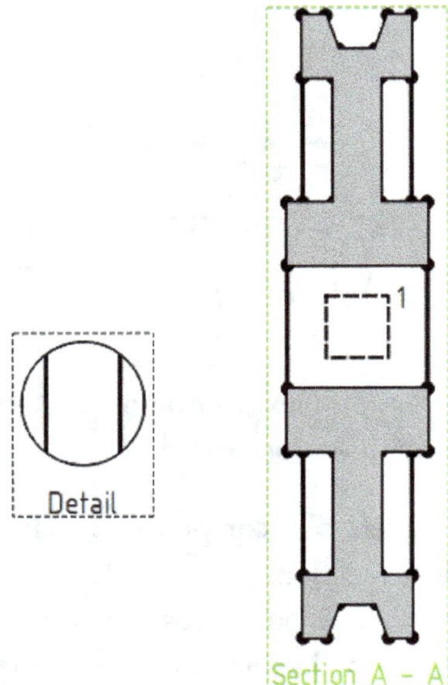

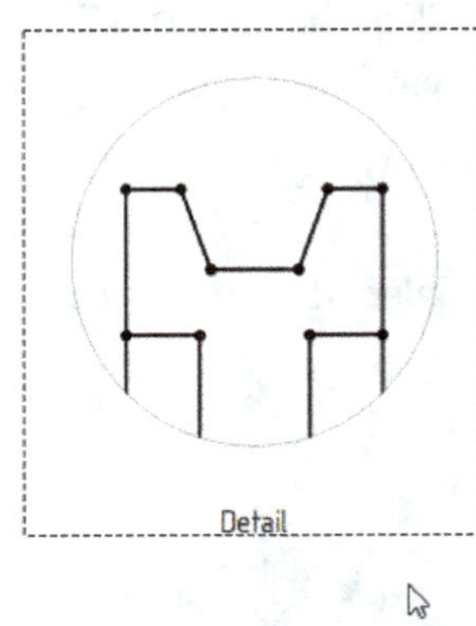

Adding Dimensions

Now, you add dimensions to the drawing.

1. Select the outer circular edge of the base view.

2. Click the **Diameter dimension** icon on the **TechDraw Dimensions** toolbar.

3. Click and drag the dimension outside the view.

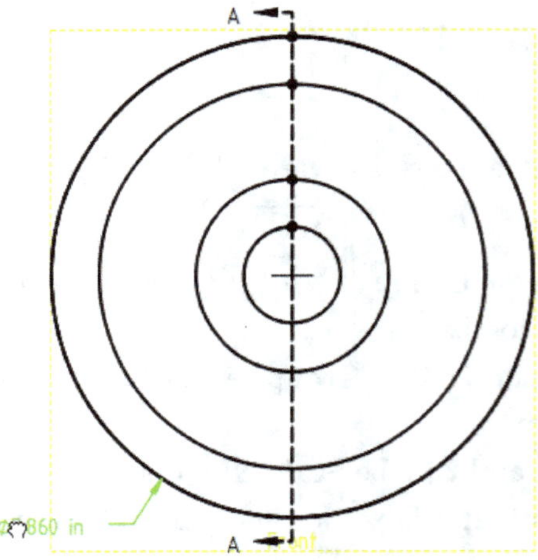

3. Select the detailed view.
4. In the **Properties** section, expand the **Anchor point** drop-down in the **Detail** section.
5. Type **95** in the **y** box.
6. Type **20** in the **Radius** box.
7. Type **1.5** in the **Scale** box.

4. Likewise, add remaining dimensions to the base view, as shown.

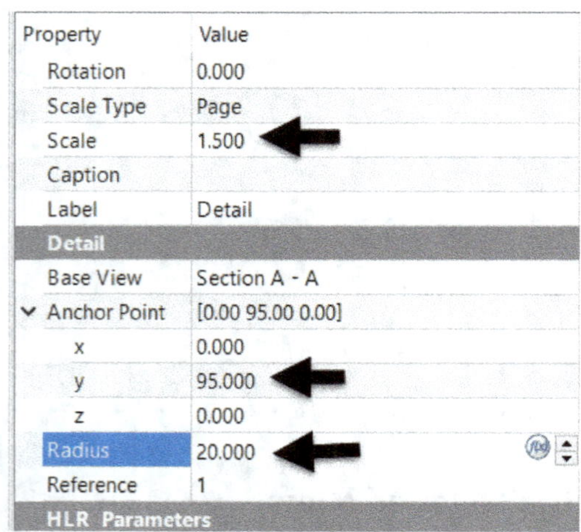

Property	Value
Rotation	0.000
Scale Type	Page
Scale	1.500
Caption	
Label	Detail
Detail	
Base View	Section A - A
Anchor Point	[0.00 95.00 0.00]
x	0.000
y	95.000
z	0.000
Radius	20.000
Reference	1
HLR Parameters	

8. Drag the detailed view to the right side on the drawing sheet.

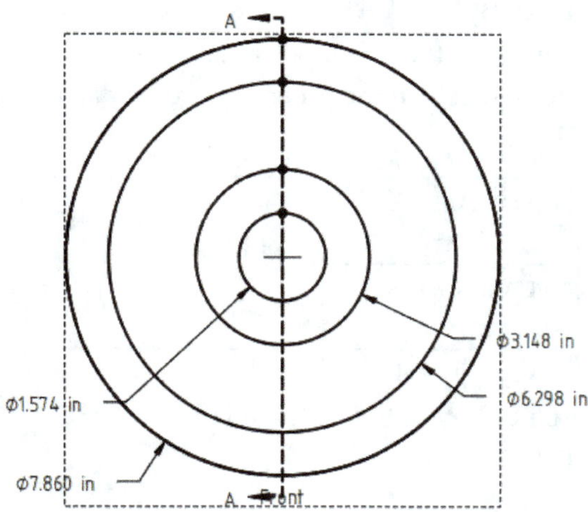

5. Press and hold the Ctrl key and select the vertices of the section view, as shown.

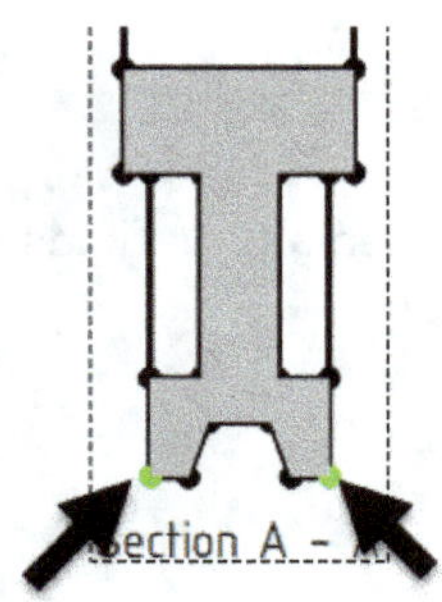

6. Click the **Horizontal-distance dimension** icon on the **TechDraw Dimensions** toolbar.
7. Press and hold the Ctrl key and select the vertices of the section view, as shown.

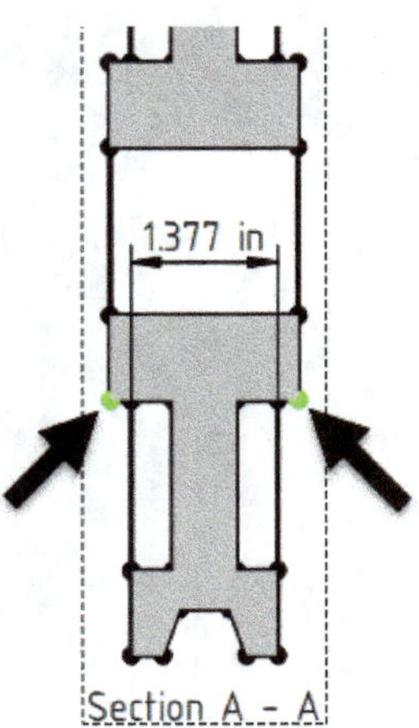

8. Click the **Horizontal-distance dimension** icon on the **TechDraw Dimensions** toolbar.

9. Drag the dimensions downward, as shown.

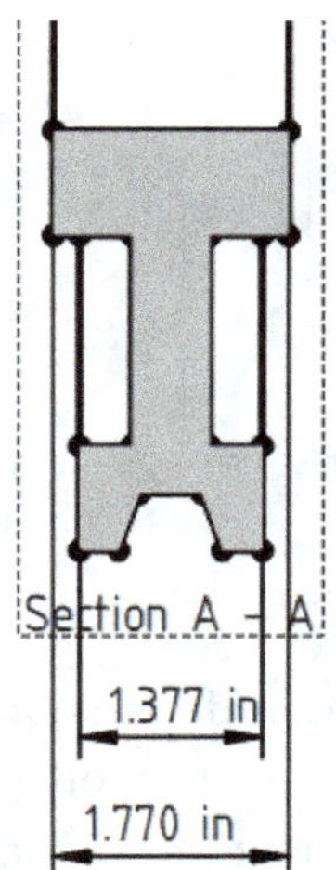

10. Press and hold the Ctrl key and select the two inclined lines in the detailed view, as shown.

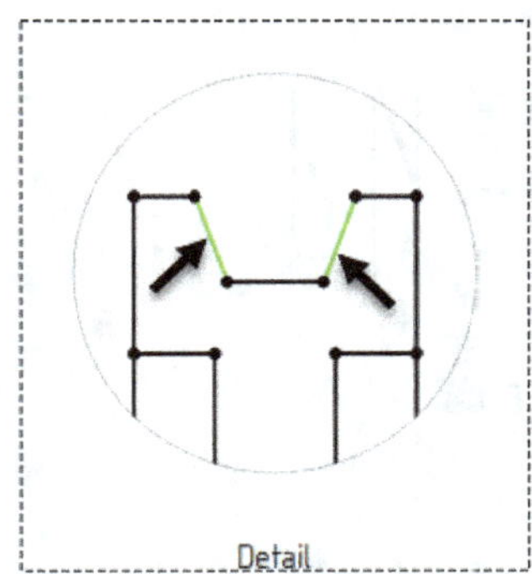

11. Click the **Angle Dimension** icon on the **TechDraw Dimensions** toolbar.

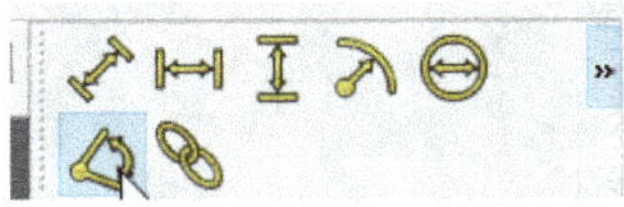

12. Press and hold the Ctrl key and select the vertices of the detailed view, as shown.

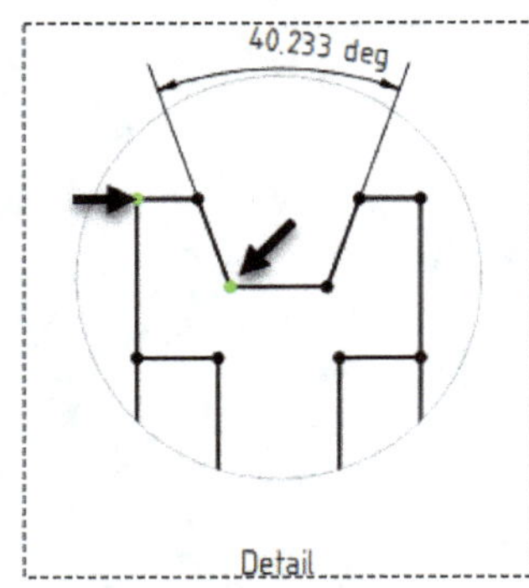

13. Click the **Vertical-distance dimension** $\mathcal{I}$ icon on the **TechDraw Dimensions** toolbar.

14. Create the remaining dimension, as shown.

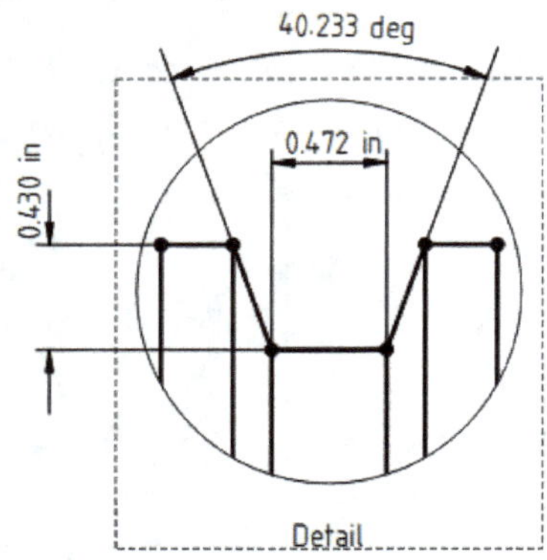

Populating the Title Block

1. Zoom in to the title block area.

2. Double-click on the green square displayed on TITLE.

3. Type **Pulley** in the **Value** box.

4. Click **OK**.

5. Likewise, add data to the remaining fields in the Title block.

6. Save and close the file.

Chapter 7: Sheet Metal Modeling

TUTORIAL 1

In this tutorial, you create the sheet metal model shown in the figure.

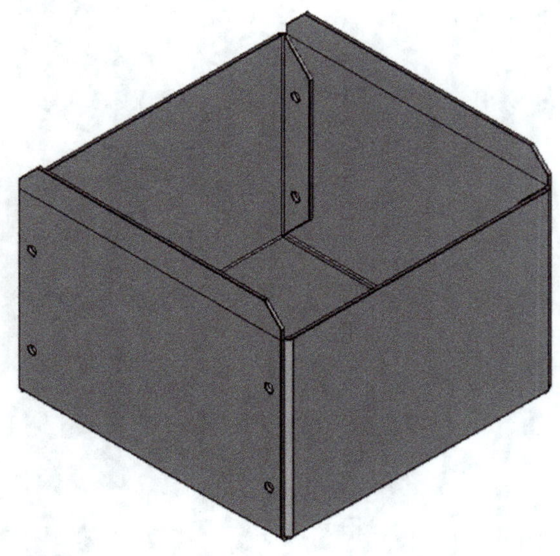

Creating the Base Feature

1. Open a new FreeCAD file.
2. Click **Tools > Addon Manager** on the Menu bar.
3. On the **Addon Manager** dialog, click the **Workbenches** tab.
4. Select **sheetmetal** from the list.
5. Click **Install/Update**.
6. Click **Close**.
7. Close the FreeCAD application, and then restart it.
8. Select **Part Design** from the **Workbenches** drop-down.
9. Click the **Create Sketch** icon on the **Part Design Helper** toolbar.
10. Select the XY plane and click **OK**.
11. Click the **Create Polyline** icon on the **Sketcher geometries** toolbar.
12. Create a closed sketch, as shown.

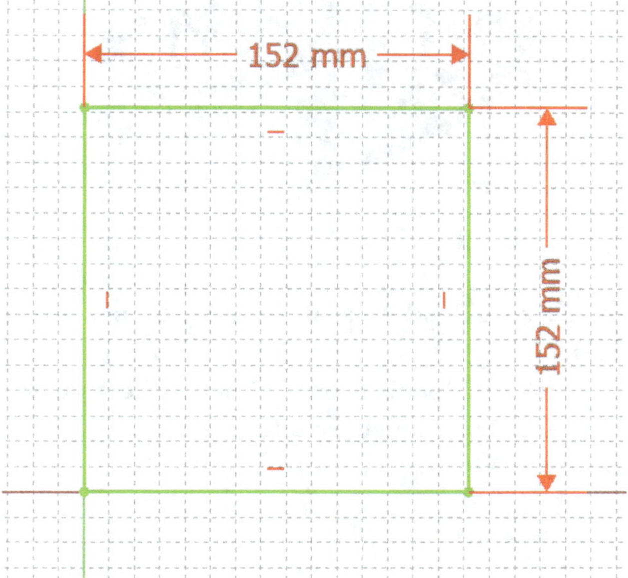

13. Click the **Close** button on the **Combo View** panel.
14. Click the **Pad** icon on the **Part Design Modeling** toolbar; the sketch is selected automatically.
15. Type **1.5** in the **Length** box.
16. Click **OK**.

Creating the flange

1. Select **Sheet Metal** from the **Workbenches** drop-down.
2. Press and hold the CTRL key and select the edges on the top face, as shown.

3. Click the **Bend** icon on the **My Commands** toolbar.
4. Click the **Model** tab on the **Combo View** panel.
5. Select **Bend** from the model tree.

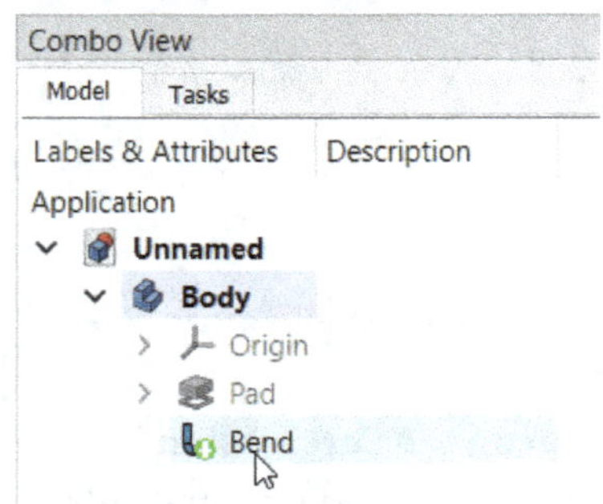

6. On the **Properties** panel, enter **100** and **1** in the **length** and **radius** boxes, respectively.
7. Select **Bend Type > Offset**.
8. Enter **1.75** in the **offset** box.
9. Select **invert > true**.

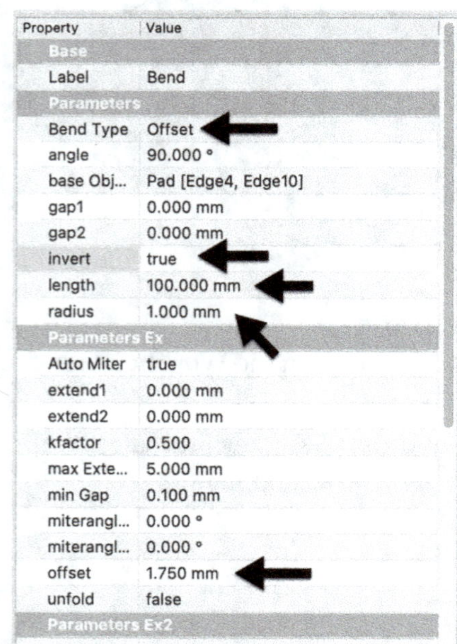

10. Press and hold the CTRL key and select the edges on the top face, as shown.

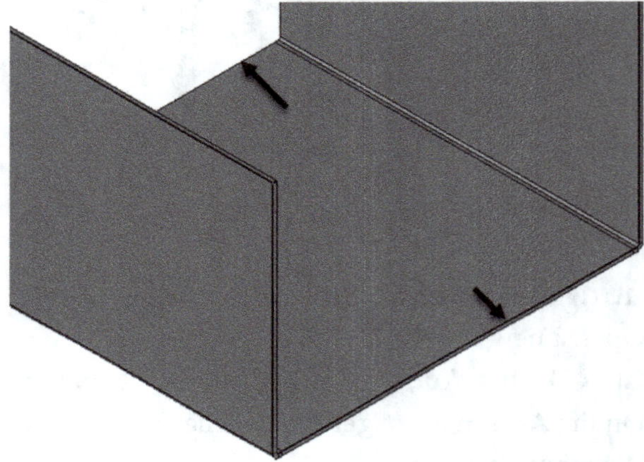

11. Click the **Bend** icon on the **My Commands** toolbar.
12. Select **Bend001** from the **Model** tab of the **Combo View** panel.

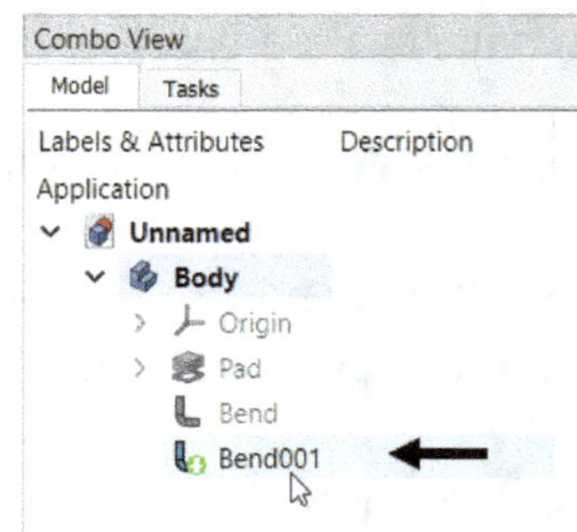

13. Select **Bend Type > Material Outside**.
14. Type **100** in the **length** box.

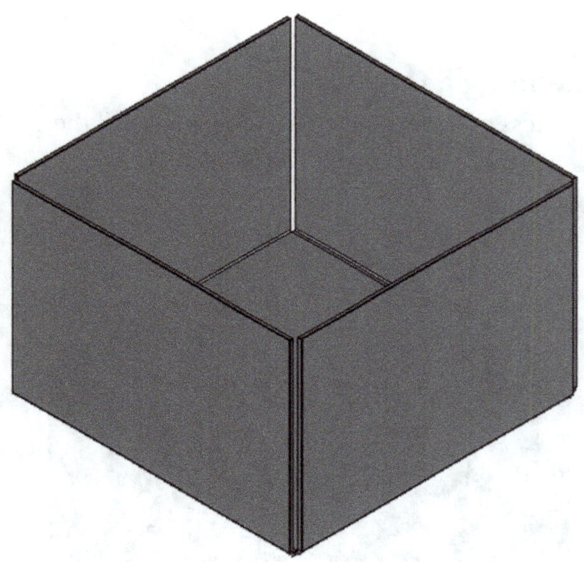

Property	Value
Base	
Label	Bend001
Parameters	
Bend Type	Material Outside
angle	90.000 °
base Obj...	Bend [Edge33, Edge30]
gap1	0.000 mm
gap2	0.000 mm
invert	true
length	100.000 mm
radius	1.000 mm
Parameters Ex	

15. Select the inner edge of the flange, as shown.

16. Click the **Bend** icon on the **My Commands** toolbar.
17. Select **Bend002** from the **Model** tab of the **Combo View** panel.
18. Select **Bend Type > Material Outside**.
19. Type **15** in the **length** box.
20. Select **invert > true**.
21. In the **Parameters Ex** section, select **Auto Miter > False**.
22. Type **45** in the **miterangle1** and **miterangle2** boxes, respectively.

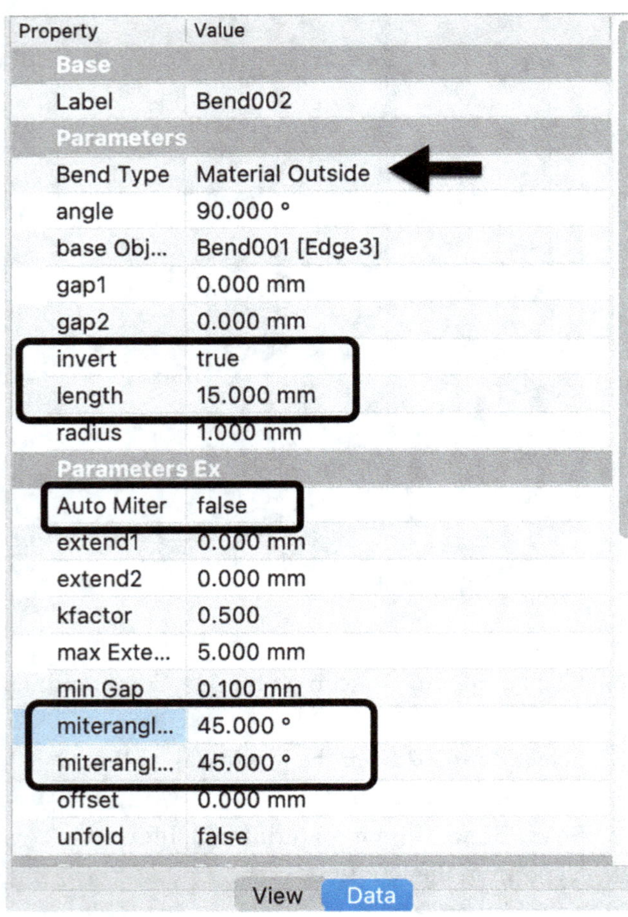

Property	Value
Base	
Label	Bend002
Parameters	
Bend Type	Material Outside
angle	90.000 °
base Obj...	Bend001 [Edge3]
gap1	0.000 mm
gap2	0.000 mm
invert	true
length	15.000 mm
radius	1.000 mm
Parameters Ex	
Auto Miter	false
extend1	0.000 mm
extend2	0.000 mm
kfactor	0.500
max Exte...	5.000 mm
min Gap	0.100 mm
miterangl...	45.000 °
miterangl...	45.000 °
offset	0.000 mm
unfold	false

View Data

23. Press and hold the middle mouse button and the right mouse button.
24. Drag the pointer toward left such that the other end of the flange is displayed.

The flange is displayed.

25. Likewise, create three more miter flanges, as shown.

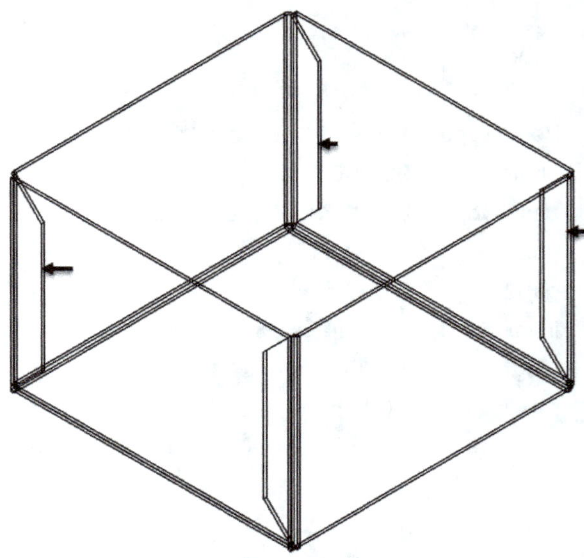

Extending a face

1. Press and hold the CTRL key and select the outer edges of the flanges, as shown.

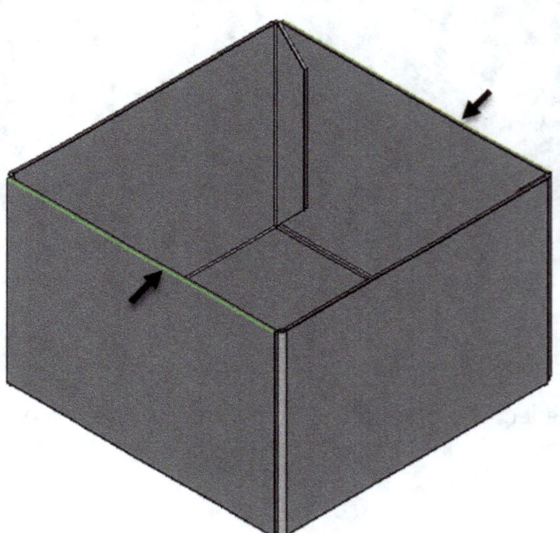

2. Click the **Extend a face along normal** icon on the **My Commands** toolbar.
3. Select **Extend** from the **Model** tab of the **Combo View** panel.
4. Type **15** in the **Length** box of the **Properties** panel.

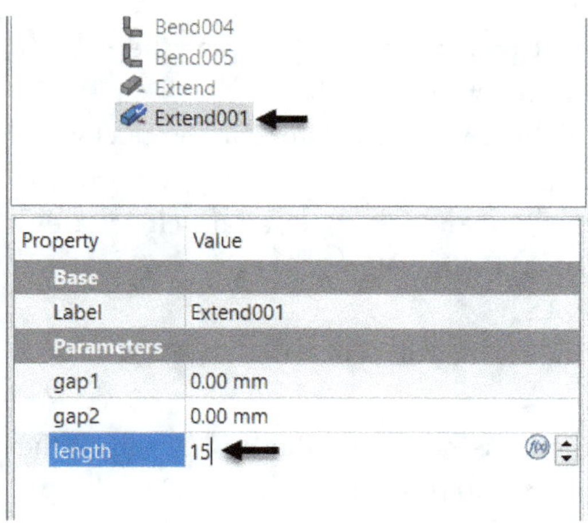

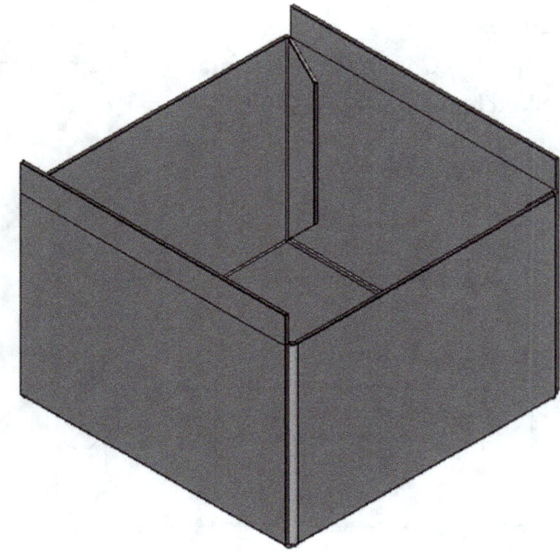

5. Select **Part Design** from the **Workbenches** drop-down.
6. Select the edge of the extended face, as shown.

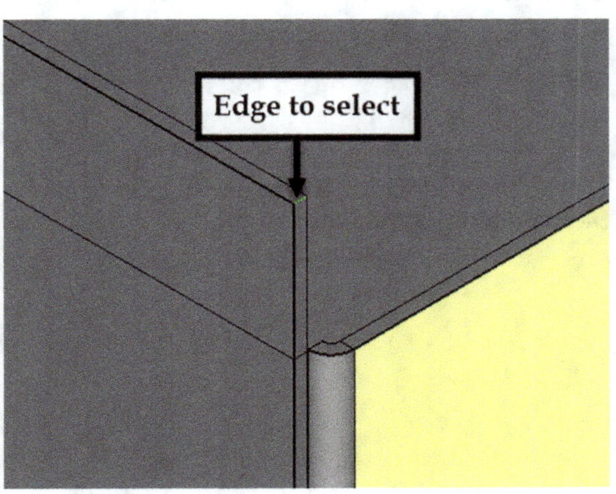

7. On the **Part Design Modeling** toolbar, click the

Chamfer  icon.

8. On the **Chamfer parameters** dialog, click the **Add ref** button.
9. Select the corner edge of the extended face, as shown.

10. Likewise, use the Add ref button and select the corner edges of another extended face.

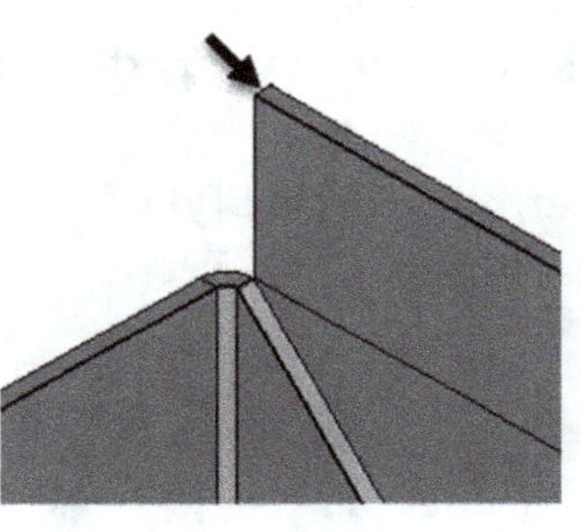

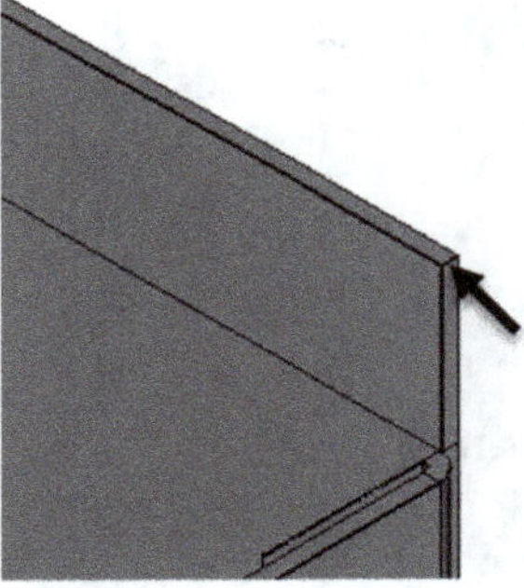

11. Type **10** in the **Size** box and click **OK**.

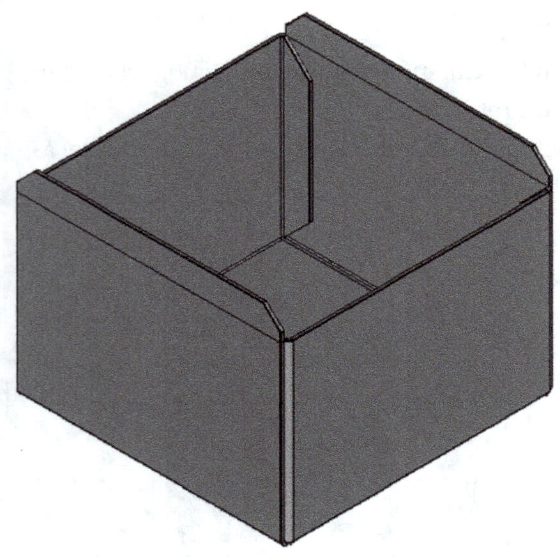

Creating the Pockets

1. Select the flat face of the flange.
2. Click the **Create Sketch** icon on the **Part Design Helper** toolbar.
3. On the **View** toolbar, click **Draw Style** drop-down > **Wireframe Mode**.

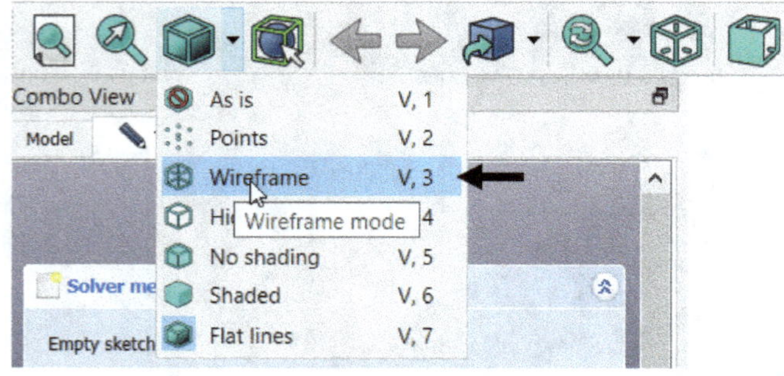

4. Create four circles, as shown.

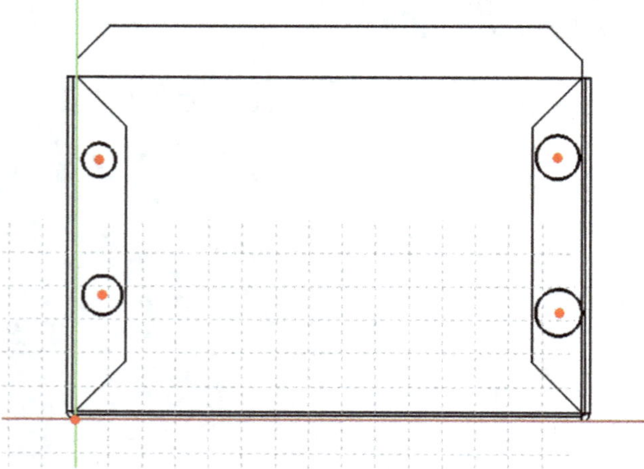

5. Click the **Constrain equal** icon on the **Sketcher constraints** toolbar.
6. Select all the circles one-by-one in the clockwise direction.
7. Select the first and last circle; all the circles are made equal in diameter.
8. Press ESC.
9. Select the center points of the two circles, as shown.
10. Click the **Constrain horizontally** icon on the **Sketcher constraints** toolbar.
11. Select the center points of the remaining two circles.
12. Click the **Constrain horizontally** icon on the **Sketcher constraints** toolbar.

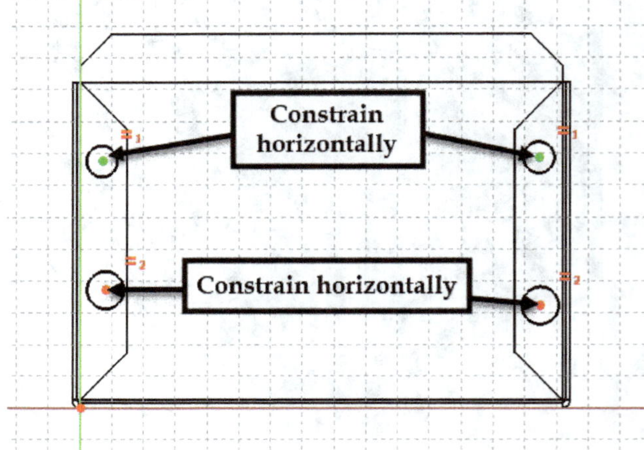

13. Select the centerpoints of the two circles, as shown.
14. Click the **Constrain vertically** icon on the **Sketcher constraints** toolbar.
15. Select the centerpoints of the two circles, as shown.
16. Click the **Constrain vertically** icon on the **Sketcher constraints** toolbar.

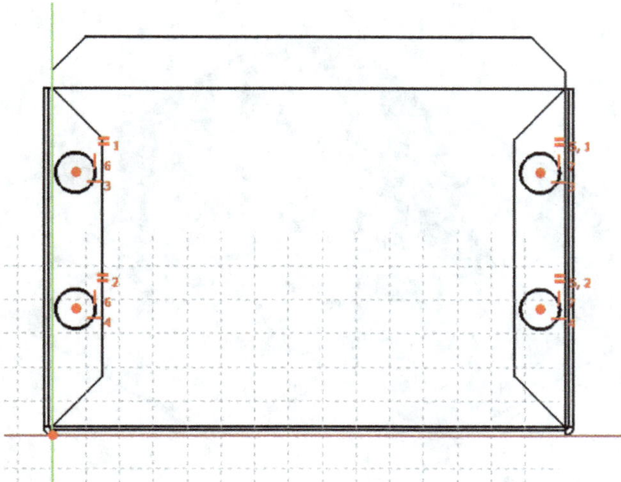

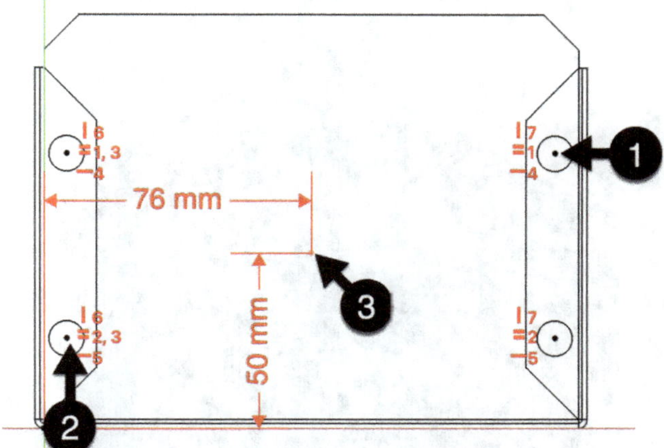

17. Click the **Create point** ● icon on the **Sketcher geometries** toolbar.
18. Click in the center of the model.
19. Add vertical and horizontal dimensions to the point, as shown.

24. Create horizontal and vertical distance constraints, as shown.
25. Create the diameter constraint, as shown.

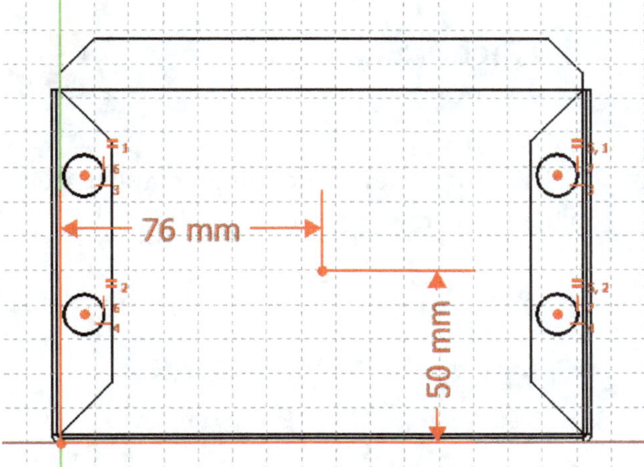

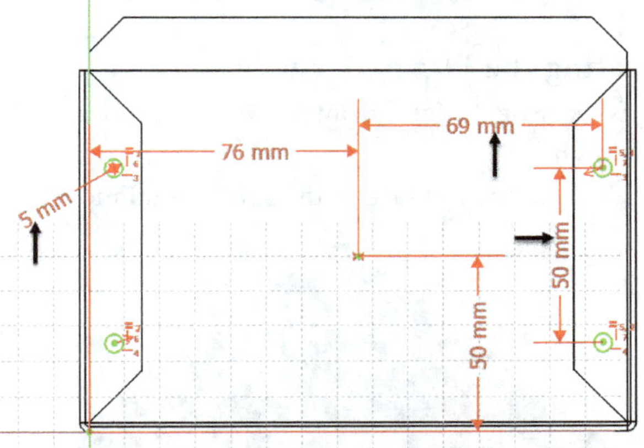

20. Click the **Constrain symmetrical** ⧓ icon on the **Sketcher constraints** toolbar.
21. Select the center point of the top-right circle.
22. Select the center point of the bottom-left circle.
23. Select the newly created point.

26. Click **Leave Sketch** on the **Sketcher** toolbar.
27. On the **Part Design Modeling** toolbar, click the **Pocket** 🟦 icon.
28. On the **Pocket Parameters** dialog, select **Type > Through All**.
29. Click **OK**.
30. On the **View** toolbar, click **Draw Style** drop-down > **Flat Lines**.

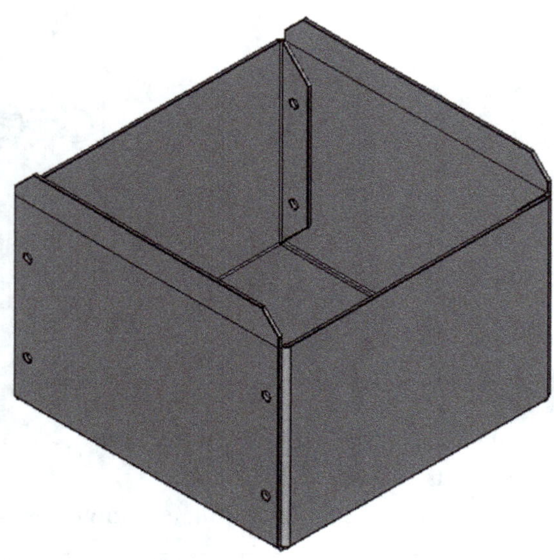

Creating the Flat Pattern

1. Select **Sheet Metal** from the **Workbenches** drop-down.
2. Click on the flat face of the sheet metal model.

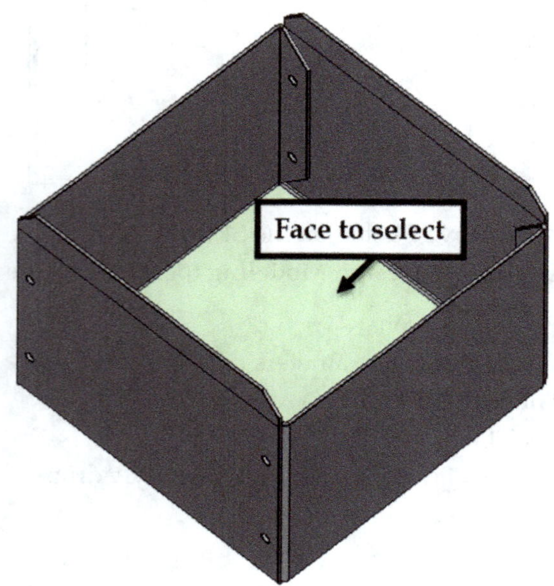

3. Click the **Flatten folder sheet metal object** icon on the **My Commands** toolbar.
4. Keep the **Manual K-factor** option checked on the **Unfold sheet metal object** dialog.
5. Select the **ANSI** option.
6. Click **OK**.

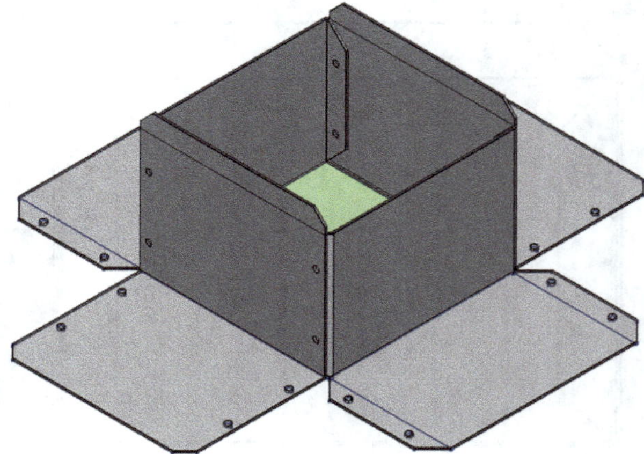

7. Save the sheet metal part.

Creating 2D Drawing of the sheet metal part

1. Select **TechDraw** from the **Workbenches** drop-down.

2. Click the **Insert new Page using Template** icon on the **TechDraw pages** toolbar.

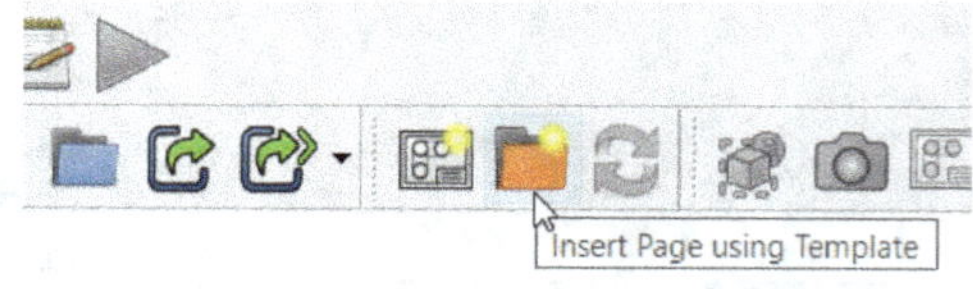

3. Double-click on the **A2_Landscape_ISO7200TD** template.
4. Select **Body** from the **Model** tab.

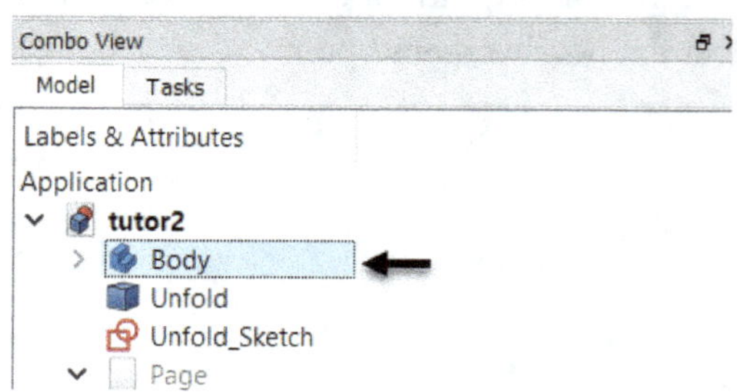

5. Click the **Insert multiple linked views of the drawing object(s)** icon on the **Techdraw Views** toolbar.

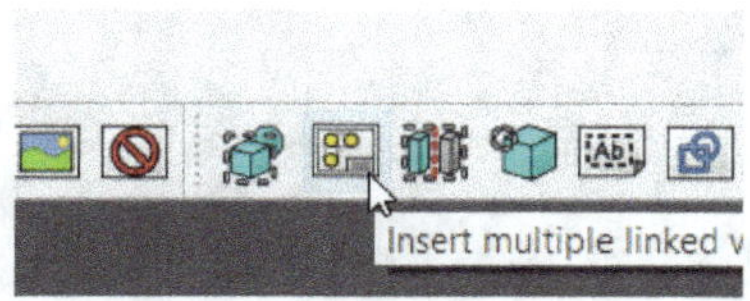

6. On the **Projection Group** dialog, select **Scale > Custom**.
7. Type **1** and **2** in the **Custom Scale** boxes, respectively.

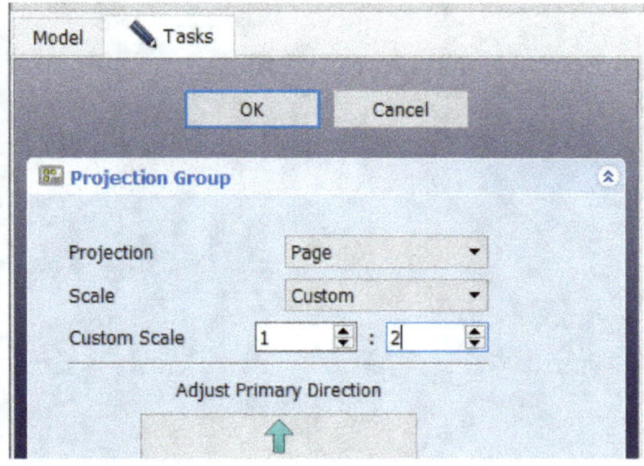

8. Click **OK** on the **Projection Group** dialog.
9. Click the **Refresh** icon on the **File** toolbar.
10. Switch to the drawing sheet tab.
11. Click and drag the view to the bottom right corner, as shown.

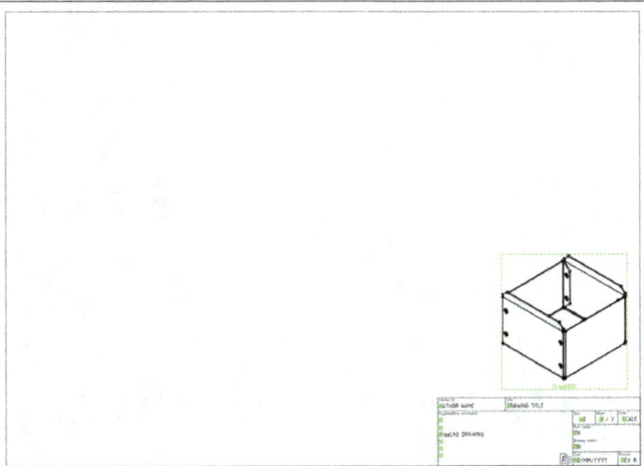

12. Switch to the sheet metal model file.
13. On the **View** toolbar, click the **Set to top view** icon.

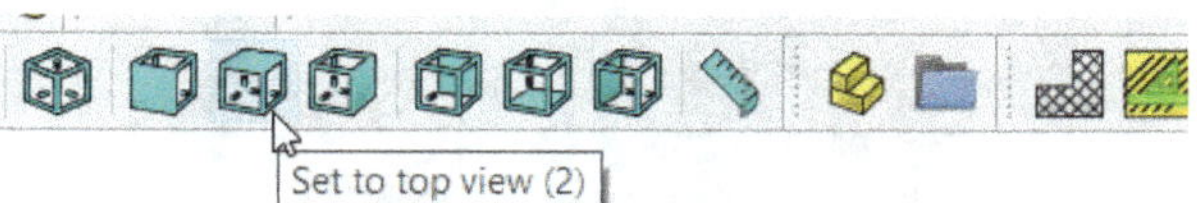

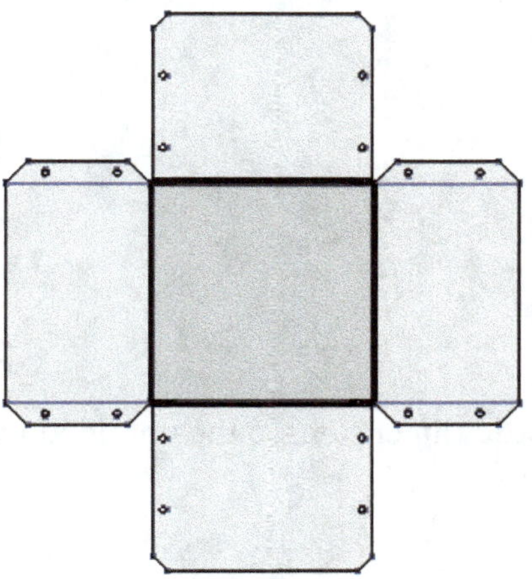

14. Switch to the drawing view.
15. Select **Body** from the **Model** tab.

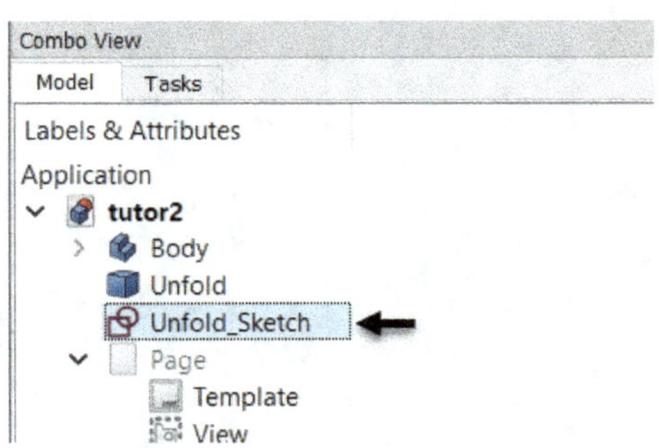

16. Click the **Insert multiple linked views of the drawing object(s)** icon on the **Techdraw Views** toolbar.
17. On the **Projection Group** dialog, select **Scale > Custom**.
18. Type **3** and **4** in the **Custom Scale** boxes, respectively.
19. Click **OK** on the **Projection Group** dialog.
20. Click the **Refresh** icon on the **File** toolbar.

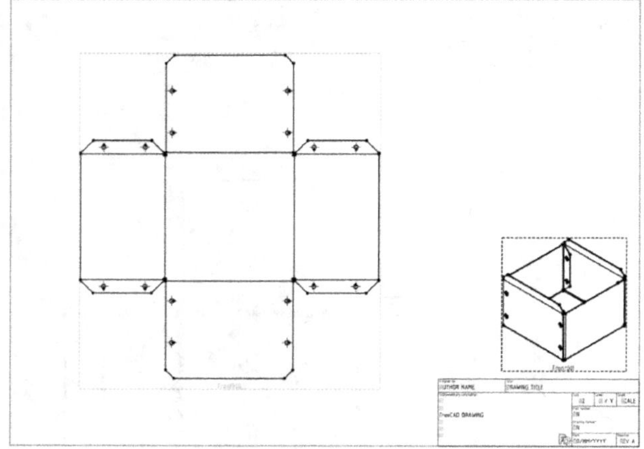

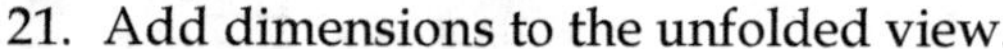

21. Add dimensions to the unfolded view.

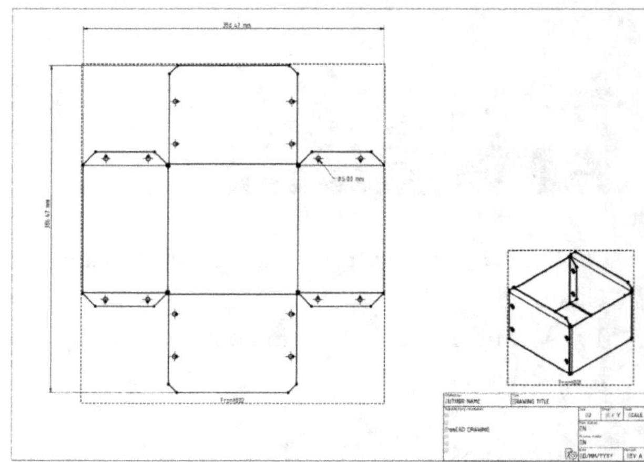

22. Save and close the sheet metal files.